Communications
in Computer and Information Science   1679

More information about this series at https://link.springer.com/bookseries/7899

Davor Svetinovic · Yin Zhang · Xiapu Luo ·
Xiaoyan Huang · Xingping Chen (Eds.)

Blockchain and Trustworthy Systems

4th International Conference, BlockSys 2022
Chengdu, China, August 4–5, 2022
Revised Selected Papers

 Springer

Editors
Davor Svetinovic
Vienna University of Economics
and Business
Vienna, Austria

Yin Zhang
University of Electronic Science
and Technology of China
Chengdu, China

Xiapu Luo (iD)
Hong Kong Polytechnic University
Kowloon, Hong Kong

Xiaoyan Huang
University of Electronic Science
and Technology of China
Chengdu, China

Xingping Chen
Sun Yat-sen University
Guangzhou, China

ISSN 1865-0929   ISSN 1865-0937 (electronic)
Communications in Computer and Information Science
ISBN 978-981-19-8042-8   ISBN 978-981-19-8043-5 (eBook)
https://doi.org/10.1007/978-981-19-8043-5

This Springer imprint is published by the registered company Springer Nature Singapore Pte Ltd.
The registered company address is: 152 Beach Road, #21-01/04 Gateway East, Singapore 189721, Singapore

Preface

Blockchain has become a hot research area in academia and industry. The blockchain technology is transforming industries by enabling anonymous and trustful transactions in decentralized and trustless environments. As a result, blockchain technology and other technologies for developing trustworthy systems can be used to reduce system risks, mitigate financial fraud, and cut down operational cost. Blockchain and trustworthy systems can be applied to many fields, such as financial services, social management, and supply chain management.

This volume contains the papers from the proceedings of 4th International Conference on Blockchain and Trustworthy Systems (BlockSys 2022). This conference was held with an emphasis on the state-of-the-art advances in blockchain and trustworthy systems. The main conference received 56 paper submissions, out of which 26 papers were accepted as regular papers. All papers underwent a rigorous single-blind peer review process – each paper was reviewed by two to three experts. The accepted papers together with our outstanding keynote and invited speeches led to a vibrant technical program. We are looking forward to future events in this conference series.

The conference would not have been successful without help from so many people. We would like to thank the Organizing Committee for their hard work in putting together the conference. First, we would like to express our sincere thanks to the General Chairs, Yan Zhang and Danny Tsang, for their guidance, support, and promotion of this event. We also extend our deep gratitude to the Program Committee members whose diligent work in reviewing the papers lead to the high quality of the accepted papers. We greatly appreciate the excellent support and hard work of the Publicity Chairs, Jinjia Zhou, Kun Wang, Yueyue Dai, and Neng Zhang; Organizing Chairs, Ke Zhang, Fan Wu, and Dan Li; and Advisory Board, Michael R. Lyu, Jiannong Cao, Kuan-Ching Li, Huaimin Wang, and Zibin Zheng. Most importantly, we would like to thank the authors for submitting their papers to BlockSys 2022 conference.

We believe that the BlockSys conference provides a good forum for both academic researchers and industrial practitioners to discuss all technical advances in blockchain and trustworthy systems. We also expect that the future BlockSys conferences will be as successful as this year's, as indicated by the contributions presented in this volume.

October 2022

Davor Svetinovic
Yin Zhang
Xiapu Luo
Xiaoyan Huang
Xiangping Chen

Organization

General Chairs

Yan Zhang   University of Oslo, Norway
Danny Tsang   HKUST, Hong Kong

Program Chairs

Yin Zhang   University of Electronic Science and Technology
                          of China, China
Davor Svetinovic   Vienna University of Economics and Business,
                          Austria
Xiapu Luo   The Hong Kong Polytechnic University,
                          Hong Kong

Organizing Chairs

Ke Zhang   University of Electronic Science and Technology
                          of China, China
Fan Wu   University of Electronic Science and Technology
                          of China, China
Dan Li   Sun Yat-sen University, China

Publicity Chairs

Jinjia Zhou   Hosei University, Japan
Yueyue Dai   Nanyang Technological University, Singapore
Kun Wang   UCLA, USA
Neng Zhang   Sun Yat-sen University, China

Publication Chairs

Xiaoyan Huang   University of Electronic Science and Technology
                          of China, China
Xiangping Chen   Sun Yat-sen University, China

Advisory Board

Michael R. Lyu	The Chinese University of Hong Kong, Hong Kong
Jiannong Cao	The Hong Kong Polytechnic University, Hong Kong
Kuan-Ching Li	Providence University, Taiwan
Huaimin Wang	National University of Defense Technology, China
Zibin Zheng	Sun Yat-sen University, China

Program Committee

Alexander Chepurnoy	IOHK Research, USA
Ali Vatankhah	Kennesaw State University, USA
Andreas Veneris	University of Toronto, Canada
Ao Zhou	Beijing University of Posts and Telecommunications, China
Bahman Javadi	Western Sydney University, Australia
Bu-Qing Cao	Hunan University of Science and Technology, China
Chang-Ai Sun	University of Science and Technology Beijing, China
Claudio Schifanella	University of Turin, Italy
Debiao He	Wuhan University, China
Fangguo Zhang	Sun Yat-sen University, China
Gerhard Hancke	City University of Hong Kong, Hong Kong
Guobing Zou	Shanghai University, China
Han Liu	Tsinghua University, China
Jan Henrik Ziegeldorf	RWTH Aachen University, Germany
Jiwei Huang	China University of Petroleum, China
Kai Lei	Peking University, China
Kenneth Fletcher	University of Massachusetts Boston, USA
Laizhong Cui	Shenzhen University, China
Mario Larangeira	IOHK/Tokyo Institute of Technology, Japan
Muhammad Habib ur Rehman	King's College London, UK
Pengcheng Zhang	Hohai University, China
Qianhong Wu	Beihang University, China
Qinghua Lu	CSIRO, Australia
Quanqing Xu	Alibaba, China
Sabah Suhail	University of Tartu, Estonia
Shangguang Wang	Beijing University of Posts and Telecommunications, China

Contents

Private Computing

Trustworthy Systems

Secure and Efficient Agreement Signing Atop Blockchain and Decentralized Identity

Songlin He[1(✉)], Tong Sun[2], Qiang Tang[3], Chase Wu[1], Nedim Lipka[2], Curtis Wigington[2], and Rajiv Jain[2]

[1] New Jersey Institute of Technology, Newark 07102, USA
{sh553,chase.wu}@njit.edu
[2] Adobe Research, San Jose 95110, USA
{tsun,lipka,wigingto,rajijain}@adobe.com
[3] University of Sydney, Camperdown, NSW 2006, Australia
qiang.tang@sydney.edu.au

Abstract. In recent years, we have witnessed an exorbitant growth of online interactions, especially during the pandemic of COVID-19, which requires diversified digital agreements in different application scenarios. In essence, multi-party agreement signing (MPAS) can be reckoned as a special case of the multi-party fair exchange (MPFE) for signatures over a digital agreement. However, such general MPAS protocols have not seen wide adoptions in practice, possibly due to the lack of incentives to maintain the signing platform. Practically, monetary-incentivized enterprises exist to act as a trusted third party (TTP) and provide signing services. However, such an agreement signing flow still suffers from certain limitations in terms of insecure and inefficient operations. To this end, we propose a secure and efficient framework for multi-party agreement signing based on decentralized identity, blockchain and decentralized storage network (DSN). The framework consists of two subsystems where the identity subsystem contains an extensible three-tier user identity model atop decentralized identity, and the agreement signing subsystem, empowered by the identity subsystem, DSN and several novel designs, achieves security and efficiency design goals. For the convenience of explanation, we suppose that a centralized signing service provider (SSP) is properly involved, i.e., sensitive information is still protected against the SSP, and acts as a TTP to ensure the crucial properties such as fairness and coordinate the signing activities. Our design is also compatible with other methods, e.g., ensuring fairness via blockchain, which removes the single point of failure of SSP. We prototype the framework and the performance evaluation shows effectiveness and efficiency.

Keywords: Agreement signing · Decentralized identity · Self-sovereign identity · Blockchain · Decentralized storage networks

D. Svetinovic et al. (Eds.): BlockSys 2022, CCIS 1679, pp. 3–17, 2022.
https://doi.org/10.1007/978-981-19-8043-5_1

1   Introduction

In recent years, we have witnessed an explosive growth of online interactions between Internet users, especially during the pandemic of COVID-19, which require diversified *agreements*[1] ranging from sales contracts and offer letters to invoices and non-disclosure agreements (NDAs). To ensure the validity of agreements, involved parties are usually required to digitally sign the agreement.

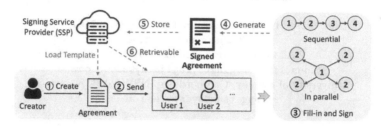

Fig. 1. Existing digital agreement signing model.

In essence, multi-party agreement (or contract) signing can be considered as a special case of *multi-party fair exchange* (MPFE) protocols [1] where the exchanged items are signatures over a common message, viz. the agreement. One of the most crucial properties required by an agreement signing protocol is *fairness*, indicating that either all honest parties obtain a valid signed agreement or nothing useful at the end of the protocol. It is well known that in a fair exchange scenario, a trusted third party (TTP) is needed to ensure complete fairness [15]. An MPFE can further be applied to *secure multi-party computation* (SMPC) if the privacy is also preserved against the TTP. A bevy of literature has studied the agreement/contract signing problem and the solutions mainly include: (i) TTP-free protocols such as gradual release-based [6] or trustworthy timestamping-based [19]; (ii) (optimistic[2]) TTP-based [12]; and (iii) blockchain-based [18]. However, practically we did not see a wide adoption of these protocols in real social or commercial activities. One intuitive reason may lie in these general designs provide no incentive for one to maintain a platform coordinating the agreement signing. Practically, TTP is oftentimes played by monetary-incentivized enterprises who provide signing services.

In this paper, instead of focusing on a general design of agreement signing, we switch to a new perspective and concentrate on the existing real-life agreement signing model with the goal of improving its security and efficiency. As illustrated

---

[1] An *agreement* indicates a promise that embodied by a *digital document* among n ($\geq$ 2) parties regarding a common intention and is a more general term for *contract*, which creates a mutual obligation and is enforceable by law. In the landscape of distributed computing, agreement also often refers to a key property of a consensus mechanism, stating that all honest peers in a network agree on the same value [11].

[2] An *optimistic* TTP is offline and only involved when a violation of fairness occurs.

in Fig. 1, a *creator* first creates or loads a template of an agreement from a *signing service provider* (SSP), and then sends the "empty" agreement to *signers* (possibly including the creator itself). During creation, the creator can even specify the signing order of signers. All designated signers fill in required data fields and sign, and the signed agreement is typically maintained by the SSP for backup or subsequent management.

Problems. However, the existing agreement signing flow exhibits a set of limitations in terms of *inefficient* and *insecure* operations. In particular,

- **Manual data fill-in.** Signers need to manually and repeatedly fill in all data fields required for every agreement, resulting in inefficiency.
- **Time-consuming information check.** Some information provided by signers lacks verification, or the verification procedure is time-consuming as it involves onerous operations and various auxiliary documents.
- **Leaking sensitive information.** Some data provided in the agreement may leak private information, e.g., in a house leasing scenario, a tenant only needs to show that his or her income is more than 5,000 USD instead of revealing the actual amount.
- **Hard to scale for content-intensive agreements.** An agreement, especially in B2B scenarios, usually contains a large volume of linked documents and multi-modal contents. However, it remains unclear how to securely attach these contents to the agreement and efficiently sign regardless of the quantity and size of the attachments.
- **Unguaranteed clause execution.** It is generally difficult to enforce and trace the clause execution in a signed agreement, and sometimes it may lead to inefficient and complex workflows or even disputes and expensive lawsuits.

Contributions. We attempt to tackle the above limitations to improve the existing signing procedure with benefits for both SSP and signers. To this end, we propose a secure and efficient framework for multi-party agreement signing and address the aforementioned issues via decentralized identity, blockchain and DSN. Our contributions are summarized as:

1) We propose a secure and efficient framework for practical multi-party agreement signing, which contains two sub-systems: an *identity* system and an *agreement signing* system. The framework is compatible with the existing real-life agreement signing flow where signing service providers are incentivized and properly involved in the agreement signing process.
2) We propose a decentralized identity-based three-tier user identity model, which allows users to manage and control their own identity information.
3) We propose a signing system with the following designs: (i) a computational representation model for an agreement; (ii) privacy-preserved auto-filling with verifiable identity information; (iii) DSN-enabled scalability to content-intensive agreements; (iv) guaranteed execution of agreement clauses; and (v) minimized signing data and reduced agreement verification complexity.

2   Background

Blockchain and Smart Contract. Blockchain is an immutable ledger for recording transactions in a distributed system among mutually untrusting peers. Nowadays, blockchain has been widely adopted in many scenarios [10,11] beyond its initial popularization in cryptocurrency [14]. Two main functionalities provided by blockchain are storage and computation. The storage via blockchain, especially in permissioned blockchains [2] where participants are identified and known to each other, resembles the conventional distributed database by achieving not only crash fault tolerance (CFT) but also byzantine fault tolerance (BFT). For computation, blockchain supports smart contract, which is a piece of pre-agreed logic that can be developed via Turing-complete programming languages [20].

Decentralized Identity. Decentralized identity, also referred to as *self-sovereign identity* (SSI) is a new online identity model highlighting that users possess full control and management of their identity information. As specified by initiatives such as Decentralized Identity Foundation[3] and Decentralized Identifier group of World Wide Web Consortium (W3C)[4], the basic elements contained in decentralized identity are:

– **Decentralized Identifier (DID).** A globally unique decentralized identifier, e.g., did : DID_Method : 123 . . . abc . . ., where did is fixed, DID_Method describes the concrete interaction mechanism between DIDs and a specific blockchain, and 123 . . . abc . . . is the identifier in a specific DID method.
– **DID Document Object (DDO).** Each DID is associated with a DDO, which contains the DID itself, the linked public keys (e.g., for authentication) and other metadata. A DID can be resolved to obtain a DDO via specific ways defined in the corresponding DID method.
– **Claim.** A claim is a statement about an entity, denoted by claim = $\{a, v\}$ where a is the attribute and v means the value, e.g., claim = { "name", "Bob" }.
– **Verifiable Credential (VC).** Based on the definition of W3C[5], a VC is a set of claims issued by an issuer. The authenticity of claims is verifiable.

Note that both DDO and VC can be represented by JSON-LD document[6] but they serve distinct purposes: A VC attests to claims of entities while a DDO associated with a DID is mainly for connection or authentication.

Decentralized Storage Network. A decentralized storage network (DSN) aggregates storage offered by multiple independent storage providers and self-coordinate to provide data storage and data retrieval to clients. Informally, a DSN mainly satisfies two properties: *data integrity* and *retrievability*. We use the popular InterPlanetary File System (IPFS) [3] as an instantiation of DSN.

---

[3] https://identity.foundation/.
[4] https://www.w3.org/TR/did-core/.
[5] https://www.w3.org/TR/vc-data-model/.
[6] https://www.w3.org/TR/did-core/bib-json-ld11/.

3 System and Security Models

3.1 System Model

As depicted in Fig. 2, our framework involves the following parties: (i) a *creator* who creates a to-be-signed agreement; (iii) *signers* who fill in and sign agreements, possibly containing the creator itself; (iii) *issuer* who issues VCs for signers and creators; and (iv) *verifiers* who can verify VCs or signed agreements.

3.2 Security Model

Adversarial Model. The adversary is considered efficient in the sense of being *static* and restricted to *probabilistic poly-time* (P.P.T) algorithms.

Communication Model. We consider the *authenticated asynchronous* communication channel. Nevertheless, for some system components, the communication requirements may vary, e.g., the specific consensus mechanism in blockchain network may require either *partial synchronous* or *asynchronous* [8]; the distributed key generation protocol for setting up the decentralized issuer committee in a decentralized identity scheme requires *weak synchrony* for liveness [13].

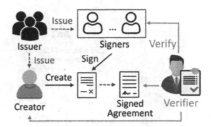

Fig. 2. System model.

Security Properties. Our framework aims to meet the security properties that:

- **Effectiveness.** Conditioned that all signers are honest, the system ensures that signing completes and the signers receive the valid signed agreement.
- **Fairness.** Upon finalization of the multi-party agreement signing protocol, either all honest signers obtain the evidence that the agreement is signed, or none of them does. A weaker fairness definition states that either the aforementioned fairness is met or all honest parties can prove that they have behaved correctly.
- **Timeliness.** Any party in the multi-party agreement signing protocol can assure that the protocol would terminate in a finite time, and once the protocol aborts or completes, the fairness for any honest party maintains.
- **Non-repudiation.** Upon finalization of the multi-party agreement signing protocol, none of the participants can deny having participated.

The above security properties are mandatory for a multi-party agreement signing protocol. In addition, two more properties can be optionally satisfied:

- **Confidentiality.** No external parties except the involved signers (including the creator) have access to the agreement content.

– **Abuse-free.** A signer P_i, if knowing another involved signer P_j's signature (but not all), cannot convince others but himself that the received signature is from P_j, i.e., P_i cannot leverage the commitment intention to misbehave.

We focus on the existing practical agreement signing model (§ 1) where a signing service provider (as a TTP) is incentivized to coordinate the signing operations. Intuitively, the above mandatory and optional properties can be readily satisfied. However, we highlight that our main contribution lies in improving the efficiency and security during the filling and signing procedure. Thus, in principle our designs are compatible with the methods concentrating on ensuring fairness, e.g., blockchain-based [18], which remove the centralized SSP. Such an integration naturally forms an interesting future extension. Besides the above properties, our system aims to further satisfy the following properties.

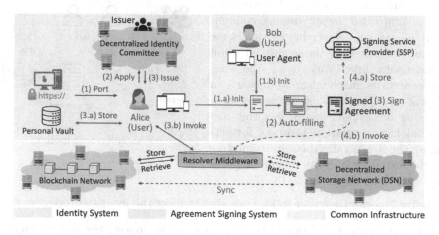

Fig. 3. An overview of the secure and efficient framework for agreement signing.

– **Privacy against signers.** The agreement contents are confidential to external parties (i.e., the confidentiality property), and the sensitive information is kept private even against malicious signers.
– **Scalability.** The framework is scalable to content-intensive agreements.

4   System Design

As shown in Fig. 3, the framework contains two subsystems: identity system and agreement signing system. The former allows a user/signer to obtain the credentials that can be utilized for agreement signing, while the latter presents the improved agreement signing flow. The common infrastructure is constructed by a permissioned blockchain and DSN to provide robust storage [9], e.g., storing users' issued VCs or signed agreements (instead of storing on the SSP side). For efficient retrieval, a signer can also cache some frequently used VCs in the personal vault, which though may not be robust as the blockchain-DSN based storage. The resolver middleware is deployed on each full node in the blockchain network for connection initialization, requests' and outputs' forwarding.

4.1 Identity System

The identity system is based on decentralized identity. We first introduce one specific instantiation via CanDID [13] and then present the proposed three-tier identity model. Note that other decentralized identity schemes, e.g., Coconut [16], can also be integrated as a underlying building block of our system.

CanDID allows users (namely, signers) to convert online legacy identity information, via oracle protocols [21], to so-called *pre-credentials*, which can then be submitted to a decentralized issuer committee to obtain VCs. Via CanDID, a *master credential* binding with a real-world unique identity, e.g., social security number (SSN) in the US, can be used to uniquely identify a user while various *context-based credentials* can be utilized in different application scenarios. The credential issuance procedure is private against corrupted issuers via zero-knowledge proof of knowledge and SMPC. Importantly, the security properties enabled by CanDID identity system are:

- **Sybil resistance.** An adversary cannot obtain more credentials than the number of users it controls.
- **Unforgeability.** An adversary cannot forge the credentials of honest users.
- **Credential issuance privacy.** An adversary controlling partial issuer committee members cannot learn the values of the claims contained in the pre-credentials during credential issuance procedure.
- **Credential validity.** An adversary can obtain credentials only for real-world identities it controls.
- **Unlinkability of applications.** An adversary corrupting multiple applications cannot link the transactions of any given user.
- **Credential verification privacy.** An adversarial verifying party cannot glean more information about the user than what is presented.

A Three-Tier User Identity Model. Based on the decentralized identity scheme, we propose an extensible three-tier user identity model, as detailed below.

- **Layer I.** This layer contains the user's decentralized identifier (DID) and master credential, which serves the purpose of **uniquely identifying a user**. Note the master credential is not intended for use in interactions with applications due to the *linkability* issue, i.e., a user's activities may be tracked if one identity is always used. Instead, context-based credentials are used.

– **Layer II.** This layer includes all context-based VCs of a user, which are used when **participating in a specific activity**. Essentially each VC is composed of one or a set of claims, e.g., "Name : Alice" and its validity proof, i.e., the issuer committee's joint signature $\sigma^{\mathcal{C}}$. For agreement signing, a user can apply for a "signing" credential with needed claims in advance.

– **Layer III.** This layer consists of **any yet verified claims of a user**. It is useful as there may exist no ground-truth for some claims, e.g., a user's hobby. Additionally, the value v_i of a claim can be various formats like image, audio, or video. E.g., the attribute of a claim is "Vaccination_Record" and the corresponding value is a picture of the vaccination record.

Extensible Identity Model. Moreover, some claims can be extracted from signed agreements, e.g., a user (as an employee) who signed an offer from a company X can extract a claim stating that "I am the employee of company X". Such an unverified claim resides in layer III initially. Later, the user can submit this claim to apply for a context-based credential, where the context can be "a discount for any employee in company X", and join in the corresponding activity. In that case, such a VC containing the claim "Employment_Affiliation : Company_X" would be categorized into layer II.

4.2 Agreement Signing System

Empowered by the decentralized identity-based identity model, our overarching goal of the agreement signing system lies in improving the existing signing flow in a secure and efficient way. Now we present the key designs in the signing flow.

Computational Representation Model of an Agreement. Inspired by the Accord project[7] and a common web application design pattern of model-view-controller (MVC), we split an agreement into three components: (i) Text $\mathcal{T}$: the textual part of an agreement, which is unchangeable and acts as a template; (ii) Model $\mathcal{M}$: the data fields (typically represented in JSON format) populated in an agreement; (iii) Logic $\{\mathcal{L}_i\}$: the execution logic of a set of clauses in an agreement. A specific clause logic is denoted as $\mathcal{L}_i$. An agreement is denoted as a tuple $(\mathcal{T}, \mathcal{M}, \{\mathcal{L}_i\})$.

In an agreement signing instance, upon a signer receives the agreement, the three components are presented for signers as follows: (i) the text $\mathcal{T}$ is shown as plaintext on the webpage after replacing each fillable data filled in the agreement data $\mathcal{M}$ as an input box; (ii) the model $\mathcal{M}$ extracts the fillable data fields as a JSON template whose values will be updated when the signer fills in; (iii) each clause $\mathcal{L}_i$, shown with a natural language description on the webpage, corresponds to a pre-determined executable smart contract function.

Furthermore, we propose to construct a *global agreement template library* and a *global clause template library*, which are deployed in a consortium blockchain maintained by organizations of interest, e.g., the same committee of the credential issuer. Such designs bring multi-fold benefits: (i) the unchangeable textual

---

[7] https://github.com/accordproject/.

description of an agreement usually accounts for a large proportion. Similarly, the clauses are typically common business logic, and extracting them as public templates exhibits a modular design, thus enabling efficient management; (ii) the publicly auditable template for agreements or clauses would be beneficial to establish the standard of the agreement signing ecosystem; (iii) blockchain-enabled storage of the libraries enjoys the advantages offered by blockchain including availability, consistency, and byzantine fault tolerance [9]. As an added benefit, the clauses $\{\mathcal{L}_i\}$ in an agreement can be parameterized and enabled for execution in smart contract, which provides guaranteed execution.

Privacy-Preserved Auto-Filling with Verifiable Data. The signing system supports auto-filling via a *fuzzy matching* algorithm, as shown in Algorithm 1. Specifically, the agreement data $\mathcal{M}$ are represented in JSON where each entry (i.e., a key-value pair) binds with a redactable data field in the agreement. Once the user agent loads the to-be-signed agreement, the fuzzy matching algorithm, by taking as input the key of the input box, e.g., userName, and a VC in this context, e.g., cred$_{signing}$ containing the claims $\{\{$ "name": "Alice"$\}, \{$ "address": "123, Main Street"$\}, \{$ "state": "NY"$\}\}$, from the user's information vault, would return the best matched value y (i.e., Alice) and automatically fill in. A user can selectively fill in even though some fields are auto-filled, and for those unfilled fields, the user can manually fill in as usual.

Algorithm 1. The fuzzy matching algorithm for auto-filling

Input: target, the key of the input box, which is derived from the agreement model
　　data $\mathcal{M}$; the VC cred$_{signing}$ for the context of agreement signing.
Output: y, the most possible value contained in VC for the key target
1: **Initialization:** $y := \bot$, and max_possibility $:= 0$;
2: $\{$claim$_i = (a_i, v_i)\} \leftarrow parse(\text{cred}_{signing})$;
3: **for** each claim$_i$ in $\{$claim$_i\}$ **do**
4: 　　find the *longest common substring* (lcs) between claim$_i.a_i$ and target;
5: 　　$\theta_1 :=$ lcs.length/claim$_i.a_i$.length; $\theta_2 :=$ lcs.length/target.length;
6: 　　$\theta := \max\{\theta_1, \theta_2\}$;
7: 　　**if** $\theta \equiv 0$ **then**
8: 　　　　continue;
9: 　　**else**
10: 　　　**if** $\theta >$ max_possibility **then**
11: 　　　　　max_possibility $:= \theta$; $y :=$ claim$_i$;
12: **return** y;

Algorithm 2. Verification of auto-filled identity information

---

Input: The user inputs the context-based VC, e.g., $\mathsf{cred}_{\mathsf{signing}}$, that is used for auto-filling. The verifier $\mathcal{V}$ inputs a random challenge c. The public key $pk^{\mathcal{C}}$ of the issuer committee and the context-specific public key $pk^{\mathcal{U}}_{\mathsf{ctx}}$ of the user are public inputs.
Output: The verifier $\mathcal{V}$ outputs $true/false$.
1: <u>For the user $\mathcal{U}$:</u>
2: Send $(\mathsf{cred}_{\mathsf{signing}}, \sigma)$ to the verifier $\mathcal{V}$ where $\sigma := \mathsf{Sign}(sk^{\mathcal{U}}_{\mathsf{ctx}}, c)$

3: <u>For the verifier $\mathcal{V}$:</u>
4: Output $\mathsf{Verify}(pk^{\mathcal{U}}_{\mathsf{ctx}}, c, \sigma) \wedge \mathsf{Verify}(pk^{\mathcal{C}}, \mathsf{cred}_{\mathsf{signing}} \backslash \sigma^{\mathcal{C}}, \sigma^{\mathcal{C}})$? $true : false$

It is worth pointing out that the auto-filled data fields come from layer II in the user identity model, where the validity of each claim in the credential is trusted in the sense of publicly verifiable via the issuer committee's signature $\sigma^{\mathcal{C}}$. Algorithm 2 elaborates the verification of auto-filled identity information. Moreover, the filling is privacy-preserved, because instead of sensitive identity information, a *statement* would be filled in. For example, in a *loan application* scenario, the user needs to sign the agreement with the bank and prove that his or her age is qualified. In this case, instead of a specific age, e.g., "Age : 23", the pre-credential for the statement "Age : Over_18" would be submitted to the issuer for VC issuance. Such a proof can be generated via zero-knowledge proof, e.g., Bulletproofs [5] for range proof.

Handling Content-Intensive Agreements. During agreement filling, many agreements, e.g., in B2B setting, are associated with attachments of large size. To handle this situation, we propose the introduce the DSN that instantiated by private IPFS cluster. Specifically, the following steps operate: (i) the signer selects the attachment in the user agent; (ii) each attachment is encrypted via $c_{\mathsf{att}_i} \leftarrow \mathsf{Enc}(sk_i, \mathsf{att}_i), sk_i := \mathcal{H}(\mathsf{session\_ID}||mk||i)$ where c_{att_i} is the encrypted attachment; $\mathsf{Enc}(\cdot)$ is the symmetric encryption scheme; sk_i is the secret key for the i-th attachment that can be derived by hashing the unique $\mathsf{session\_ID}$, a randomly sampled master key mk, and the index i; (iii) the array of encrypted attachments are uploaded to IPFS cluster, which returns an array of content identifiers, i.e., $\{cid_{\mathsf{att}_i}\}$. The array $\{cid_{\mathsf{att}_i}\}$ is then added to the agreement data model $\mathcal{M}$ as one of it entries. Alternatively, the attachments can be submitted to IPFS as one file, thus only one cid needs to be added to agreement data $\mathcal{M}$.

Minimized Agreement Signing Data. With the computational representation model and further scalable design for content-intensive agreements, the agreement signing data can be minimized for better signing efficiency. In sum, the following designs make the contributions: (i) a short agreement template ID string instead of the entire unchangeable agreement textual template $\mathcal{T}$; (ii) clause instances (i.e., short clauses' textual template IDs and their parameters in JSON format) instead of the whole textual template and parameters of clauses; (iii) short attachments' IDs instead of attachments of large size. These information are added in agreement model data $\mathcal{M}$ for signing. Listing 1.1 gives an example of the model data $\mathcal{M}$ for a copyright license agreement.

```
 1    {
 2      "agreement_template_id": "AGREEMENT-8dd14d0adbc8...",
 3      "agreement_data_fields": [
 4        "licenseeName": "Alice",
 5        "licenseeState": "NY",
 6        "licenseeEntityType": "individual",
 7        "licenseeAddress": "123 Main Street",
 8        "licensorName": "Bob",... ],
 9      "attachment_id": [
10        "QmeGPbyGuz3vSLegSYkz92KHfuVJj6Dz5gGWnPXaSaww4J",...],
11      "clause_instance": [{
12        "clause_id": "CLAUSE-930497c469f53d...",
13        "params": [
14          "amount": "100",
15          "amount_text": "one_hundred",
16          "payment_method": "bank_transfer" }},...],
17      "matadata": [
18        "agreement_creation_timestamp": "2022/03/06",...],
19      "signature_info": [{
20        "licenseeSignature": { ... },
21        "licenseeSignDate": "16:10:50/March 10 2022" }, {
22        "licensorSignature": { ... },
23        "licensorSignDate": "11:20:31/March 11 2022"}]
24    }
```

Listing 1.1. An example of a copyright license agreement model data $\mathcal{M}$, which mainly contains six aspects: (i) agreement template id; (ii) agreement data fields that can be updated by signers; (iii) attachment id(s); (iv) clause instances; (v) metadata; and (vi) signature information.

Reduced Verification Complexity for an Agreement. The signatures from n parties typically result in $O(n)$ verification complexity. To this end, we propose to leverage the cryptographic primitive *BLS (Bohen-Lynn-Shacham) multisignature aggregation scheme* [4] so that the TTP can aggregate the signatures and reduce the verification complexity. The scheme utilizes the following ingredients: (i) *a bilinear pairing* $e : \mathbb{G}_0 \times \mathbb{G}_1 \to \mathbb{G}_T$. The group $\mathbb{G}_0$, $\mathbb{G}_1$ and $\mathbb{G}_T$ all have a large prime order q. The pairing is efficiently computable and non-degenerate. We let g_0 and g_1 be generators of $\mathbb{G}_0$ and $\mathbb{G}_1$ respectively; (ii) *hash functions*. Two hash functions are used: (i) $\mathcal{H}_0 : \{0,1\}^* \to \mathbb{G}_1$; and (ii) $\mathcal{H}_1 : \{0,1\}^* \to \mathbb{Z}_q$. With the basis above, the agreement signing scheme works as follows:

- Setup(1^λ) $\to$ pp: The setup algorithm that given the security parameter λ outputs a set of public parameters pp := $(\mathbb{G}_0, \mathbb{G}_1, \mathbb{G}_T, e, g_0, g_1, q, \mathcal{H}_0, \mathcal{H}_1)$;
- KeyGen(pp) $\to$ (pk, sk): The key generation algorithm randomly and uniformly chooses a secret key $sk \leftarrow_\$ \mathbb{Z}_q$, computes the public key $pk \leftarrow g_1^{sk}$ and outputs (pk, sk);
- KeyAggr($\{pk_1, \cdots, pk_n\}$) $\to$ apk: The key aggregation algorithm takes as input the n signing parties' public keys $\{pk_1, \cdots, pk_n\}$ and outputs an aggregated key $apk \leftarrow \prod_{i=1}^{n} pk_i^{\mathcal{H}_1(pk_i, \{pk_1, \cdots, pk_n\})}$;
- SignAgreement(pp, $\{pk_1, \cdots, pk_n\}, sk_i, \mathcal{M}$) $\to$ σ: The signing algorithm takes as input the public parameters pp, the parties' public keys $\{pk_1, \cdots, pk_n\}$, the signer's secret key sk_i and the agreement model data $\mathcal{M}$, and outputs the aggregated signature σ where $\sigma \leftarrow \prod_{i=1}^{n} \mathcal{H}_0(\mathcal{M})^{sk_i \cdot \mathcal{H}_1(pk_i, \{pk_1, \cdots, pk_n\})}$;

- VerifySignature(pp, $apk, \mathcal{M}, \sigma$) $\rightarrow$ 1/0: The signature verification algorithm takes as input the public parameters pp, the aggregated key apk, the agreement data $\mathcal{M}$ and the resulting signature σ, and outputs 1 iff $e(g_1, \sigma) \equiv e(apk, \mathcal{H}_0(\mathcal{M}))$.

The agreement signing scheme satisfies the *correctness* so that, informally speaking, the honest party can be convinced that indeed σ is a valid signature on the agreement model data $\mathcal{M}$ relative to the n parties' public keys. Also, the signature is *unforgeable* in the sense that given an oracle that generates valid signatures, it is infeasible for an efficient adversary to output a valid signature on a message that has not been queried to the oracle [7].

4.3 Security Sketch

Theorem 1. *Conditioned that the underlying cryptographic primitives are secure, and the signing service provider is trusted, our framework satisfies the properties of effectiveness, fairness, timeliness, non-repudiation, confidentiality, abuse-free, privacy against signers and scalability.*

Proof. As we consider the signing service provider (SSP) as a TTP for coordinating the signing activity, the basic properties including effectiveness, fairness, timeliness, non-repudiation, confidentiality and abuse-free can be readily ensured. For the privacy against signers, it reduces to the credential verification privacy in the identity model, i.e., a signer $\mathcal{P}_i$ cannot glean more information than that the other signer $\mathcal{P}_j$ meant to reveal. It further reduces to the *zero-knowledge* property of zero-knowledge proof for a claim during the process of credential issuance. For the scalability, the attachments (of any size) associated with an agreement are uploaded to DSN while only a short string is embedded into agreement model data for signing.

5 Experiments

Prototype System Implementation. We implemented[8] a prototype of the framework with the following instantiation: (i) Blockchain is instantiated by Hyperledger Fabric with BFT-SMaRt-enabled byzantine fault tolerant consensus [17], instead of Fabric's default version that only supports CFT consensus such as Raft. (ii) DSN is instantiated by an IPFS cluster[9] as the data stored in public IPFS may eventually fade away if no one accesses it. (iii) The PKI-like infrastructure for mapping users' DIDs and public keys is instantiated by Microsoft Identity Overlay Network (ION)[10]. Since ION is anchored on Bitcoin, to accommodate our framework, we only leverage its interfaces to generate the DDOs while the underlying blockchain platform is switched to the Fabric-based

---

[8] https://github.com/Blockchain-World/Agreement-Signing.git.
[9] https://cluster.ipfs.io/documentation/guides/pinning/.
[10] https://github.com/decentralized-identity/ion/.

architecture we developed. (iv) As the CanDID implementation has not been made publicly available at present, we simplified the credential issuance procedure by allowing one node to represent the issuer committee to sign VCs. (v) The computational representation model is instantiated by Accord, and we integrated it with the Fabric-based blockchain platform we developed to guarantee the execution of clauses enabled in the agreement.

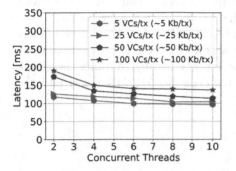

Fig. 4. Latency of writing VCs to Fabric ledger with varied TX size.

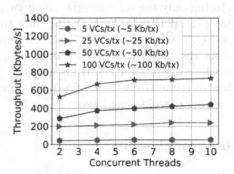

Fig. 5. Throughput of writing VCs to Fabric ledger with varied TX size.

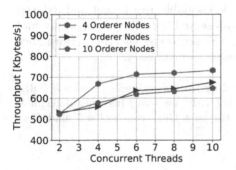

Fig. 6. Throughput with different number of orderers in Fabric ledger.

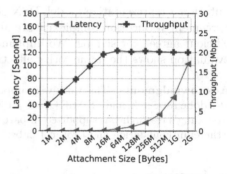

Fig. 7. Latency and throughput of data writing to IPFS cluster.

Experiment Environment. We run experiments on a small-scale cluster consisting of four Virtual Machines (VMs) residing on two servers (both are Dell PowerEdge R740), representing four nodes to form a permissioned blockchain and an IPFS cluster. Each VM has 8 vCPUs, 24 GB memory, and 800 GB hard drive, and the bandwidth between the VMs is about 10 Gbits/s.

Performance Evaluation. Figures 4 and 5 illustrate the latency and the corresponding throughput of writing VCs to the ledger (i.e., the state database in Fabric) where each VC in our experiment is about 1 KBytes (containing two claims). The measurements show that the throughput reaches about 800 KBytes/s. In addition, as shown in Fig. 6, we evaluate the scalability on the number of orderer nodes for the BFT consensus in the blockchain network. The results show that the throughput decreases slightly with more orderers. This is reasonable since more ordering nodes reaching consensus would yield more communication latency. Moreover, the Fabric-IPFS architecture reduces the storage costs in the ledger by storing the data (e.g., attachments, VCs) in IPFS while storing only the reference (i.e., content ID) in the ledger. Thus, we further evaluate the performance of writing data to the private IPFS cluster, as illustrated in Fig. 7, where the throughput stably reaches 20 MBytes/s. The query latency from the blockchain network is about 89 ms since only the short content ID is retrieved, while for the IPFS network, the latency mainly contains the chunk lookup time (from 23 ms for 1 MB data to 95 ms for 512 MB data) and the ensuing downloading latency.

6   Conclusion

We proposed a secure and efficient framework to improve the existing agreement signing flow. The identity subsystem based on decentralized identity schemes allows a user to apply, control, manage and selectively reveal their credentials. Based on it, the agreement signing subsystem realizes privacy-preserved auto-filling with verifiable identity information. Other critical designs such as the computational representation model, DSN-enabled scalable attachment and reduced agreement verification complexity are also presented to facilitate the secure and efficient agreement signing. We implement the prototype and the performance evaluation shows the framework's effectiveness and efficiency.

Acknowledgments. This work was supported by Document Intelligence Labs (DIL) at Adobe Research, and US NSF Grant #1801492 with New Jersey Institute of Technology. Tang's research was supported in part by Research Gifts from Stellar Foundation, Ethereum Foundation and Protocol Labs.

References

1. Alper, H.K., Küpçü, A.: Optimally efficient multi-party fair exchange and fair secure multi-party computation. ACM Trans. Priv. Secur. **25**, 1–34 (2021)
2. Androulaki, E., Barger, A., Bortnikov, V., Cachin, C., Christidis, K., et al.: Hyperledger fabric: a distributed operating system for permissioned blockchains. In: Proceedings of the 13th EuroSys, pp. 1–15 (2018)
3. Benet, J.: IPFS-content addressed, versioned, P2P popfile system. arXiv preprint arXiv:1407.3561 (2014)
4. Boneh, D., Drijvers, M., Neven, G.: Compact multi-signatures for smaller blockchains. In: Peyrin, T., Galbraith, S. (eds.) ASIACRYPT 2018. LNCS, vol. 11273, pp. 435–464. Springer, Cham (2018). https://doi.org/10.1007/978-3-030-03329-3_15

5. Bünz, B., Bootle, J., Boneh, D., Poelstra, A., Wuille, P., Maxwell, G.: Bulletproofs: short proofs for confidential transactions and more. In: Symposium on Security and Privacy (SP), pp. 315–334. IEEE (2018)
6. Garay, J., MacKenzie, P., Prabhakaran, M., Yang, K.: Resource fairness and composability of cryptographic protocols. In: Halevi, S., Rabin, T. (eds.) TCC 2006. LNCS, vol. 3876, pp. 404–428. Springer, Heidelberg (2006). https://doi.org/10.1007/11681878_21
7. Goldwasser, S., Micali, S., Rivest, R.L.: A digital signature scheme secure against adaptive chosen-message attacks. SIAM J. Comput. **17**, 281–308 (1988)
8. Guo, B., Lu, Z., Tang, Q., Xu, J., Zhang, Z.: Dumbo: faster asynchronous BFT protocols. In: Proceedings of the ACM CCS, pp. 803–818 (2020)
9. He, S., et al.: Blockchain-based automated and robust cyber security management. J. Parallel Distrib. Comput. (JPDC) **163**, 62–82 (2022)
10. He, S., Lu, Y., Tang, Q., Wang, G., Wu, C.Q.: Fair peer-to-peer content delivery via blockchain. In: Bertino, E., Shulman, H., Waidner, M. (eds.) ESORICS 2021. LNCS, vol. 12972, pp. 348–369. Springer, Cham (2021). https://doi.org/10.1007/978-3-030-88418-5_17
11. He, S., Tang, Q., Wu, C.Q., Shen, X.: Decentralizing IoT management systems using blockchain for censorship resistance. IEEE Trans. Ind. Inform. **16**, 715–727 (2019)
12. Kordy, B., Radomirovic, S.: Constructing optimistic multi-party contract signing protocols. In: 2012 IEEE 25th Computer Security Foundations Symposium, pp. 215–229. IEEE (2012)
13. Maram, D., et al.: CanDID: can-do decentralized identity with legacy compatibility, sybil-resistance, and accountability. In: 2021 IEEE Symposium on Security and Privacy, pp. 1348–1366 (2021)
14. Nakamoto, S.: Bitcoin: a peer-to-peer electronic cash system (2008)
15. Pagnia, H., Gärtner, F.C., et al.: On the impossibility of fair exchange without a trusted third party. Technical report, Darmstadt University of Technology (1999)
16. Sonnino, A., Al-Bassam, M., Bano, S., Meiklejohn, S., Danezis, G.: Coconut: threshold issuance selective disclosure credentials with applications to distributed ledgers. In: Proceedings of NDSS (2019)
17. Sousa, J., Bessani, A., Vukolic, M.: A Byzantine fault-tolerant ordering service for the hyperledger fabric blockchain platform. In: DSN, pp. 51–58. IEEE (2018)
18. Tian, H., He, J., Fu, L.: Contract coin: toward practical contract signing on blockchain. In: Liu, J.K., Samarati, P. (eds.) ISPEC 2017. LNCS, vol. 10701, pp. 43–61. Springer, Cham (2017). https://doi.org/10.1007/978-3-319-72359-4_3
19. Wan, Z., Deng, R.H., Lee, D.: Electronic contract signing without using trusted third party. In: NSS 2015. LNCS, vol. 9408, pp. 386–394. Springer, Cham (2015). https://doi.org/10.1007/978-3-319-25645-0_27
20. Wood, G.: Ethereum: a secure decentralised generalised transaction ledger. Ethereum Proj. Yellow Pap. **151**, 1–32 (2014)
21. Zhang, F., Maram, D., Malvai, H., Goldfeder, S., Juels, A.: DECO: liberating web data using decentralized oracles for TLS. In: ACM CCS, pp. 1919–1938 (2020)

A Privacy-Preserving Credit Bank Supervision Framework Based on Redactable Blockchain

Xinzhe Huang[1], Yong Ding[1,2(✉)], Haibin Zheng[3], Decun Luo[3], Yujue Wang[1], Junfu Wu[1], and Luyi Zhang[1]

[1] Guangxi Key Laboratory of Cryptography and Information Security, School of Computer and Information Security, Guilin University of Electronic Technology, Guilin 541004, China
stone_dingy@126.com
[2] Cyberspace Security Research Center, Pengcheng Laboratory, Shenzhen 518038, China
[3] Hangzhou Innovation Institute, Beihang University, Hangzhou 310053, China

Abstract. Credit bank plays a vital role in constructing a lifelong education system. However, it confronts many security and privacy issues, and it is difficult to maintain the records. Thus, the blockchain technology has been introduced to achieve automatic management of credit bank. Unfortunately, the immutable nature of blockchain makes it impossible for students to delete their private data when they leave, which would bring data leakage risks. As an effective way to protect private data, redactable blockchain allows user to modify the data on the blockchain. However, existing redactable blockchains lack a trusted third party regulatory mechanism to ensure the legality and compliance of delete operations. To addresses these issues, based on redactable blockchain and threshold signature, this paper provides a data management scheme with privacy protection for credit bank, which supports external supervision, and allows secure and efficient deletion of student's private data on the blockchain while ensuring the privacy data of students. Theoretical analysis and experiments show that the proposed scheme can effectively resist malicious behaviors and has practical performance.

Keywords: Credit bank · Chameleon hash · Redactable blockchain · Threshold signature · Privacy protection

1 Introduction

With the increasing awareness of lifelong learning and the improvement of vocational skill requirements, more and more people choose to take training courses related to career growth after completing academic education. In order to meet the needs of professional talent promotion, the credit bank was introduced. It mainly provides professional training guidance and multi-level skill courses to help students improve their skills and get employed quickly.

Blockchain is a distributed ledger [1], with advantages of decentralization, tamper-proof security, traceability, openness, transparency, and anonymity. It can effectively solve the record management problems of traditional credit bank, promote the input, conversion, and verification of learning achievements, ensures the trusted storage of learning achievements. Blockchain also can promote trust with employers, significantly improving learning and employment efficiency [2, 3].

With the rise of privacy awareness, the 'Right to be Forgotten' has recently been imposed as an essential Data Subject Right by the GDPR of the European Union, which means that people have the right to ask to delete their private data. Thus, the private data recorded on the blockchain that cannot be tampered with will no longer be legal. As the Open Data Institute reports [4], private data can be leaked from the blockchain. For example, in a healthcare system based on blockchain, where a large amount of patient disease data is stored on the blockchain, the system should remove that if no longer needed. At the same time, the immutable nature of the blockchain enables student's private data to be permanently stored on the blockchain [5], which would bring great privacy and security risks to students [6, 7].

Fortunately, the Chameleon hash [8] provides a way to edit the content of the given block with a 'trapdoor'. The deletion of data on the blockchain needs to be supervised by a trusted third party, which can ensure the deletion has not been abused. However, the supervision will likely bring privacy leakage issues [9, 10]. Due to the structural differences between redactable and traditional blockchains, privacy protection methods on traditional blockchains cannot be applied to redactable blockchains. Therefore, it is necessary to design an effective supervision mechanism for protecting private data on the redactable blockchain in credit bank.

1.1 Related Works

Many studies have been conducted on implementing blockchain modifications in different scenarios. Ateniese et al. [11] first introduced the concept of a redactable blockchain by using the Chameleon hash function. It allows the user holding the trapdoor to modify any block's content without affecting the original block's hash value. Thus trusted supervisor holding a trapdoor can supervise the content of any block on the blockchain. Deuber et al. [12] proposed to modify a confirmed block by publishing a new block and replacing it when the new block gets enough votes. However, this modification can only solve the problem at the block level. In this process, personal data is easily modified by malicious users. Alla et al. [13] presented a redactable medical blockchain based on the Chameleon hash function, enabling the sharing of medical data and modifying error data. Xu et al. [14] proposed an identity management scheme based on a redactable blockchain. It implemented lightweight user authentication using blockchain and enabled users to log out their identity data after leaving the network but did not introduce third-party trusted supervision.

For blockchain supervision, Deuber et al. [12] proposed a dual-chain architecture for blockchain supervision in a public blockchain environment. Li et al. [15] designed a two-layers supervision framework based on adaptive blockchain for the supervision problems in off-site modular housing production. Wen et al. [16] proposed a privacy protection supervision framework in a multi-party environment, which can monitor sensitive data on the business blockchain.

However, redactable blockchain in existing scenarios does not consider external supervision mechanisms, and most blockchain supervision schemes do not support private data deletion in credit bank scenarios. Thus, it is necessary to design a management scheme based on redactable blockchains for supporting credit bank scenarios.

1.2 Our Contributions

To address the above challenges faced by the credit bank blockchain, we propose a privacy-preserving credit bank supervision framework based on the redactable blockchain (PCR), where a supervision chain (SC) is introduced to manage the credit bank chain (CBC).

When students request an data deletion request, the supervisors on SC are responsible for reviewing whether the request is reasonable through threshold signature. The threshold signature is generated for the deletion request only when the signature shares reach the threshold. The smart contract will verify the correctness of this signature and remove the student's private data on the CBC after successful verification.

In the PCR system, the management of trapdoors is separated from business transactions, which can reduce the burden and improve the operations efficiency of CBC. The main contributions are summarized as follows.

- We provide a trusted and supervisable data management solution for CBC, which can enhance the scalability of the CBC by employing the redactable blockchain with Chameleon hash. Thus, the data on CBC can be effectively maintained.
- A dual-chain supervisory architecture is designed based on a redactable blockchain to separate the data storage and management. The management process of private data is executed on SC without the involvement of CBC, which improves the efficiency of the PCR system.
- A new approach to protect the private data of students is proposed. In CBC, students can remove their private data from CBC when they leave. In addition, the threshold signature is also used to protect the real identity for the supervisor on SC. No one can recover the real identity of the supervisor from the aggregated signature.
- An instantiation is presented, which is analyzed through theoretical analysis and experiments. It confirms that the proposed method can effectively guarantee the privacy of students and supervisors. Experiments show that the dual-chain separation architecture can improve system efficiency.

1.3 Paper Organization

The remainder of this paper is organized as follows Sect. 2 provides some preliminaries, and Sect. 3 presents the system model and security requirements. A PCR construction is designed in Sect. 4, which security is analyzed in Sect. 5. Section 6 evaluates the performance, and Sect. 7 concludes the paper.

2 Preliminaries

2.1 Chameleon Hash

A Chameleon hash scheme [8] consists of five polynomial-time algorithms $CH = (ParGen, KGen, Hash, Forge, Check)$.

- $pp \leftarrow ParGen(1^\lambda)$: The public parameter generation algorithm $ParGen_{CH}$ takes a security parameter λ, and outputs a public parameter pp.
- $(pk, tk) \leftarrow KGen(pp)$: The key generation algorithm $KGen$ takes a public parameter pp, and outputs public key and trapdoor key (pk, tk).
- $(h, r) \leftarrow Hash(pk, m)$: The Chameleon $Hash$ algorithm takes the public key pk and message m, and outputs a hash value h and a checking string r.
- $(h, s') \leftarrow Forge(tk, (h, m, r), m')$: The Chameleon hash collision algorithm $Forge$ takes trapdoor key tk, hash h, message m, and new message m', and outputs checking string s'.
- $\{0, 1\} \leftarrow Check(pk, (h, r, s))$: The deterministic verification algorithm $Check$ takes the public key pk, hash value h, message m. If (h, s) is valid hash and checking string for message m, then returns 1, otherwise 0.

2.2 Smart Contract

The smart contract [17] is a computer protocol that automatically executes predefined rules and procedures as transactions occur. The transparent script code of the smart contract is automatically performed under the supervision of all nodes and follows the conditions. The performance process of the transaction cannot be manipulated or tampered with, which ensures the reliability of the automatic operation results of the predefined programs.

2.3 Threshold Signature

A (t, n) threshold signature scheme [18] consists of four polynomial-time algorithms $TS = (Setup, Sign, Refactor, Verify)$.

- $(PK, \{PartSigSK_i\}_{i=1,\cdots,n}) \leftarrow Setup(s, t, n)$: The common parameter generation algorithm $Setup$ takes a security parameter s, threshold value t and total number of users n, and outputs the public key PK and private key fragment $PartSigSK_i$ for each user $i = 1, 2, \cdots, n$.

- $ThresholdSig_i \leftarrow Sign(msg, PartSigSK_i)$: The signature fragment generation algorithm $Sign$ takes a message msg and a user private key fragment $PartSigSK_i$ for some $i \in \{1, 2, \cdots, n\}$, and outputs a signature share $ThresholdSig_i$.
- $ThresholdSig \leftarrow Refactor(\{PartSigSK_i\}, t)$: The signature collection algorithm $Refactor$ requires a minimum of t signature shares $\{PartSigSK_i\}$, and outputs a signature $ThresholdSig$.
- $\{1, 0\} \leftarrow Verify(msg, PK, ThresholdSig)$: The threshold signature verification algorithm $Verify$ takes a message msg, the public key PK, and a signature $ThresholdSig$. It outputs 1 if the verification is passed; otherwise 0.

2.4 Bilinear Mapping

Let G_1, G_2 and G_T be three cyclic groups with the prime order p, where g_1 is a generator of G_1 and g_2 is a generator of G_2. $e : G_1 \times G_2 \to G_T$ is a bilinear map if it satisfies the three properties:

1) Bilinearity: For all $g_1 \in G_1, g_2 \in G_2$ and $a, b \in Z_p$, we have $e(g_1^a, g_2^b) = e(g_1, g_2)^{ab}$.
2) Non-degeneracy: There exists $g_1 \in G_1, g_2 \in G_2$ such that $e(g_1, g_2) \neq 1$.
3) Computability: There exists efficient algorithm to compute $e(g_1, g_2)$ for all $g_1 \in G_1, g_2 \in G_2$.

3 System Model and Requirements

3.1 System Model

As shown in Fig. 1, we design a secure and efficient redactable blockchain management system to achieve private data management in CBC. The PCR system has five main entities: student, supervisor, key generation center (KGC), system manager and executor. Their definitions are as follows.

The system manager deploys the blockchain and generates system parameters. After completing the initialization procedure, system manager will be offline and no longer participate in subsequent operations. The student is the core user of the CBC. Students can obtain learning results through courses, apply for the completion certificate after meeting the graduation conditions, and request to remove the private data on the CBC when leaving it. KGC is a trusted third party that initializes system parameters for SC and CBC, generates a trapdoor for Chameleon hash transactions and private key fragments for the supervisor. The supervisor on SC is responsible for reviewing deletion requests from the student on CBC. The executor on CBC is responsible for executing the delete operation and removing the private data of the specified student.

CBC is a redactable blockchain based on the Chameleon hash. It is responsible for the core business of credit bank, such as learning achievements management, learning file storage and dealing with malicious users on the blockchain.

SC is a standard blockchain composed of multiple supervisor nodes, which uses smart contracts and threshold signatures to review deletion requests for the CBC. In the PCR system, the student's deletion request is first submitted to the supervisor, where the request is reviewed through the threshold signature. If the final review is approved, the deletion request with the threshold signature is sent to the executor responsible for deleting the specified private data.

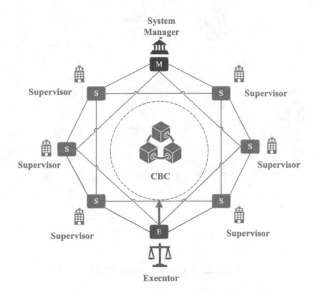

Fig. 1. System model.

3.2   Security Requirements

- Data security: The private data of the student's identity can only be deleted by themselves when leaving CBC.
- Privacy protection: The student's private data and the supervisor's real identity should be encrypted and stored on the chain.

4   PCR Construction

In this section, the PCR system has three phases: the initialization phase, the storage phase and the deletion phase (Fig. 2).

4.1   Initialization Phase

This phase consists of three parts including the initialization of CBC, SC and smart contract.

  1) **CBC Initialization**

System manager deploys a redactable blockchain on Chameleon hash with the help of KGC. KGC selects big prime numbers p and q such that $p = kq + 1$, where q is a large enough prime factor. The element g is of order q in Z_p^*. Then KGC selects a random $x \in Z_q^*$ and calculates $y = g^x$. KGC gives the trapdoor key and public key $(tk, pk) = (x, y)$ to the system manager.

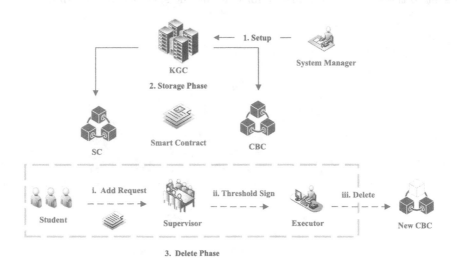

Fig. 2. A procedure of PCR.

The system manager deploys executor node on CBC and writes the parameters $pp = (p, q, g)$ and secure Chameleon hash function h onto the smart contracts of PCR.

2) SC Initialization

System manager deploys an blockchain based on tradition hash, and initializes threshold signature on SC with the help of KGC.

KGC chooses a bilinear pairing $e : G_1 \times G_2 \to G_T$, where G_1, G_2 and G_T have prime order p, and chooses random generators $g_1 \in G_1$ and $g_2 \in G_2$. Then the KGC generates a master public/secret key pair. Let $x \in Z_p$ be the master secret key as msk and $v = g_2^x \in G_2$ be the master public key as mpk. The KGC picks a random polynomial $w \in Z_p[X]$ of degree at most $t - 1$ such that $w(0) = x$. For $i = 1, ..., n$, the KGC gives supervisor i the value $x_i = w(i)$, its share of the private key. KGC selects a secure hash function $H : \{0, 1\}^* \to G_1$ for the supervisor to calculate the signature share.

The system manager deploys supervisor nodes on SC. Then he writes the system parameters, the master public key, the supervisor's public key shares and secure hash function H into smart contracts of PCR.

3) Smart Contract Initialization

The system manager initializes the genesis block CB_0 on CBC, which is the only one immutable block on CBC. CB_0 contains the address of central management contract SC_{center} of PCR, where SC_{center} contains all of SC's addresses for editing CBC block information, identity verification contract $SC_{identity}$, trapdoor management contract $SC_{trapdoor}$, and threshold signature verification contract $SC_{threshold}$.

4.2   Storage Phase

When a student registers on CBC, the student's all private data will be combined and transferred to point m on Z_q^*. Then the student node calculate the Chameleon hash value h_{ch} as follow.

$$h_{ch} = g^m \Delta y^r \quad \text{mod } p \tag{1}$$

Once the identity transaction is verified and confirmed, the identity verification smart contract $SC_{identity}$ is automatically triggered. The transaction data m is converted into private data and written on CBC, which will be used as the student's identity proof for subsequent operations on CBC.

4.3   Delete Phase

1) Delete Request
   The student can submit a deletion request $msg = (m, t) \in \{0, 1\}^*$ when leaving PCR, where m is the point of student's private data on Z_q^* and t is the request's timestamp. Then msg is forwarded to SC for review by CBC through a secure cross-chain information transmission mechanism.
2) Threshold Sign
   When SC receives the deletion request, SC will automatically start the threshold signature algorithm for msg. Each supervisor will generate and broadcast the signature share σ_i of msg as follows.

$$\sigma_i = H(msg)^{x_i} \in G_1 \tag{2}$$

When the number of signature share reaches the threshold t, the threshold signature σ is constructed as follows

$$\sigma = \prod_{i=1}^{t} \sigma_i^{\lambda_i} \tag{3}$$

where

$$\lambda_i = \frac{\prod_{i=1, j \neq i}^{t} (0 - j)}{\prod_{i=1, j \neq i}^{t} (i - j)} \quad \text{mod } p \tag{4}$$

To verify threshold signature σ, threshold verification contract $SC_{threshold}$ is invoked, only when the equality in (5) holds the threshold signature is valid.

$$e(\sigma, g_2) = e(H(msg), mpk) \tag{5}$$

Then the final deletion request $msg' = (m, t, \sigma)$ is generated and sented to the executor on CBC using a secure cross-chain mechanism.

3) Delete Phase

Upon receiving the final deletion request msg' by the executor, the threshold signature verification contract $SC_{threshold}$ will be automatically triggered, where the equality (5) is checked. The executor uses the $SC_{trapdoor}$ to obtain the trapdoor tk of the specified transaction and calculates the new random number r' as follows

$$r' = (m - m')x^{-1} + r \mod q \tag{6}$$

and modifies the messages m to m' if the following condition is satisfied

$$g^m \cdot y^r = g^{m'} \cdot y^{r'} \mod p \tag{7}$$

where m' is the point on Z_q^* with no identity data.

After deletion by the executor, the random number r' and content m' of the modified block CB_i on CBC should be published on the SC's core smart contract SC_{center}, so that CBC can determine the latest blockchain content. To address the growing performance issue of PCR, the content m' is only broadcasted on CBC, whose hash is stored on SC for subsequent audit trail while saving storage space on the PCR system. After the deletion operation is completed, all the private data of the specified student on the CBC will be removed.

5   Security Analysis

Theorem 1. *If threshold signature and Chameleon hash are secure, then our proposed PCR supervision system is secure.*

Proof. Our PCR supervision system is constructed based on the Chameleon hash [8] and threshold signature [18] technologies, where the threshold signature is employed to manage the 'trapdoor' of the Chameleon hash to avoid malicious users from obtaining the 'trapdoor' and directly modifying the blockchain data. As demonstrated in [8] and [18], respectively, that Chameleon hash and threshold signature are secure, and a secure cross blockchain mechanism is adopted between two blockchains, thus the proposed PCR supervision system is secure.

Theorem 2. *The data of the proposed PCR supervision system is secure, anyone cannot delete student's private data on CBC.*

Proof. For other CBC students, the smart contract determines that applying for deletion of private data other than themselves is impossible. For the supervisor on the SC, he can review deletion requests whether they are valid with threshold signature, but supervisor cannot directly edit the data on the CBC. For executor on the CBC, he can delete specified transactions with trapdoor only after receiving a valid deletion request with a threshold signature. However, executor has no right to delete transactions at other times. In summary, by restricting individual entities in the PCR supervision system, the student's private data on CBC cannot be arbitrarily deleted by others.

Theorem 3. *The proposed PCR supervision system can effectively protect the private data of students and supervisor's real identity.*

Proof. The student's private data and the supervisor's real identity must be protected in the PCR supervision system. The student's private data is only visible to himself by default, which should be authorized if others ask for access. Furthermore, the student's private data deletion request can only be made by himself. The threshold signatures ensure that a third party cannot recover the supervisor's real identity from the constructed signature. In this process, the private data of students and supervisor's real identity can be effectively protected.

6   Evaluation

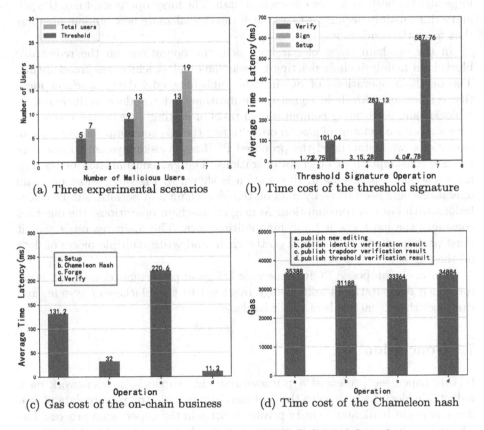

(a) Three experimental scenarios

(b) Time cost of the threshold signature

(c) Gas cost of the on-chain business

(d) Time cost of the Chameleon hash

Fig. 3. The performance of our system in the off-chain and on-chain parts.

To evaluate the performance and effectiveness of our approach, we simulated the proposed PCR supervision system on a platform, where the configuration contains a ubuntu20.04 system with 2.2 GHz and 16G RAM. We used Java to construct CBC and SC and simulate the computation process on-chain and off-chain. The security parameter of the system was set to 256 bits. We simulated the execution process of the solution in different scenarios and tested the time overhead of off-chain businesses and the gas consumption of on-chain businesses.

In the off-chain stage, we simulated three different test environments. As shown in Fig. 3(a), the number of malicious users is f, the threshold number $th = 2 * f + 1$, and the total number of users $n = 3 * f + 1$. The threshold signature mainly includes three phases: initialization, signing and verification. The test results in the three test environments are shown in Fig. 3(b). The verification part of the threshold signature has the primary time cost because the corresponding computing cost will increase synchronously with the increase of the signature shares. As shown in Fig. 3(c), for the CBC based on redactable blockchain, whose primary time overhead includes four operations of setup, hash, forge and verification on the Chameleon hash. The forge operation takes the primary time, mainly because it takes much time to calculate new random numbers that meet the conditions.

In the on-chain stage of our approach, the operations on the redactable blockchain mainly include deleting transactions and synchronous broadcasting. The on-chain operations of SC include publishing edit data, on-chain identity verification, threshold signature verification and trapdoor verification. In a blockchain, performing computational tasks or storing data on the chain consumes a certain amount of gas. In order to test the gas consumption of on-chain operations, we instantiated the proposed PCR supervision system to calculate the gas consumption of on-chain operations. The gas consumption of the primary on-chain operations in this system is shown in Fig. 3(d). Most on-chain operations only need to verify data on the blockchain and perform simple calculations with low gas consumption. Among all on-chain operations, the one that consumes the most gas is publishing editing data. The main reason is that it must perform many calculations on the chain and write multiple pieces of data on the CBC.

Hence, our proposed PCR framework has good performance, does not bring too much computational and storage overhead to the blockchain system, and can meet the actual needs of credit banks.

7 Conclusion

In this paper, we presented a privacy-preserving supervision framework on a redactable blockchain to solve the problems of removing the private data of students in credit bank and identity privacy leakage in the supervision process. The Chameleon hash and threshold signature technologies are employed to achieve the deletion of student's private data and privacy protection of the identities of supervisors. The executor can only delete the specified data after obtaining a deletion request with a threshold signature in the deletion process. Security analysis and experiments demonstrated the effectiveness and practicality of our PCR supervision system.

Acknowledgments. This article is supported in part by the National Key R&D Program of China under project 2020YFB1006004, the Guangxi Natural Science Foundation under grants 2019GXNSFFA245015 and 2019GXNSFGA245004, the National Natural Science Foundation of China under projects 62162017 and 62172119, the Guangdong Key R&D Program under project 2020B0101090002, the Zhejiang Soft Science Research Program under 2021C35044, the China Postdoctoral Science Foundation under 2021M700347, and the Major Key Project of PCL under grants PCL2021A09, PCL2021A02 and PCL2022A03.

References

1. Zheng, Z., Xie, S., Dai, H., Chen, X., Wang, H.: An overview of blockchain technology: architecture, consensus, and future trends. In: 2017 IEEE International Congress on Big Data (BigData Congress), pp. 557–564. IEEE (2017)
2. Yan, N.: Application of blockchain in academic credit bank system. In: Lee, L.-K., U, L.H., Wang, F.L., Cheung, S.K.S., Au, O., Li, K.C. (eds.) ICTE 2020. CCIS, vol. 1302, pp. 337–348. Springer, Singapore (2020). https://doi.org/10.1007/978-981-33-4594-2_28
3. Alharby, M., Aldweesh, A., Van Moorsel, A.: Blockchain-based smart contracts: a systematic mapping study of academic research. In: 2018 International Conference on Cloud Computing, Big Data and Blockchain (ICCBB), pp. 1–6. IEEE (2018)
4. Smith, J., Tennison, J., Wells, P., Fawcett, J., Harrison, S.: Applying Blockchain Technology in Global Data Infrastructure. Open Data Inst. (2016)
5. Jia, Y., Sun, S.-F., Zhang, Y., Liu, Z., Gu, D.: Redactable blockchain supporting supervision and self-management. In: Proceedings of the 2021 ACM Asia Conference on Computer and Communications Security, pp. 844–858 (2021)
6. Cai, X., Ren, Y., Zhang, X.: Privacy-protected deletable blockchain. IEEE Access **8**, 6060–6070 (2019)
7. Feng, Q., He, D., Zeadally, S., Khan, M.K., Kumar, N.: A survey on privacy protection in blockchain system. J. Netw. Comput. Appl. **126**, 45–58 (2019)
8. Krawczyk, H., Rabin, T.: Chameleon hashing and signatures. Cryptology ePrint Archive, Paper 1998/010 (1998). https://eprint.iacr.org/1998/010
9. Pandey, P., Litoriya, R.: Implementing healthcare services on a large scale: challenges and remedies based on blockchain technology. Health Policy Technol. **9**(1), 69–78 (2020)
10. Jiang, J.X., Bai, G.: Evaluation of causes of protected health information breaches. JAMA Intern. Med. **179**(2), 265–267 (2019)
11. Ateniese, G., Magri, B., Venturi, D., Andrade, E.: Redactable blockchain-or-rewriting history in bitcoin and friends. In: 2017 IEEE European Symposium on Security and Privacy (EuroS&P), pp. 111–126. IEEE (2017)
12. Deuber, D., Magri, B., Thyagarajan, S.A.K.: Redactable blockchain in the permissionless setting. In: 2019 IEEE Symposium on Security and Privacy (SP), pp. 124–138. IEEE (2019)
13. Alla, S., Soltanisehat, L., Tatar, U., Keskin, O.: Blockchain technology in electronic healthcare systems. In: Proceedings of the IIE Annual Conference, pp. 901–906. Institute of Industrial and Systems Engineers (IISE) (2018)
14. Xu, J., et al.: An identity management and authentication scheme based on redactable blockchain for mobile networks. IEEE Trans. Veh. Technol. **69**(6), 6688–6698 (2020)

15. Li, X., Wu, L., Zhao, R., Lu, W., Xue, F.: Two-layer adaptive blockchain-based supervision model for off-site modular housing production. Comput. Ind. **128**, 103437 (2021)
16. Wen, B., Wang, Y., Ding, Y., Zheng, H., Liang, H., Wang, H.: A privacy-preserving blockchain supervision framework in the multiparty setting. Wirel. Commun. Mob. Comput. **2021** (2021). Article ID 5236579
17. Hegedűs, P.: Towards analyzing the complexity landscape of solidity based ethereum smart contracts. Technologies **7**(1) (2019)
18. Boldyreva, A.: Threshold signatures, multisignatures and blind signatures based on the Gap-Diffie-Hellman-group signature scheme. In: Desmedt, Y.G. (ed.) PKC 2003. LNCS, vol. 2567, pp. 31–46. Springer, Heidelberg (2003). https://doi.org/10.1007/3-540-36288-6_3

A Trusted Storage System for Digital Object in the Human-Cyber-Physical Environment

Xiang Jing[1], Yueyang Hu[1], Chaoran Luo[2], Xingchun Diao[3], Gang Huang[2], and Haiou Jiang[3(✉)]

[1] School of Software and Microelectronics, Peking University, Beijing 102600, China
{jingxiang,yueyanghu}@pku.edu.cn
[2] Peking University, Beijing 100871, China
luochaoran@pku.edu.cn
[3] Advanced Institute of Big Data Beijing, Beijing 100195, China
jiangho@aibd.ac.cn

Abstract. The continuous development of the information technology has driven the deep integration of various networks such as the Internet, Internet of Things, and mobile networks, promoting the fusion of human society, information space, and the physical world and the development of the human-cyber-physical (HCP) environment. In the HCP environment, applications usually need to use heterogeneous resources belonging to multiple systems and participants. The Digital Object Architecture (DOA), a data-centric software architecture proposed by Dr. Robert Kahn and aims to enable interoperability across systems, is useful in the HCP environment. HCP resources can be uniformly abstracted and modeled as digital objects (DOs), and all the operations and interactions of HCP resources can be transformed into the DO operations and interactions. There are two challenges of using DOA in the HCP environment, the first is the trust DO governance because of the "digital" nature of DO, making itself easily copied; the second is the dynamic characteristics of HCP resources, making it necessary to store the history state of resource DOs. In this paper, a trusted storage system for resource DOs in the HCP environment is proposed. By using blockchain technology, the change records of DOs can be stored in blockchain nodes, maintained by committee constituted by authoritative participants in the HCP environment. Two algorithms are proposed in the block generation and consensus stage to improve the whole performance of the system. In the block generation stage, the Periodic-Adjusted Merkle (PA-Merkle) tree is proposed and reduces time consumption by 27.8%. In the consensus stage, the Tree Spread PBFT (TS-PBFT) algorithm is proposed and reduces the time consumption by more than 20% under 100 Mbps bandwidth. The overall performance of the system improves by 24.2% in the case of four nodes with 100 Mbps bandwidth.

Keywords: Human-cyber-physical · Digital object architecture · Trust DO governance · Trusted storage system · Blockchain

1 Introduction

With the development of information technology, various networks, such as Internet, Internet of things and mobile network have deeply integrated and have promoted the mutual integration of human society, information space and physical world [1]. In such human-cyber-physical (HCP) environment, the ability to use heterogeneous resources belonging to multiple systems belonging to different participants seamlessly is an essential requirement for a successful application. For example, smart city applications need to aggregate affairs data from governments, society data from commercial applications and even personal data from individuals, so as to achieve intelligent decision-making and efficient governance. Manufacturing applications need to get through the data of the industrial chain, various departments of enterprises and production equipment in factories, to monitor and control the entire manufacturing process accurately.

The Digital Object Architecture (DOA) was proposed by Dr. Robert Kahn in 1995 and designed to enables interoperability across systems [2]. In HCP environment, any resource can be uniformly abstracted and modeled as a digital object (DO). A DO can be serialized as a byte array.

As shown in Fig. 1, Each DO is assigned to an identifier, namely DOI, and three elements, namely metadata, API of the HCP resource [3], the status information, are stored and maintained in the Registry, Repository, and Identifier/Resolution system respectively. Two protocols, namely Digital Object Interface Protocol (DOIP) and Digital Object Identifier Resolution Protocol (DO-IRP) are used to interact with the three components.

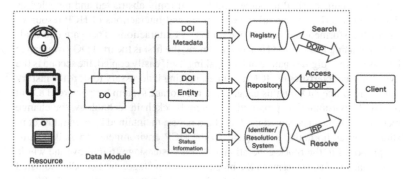

Fig. 1. DOA in HCP environment

However, there are two challenges to use DOA in the HCP environment. First, the "digital" nature of DO makes itself easily copied and modified. The provider of the resource needs to trace and understand how the resource is used by other applications, and the applications also need to ensure that the DO is exactly the one provided by the provider and not tampered [4]. Second, in traditional Internet environment, DOs are usually files and stored statically in the hosts. In contrast, DOs in the HCP environment changes dynamically. The change states of resource DO are also useful to applications. So, a trusted system is needed to ensure that the changes of DOs are securely traceable, auditable, and tamper resistant.

In this paper, a trusted storage system for resource DOs in the HCP environment is proposed. By using blockchain technology, the changes of DOs can be stored in blockchain nodes. The blockchain nodes are maintained by committee constituted by authoritative participants. When a DO changes, the change record is sent to the record buffer of the authority node which stores unpackaged records, the node that has the right to pack package records into blocks and makes block consensus among all nodes in blockchain network. Two algorithms are proposed in the block generation and consensus stage to improve the whole performance of the system. In the block generation stage, a Periodic-Adjusted Merkle (PA-Merkle) tree based on DO change features periodically analyzed by KMeans algorithm is proposed. It reduces time consumption by 27.8%. In the consensus stage, the Tree Spread PBFT (TS-PBFT) algorithm is proposed, which divides the pre-preparation stage of PBFT algorithm into proposal stage and pre-block stage based on the Gossip protocol idea. It reduces the time consumption by more than 20% compared with PBFT under 100 Mbps bandwidth. The overall performance of the system improves by 24.2% in the case of four nodes with 100 Mbps bandwidth.

2 Related Work

This section describes the digital object architecture's current application, and investigates the solutions proposed in different fields by the trusted storage technology based on blockchain.

2.1 Digital Object Architecture's Application

DOA has been widely and successfully used since it was born from the Corporation for National Research Initiatives (CNRI) of the U.S. in 1990s [5]. The first and most successful application is the DOI System in the publishing industry with approximately 275 million DOIs assigned in the electronic publications, such as papers, movies, and music by the end of 2021 [6]. In the entertainment industry, the Entertainment Identifier Registry Association (EIDR) [7] based on DOI system is used to assign the uniform Resource Identifier to the entertainment digital resources. In the financial industry, ANNA developed the DSB system to assign a unique ISIN (International Securities Identification Number) to the derivative trading records [8]. In Industrial Internet area, China began to construct Identifier/Resolution System since 2018, and more than 60 billion identifiers have been registered on the system so far, covering a wide range of areas, such as manufacturing, supply chain, aerospace industry, and so on [9]. DOA is also used in IoT area, where DO is used to represent and identify the smart governance elements of the heterogeneous Internet of Things systems [10–12]. Most of the applications of DOA in the industry are implemented by modeling the data resource as DOs, and access DOs by DOIs instead of URLs, avoiding the failure of URLs and ensuring QoS.

Some researches apply DOA to more complex environments. Huang et al. and Liu et al. introduced DOA to construct data centric infrastructure in the big data, service computing and HCP area. Huang et al. designed a decentralized software-defined data lifecycle governance infrastructure based on DOA [3]. Liu et al. [4] designed a decentralized services computing paradigm based on DOA and blockchain to ensure data governance as well as programmability, interoperability, and intelligence. The key principle of the design is to separate the data and applications and make the data as application independent resources, namely DO, that are fully controlled by the data owners. The researches lack complete mechanism to guarantee the trust governance and storage of DOs.

2.2 Trusted Storage Technology Based on Blockchain

The concept of blockchain technology comes from Bitcoin [13], which can achieve decentralization of data storage, enhance data security and perform trusted storage of data [14]. It has been applied in many fields.

Han Liu et al. designed a blockchain-based Vehicular Networks (VANETs) trust (Management) model [15], aiming at the problem that vehicles may send false messages in the VANETs. The HMM algorithm is used to evaluate whether the vehicle is trustworthy, and the system performs trust score update and query operations by calling smart contracts. Liu et al. proposes a solution for VoIP systems based on blockchain technology [16], aiming at the trust problem between multiple CAs in the STIR/SHAKEN framework. All user certificates are stored on the blockchain, and by reading the Data to verify the identity of the phone can guarantee the authenticity of the number in an end-to-end manner. Peng Zhu et al. proposed a method for the storage and traceability of disease information data [17], which uses blockchain technology to trusted store disease information. The information stored for tracking of the spread of infectious diseases is transparent, which can be accessed and maintained through any node of the system. Christian et al. proposed to use blockchain platform in smart city applications by defining block structures and smart contracts to implement the trusted storage of security policies [18]. Lei et al. have built a distributed electricity trade platform based on blockchain technology [19], standardizing the business process of distributed electricity trade. The process and flow of electricity trade data is stored on the blockchain to promote fair and open distributed electricity trade. Jing et al. proposed a blockchain-based code copyright management system [20], and designed a blockchain network to reliably store the copyright information of the original code. The block structure and the consensus and the verification algorithm are designed according to the characteristics of the application scenario. In the HPC scenario, the state of DO is quickly and continuously changed, the speed of block generation and consensus phases is the bottleneck. So, algorithms should be proposed to improve the efficiency.

3 Trusted Storage System

In this section, the trusted storage system for resource DOs in the HCP environment is described in detail. Authoritative participants in the HCP environment constitute the committee and maintains a network of blockchain nodes. The DO changes are recorded in the blockchain and can be inspected when the dispute occurs. The Periodic-Adjusted Merkle (PA-Merkle) tree and the Tree Spread PBFT (TS-PBFT) algorithm is proposed in the block generation and consensus stage to improve the whole performance of the system.

3.1 System Description

The trusted storage system uses blockchain technology to credibly storage the changes of DOs. A committee constituted by authoritative participants is set up to be responsible for the maintenance of the authoritative nodes of the blockchain. As shown in Fig. 2, when a DO changes, the record includes information such as time, DO serialized hash value, etc. will be sent to the blockchain node's buffer pool. After block generation and consensus stage, records are stored in the blockchain. When a dispute occurs, partied to the dispute can check and inspect the historical change records of the DOs from the blockchain.

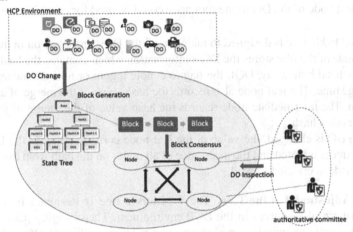

Fig. 2. System architecture

DO Change Record. When a DO changes, the record will be sent to the blockchain node's buffer pool. A record is a vector in the form < *time, hash, type* >, where *time* represents the change time, *hash* represents the hash value of the DO serialized byte array, *type* represents the type of operation including add, update and logout. After block generation and consensus, records are stored in the blockchain.

Block Generation. First, a node that has the user rights to generate a block reads the DO change records. Then, the node updates the PA-Merkle tree with these records and calculates the tree's root hash. Finally, the node generates complete blocks. The block header contains the tree's root hash, the height of the block and hash of the block, etc. The block body contains the change records.

Block Consensus. The block consensus is responsible for reaching a consensus among all nodes. After the block is generated, the consensus algorithm is used to verify the block data among all nodes of the blockchain. A single committee member cannot modify the change records of DOs that have been stored on the blockchain without authorization.

DO Inspection. When a dispute occurs, parties to the dispute can check the latest status of the DOs and obtain the historical change records of the DOs reply on the data stored in the system.

3.2 Block Generation

When a DO changes, the PA-Merkle tree is updated in the block generation stage. New blocks are generated when the unpacked record buffer reaches the threshold or the upper limit of the recent non-block generation time. There are three operations in the block generation based on PA-Merkle tree.

Construction and Update of the PA-Merkle Tree. The PA-Merkle tree is a modification of the Merkle tree, which is widely used in distributed systems to meet the needs of verifying data integrity. Getting the root of the Merkle tree in the block and the Merkel path from leaf node of the DO to the root node could be used for checking the state of a DO.

The PA-Merkle tree is designed to maintain all the DOs' information in the system. Each leaf node of the tree stores the DO's information which contains the hash value of the DO serialized byte array, DOI, the flag to denote logout or not, the owner, and the latest change time. The leaf node also records the hash value of the merge of all the DO information. The intermediate node records the hash value of the merge of its left and right child node's hash.

When a DO is changed, the value of the leaf node corresponding to the DO in the PA-Merkle tree is updated and the hash value of all nodes on the path from the leaf node to the root node is updated as well.

Periodical Adjustment of the Tree. The PA-Merkle tree is designed based on the changing pattern of resources in the HCP environment. The changing patterns of the same DO is continues within a period and varies among different DOs of different resource type. For example, the DO of the takeaway electric car needs to update its own location information every five seconds, and the DO of the air detection machine needs to report its own collection information every two seconds.

According to the update patterns of DOs, placing nodes with similar update patterns under the same subtree can effectively reduce the number of hash calculations. As shown in the Fig. 3, the green nodes are the DOs that have changed and the red nodes are the nodes to recalculate the hash value during the PA-Merkle tree update. In the left, the two green nodes are under different subtrees. If the leaf node is not included, the number of nodes that need to recalculate the hash is five. In the right, if the two green nodes are under the same subtree, then the number of nodes that need to recalculate the hash is three. In this way, the number of hash recalculations can be reduced and the storage overhead of intermediate nodes can be reduced.

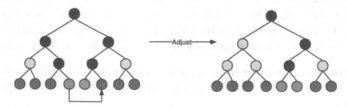

Fig. 3. The adjustment of Merkle tree

PA-Merkle tree analyze the past change records and classify the DOs with the same change pattern periodically to adjust itself. In this work, the KMeans algorithm, a distance-based clustering algorithm [21] is used to analyze and cluster DOs with similar changing patterns in blocks in the past period. For each DO, its change records in n blocks can be mapped to an n-dimensional space $\alpha = (a_0, a_1, \ldots, a_i \ldots, a_n)$. a_i represents whether DO has changed in block i. R^n represents all the possible values of n-dimensional space.

For all DOs, the corresponding mapping can be obtained in the same way, and constitute the dataset required by KMeans. For A, finding the closest center point C, then the hamming distance between A and the center point C is calculated, as shown in Eq. (1).

$$d(A, C) = \sum_{i=1}^{n}(a_i \wedge c_i) \tag{1}$$

The target is to find the minimum value of distance sum of each DO in the system to each center of the k the clusters. And the optimal number of clusters k is gained with the grid search.

After the classification, the leaf nodes belonging to the same cluster are placed under the same subtree of the PA-Merkle tree. The PA-Merkle tree is updated by recalculating the hash value on paths from the adjusted leaf nodes to the root node. The adjustment record, consisting of the position before and after adjustment of each leaf node, is obtained. The adjustments records should synchronize between all nodes in blockchain network, so that other nodes can make the same tree adjustment to ensure the consistency of the tree.

Block Generation. There are two types of blocks generated in this stage. The normal block is to pack the DO change records to be stored. The adjustment block is generated periodically in the adjustment of the PA-Merkle tree. The block header contains the type of the block and hash of PA-Merkle Tree's root node etc. The block body stores the records. According to the type of records, records are processed respectively, and the root of the PA-Merkle tree after the execution of these records is obtained.

When the unpacked record buffer reaches the threshold or the upper limit of the recent non-block generation time, the normal block will be triggered generate action. The block generation component reads a certain number of records from the buffer and generates a normal block.

The adjustment blocks are generated according to the periodic adjustment of tree. The adjustment blocks will synchronize among all nodes in blockchain network, so that other nodes can make the same adjustment to ensure the consistency of the PA-Merkle tree.

3.3 Block Consensus

In this section, the Tree Spread PBFT (TS-PBFT) algorithm is designed to improve the PBFT algorithm performance. The block consensus is responsible to reach the consensus among all nodes. The PBFT is a widely used consensus algorithm with the ability tolerate

Byzantine nodes. The algorithm consists three stages, namely the pre-prepare stage, the prepare stage, and the commit stage [22]. In the pre-prepare stage, the master node that has the right to generate blocks in this consensus round broadcasts pre-prepare messages carrying complete block data to the other nodes in the blockchain network. The time consumption replies on the network bandwidth and is linearly related to the number of nodes in the blockchain network.

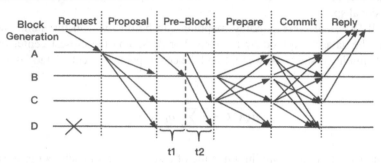

Fig. 4. TS-PBFT algorithm

The gossip protocol is widely used in distributed networks [23]. It uses a rumor-like way to spread the message to every node in the network effectively. The time complexity is logarithmic to the number of nodes. The TS-PBFT algorithm is proposed based on Gossip protocol. As shown in Fig. 4, the pre-prepare stage of PBFT is split into the proposal stage and the pre-block stage. The complete block is divided into the block head and the block body and transmitted separately. Then can be assembled by the nodes after receiving them.

Algorithm 1: Tree Propagation Graph Algorithm
Input: *mainNode* /*the main node in current view*/
nodes /*nodes waiting to propagate*/
Output: *boardcast* /*propagation graph two-dimensional array*/
1 **function** GenBoardcast(*mainNode*, *nodes*):
2   Init(*boardcast*) /*Used to record which nodes each node needs to propagate to*/
3   Init(*nowRound*) /*Record the nodes that can receive blocks in the current round*/
4   Init(*nextRound*) /*Record the nodes that will receive blocks in the next round*/
5   *nowRound.**push**(mainNode)*
6   **for** *i*=0; *i*< len(*nodes*):
7   *nextRound ← null*
8   **for** *node* **in** *nowRound*:
9   nextRound.***append**(node)*
10   nextRound.***append**(nodes[i])*
11   *i ← i+1*
12   **end for**
13   *nowRound ← nextRound*
14   **end for**
15   **return** *boardcast*
16 **end function**

In the proposal stage, the master node broadcasts the block header to the other nodes first, so that the other nodes know which block is in the consensus progress. The form of the proposal message is shown in Eq. (2). *view* represents the master node, *n* represents the sequence number of the message, *digest* represents the digest of the message, *sign* represents the node's signature on the message. Different from the pre-prepare message, the proposal message changes from a complete block to a block header.

$$<< proposal, \; view, \; n, \; digest >, \; Block_{header}, \; sign > \tag{2}$$

In the pre-block stage, a tree-like propagation graph is generated according to the current blockchain network information. The block body is propagated to each node in the network by means of the tree-like propagation. The message format of the pre-block stage is shown in Eq. (3).

$$<< pre - block, \; view, \; n, \; digest >, \; Block_{body}, \; sign > \tag{3}$$

The algorithm for generating the tree propagation graph is as follows. The *boardcast* is a two-dimensional array, each element in the array records to which nodes a node should propagate messages. Line 5 means *nowRound* initially has only one element *mainNode*. Line 8 to Line 13 menas the algorithm iterates over the elements in *nowRound*, adds it to *nextRound*, and adds a node waiting to propagate into *nextRound*. Then, use *nextRound* to assign *nowRound* and set *nextRound* to null.

As shown in Fig. 5, the left side is the original block propagation method. Node A first needs to propagate blocks to B in round 1, propagate blocks to C in round 2, and propagate blocks to D in round 3. The right side is the optimized way. Node A propagates the block to B in round 1, A propagates to C, and B propa-gates to D in round 2. Since the node has already received the block header in the Proposal stage, it can be judged whether the message is correct by verifying whether the block body received in the Pre-Block stage matches the block header received in the Proposal stage.

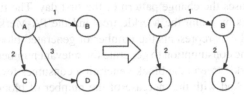

Fig. 5. Example of tree propagation graph algorithm with four nodes

In case of the Byzantine and crash nodes, a timeout mechanism id proposed. If a node has not received a block within a certain period after entering the pre-block status, it sends a request to the master node, and the master node will re-transmit the pre-block message, as shown in Fig. 6.

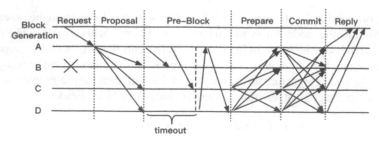

Fig. 6. Timeout mechanism of TS-PBFT

4 Experiment and Analysis

This section presents the experiments and then analyze the performance of the trusted storage system.

4.1 The Experiment Setting

In the experiment, we deploy the trusted storage system on 10 hosts rent from Alibaba Cloud. Each host has 2 vCPUs, 8G memory. System is ubuntu 18.04 and bandwidth is 100 Mbps. We simulate 10,000 DOs of different type of resources, including people, online car hailing, air purifiers, etc. The change frequency varies according to the resource type during the daytime. The record lasts two days.

4.2 The Performance in the Block Generation Stage

IN this experiment, we record and compare the time consumption of generating different numbers of blocks in the block generation stage using Merkle tree and the PA-Merkle tree. The block size is set 1 MB and each block contains 1000 DO change records. The PA-Merkle tree uses the change pattern of the first day. The time consumption of generating 100 blocks by using the Merkle tree and the PA-Merkle tree is shown in Fig. 7. The horizontal axis represents the number of generated blocks, and the vertical axis represents the time consumption to generate the relevant number of blocks. It shows that using the PA-Merkle tree in the block generation consumes fewer time than that of the Merkle tree and. And with the increase of the number of blocks, the reduction of time consumption is more significant with the number of block increases. The average generation time of the 100 blocks was 64.49 ms using the Merkle tree and 46.53 ms using the PA-Merkle tree, reduced by 27.8%.

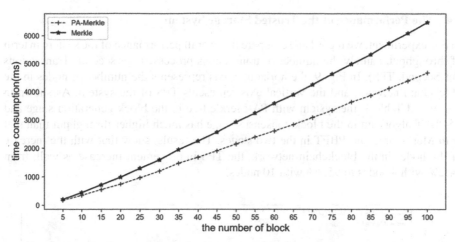

Fig. 7. The time consumption in the block generation stage

4.3 The Performance in the Block Consensus Stage

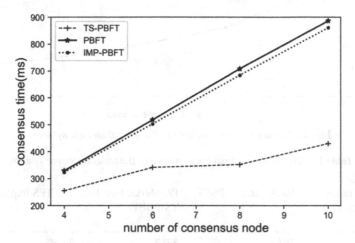

Fig. 8. The consensus time in the block consensus stage

In this experiment, we record and compare the consensus time with different numbers of consensus nodes in the block consensus stage using PBFT algorithm, TS-PBFT algorithm and IMP-PBFT algorithm [24]. As shown in Fig. 8, the horizontal axis represents the number of consensus nodes in the blockchain network, and the vertical axis represents the time consumption to finish the consensus. It shows that TS-PBFT algorithm cost much less time than PBFT algorithm and IMP-PBFT algorithm, and the time reduction is more significant with the increase of consensus nodes. Total node consensus time is reduced by 22.4% in the 4-node blockchain network. Whereas total node confirmation time on the 10-node blockchain network is reduced by 51.5%.

4.4   The Performance of the Trusted Storage System

In this experiment, we record and compare the overall performance of the system in term of throughput, namely the number of transactions processed per second (Transactions Per Second, TPS). In Fig. 9, the horizontal axis represents the number of nodes in the blockchain network, and the vertical axis represents TPS of the system. As shown in Fig. 9 and Table 1, the system with PA-Merkle tree in the block generation stage and TSPBFT algorithm in the block consensus stage has much higher throughput than that with Merkle tree and PBFT in the two stages. The results show that with the increase of the nodes in the blockchain network, the TPS improvement increase as well, from 24.2% with 4 nodes to 95.2% with 10 nodes.

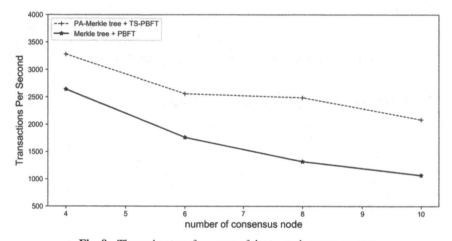

Fig. 9. Throughout performance of the trusted storage system

Table 1. Table of throughput performance of the trusted storage system

Number of nodes in the blockchain network	Merkle tree + PBFT	PA-Merkle tree + TS-PBFT	The TPS improvement
4	2643	3282	24.2%
6	1762	2558	45.2%
8	1319	2488	88.6%
10	1068	2085	95.2%

5   Conclusion

In this paper, a trusted storage system for DO in the HCP environment is proposed. Authoritative participants in the HCP environment constitute the committee and maintains a network of blockchain nodes. The change records of DOs can be stored in the blockchain nodes to ensure that DOs used by the applications in the HCP environment are securely traceable, auditable, and tamper resistant. When a DO changes, the change record is sent to the record buffer of the authority node which stores unpackaged records, the node that has the right to pack package records into blocks and makes block consensus among all nodes in blockchain network. In the block generation stage, the Periodic-Adjusted Merkle (PA-Merkle) tree is proposed. The state tree adjustment block is generated based on DO change features periodically analyzed by KMeans algorithm. It improves the efficiency of block generation and reduces time consumption by 27.8%. In the consensus stage, the Tree Spread PBFT (TS-PBFT) algorithm is proposed. It divides the pre-preparation stage of PBFT algorithm into proposal stage and pre-block stage based on the Gossip protocol idea. The proposal stage propagates the block head, and the pre-block stage propagates the block body in a tree-like manner. It reduces the time consumption for all nodes to confirm by more than 20%. The two algorithms improve the overall performance of the system, where the time consumption is reduced by 24.2% in the case of four nodes with 100 Mbps bandwidth.

In the future work, we will use sharding technology to improve the system performance. Since resources in the HCP environment have geographic location attributes, nodes with similar physical locations often require smaller routing hops for communication. The nodes in the network are grouped according to the physical location information, and a consensus group is used to credibly store records in a shard. Within the consensus group, an algorithm with higher consensus efficiency can be considered to improve the efficiency of the system.

Acknowledgments. This work was supported by the National Key R&D Program of China (No. 2021YFF0901100), the Beijing Outstanding Young Scientist Program (No.BJJWZYJH01201910001004), the Beijing Nova Program Z211100002121159.

References

1. Mei, H., Cao, D.G., Xie, T.: Ubiquitous operating system: toward the blue ocean of human-cyber-physical ternary ubiquitous computing. Bull. Chin. Acad. Sci. **37**(1), 30–37 (2022). (in Chinese)
2. Kahn, R., Wilensky, R.: A framework for distributed digital object services. Int. J. Digit. Libr. (2006). First published by the authors May 1995, A Framework for Distributed Digital Object Services. http://hdl.handle.net/4263537/5001)
3. Huang, G., Luo, C., Wu, K., Ma, Y., Zhang, Y., Liu, X.: Software-defined infrastructure for decentralized data lifecycle governance: principled design and open challenges. In: The 39th IEEE International Conference on Distributed Computing Systems (ICDCS 2019) (2019)
4. Liu, X., Sun, S.X., Huang, G.: Decentralized services computing paradigm for blockchain-based data governance: programmability, interoperability, and intelligence. IEEE Trans. Serv. Comput. **13**(2), 343–355 (2020)
5. Lyons, P.A., Kahn, R.E.: Blocks as digital entities: a standards perspective. Inf. Serv. Use **38**(3), 1–13 (2018)
6. For description of DOI System, see DOI Handbook. http://www.doi.org/
7. Entertainment Identifier Registry Association (EIDR). https://eidr.org/about-us/. Accessed 2 Sep 2018

8. ANNA Presents Demo Version of the Derivatives Service Bureau. https://www.anna-web. org/anna-presents-demo-versionderivatives-service-bureau/. Accessed 2 Sep 2018
9. Identifier/Resolution System for Industrial Internet of China. http://www.aii-alliance.org/upl oad/202102/0222_094332_553.pdf
10. Ruiz-Zafra, A., Pigueiras, J., Millan-Alcaide, A., Larios, V.M., Maciel, R.: A digital object-based infrastructure for smart governance of heterogeneous internet of things systems. In: 2020 IEEE International Smart Cities Conference (ISC2). IEEE (2020)
11. Sazonov, D., Kirichek, R.: Identification system model for energy-efficient long range mesh network based on digital object architecture. In: Vishnevskiy, V.M., Samouylov, K.E., Kozyrev, D.V. (eds.) Distributed Computer and Communication Networks: Control, Computation, Communications, vol. 1337, pp. 497–509. Springer, Cham (2020). https://doi.org/10. 1007/978-3-030-66242-4_39
12. Ruiz-Zafra, A., Magán-Carrión, R.: A distributed digital object architecture to support secure IoT ecosystems. In: Dorronsoro, B., Ruiz, P., de la Torre, J., Urda, D., Talbi, E.G. (eds.) Optimization and Learning, vol. 1173, pp. 195–205. Springer, Cham (2020). https://doi.org/ 10.1007/978-3-030-41913-4_16
13. Nakamoto, S.: Bitcoin: a peer-to-peer electronic cash system (2008)
14. Liu, R., et al.: Research and application UAV operation data trusted storage technology based on blockchain. In: 2020 IEEE 2nd International Conference on Civil Aviation Safety and Information Technology (ICCASIT). IEEE (2020)
15. Liu, H., Han, D., Li, D.: Blockchain based trust management in vehicular networks. In: Zheng, Z., Dai, H.N., Fu, X., Chen, B. (eds.) Blockchain and Trustworthy Systems, vol. 1267, pp. 333–346. Springer, Cham (2020). https://doi.org/10.1007/978-981-15-9213-3_26
16. Liu, F., Yang, B., Su, L., Wang, K., Yan, J.: A blockchain based scheme for authentic telephone identity. In: Zheng, Z., Dai, H.N., Fu, X., Chen, B. (eds.) Blockchain and Trustworthy Systems, vol. 1267, pp. 675–682. Springer, Cham (2020). https://doi.org/10.1007/978-981-15-9213-3_52
17. Peng, Z.A., et al.: Enhancing traceability of infectious diseases: a blockchain-based approach. Inf. Process. Manag. 58(4), 102570 (2021)
18. Esposito, C., Ficco, M., Gupta, B.B.: Blockchain-based authentication and authorization for smart city applications. Inf. Process. Manage. 58(2), 102468 (2021)
19. Lei, Y., Liu, T., Zhu, H.: Research on the business model of distributed power trading based on blockchain technology. J. Phys.: Conf. Ser. 1800(1), 012014 (8pp) (2021)
20. Jing, N., Liu, Q., Sugumaran, V.: A blockchain-based code copyright management system. Inf. Process. Manag. 58(3), 102518 (2021)
21. Xu, J.H., Hong, L.: Web user clustering analysis based on KMeans algorithm. In: International Conference on Information. IEEE (2010)
22. Castro, M., Liskov, B.: Practical byzantine fault tolerance. In: Proceedings of the 3rd Symposium on Operating Systems Design and Implementation, OSDI, New Orleans, USA, pp. 173–186 (1999)
23. Boyd, S., et al.: Randomized gossip algorithms. IEEE/ACM Trans. Netw. 52, 2508–2530 (2006)
24. Gao, Z., Yang, L.: Optimization scheme of consensus mechanism based on practical byzantine fault tolerance algorithm. In: Blockchain Technology and Application, vol 1176, pp. 187–195. Springer, Singapore (2019). https://doi.org/10.1007/978-981-15-3278-8_12

The Role of Absorptive Capacity in the Blockchain Enabled Traceability Alignment: An Empirical Investigation

Kai Wu[1], E. Bai[2], Baiqing Sun[3]([✉]), and Haifeng Guo[4]

[1] Business School, Harbin University of Commerce, Harbin 150028, China
[2] Business School, Harbin University of Commerce, Harbin 150001, China
[3] Management School, Harbin Institute of Technology, Harbin 150001, China
baiqingsun@hit.edu.cn
[4] Department of Finance, Harbin Institute of Technology, Harbin 150001, China

Abstract. The food supply chain argues as one of the most complex and challenge systems and plays a major role in human societies for thousand years, but still faces some fundamental challenges on the data storage, forward and access. Current research indicates that blockchain is a promising technology for handling these challenges, as various nodes (actors) are connected through the network with efficiency, feasibility, and trust. However, as a novel technology, many mysteries are still waiting for discover urgently, such as information sharing, dynamic context, and emerging network scale. This study adopted absorptive capacity, as the theoretical lens, investigates a blockchain network in a longitudinal perspective, which contributes to the IS literature by providing an account of the blockchain network from the knowledge processing perspective by considering the interplay among the actors and uncover the dynamics of absorptive capacities in a loose connected network.

Keywords: Absorptive capacity · Blockchain · Food supply chain · Traceability · Trustworthy systems

1 Introduction

Food supply chain is the primary section in human society, in which the food quality, safety and trust have become a major issue in public health in the last twenty years, such as the foot-and-mouth Disease in Europe in 2001, the Escherichia Coli outbreak in Spinach in 2006 in USA, the South African listeriosis outbreak in 2017, and even the COVID-19 spread in 2019. Moreover, with numerous different actors involved like farmers, logistic companies, distributors and retailers, the supply chain is highly multi-actor based and distributed. During these food epidemic incidents, lack of traceability among any actors has been identified as a major challenge for controlling these incidents and establishing the trust and transparency. (Manski 2017, Ringsberg 2014, Marabelli and Newell 2019). Thus, a faceable solution to the existing challenge is offered by the blockchain whose traceability systems take advantage of providing the transparency and reliability (Demestichas et al. 2020), which has been considered as the fundamental attribute in the current supply chain system.

With transparency and fault tolerance, the blockchain gains success in cryptocurrencies, and it has been significantly applied to food traceability nowadays (Kouhizadeh et al. 2021). The blockchain is a promising technology towards a transparent traceability, which is widely adopted by both research and business for providing the 'Farm to Fork' traceability service. The blockchain provides us with a trust mechanism, as if anyone is trying to tamper or corrupt the data in one specific block, he must alter the following tampered actor of the chain. For the constantly added blocks, it is practically impossible to change a single actor in the chain (Demestichas et al. 2020, Ruoti et al. 2019). Therefore, blockchain is recognized as the reliable tracking solution and has been adopted for the food supply chain tracking system (Esmaeilian et al. 2020, Kamilaris et al. 2019). However, as a novel technology, it is remained the mystery, such as the interaction among the chain linked nodes (actors), and the nodes' collaborative respondence to the contextual changes (Demestichas et al. 2020, Esmaeilian et al. 2020). For exploring the mystery, absorptive capacity (AC) gives us a solid theoretical support (Wu et al. 2021, Dolmark et al. 2021).

AC plays a prominent role in IS research and scholars adopt it to explain how organizations learn from external source of knowledge (e.g. other firms, systems, and technology), integrate this knowledge within the organization and turn it into internal capability (Van Den Bosch et al. 1999, Todorova and Durisin 2007, Mariano and Walter 2015), response to the contextual changes with proper activities(Vasconcelos et al. 2019, Zahra and Hayton 2008), and creates the competitive advantage (Patterson and Ambrosini 2015, Zou et al. 2016). Especially for the modern for the modern companies, the external knowledge is the source of the internal knowledge and their alliance and collaboration also base on it (Tzokas et al. 2015, Saad et al. 2017). This suggests that using the AC to investigate the blockchain might shed light on the interactions among the loosely connected actors in food supply chain. It should be realized that AC is contextually sensitive and changes in context could act as triggers leading to the change of AC (Marabelli and Newell 2019, Zahra and Hayton 2008). Moreover, these contextual changes leaded by AC evolution and development has been less focused (Omidvar et al. 2017, Ferreras-Méndez et al. 2015, Wu et al. 2022). Indeed, how it develops in a loose connected context, such as the blockchain, has never been touched. This paper presents an empirical study to investigate the collective activities among the blockchain connected actors for responding to the contextual change.

Our methodological approach to AC analysis and food traceability system practice is qualitative. Compared to quantitative method frequently used in AC analysis (Gao et al. 2017), qualitative one allows an in-depth analysis of learning and practice over time (Neuman 2010, Denicolai et al. 2016). Moreover, this paper is structured as follows: Section two provides the literature review and highlights critical gaps. Section three presents the chosen case study and offers some in-depth insights about the role of AC in the blockchain food traceability system. With a timeline adopted to show the interplay and syntheses between AC, traceability system and work practice. Section four demonstrates the indeed analyses dynamics among the blockchain connected nodes in a traceability system. Conclusion and avenues for future research are given in the section five.

2   Literature Review

Traceability is the ability to trace the history, application, or location of that is under consideration (GalvÃ£o et al. 2010, Mann et al. 2018), which received wide application in mining, software, manufacture and even food (Maouchi et al. 2019, Mann et al. 2018, Lin et al. 2018.a). Nowadays, in case the food crises occur, the traceability of the food supply chain has been highlighted, as it embodies all food information identified through food's entire life circle. Besides, traceability is also able to track along the supply chain, since the downstream path of a product can be followed by the supply chain shareholders to trace the origins (Maouchi et al. 2019). To sum up, the food traceability includes all information about food ingredients, sources, processing, transportation, and storage and so on, which ensures the safety in food supply chains at least for four major areas: 1) information management for transparency and interpretability, 2) quality management for food quality and safety requirements, 3) production management for in-house production and outsourcing, and 4) logistics management for food supply chain complexity (Ringsberg 2014, GalvÃ£o et al. 2010, Demestichas et al. 2020). Combining interconnecting process with a re-constructing procedure of certain food is the blockchain which bases on food traceability. (Aung and Chang 2014). Subsequently, in order to produce a trustworthy outcome of traceability, all actors in the food supply chain must coordinate with others.

A blockchain was initially introduced by Stuart Haber and W. Scott Stornetta 1991 in their article " How to Time-Stamp a Digital Document", and then because Satoshi Nakamoto (a name used by an unknown person or group of people) defined it a cryptocurrency and developed the first blockchain database, the blockchain has been well recognized since 2008 (Luther 2019). In general, blockchain is defined and accepted as " digital transaction ledger, maintained by a network of multiple computing machines that are not relaying on a trusted third party" (Kamilaris et al. 2019), and its key character is the ability to keep a consistence, tractability and agreement among the nodes. Moreover, the agriculture traceability system contains the food information from "farm to fork" with security, transparency and stability. Therefore, to guarantee the food safety and quality through entire supply chain, the blockchain network is well accepted and further developed in this area (GalvÃ£o et al. 2010, Ringsberg 2014). In agriculture traceability, the blockchain is suggested in HACCP (Hazard Analysis Critical Control Point) system to produce, transport, and preserve food (Tian 2017). China developed the blockchain base on food supply chain system so as to improve food safety by providing the information and transaction security among all involved parties (Tse et al. 2017). The blockchain has been more applied into agriculture supply chain and traceability system since 2018, such as the Food Trading System with Consortium blockchain (FTSCON) to upgrade transaction security and privacy (Mao et al. 2018); a application of the blockchain technology in the existing ERP project (enterprise resource planning) for promoting the traditional agri-food supply chain. (Lin et al. 2018.b); and adoption of the blockchain in supply chain for achieving the future industry (Esmaeilian et al.

2020). Traceability of blockchain provides itself with more attention, but there is still a lack of research on its inside dynamics among the nodes and its interactions with continuous contextual changes (Demestichas et al. 2020), which plays an essential role for organization's long-term IS project success (Saad et al. 2017, Ranjan et al. 2016). Therefore, it is necessary for scholars to conduct the blockchain traceability research on the dynamic interactions and contextual changes. Blockchain in the meantime may play an important part in enhancing the supply chain resilience before a pandemic or other supply chain disruptions (Collart and Canales 2020). By virtues of immutability, openness, decentralization and anonymity, blockchain traceability system can significantly affect consumer trust, enhance purchase motivation, and provide a competitive advantage under the COVID-19 epidemic (Lin and Chang 2021). Blockchain as a promising technology has the potential to revolutionize food traceability by providing immutable, shared, and up-to-date information in the agricultural product supply chain, which also poses a number of untouched challenges that are related to the blockchain's retail application and how the blockchain benefits the consumers (Garaus and Treiblmaier 2021).

During the last two decades, IS scholars have recognized absorptive capacity (AC) as a significant construction to study how capture external knowledge and learn from it to fit into the business environment and generate the new knowledge. Cohen and Levinthal (1990) first introduced AC as "the ability of a firm to recognize the value of new, external information, assimilate it, and apply it to commercial ends". Later, the definition of AC is a substantive organizational capability (a high-level routine or set of routines) that gains and releases resources (Zou et al. 2016). In studying IS, AC is an important theory to understand the knowledge processes in organization. Focusing on the construct of AC, a method is proposed by Dyer and Singh (1998) who view AC as an iterative process of exchange (modifying assumptions), which contrasts with the single loop learning process described by Cohen and Levinthal. Lane and Lubatkin (1998) develop the idea of "relative absorptive capacity" and assess AC as a learning dyad –in which a firm's ability to learn from another firm depends on similarities in their knowledge bases, organizational structures, and dominant logics. Zahra and George (2002) view AC as a dynamic capability and indicate that the construct has potentially two general states—firms acquire and assimilate new knowledge and firms transform and exploit new knowledge. The construct of AC has been widely adopted in IS study for understanding organization capability for knowledge processing and contextual change respondence (Grandinetti 2016, Mariano and Walter 2015, Liu et al. 2013, Agramunt et al. 2020), and this study also adopts it to uncover the mystery of blockchain traceability system.

Despite the popularity of the blockchain technology on both research and industry, only few studies briefly touched the blockchain's dynamic internal interaction and co-responding to the contextual changes. However, the AC has been well adopted to understand the inter-organizational knowledge processing capacity and organization's capability for processing the contextual changes (Vasconcelos et al. 2019, Zahra and George 2002), which is also applicable for us to understand what are the interactions among the blockchain connected nodes and how these nodes collaboratively response to the contextual changes.

3   Research Setting and Method

In line with Walsham (1993), this study adopts an approach that assumes that reality, including the organizational actor domain, is a social construct. This approach is consistent with our aims which regard AC as an essential dynamic capacity of an organization and realized in an empirical context. This research moves beyond the traditional view that treats AC as an objective reality (defining antecedents and drivers) with predictable outcomes that contribute to organizational learning (measuring the outcomes). We believe that observing the blockchain traceability system from the longitudinal view provides an insightful way to understand the role of AC in the loose connected inter-organizational context and underpins the co-evolving between AC and system use in a dynamic context.

The collection of the data was based upon a blockchain food supply chain enabled loose connected network. During the period September 2019 - December 2021, project data was collected from four organizations, Alpha, Beta, Omega and Delta, which all have been connected into one blockchain connected network. Alpha is IT company and particularly providing the service in the food supply chain. In September 2019 it released a blockchain technology-based food traceability system and named ETS in this study. Beta is a local supermarket company with about 3,000 employees, ten supermarkets and about 100 mini supermarkets in one city. Omega is a farm with about 2,000 pigs, 3,000 ducks and 1,500 chicken, and most of its animal supply to Beta. Delta is agriculture company with planning vegetables and feeding the pigs, and a Chinese medicine producer as well. Moreover, it has about 500 contracted farmers for supplying the vegetables and pigs.

Since the ETS was being rolled out and the system is continuously updated as the new functionalities added; in particular, these functions are for meeting the predictable and unpredictable requirements come from internal demanding and external force. For meeting the research purpose, we regarding these four actors as a single case and have the close observation of daily practice (Klein and Myers 1999, Doolin and McLeod 2012). Also we adopt the interpretive approach for data collection and analysis (Walsham 1993, Walsham 2006).

This case extremely interesting and appropriate as an object for this research aim, as it provides us with a unique opportunity to access the data from 'farm to fork' to uncover the entire food circle and food supply chain. The data are collected qualitative way from several sources: interview, non-participant observations, official documents, meeting minutes, and steering committee presentations. During our two years retrospective data collection, judgment and snowball sampling method were mainly employed to select interviewees (Marshall 1996, Taherdoost 2016), while the interviews guided by the research objectives and questions were semi-structured (Wright and Wright 2002, Kallio et al. 2016). Structured questions with prompts to guide the interviewee were used.

The next section shows our interpretive approach and its advantages here: 1) it is helpful to understand the dynamics between absorptive capacity and blockchain traceability system; 2) it is necessary to uncover the dynamics of ACs among the loose-connected actors; and 3) it is able to provide an integrated view about the influence of contextual changes on the interconnected ACs and the related working practices.

4 Data Interpretation

This section provides a narrative of the blockchain food traceability system deployment and upgrade crossing various actors at different time of period. In September 2019, Alpha rolled out its ETS system to market. This ETS system adopted the blockchain technology and provided the traceability service for tracing the food from its origin, logistics, distribution, into retail store. At end of 2019 Alpha was starting to connect Beta and Omega into the ETS blockchain network. Although Alpha had the experience to connect the vegetable, chicken, and online shop into the traceability system, but first time to connect the pig and supermarket data.

Alpha reconfigured the chain for Omega uploading its pig data, such as the ID (bar code on ear tag), specs, days, weight, and location, into the system. However, at that moment, Omega did not use any farming software and all these data have been recorded on Office Excel. Therefore, its staff had to manually copy and paste the data into ETS on the daily base. Compared with Omega, Beta was better, as it has a small IT team and running an ERP system. It took Alpha three months to collaborate with the ERP system vendor to access the database and share certain the data on the blockchain. In June 2020 Alpha released its smart e-tag for pig. This smart e-tag is an innovative product, which can record the pig temperature and movement in 24 h for 6 months and help us to monitor and predict pig's health condition. It received great welcome from Omega, as the plague has become severe issue. Applying the e-tag allowed to add some new data into the chain. At the end of 2020, local government also provided the financial support for firm to adopt the new technology in the business. With this financial support, the ETS was further adopted by these three actors, and Delta was connected into the network.

From the project documentation, interview with key actors, and on-site observation, three project phases were identified. There three phases are not strictly sequential but overlap in certain time of period as shown in Fig. 1.

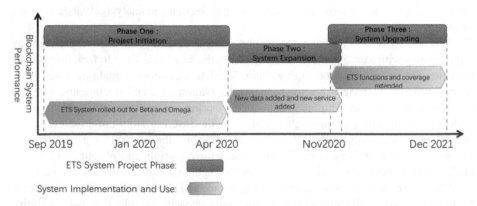

Fig. 1. The three phases of ETS blockchain traceability system project

In Fig. 1, the grey rectangle demonstrates the project phases, and the orange hexagon presents the ETS system practices. The system implementation and use are in sequence but can also overlap. For example, when Alpha developed e-tag applied at Beta and system expansion is not fully updated, the local government already provided the financial support for these three companies to upgrading their blockchain system. Hence, Phase Two and Phase Three overlap during certain time of period. A deeper analysis is conducted in the next section. We take another look at the three phases under the theoretical lenses of AC to discover the interactions between the blockchain nodes (actors) and their respondence on the contextual changes.

Phase One: Project Initiation

In May 2019, Alpha decided to extend its product line from the vegetable and fish to into pig and cattle section. Based on the existing blockchain traceability system, it took Alpha three months to extend the system into pig and cattle farm. This new system was released on September 2019 as ETS, which acted as a trigger leading to a serial of following practices. Alpha's existing client, Beta, became the first user of ETS, as it agreed to connect the ETS into its existing system. Beta had its own ERP system for managing the supermarket. To connect the traceability system into the ERP system is not easy as well, which took Alpha and the ERP vendor three months. Alphas' agriculture blockchain is private and required a series of work to connect any new node into the chain, as Alpha Engineer Vincent explained:

> "This blockchain based farm management system is not just a software system to actually implied it into the actual work, we need to set up the new business policy for managing the system, the right of data access for sharing and communicate with the other actors in the blockchain network."

Instead of joining the chain itself, Beta also introduced its meat supplier Omega into the chain. Omega owns a pig farm and most pigs are supplied to Beta's supermarket. At that time, as Omega has low IT capacity, this blockchain system did not really bring any benefit to it and only added extra working load. As its accountant June explained:

> "My manager asked me to input the pig data into the system on the daily basis. I have manually copy and paste the data from excel document into the system, which only added my working load, but did not bring any benefit to us. Also, there was once I made a mistake as input the misdate into system, which did take us lots of time to correct it. I thought maybe Beta is our major customer, so we have to do it."

Except interviewing with key persons, we also collected the project documents and conduct the onsite observation for indeed understanding. In this blockchain project, the ETS system acting acted as the Contextual trigger (Zahra and George 2002) caused a serial of practices. These practices leaded different absorptive capacity changes on both potential and realized aspects for various nodes. Moreover, the practice also caused different blockchain performances of each actor, which accumulated the ETS performance. Table 1 offers synthesis of the ETS practice from these three actors through the AC perspective.

Table 1. Phase one AC and Practice analysis

Node (Actor)	Absorptive capacity		Blockchain related practice
	Potential absorptive capacity	Realized absorptive capacity	
Alpha	Alpha CEO realized the market of the blockchain system in pig and cattle industry	Added the blockchain knowledge into the new industry,	The ETS was developed; Alpha started to market this blockchain system
Beta	Beta management team learn the benefit of joining the blockchain network	Its staffs learned the basic system knowledge from ETS	Beta agreed to join the blockchain and became one actor in the chain; The ETS started to provide data service for ETS customers
Omega	None	Only one staff in Omega learn to input data into the system	ETS added working load at Omega; Omega did not need to access the ETS

Based on the above discussion, it can be systematical to analyze the dynamics between the absorptive capacities and blockchain adaptation. The blockchain traceability system connected various actors into the network, and impacted actors differently. From AC perspective, each actor took a different role in the chain, whose capacity for acquiring, assimilating (Potential AC), transforming, and exploiting (Realized AC) were different as well. Therefore, the performance and benefit of joining the chain varies significantly. In this case, though Alpha and Beta benefit from join the chain, but Omega did not receive any benefit yet.

Phase Two: System Expansion

In 2019, almost eight million pigs, amounting to about half of China's pig totals, were killed because of the re-emerging African swine fever (Mighell and Ward 2021) which also caused about 1,000,000 pigs killed in the neighbor town. The prior study has indicated the accurate adoption of the IoT technology, such as the accelerometer, temperature, GPS, in tagging pigs to judge their health condition (Kamminga et al. 2018). By combining the Neural Network and online activity recognition system, it will be practical to monitor the animal health condition in the real-time, including in the African swine fever. (Kamminga et al. 2017, Tran et al. 2021). In order to solve the pig health issue, Alpha has extended its research focus from the blockchain traceability to the IoT based solution. In May 2020, Alpha released a new product, the electrical pig ear tag sensor with following measurement in Table 2:

Table 2. Ear tag measurement

Weight	Temperature accuracy	Working time	Communication standard	Waterproof
15 g	±0.2 °C	200 days	Bluetooth & Lora	IP 67

Through this e-tag and ETS, the pig farmer was able to know their pig health condition in the real time. Also, each e-tag has a blockchain ID for the following supply chain activities. This e-tag caused great attention for Omega, as it could reduce their risk dramatically for the swine fever. For testing purpose, Omega tapped the e-tag for each sow for two weeks and then was satisfied about the test results and later put it on each its pig.

Beat's sale team noticed that this meaningful data could strengthen its market competition. Beta collaborated with Alpha expanded the ETS system to share the pig health data the pig temperature and working steps with the supermarket customers. Moreover, for certain pig cuts, the customer can know the pig health data by scan bar code on the meat box. It is helping Omega to earn their customer trust and develop its market competitive ability. Table 3 demonstrates synthesis of the ETS practice and the AC adaptation.

Table 3. Phase two AC and practice analysis

Node (Actor)	Absorptive capacity		Blockchain related practice
	Potential absorptive capacity	Realized absorptive capacity	
Alpha	Alpha noticed the blockchain traceability system was not enough for its development	The ear e-tag was developed for recording the pig and cattle temperature and movement;	The blockchain data was extended with the pig and cattle health data added;
Beta	Beta's marketing team noticed the value of the e-tag data	E-tag data was shared on the blockchain	The real-time pig health data was projecting on the screen in the supermarket The pig health data was shared to the meat purchasing customers
Omega	Omega management team noticed the importance of IT technology in farming industry	Realized the value of monitoring the pig temperature and movement in the real time	Catching up the pig health data and share the data with the other actors in the blockchain

Table 3 summarized the trigger (e-tag) that caused the sequenced changes on these three nodes' AC and blockchain related practice. This e-tag first changed the blockchain practice on Alpha, as it added the function of recording health data into the ETS, then Omega applied the e-tag and uploaded the health data into the blockchain, later Beta shared these data with customers to improve its reputation. Their ACs are developed sequentially.

Phase Three: System Upgrading
In later 2020, the local government started to provide the fund for supporting organization's technology application in agriculture industry. Alpha, Beta and Omega all received the government technology fund with varied amount and applied the fund variously. This fund also added a new actor 'Delta' joined this network by adopting ETS system at their business. Based on the interviews and company documents from these four actors, they have applied the fund differently as the followings:

- Alpha had applied this funding to develop the mobile app for the providing traceability service, named ETS APP. Project document recorded that Alpha's ETS mobile app provides the services on three aspects: *1. Pig's health situation for the customer who purchased the meat; 2. Traceability information 'from the farm to plate' for covering entire supply chain; 3 Services for the related auditing institutes.*
- Beta had used the fund to install more sensors in their supermarket, warehouse, and delivery trucks to monitor the entire supply chain by IoT devices.
- Omega was applied the fund to payback for the e-tag installation and farming system implementation.
- Delta adopted the fund for purchasing the ETS system and implied it in their business.

Rather than purely applying the system at their daily work, Omega also regarded this is an opportunity to sale its meat and vegetables into Beta's supermarket network:

"This blockchain network enabled us to catch the products information from the growing field and feeding field at our contracted farmers. This will help us ensuring the food quality and reduce the risks. [...] We are discussing with Beta to sale our products at its supermarkets because we could provide the consistent data with their current premium products, but still working on the payment term. This is good for both parties." (CEO, Delta)

Based on data, the government technology fund leaded four actor's changes on PACAP, RACAP and related practices at phase three are summarized Table 4.

Table 4. Phase three AC and practice analysis

Node (Actor)	Absorptive capacity		Blockchain related practice
	Potential absorptive capacity	Realized absorptive capacity	
Alpha	Absorbed the external knowledge for adding the supply chain data into the system	Updated the ETS system with more functions and wider accessible	The blockchain encompass more data and more service for more actors
Beta	Learn more blockchain and supply chain knowledge	Adding more supply chain data into the blockchain	The blockchain was able to access the supply chain data
Omega	None	None	None
Delta	Adopted the ETS system knowledge; Required more system solutions	Realizing the system knowledge into the body of the organization;	Applied ETS system into the organization and required the new system solutions; Stepped into the blockchian network and developed the new market

In this phase, the government fund, act as the contextual trigger, lead to serial of actions, such as Alpha to upgrade the system with mobile app function, Beta installed more sensors at its food supply chain to extend the data coverage scale and connected the Delta into the network.

These new data and services were available for Beta's customer and extended the availability of the blockchain. Alphas absorbed the 'new' knowledge and realized the knowledge with mobile software. As the following, Beta also add the supply chain data into the blockchain for improving the customer service. Although, government funded Omega, but the fund has been applied for supporting the phase two activity, and this trigger did not lead to the AC change in Omega. This fund partially triggered Delta joined this network, adopted the ETS system knowledge, and started to apply it at its farm and even the contracted farms. Also, this may bring Delta into Beta's sale market. Therefore, we can see that one trigger may lead to a serial of activity and AC changes, may not cause any activity certain actors.

This longitudinal case study clearly illustrates the dynamics among the actors in the ETS developed blockchain network. Moreover, certain trigger may lead to the actors join or leave this network. The actor's AC and blockchain related practices are all co-constructed and co-evolved in a turbulent context The following section will discuss the dynamics in more detail.

5   Discussion and Implications

The prior data interpretation summarizes the ETS system project development, implementation and use among Alpha, Beta, Omega and Delta from later 2019 to later 2021.

This interpretation is based on Zahra's concept of absorptive capacity (2002) and adopt Marabelli's research method of applying the absorptive capacity on enterprise system study (2019, 2009). In this section, we further depict the dynamics among absorptive capacity and blockchain related changing working practices in the turbulent context. Based on the above tables and the analysis, Fig. 2 has reinterpreted these four actors' (organizations) PACAP, RACAP and blockchain related practice from the longitudinal perspective.

In Fig. 2, the ETS system network development is divided into three phases. In each phase the pentagon presents the contextual trigger, which caused the related system and business practices; the cloud shows the actual practices from various actors for responding to the contextual triggers; the rectangle indicates the actor's potential absorptive capacity (PACAP) and realized absorptive capacity (RACAP); and the arrow underpins the conditioning and enabling links. The blow figure highlights the key roles of absorptive capacity in the blockchain based traceability system project; it points out the co-constructed and co-evolved of the PACAP and RACAP among the connected actors in the turbulent context; and it underpins the role of the contextual trigger in the traceability network. Below table has discussed each of these three perspectives in details.

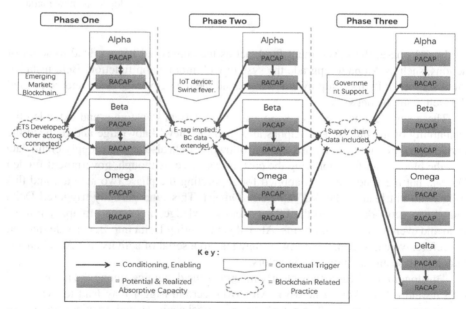

Fig. 2. Interactions among blockchain related practice and absorptive capacity at ETS system project

1. The role of AC in the blockchain network enabled enterprise system project- the above vignettes and analysis illustrate the key role of AC in blockchain traceability system adaptation. Compared with the majority study of AC in a large single organization, or the group (Omidvar et al. 2017, Gao et al. 2017), The blockchain provides a unique environment for the AC. Under such a 'chain' connected environment, one node's AC may interact with the others, which forms a loose connected network and this chain's AC. For example, in phase one, Alpha's RACAP heavily connected to Beta's RACAP on the system adaptation, and they worked together developed ETS. However, it did not contribute to RACAP at Omega, as Omega's accountant was still manually copying the data from Excel and pasting it into the system one figure by one figure. Also in phase two, Alpha developed pig E-Tag for monitoring the pig health condition, which developed the RACAP at Beta and Omega differently, as Beta demonstrate the data at its supermarket for the customer and applied the E-Tag at its farm. In phase three, Alpha and Beta RACAP play the determinate role on Omega AC and system practice. Various actors play different roles in the blockchain, their absorptive capacity condition the practices. In this network, the AC still plays the mediate role between the context and practice, but the AC is a dynamic capacity and interact among various actors.

2. The interaction of the blockchain connected ACs - Rather than linear linked from PACAP to RACAP, in this case, the PACAP development at one actor not only led to its RACAP development, but also causes the PACAP and RACAP development at the other actors. For example, Alpha for recognizing the market opportunity for adopting blockchain on food traceability, not only lead to its RACAP development for developing the ETS system, but also cause the PACAP and RACAP development at Beta to use this system; Alpha's e-tag, act as the contextual trigger, brought IT into Beta daily management. Beta staffs can monitor their pig health condition through the ETS, rather than visit the pig farm for onsite observation and personal judgement; and Beta added the pig health data into the blockchain, Omega's changes its potential AC, as adopted the data differently for improving its customers trust with the realized AC. Alpha also collaborates with Omega extended the ETS system scale into the vegetable growing up. The scale of this blockchain network is flexible at phase three, as Delta was connected into the network and its AC join the network as well. During this process, Alpha's PACAP transferred the system knowledge into Delta. Controversially, Delta's business demanding on connecting the contract farmer data into the network leaded to the extending of PACAP at Alpha. We call this blockchain linked absorptive capacity as the loose-connected absorptive capacity.

3. The role of contextual trigger in blockchain traceability system – This figure demonstrates the contextual triggers initiate a series of practices, the triggers are either predictable or unpredictable, and the triggers could come from both internal or external; more over one actors internal trigger may other actor's external trigger; even the same trigger even the same trigger may play different roles for various actors. In this case, we noticed that the emerging blockchain technology and market demanding on traceability system triggered Alpha to develop the ETS system and explore the market. Through the implementation of the ETS at various actors, Omega also noticed the farm demanding and business opportunity for the E-tag. The re-emerging African swine fever in 2019 almost killed eight million pigs for about half of China's pig population (Mighell and Ward 2021), which caused the demanding for monitoring the pig health for 24 h. Alpha developed the e-tag for monitoring the pig's temperature and movement in real time. Omega showed the great interests for adopting this e-tag at their pigs, by the way it enabled it to adopt the ETS system on its farm management. This e-tag also created the 'new' business opportunity for Beta to demonstrate the pig health condition on their supermarket to build up the customer confidence. In 2020, the financial support from local government for the technology development and adaptation also acted as the trigger caused Alpha and Omega to further develop their technology development and adaptation. This trigger also lead Delta join the network as a new actor. Combining the Join of Delta, Alpha transferred its knowledge into Delta through the system use. Delta was also trying to extend its absorptive capacity into Beta as sale its products at its supermarket. Therefore, the contextual trigger may come from quite wide background, and even the same trigger may play different roles for various actors. For example, the same government funding adopted by Alpha for developing the mobile app, by Beta to payback for the prior investment, and by Omega to develop the marketing software. Even the same trigger may play different roles for various actors. For example, the same government funding adopted by Alpha for developing the mobile app, by Beta to payback for the prior investment, and by Omega to develop the marketing software. This trigger also enable Delta as new actor join this network.

Drawing on the substantive model and findings, a generalized model is presented as below. The model adopts the process and social constructive perspective, which explains that the technology appropriation results from the constitution of human users, social histories and organizations (Orlikowski 2010, Gäre and Melin 2012), that is compatible with the loose connected network such as blockchain based traceability network (Garaus and Treiblmaier 2021). Figure 3 shows the dynamics among the absorptive capacity, working practice and contextual triggers in the blockchain based supply chain system from the longitudinal perspective. In this figure, the pentagon presents the contextual trigger led to the working practice change; the rectangle indicates each actor's absorptive capacity on both PACAP and RACAP perspectives; the cloud presents the blockchain based supply chain network; the arrow indicates the social integration, and the dash line shows the conditional social integration.

Change is the nature of any business and one of the most threatening aspects in information technology implementation and use (Altamony et al. 2016, Lichtenthaler 2009). Absorptive capacity is context sensitive phenomenon responsive to change (Lichtenthaler 2009), and it will developed through the changing practices (Omidvar et al. 2017). For absorptive capacity, the contextual triggers have been identified and extended from various aspects, such as the internal prior knowledge, working practice and system structure (Marabelli and Newell 2019, Martinkenaite and Breunig 2016), and the external marketing, technology, and supply chain (Golgeci and Kuivalainen 2020, Omidvar et al. 2017, Saad et al. 2017). Therefore, to understand the dynamics among the AC and working practice in the loose connected network like blockchain, we cannot avoid the impact of contextual changes in our modelling. Through this study, these contextual triggers are further defined as activation triggers, which caused serial dynamic changes in the network.

The prior AC studies majority focus on one organization or group, but the blockchain connected actors come from quite different background, such as IT, farming, retail, government, and others. Compared with one organization's activation trigger, the loose connected network (blockchain network) activation trigger comes from wider background and could be internal, external, predictable, and unpredictable. For example, in this case

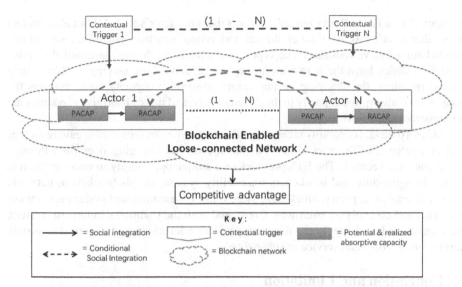

Fig. 3. Dynamics of blockchain related practice and absorptive capacity

the technology funding from triggers come from external government support, internal development and other network connected organization demands. Also, a trigger may play external role for one actor, but the internal role for another trigger, such as the Alpha developed electric ear tag internally, but it played as the external trigger for Beta to apply this technology. Moreover, the electrical ear tag and government support are acted together caused the Delta to join this network. Compared with lined connected actions, in the loose connected network, the triggers may interconnect or overlap to enable the change of practices, even the same trigger may play different roles for various actors.

The trigger leaded change of practice is conditioned by the actor's AC. However, the AC is not only a conditioning agent, but itself is also liable for change and transformation in the practice. The changing practice as new knowledge is acquired and assimilated into the adopting actor and the related practice too develops the AC. This has been identified as the endless process of revisions and enhancements (Markus et al. 2000) where each process encompasses different degrees of knowledge exploration and exploitation (Marabelli and Newell 2019). From the longitudinal perspective, in this case the blockchain based supply chain network, the practice and the AC are overlappingly developing on multiple actors. This is because the loose connected network also provides a data and knowledge sharing channel. The information technologies can develop knowledge management and learning in organization (Iyengar et al. 2015), through implementing knowledge management systems (Kuo and Lee 2009, Wang et al. 2007, Lee et al. 2007) and enterprise system (Chadhar and Daneshgar 2018, Acar et al. 2017), but the blockchain creates an unique environment which is composed from organizational level to operational level (Agrawal et al. 2021), and from one to rack all the entire supply chain (Madhwal et al. 2021, Xu et al. 2021). This study has clearly shown that, in the blockchain enabled supply chain, one actor's PACAP and RACAP are not linear connected. One PACAP may not only impacts the same actor's RACAP, but also interact with other actor's PACAP through the network related practice. Therefore, we call this blockchain linked various actor's absorptive capacity as the 'loose-connected absorptive capacity', which form the network's absorptive capacity. Companying the blockchain related practices, the changing on one actor's absorptive capacity could impacts the other actors' absorptive capacity in the different way, and these absorptive capacities are co-construct and co-evolved.

AC as a dynamic capability receive the advantage when its dimensions gain resources and competencies (Teece et al. 1997), that means AC changing over time through loose connected actors.. The ETS provides us a unique opportunity to uncover the role of AC in agriculture and blockchain traceability system. In this blockchain network, actor's absorptive capacity, blockchain system implementation and system use are co-construct and co-evolving overtimes. Compared with the traditional enterprise system, the blockchain based supply chain system provides a loose-connected network, as only certain limited data and service are connected.

6 Conclusion and Limitation

Blockchain is an immutable digital ledger, which provides the unique strength for traceability (Demestichas et al. 2020), as a novel technology, applying the blockchain technology still has many mysteries waiting for unveil. In this study blockchain enabled traceability network provides a quite different environment for the knowledge transferring and working practice. This study uncover that 1) the blockchain enabled system connected the actors come from quite different industry, such as the farm, manufacture, logistics and even retails; 2) all the actors are loosely connected by the certain data access crossing entire network; 3) the network may shift quick as the nodes (actors) added or lose connect for quickly change; and 4) this network can enable certain actions outside of the system application, in which one actor could build up new services with the others In our case, blockchain network builds a unique environment called "loose connected network" waiting for the future study.

This research adopted the AC as the theoretical lens for understanding the knowledge absorption and development under the loose connected network. It also uncovered the importance and complexity of the knowledge processing capacity in this network. Adopting AC as the theoretical lens enlighten the research on blockchain technology application in traceability. From this longitudinal perspective the benefit of blockchain based traceability system emanates from the co-construction and co-evolution among the contextual trigger, system use and AC. In this process, the AC plays a mediator role, as it conditions the interaction between the contextual trigger and the related working practice. The co-construction and co-evolution also provide a unique circumstance for AC, in which it is not lined developed from PACAP to RACAP, but one actor's PACAP improvement may also cause the other actors' PACAP and RACAP changes. Same as well, the PACAP development in one actor, may cause the changes of PACAP and RACAP in the others. The development of loose connected network relays on the accumulated knowledge processing capacity of the connected actors. Even the nodes' (actors) AC determinates the blockchain performance. Therefore, the loosed connected network has its own AC waiting for the future research.

This study also uncovered the complex and the importance of the contextual trigger. As we noticed, the blockchain connected nodes may come from various background. Compared with the single organization, this network is more sensible for various contextual changes and responsible the changes with different actions. In this case, the four actors have quite different AC and business background, the government technology funding lead to the various actions, and even continuous changing practices on certain actors. Although previous study about AC uncovered its context sensitive characteristics (Volberda et al. 2010, Todorova and Durisin 2007). Our results further this finding and suggests that one trigger may play different roles for the actors at the loose connected network and the responding practices may interacted as well.

This study has some inherent limitations, but it indicates some future research possibilities. The data were gathered at only one blockchain food traceability system in early stage. A broader survey from various blockchains traceability may provide further insight into the dynamics of AC and adding more detail interactions among the actors. Moreover, the research focus is on the high-level process and construct amongst this loose connected network and related blockchain working practice. More elaborate studies into finer elements of those construct and process are likely to add further value for applying this discovery in real word applications.

Acknowledgments. This paper is supported by The National Key Research and Development Program of China (2020YFB1006104); Educational Science Planning Key Project in Heilongjiang Province (No. GJB1421045); National Key Research and Development Program for National Major Project Provincial Funded Project (No. GX18A031); State Grid Corporation Science and Technology Project; Harbin Science and Technology Innovation Talents Research Fund (No.2017RAXXJ026).

References

Acar, M.F., Tarim, M., Zaim, H., Zaim, S., Delen, D.: Knowledge management and ERP: complementary or contradictory? Int. J. Inf. Manag. **37**, 703–712 (2017)

Agramunt, L.F., Berbel-Pineda, J.M., Capobianco-Uriarte, M.M., Casado-Belmonte, M.P.: Review on the relationship of absorptive capacity with interorganizational networks and the internationalization process. Complexity **2020**, 20 (2020)

Agrawal, T.K., Kumar, V., Pal, R., Wang, L., Chen, Y.: Blockchain-based framework for supply chain traceability: a case example of textile and clothing industry. Comput. Ind. Eng. **154**, 107130 (2021)

Akkermans, H., Helden, K.V.: Vicious and virtuous cycles in ERP implementation: a case study of interrelations between critical success factors. Eur. J. Inf. Syst. **11**, 35 (2002)

Altamony, H., Al-Salti, Z., Gharaibeh, A., Elyas, T.: The relationship between change management strategy and successful enterprise resource planning (ERP) implementations: a theoretical perspective. Int. J. Bus. Manag. Econ. Res. **7**, 690–703 (2016)

Aung, M.M., Chang, Y.S.: Traceability in a food supply chain: safety and quality perspectives. Food Control **39**, 172–184 (2014)

Chadhar, M., Daneshgar, F.: Organizational learning and ERP post-implementation phase: a situated learning perspective. J. Inf. Technol. **19**, 138–156 (2018)

Cohen, W., Levinthal, D.: Absorptive capacity: a new perspective on learning and innovation. Adm. Sci. Q. **35**, 128–152 (1990)

Demestichas, K., Peppes, N., Alexakis, T., Adamopoulou, E.: Blockchain in agriculture traceability systems: a review. Appl. Sci. **10**, 4113 (2020)

Denicolai, S., Ramirez, M., Tidd, J.: Overcoming the false dichotomy between internal R&D and external knowledge acquisition: absorptive capacity dynamics over time. Technol. Forecast. Soc. Chang. **104**, 57–65 (2016)

Dolmark, T., Sohaib, O., Beydoun, G., Wu, K.: The effect of individual's technological belief and usage on their absorptive capacity towards their learning behaviour in learning environment. Sustainability **13**, 718 (2021)

Doolin, B., McLeod, L.: Sociomateriality and boundary objects in information systems development. Eur. J. Inf. Syst. **21**, 570–586 (2012). https://doi.org/10.1057/ejis.2012.20

Esmaeilian, B., Sarkis, J., Lewis, K., Behdad, S.: Blockchain for the future of sustainable supply chain management in Industry 4.0. Resour. Conserv. Recycl. **163**, 105064 (2020)

Ferreras-Méndez, J. L., Newell, S., Fernández-Mesa, A., Alegre, J.: Depth and breadth of external knowledge search and performance: the mediating role of absorptive capacity. Ind. Mark. Manag. **47**, 86–97 (2015)

Galvã£o, J.A., Margeirsson, S., Garate, C., Viã°Arsson, J.R., Oetterer, M.: Traceability system in cod fishing. Food Control **21**, 1360-1366 (2010)

Gao, S., Yeoh, W., Wong, S.F., Scheepers, R.: A literature analysis of the use of absorptive capacity construct in IS research. Int. J. Inf. Manag. **37**, 36–42 (2017)

Garaus, M., Treiblmaier, H.: The influence of blockchain-based food traceability on retailer choice: the mediating role of trust. Food Control **129**, 108082 (2021)

Gäre, K., Melin, U.: Sociomaterial actors in the assimilation gap: a case study of web service, management and IT-assimilation. IseB **11**(4), 481–506 (2012). https://doi.org/10.1007/s10257-012-0205-9

Golgeci, I., Kuivalainen, O.: Does social capital matter for supply chain resilience? The role of absorptive capacity and marketing-supply chain management alignment. Ind. Mark. Manag. **84**, 63–74 (2020)

Grandinetti, R.: Absorptive capacity and knowledge management in small and medium enterprises. Knwl. Manag. Res. Pract. **14**, 159–168 (2016)

Iyengar, K., Sweeney, J.R., Montealegre, R.: Information technology use as a learning mechanism: the impact of IT use on knowledge transfer effectiveness, absorptive capacity, and franchisee performance. MIS Q. **39**, 615–642 (2015)

Kallio, H., Pietilä, A.M., Johnson, M., Kangasniemi, M.: Systematic methodological review: developing a framework for a qualitative semi-structured interview guide. J. Adv. Nurs. **72**, 2954–2965 (2016)

Kamilaris, A., Fonts, A., Prenafeta-Boldú, F.X.: The rise of blockchain technology in agriculture and food supply chains. Trends Food Sci. Technol. **91**, 640–652 (2019)

Kamminga, J.W., Bisby, H.C., Le, D.V., Meratnia, N., Havinga, P.J.M.: Generic online animal activity recognition on collar tags. In: Proceedings of the 2017 ACM International Joint Conference on Pervasive and Ubiquitous Computing and Proceedings of the 2017 ACM International Symposium on Wearable Computers, Maui, Hawaii. Association for Computing Machinery (2017)

Kamminga, J.W., Le, D.V., Meijers, J.P., Bisby, H., Meratnia, N., Havinga, P.J.M.: Robust sensor-orientation-independent feature selection for animal activity recognition on collar tags. Proc. ACM Interact. Mobile Wearable Ubiquit. Technol. **2**, 15 (2018)

Klein, H.K., Myers, M.D.: A set of principles for conducting and evaluating interpretive field studies in information systems. MIS Q. **23**, 67–93 (1999)

Kouhizadeh, M., Saberi, S., Sarkis, J.: Blockchain technology and the sustainable supply chain: theoretically exploring adoption barriers. Int. J. Prod. Econ. **231**, 107831 (2021)

Kuo, R.Z., Lee, G.G.: KMS adoption: the effects of information quality. Manag. Decis. (2009)

Lee, S.M., Lee, Z., Lee, J.: Knowledge transfer in work practice: adoption and use of integrated information systems. Ind. Manag. Data Syst. **107**, 501–518 (2007)

Lichtenthaler, U.: Absorptive capacity, enviromental turbulence, and the completmentarity of organizational of organizational learning processes. Acad. Manag. J. **52**, 822–846 (2009)

Lin, J., Shen, Z., Zhang, A., Chai, Y.: Blockchain and IoT based food traceability for smart agriculture. In: Proceedings of the 3rd International Conference on Crowd Science and Engineering, Singapore. Association for Computing Machinery (2018)

Lin, J., Shen, Z., Zhang, A., Chai, Y.: Blockchain and IoT based food traceability for smart agriculture (2018)

Liu, H., Ke, W., Wei, K.K., Hua, Z.: The impact of IT capabilities on firm performance: the mediating roles of absorptive capacity and supply chain agility. Decis. Support Syst. **54**, 1452–1462 (2013)

Luther, W.J.: Getting off the ground: the case of bitcoin. J. Inst. Econ. **15**, 189–205 (2019)

Madhwal, Y., Chistiakov, I., Yanovich, Y.: Logging multi-component supply chain production in blockchain. In: 2021 The 4th International Conference on Computers in Management and Business. Association for Computing Machinery (2021)

Mann, S., Potdar, V., Gajavilli, R.S., Chandan, A.: Blockchain technology for supply chain traceability, transparency and data provenance. In: Proceedings of the 2018 International Conference on Blockchain Technology and Application, Xi'an, China. Association for Computing Machinery (2018)

Manski, S.: Building the blockchain world: technological commonwealth or just more of the same? Strateg. Change **26**, 511–522 (2017)

Mao, D., Hao, Z., Wang, F., Li, H.: Novel automatic food trading system using consortium blockchain. Arab. J. Sci. Eng. **44**(4), 3439–3455 (2018). https://doi.org/10.1007/s13369-018-3537-z

Maouchi, M.E., Ersoy, O., Erkin, Z.: DECOUPLES: a decentralized, unlinkable and privacy-preserving traceability system for the supply chain. In: Proceedings of the 34th ACM/SIGAPP Symposium on Applied Computing. Limassol, Cyprus. Association for Computing Machinery (2019)

Marabelli, M., Newell, S.: Organizational learning and absorptive capacity in managing ERP implementation projects. In: ICIS 2009 Proceedings, p. 136 (2009)

Marabelli, M., Newell, S.: Absorptive capacity and enterprise systems implementation: the role of prior-related knowledge. ACM SIGMIS Database: Database Adv. Inf. Syst. **50**, 111–131 (2019)

Mariano, S., Walter, C.: The construct of absorptive capacity in knowledge management and intellectual capital research: content and text analyses. J. Knowl. Manag. **19**, 372–400 (2015)

Markus, M., Tanis, C., van Fenema, P.: Enterprise resource planning: multisite ERP implementations. Commun. ACM **43**, 42–46 (2000)

Marshall, M.N.: Sampling for qualitative research. Family Pract. **13**, 522 (1996)

Martinkenaite, I., Breunig, K.J.: The emergence of absorptive capacity through micro–macro level interactions. J. Bus. Res. **69**, 700–708 (2016)

Mighell, E., Ward, M.P.: African swine fever spread across Asia, 2018–2019. Transbound. Emerg. Dis. **68**, 2722–2732 (2021)

Neuman, W.L.: Social Research Methods: Quantitative and Qualitative Methods. Allyn and Bacon, Boston (2010)

Omidvar, O., Edler, J., Malik, K.: Development of absorptive capacity over time and across boundaries: the case of R&D consortia. Long Range Plann. **50**, 665–683 (2017)

Orlikowski, W.J.: The sociomateriality of organisational life: considering technology in management research. Cambridge J. Econ. **34**, 125–141 (2010)

Patterson, W., Ambrosini, V.: Configuring absorptive capacity as a key process for research intensive firms. Technovation **36–37**, 77–89 (2015)

Ranjan, S., Jha, V.K., Pal, P.: Literature review on ERP implementation challenges. Int. J. Bus. Inf. Syst. **21**, 388–402 (2016)

Ringsberg, H.: Perspectives on food traceability: a systematic literature review. Supply Chain Manag. **19**, 558–576 (2014)

Ruoti, S., Kaiser, B., Yerukhimovich, A., Clark, J., Cunningham, R.: Blockchain technology: what is it good for? Commun. ACM **63**, 46–53 (2019)

Saad, M., Kumar, V., Bradford, J.: An investigation into the development of the absorptive capacity of manufacturing SMEs. Int. J. Prod. Res. **55**, 6916–6931 (2017)

Taherdoost, H.: Sampling methods in research methodology; how to choose a sampling technique for research (2016)

Teece, D.J., Pisano, G., Shuen, A.: Dynamic capabilities and strategic management. Strateg. Manag. J. **18**, 509–533 (1997)

Tian, F.: A supply chain traceability system for food safety based on HACCP, blockchain & Internet of Things (2017)

Todorova, G., Durisin, B.: Absorptive capacity: valuing a reconceptualization. Acad. Manag. Rev. **32**, 774–786 (2007)

Tran, H.T.T., et al.: Genetic characterization of African swine fever viruses circulating in North Central region of Vietnam. Transbound. Emerg Dis. **68**, 1697–1699 (2021)

Tse, D., Zhang, B., Yang, Y., Cheng, C., Mu, H.: Blockchain application in food supply information security (2017)

Tzokas, N., Kim, Y.A., Akbar, H., Al-Dajani, H.: Absorptive capacity and performance: the role of customer relationship and technological capabilities in high-tech SMEs. Ind. Mark. Manage. **47**, 134–142 (2015)

van den Bosch, F.A., Volberda, H.W., de Boer, M.: Coevolution of firm absorptive capacity and knowledge environment: Organizational forms and combinative capabilities. Organ. Sci. **10**, 551–568 (1999)

Vasconcelos, A.C., Martins, J.T., Ellis, D., Fontainha, E.: Absorptive capacity: a process and structure approach. J. Inf. Sci. **45**, 68–83 (2019)

Volberda, H.W., Foss, N.J., Lyles, M.A.: Absorbing the concept of absorptive capacity: how to realize its potential in the organization field. Organ. Sci. **21**, 931–951 (2010)

Walsham, G.: Interpreting Information Systems in Organizations. Wiley, New York (1993)

Walsham, G.: Doing interpretive research. Eur. J. Inf. Syst. **15**, 320–330 (2006)

Wang, Y.-S., Wang, H.-Y., Shee, D.Y.: Measuring e-learning systems success in an organizational context: scale development and validation. Comput. Hum. Behav. **23**, 1792–1808 (2007)

Wright, S., Wright, A.M.: Information system assurance for enterprise resource planning systems: unique risk considerations. J. Inf. Syst. **16**, 99–113 (2002)

Wu, K., Beydoun, G., Sohaib, O., Gill, A.: The co-construct/ co-evolving process between organization's absorptive capacity and enterprise system practice under changing context: the case of ERP practice. Inf. Syst. Front. (2022). https://doi.org/10.1007/s10796-021-10238-1

Wu, K., Sun, B., Guo, H.: Absorptive capacity, blockchain and food traceability: an empirical investigation. In: Dai, H.N., Liu, X., Luo, D.X., Xiao, J., Chen, X. (eds.) Blockchain and Trustworthy Systems, vol. 1490, pp. 512–529. Springer, Cham (2021). https://doi.org/10.1007/978-981-16-7993-3_40

Xu, X., Zhu, D., Yang, X., Wang, S., Qi, L., Dou, W.: Concurrent practical byzantine fault tolerance for integration of blockchain and supply chain. ACM Trans. Internet Technol. **21**, 1–7 (2021)

Zahra, S.A., George, G.: Absorptive capacity: a review, reconceptualization, and extension. Acad. Manag. Rev. **27**, 185–203 (2002)

Zahra, S.A., Hayton, J.C.: The effect of international venturing on firm performance: the moderating influence of absorptive capacity. J. Bus. Ventur. **23**, 195–220 (2008)

Zou, B., Guo, F., Guo, J.: Absorptive capacity, technological innovation, and product life cycle: a system dynamics model. Springerplus **5**(1), 1–25 (2016). https://doi.org/10.1186/s40064-016-3328-5

DataAttest: A Framework to Attest Off-Chain Data Authenticity

Su Zhang[1], Ying Zhang[1,2]($\boxtimes$), Xiang Jing[3], Xingchun Diao[4], and Gang Huang[1]

[1] Key Laboratory of High-Confidence Software Technology (Peking University),
Ministry of Education, Beijing, China
{samsuzhang,zhang.ying,hg}@pku.edu.cn
[2] National Engineering Research Center for Software Engineering, Peking University,
Beijing, China
[3] School of Software and Microelectronics, Peking University, Beijing, China
jingxiang@pku.edu.cn
[4] Advanced Institute of Big Data, Beijing, China
diaoxc@aibd.ac.cn

Abstract. In recent years, more and more applications are built on blockchains for boosting security, while keeping interaction with the off-chain world. These applications usually leverage blockchain oracles to access off-chain data. However, they are still threatened by the weakness of data authenticity as the external data source system may be attacked and provide forged and malicious data. In this paper, we propose DataAttest, a framework based on remote attestation to guarantee the authenticity of off-chain data. DataAttest first instruments the data source system for collecting runtime traces. Then, it measures the static code and runtime traces in TEE to construct a Data Authenticity Proof (DAP). Finally, blockchain oracles verify the DAP to guarantee that the integrity of the specific data source system is undamaged and the provided data is actually obtained from that system. In addition, DataAttest also adopts two optimization strategies to accelerate DAP verification and minimize the overhead brought by DAP construction. We implement DataAttest and evaluate it on a real-world system. The experimental results show that DataAttest can effectively check data authenticity and the overhead is relatively low.

Keywords: Off-chain data · Data authenticity · Remote attestation · Blockchain oracle · Trusted execution environment

1 Introduction

With the widespread of blockchain technologies [12] in fields like Internet of Things (IoT) and e-health, more and more applications are built on blockchains for boosting security while keeping interaction with the off-chain world. For example, an IoT application requires off-chain device data and an e-health application requires off-chain medical data.

D. Svetinovic et al. (Eds.): BlockSys 2022, CCIS 1679, pp. 65–78, 2022.
https://doi.org/10.1007/978-981-19-8043-5_5

In such cases, blockchain oracles [10] are used for accessing off-chain data via the built-in security mechanisms. For example, the Provable oracle [6] uses the TLS-Notary [8] proof to prove the behavior correctness of web accessing, the TownCrier oracle [20] leverages the Intel SGX TEE to obtain data correctly [5], the ChainLink oracle [11] verifies data through the K-out-of-M threshold signature, and the Augur oracle [17] selects data through decentralized voting.

Unfortunately, however, the blockchain applications are still threatened by the weakness of data authenticity since the external data source system may be attacked and provides forged and malicious data to fool the oracles.

As we can see that the weak authenticity of the off-chain data itself has become the bottleneck blockchains. Therefore, how to prove the authenticity of off-chain data becomes a critical challenge to blockchain researches.

To address this problem, we draw on the idea of remote attestation (a proved method that verifies the integrity of software running on an untrusted remote device with the help of a trust anchor such as TPM [15] and TEE [14])) and propose the DataAttest framework to guarantee the authenticity of the off-chain data itself. In our approach, we regard a data source system as the software to be attested. The system will first be instrumented for collecting runtime information such as the executed Control-Flow Graph (CFG) path. Then, a Data Authenticity Proof (DAP) companioned with the provided data will be constructed by a TEE-based trusted measurement engine. Finally, oracles are able to verify the data authenticity with the DAP to attest that the integrity of the specific data source system is undamaged and the data is actually obtained from that system. In addition, DataAttest accelerates DAP verification via precisely instrumenting the program fragment corresponding to the data provision procedure, and minimizes the overhead brought by DAP construction via constructing a bypass for the program fragment to be attested.

We implement DataAttest and evaluate it on a real-world system. The experimental results show that DataAttest can effectively detect data authenticity problems of off-chian data while the modification to the data source system is slight and the overhead of DAP construction and verification is relatively low.

The main contributions of this paper are summarized as follows.

- The first work to guarantee the authenticity of off-chain data itself based on static and runtime remote attestation, which can easily combine with existing blockchain oracles.
- A precise instrumentation strategy to accelerate DAP verification and a bypass strategy to minimize the overhead brought by DAP construction.
- Implement the proposed framework and evaluate it on a real-world data source system.

The rest of the paper is organized as follows. We introduce the motivating example and our research goals in Sect. 2. We present the design of DataAttest in Sect. 3. We introduce the implementation of DataAttest and report evaluation results in Sect. 4. We discuss some issues in practical application in Sect. 5. We overview related work in Sect. 6, and conclude in Sect. 7.

2   Motivating Example and Goals

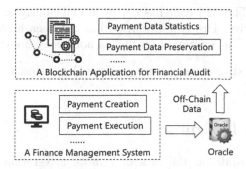

Fig. 1. Example of a blockchain application that accesses off-chain data.

Suppose there is a financial audit application that has to obtain the payment data from an off-chain financial system (as shown in Fig. 1). This application uses an oracle for guaranteeing the procedure security when data is transferred from the data source to the blockchain. However, even if the data source is under an attack which leads to a malicious data provision, these forged data will still be transferred to the blockchain without any doubt. This is a great threat to the whole blockchain security architecture since the authenticity of the incoming data is damaged from the beginning. Therefore, proving the authenticity of the off-chain data itself is necessary, no matter how well the data transferring procedure is protected.

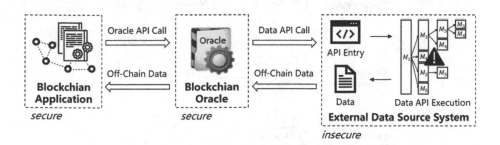

Fig. 2. Abstract view of off-chain data accessing.

Figure 2 shows the abstract view of a blockchain application accessing off-chain data through an oracle. Since that data source systems usually provide data in the form of data APIs, we regard the procedure that an oracle obtains a piece of off-chain data as the data API call phrase, while the procedure that the external data source system provides a piece of off-chain data as the data API execution phrase. We argue that the authenticity verification of the off-chain data is equal to the integrity verification of the data provision procedure, which consists of the following three parts:

1) Code Integrity: The API code has not been maliciously modified.
2) Execution Integrity: The code execution has not been hacked.
3) Result Integrity: The execution result has not been tempered with.

Therefore, in the next sections, we will propose DataAttest to provide evidences to prove them.

3   DataAttest Design

In this paper, we draw on the idea of remote attestation and propose the DataAttest framework to guarantee the authenticity of the off-chain data itself. Remote attestation is an approach to verify the integrity of software running on an untrusted remote device with the help of a trust anchor (e.g. TPM [15], TEE [14]). The attestation is accomplished by two main parts: a "prover" that has to generate an attestation report to prove itself via the trust anchor, and a "verifier" that remotely checks the prover using the report.

In our approach, we measure the API code for attesting *code integrity*, and trace the runtime CFG paths for attesting *execution integrity*, and sign the execution result (i.e. provided/returned data) at runtime for attesting *result integrity*. All these three parts will take the form of DAP and will be used as an attestation report to guarantee the authenticity of the off-chain data itself.

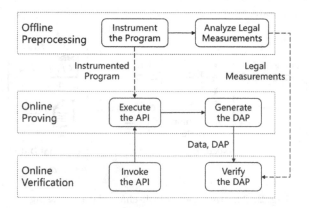

Fig. 3. Workflow of DataAttest.

DataAttest Workflow Overview. To construct and verify the DAP, we carry out the following workflow (as shown in Fig. 3), which can be divided into three stages: offline preprocessing, online proving and online verification.

In the offline stage, DataAttest will first instrument the program for constructing DAP at runtime. This program will then be further analyzed to produce the legal code measurement and the legal CFG path measurements separately for DAP verification.

In the online proving stage, DataAttest will construct the DAP containing the reports of code integrity, execution integrity and result integrity during the API execution.

In the online verification stage, DataAttest will verify the DAP to guarantee the authenticity of the data provided by the data source system.

3.1 DAP Construction and Verification

A DAP consists of three parts: the code integrity report, the execution integrity report and the result integrity report. DataAttest constructs the DAP with a measurement engine in the TEE secure world [14], which is afford to be trusted.

Code Integrity Report. In modern devices, the execution of the program is protected by the Data Execution Prevention (DEP) mechanism [18] of OS and hardware, which ensures runtime code integrity. Therefore, statically calculating the code hash of the instrumented API program is good enough to verify that the code has not been maliciously modified.

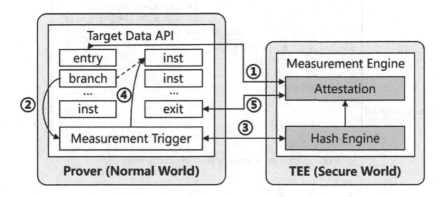

Fig. 4. Runtime CFG path measurement.

Execution Integrity Report. The execution integrity report (EIR) is a measurement of the executed CFG path of an API run. Figure 4 shows the details of the runtime CFG path measurement. First, an instrumented "Hello" message will be used for initializing the measurement engine (①). Then, whenever a basic block [2] is entered, an instrumented "measure" message will be sent with a preset unique block ID to the engine to let it mark a CFG path (②–④) by hash cumulating: $h_{cur} = H(h_{prev}, id)$, while when measuring the first basic block, the initial hash is set as: $h_{first} = H(0, id)$. The hash value will be verified against the legal CFG path measurements obtained in the offline static analysis. What should be noted is that state explosion is a common phenomenon when doing static analysis. To cope with this challenge, DataAttest carries out several optimization processes, which will be discussed detailed in the next section. Finally, a "Goodbye" message will be sent to the engine before the end of the API run and the engine will format the measurement result, do signature and send them back (⑤).

Result Integrity Report. The result integrity report (RIR) is the hash of the returned data of an API run. Whenever a "Goodbye" message is received (⑤), the measurement engine will also pack the returned data together with its RIR, and will sent them back along with the reports described above.

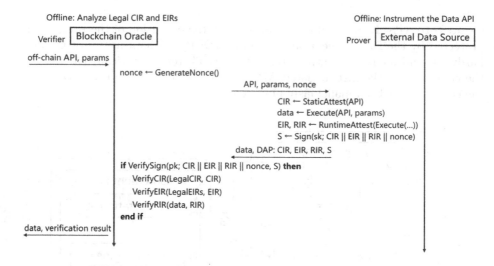

Fig. 5. Protocol interaction of DataAttest.

Protocol Interaction. Figure 5 shows the protocol interaction of DataAttest. After receiving a data request from a blockchain application, the oracle (verifier) will forward it to the external data source. A randomly generated nonce is also be sent together to avoid replay attacks [19].

Then, the data source (prover) will execute the instrumented API, construct the DAP, do signature with the hardware-protected secret key in TEE, and return.

After that, the oracle (verifier) will verify the DAP by checking the CIR, EIR and RIR respectively. For instance, the EIR will be checked against the legal CFG path measurements as above. The request data will finally be returned back to the blockchain application if all verifications are passed.

3.2 Attestation Optimization

In this section, we propose two optimization strategies used in DataAttest.

Precise Instrumentation Strategy. As discussed, the DAP generated at runtime will be verified against the legal measurements obtained offline. The calculation of the latter may explode due to the natural drawbacks of the static analysis approach. Fortunately, we find that the data API attested is usually a small code part of the data source system. Therefore, we minimize the calculated legal space of the potential CFG paths by instrumenting only the code fragment corresponding to a specific API, which is show in Algorithm 1. We also treat the loops and recursive functions as subroutines suggested by Abera et al. [9] to further accelerate verification.

Given a target system, DataAttest will profile and instrument it to identify all of the functions for runtime tracing like name, parameters, and return values (line 3–5). Then, DataAttest will ask the system to executed a specific data API to check which functions be invoked exactly during the API execution (line 6–14). The contents of the API input and output will be compared with the traced functions to locate the entry and exit ones for the API. After that, a legal CFG path can be constructed finally by the depth first traversal (line 15–19) from the entry to the exit, and the other paths will be neglected to avoid state explosion.

Algorithm 1. Locate program fragment of the data API

Require: *Program*
Ensure: *TargetFuncions*
  1: *TargetFuncions* ← empty set
  2: **function** LOCATEPROGRAMFRAGMENT(*Program*, *input*)
  3:    **for all** function f in *Program* **do**
  4:       InstrumentForLocating(f)
  5:    **end for**
  6:    *trace*, *output* ←ExecuteDataAPI(*Program*, *input*)
  7:    **for all** function record fr in *trace* **do**
  8:       **if** *entry* == *null* and Match(fr, *input*) **then**
  9:          *entry* ← fr
 10:       **end if**
 11:       **if** Match(fr, *output*) **then**
 12:          *exit* ← fr
 13:       **end if**
 14:    **end for**
 15:    *CallGraph* ←ConstructCallGraph(*Program*)
 16:    *curFunction* ← *CallGraph*.find(*entry*)
 17:    LocoateFragment(*curFunction*, *exit*, false)
 18:    *TargetFuncions*.insert(*CallGraph*.find(*exit*))
 19:    **return** *TargetFuncions*

20: **end function**
21: **function** LOCOATEFRAGMENT(*curFunction, exit, finish*)
22:     **if** *finish* or *curFunction.name* == *exit* **then**
23:         *finish* ← true
24:         **return**
25:     **end if**
26:     *TargetFuncions*.insert(*curFunction*)
27:     **for all** child *c* in *curFunction* **do**
28:         LocoateFragment(*CallGraph, c, exit*)
29:     **end for**
30: **end function**

Bypass Strategy. Furthermore, as function sharing is a common practice in model system design, the instrumented functions may be invoked by other modules unrelated to the API and thus delay their execution. Therefore, DataAttest leverages a bypass strategy to minimize this overhead.

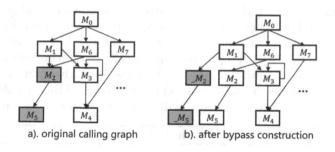

a). original calling graph   b). after bypass construction

Fig. 6. Bypass construction.

Figure 6 illustrates the process of bypass construction. DataAttest will first clone the functions related to the API fragment and rename them with the prefix of *_cfa_*. Then, it will reconstruct the incoming and outgoing relations in-between the cloned ones and also the other functions. Such refactoring makes sure that the execution of an attested API be confined in these cloned functions for performance isolation, while their states are still able to send out to keep the whole system working correctly.

4   Case Study

We built the prototype of DataAttest with about 1614 lines of Java code and about 423 lines of C++ code. It uses the ASM library [1] for instrumenting Java-based data soure systems, and it implements the measurement engine for the Intel SGX enclave [5] in C++ and uses BLAKE2s [3] as the hash function required. It also uses the Soot library [7] for carrying out offline static analysis.

4.1 Experimental Setup

We apply DataAttest to the real-world case which has been shown in Fig. 1. In this case, a financial audit application deployed on Hyperledger Fabric [4] will obtain the payment data from an external java data source system, which provides APIs to return the list and details of financial payments show in Fig. 7. We can see that these payments data is critical and cannot afford any forgery. In such cases, DataAttest will come to the rescue and can be surely useful.

API: Accredit_JB_SendReq_GetReqList

Field Name	Type	Description
id	String	Fund Application ID
voucher_no	String	Payment Application Number
bsi_code	String	Financial Classification Code
bsi_name	String	Financial Classification Name
payee_account_name	String	Payee Name
payee_account_no	String	Payee Bank Account Number
...	...	...
bp_name	String	Indicator Type
bl_name	String	Indicator Source
bl_name	String	Indicator Source

API Response

```
[
  {
    "pf_name": "Normal Payment",
    "billtype_code":"369",
    "rg_code":"3502",
    "voucher_no":"D013018-023AB-00063",
    ......
    "fromctrlid":"858730",
    "pay_summary_name":"1",
    "bsi_code":"30102 "
  },
  ......
]
```

Fig. 7. The target data API of the financial payment management system.

4.2 Effectiveness Evaluation

DataAttest first located and instrumented the API fragment, and also equipped the trusted measurement engine onto the remote device's Intel SGX enclave. After that, the financial system returned the data as well as the DAP whenever a data API was invoked. At this time, DataAttest can help to verify the DAP regrading to the data for attesting its authenticity.

As expected, the DAP is able to pass the verification when the data API was executed normally. To further verify the effectiveness of DataAttest, we simulate 3 attacks that would generate forged and malicious data.

Attack 1 is an attack on the *code integrity*. It modifies the static code of the API to return some forged data instead of the original ones. The check result reports errors when verifying the CIR in the DAP due to the attack on the static code has detected.

Attack 2 is an attack on the *execution integrity*. It modifies the destination of a goto instruction at runtime for simulating control-flow attack (Fig. 8.a). This kind of attack can easily pass the code integrity verification. However, it cannot pass the test of execution integrity because the EIR check of the DAP (Fig. 8.b) shows that an illegal CFG path has been run through.

Attack 3 is an attack on the *result integrity*. It simulates a HTTP hijacking to modify the returned data of the API. Of cource, DataAttest successfully detects the attack because the hash of the modified data is different from the RIR in the DAP.

```
45: aaload
46: invokestatic  #3
49: pop
50: goto     -90- 142
53: aload_0
54: ifnull    90
57: aload_0
58: arraylength
59: iconst_3
```

a). the attack 2

```
{"data":[{"pf_name":"Normal Payment","billtype_code":"36
9","rg_code":"3502","voucher_no":"D0130..."},...],"DAP":{"CIR
":"f993004f7f508d9b251d7b861baa405f2f1712f4d42528a6
92858951ffcacef9","EIR":"8d80b7034426c6c5528f3892a87c
7de006ad6a09eeebb19b12c33a20f220c5fb,<3e3aa7211c1
eebfce6aa03079c68d7ba66955ea0c9e753b5209921720acf
8672,{<256b91bafbdafaf32cd81b2f4ca925402117229e349
f02d722f22d21c38967eb,6>}>","RIR":"9e846cf00f0021d6ef
e4a7fb317402834f2b3f48fcab21095ea87cd3bf408bf9","Sig
nature":"C0vAnhhy07FvFqNPMGdQxuKZZhJ4ywqFjR83Hv
Ni+pHt/w+SeEF2T7piKDJgbVmDYS4yGGg06osYyEjXps..."}}
```

b). the returned data and DAP

```
{
"data":[{"pf_name":"Normal Payment","bill
   type_code":"369","rg_code":"3502
   ","voucher_no":"D0130..."},...],
"attestation": {
   "stateCode":2,
   "details":"EIR verification failed, the API
   execution may be attacked."
   }
}
```

c). the verification report

Fig. 8. The simulated control-flow attack and the attestation.

4.3   Performance Evaluation

We further conduct some experiments to evaluate the impact of applying DataAttest to determine whether the overhead can be tolerated in real-world cases. The experiment mainly focuses on the following three questions: 1) the amount of modification to the target data source system, 2) the overhead of DAP construction during the API execution, and 3) the overhead of DAP verification. Table 1 shows the experimental results.

The Amount of Modification. The target system has a total of 774,299 lines of bytecode, and DataAttest injects 2397 lines of bytecode to the system in this case. It should be noted that most of them are generated due to the code clone when constructing the bypass. Only 568 lines of bytecode are injected for the attestation. Since the instrumentation is only performed for the located API fragment, the modification to the original system is lightweight.

The Overhead of DAP Construction. In terms of the API run time, the overhead introduced by DataAttest is about 19.13%. The overhead mainly comes from the CFG path measurement whenever a new control-flow event (e.g. branch, return) happens and it is proportional to the number of control-flow events. In terms of the API memory cost, the overhead introduced by DataAttest is about 0.23%. It mainly comes from the loading of the injected bytecode and the instantiation of the classes to interact with the measurement engine.

Table 1. The impact of adopting DataAttest.

	Original	DataAttest	Overhead
Bytecode lines	774299	776696	0.31%
API run time	183 (ms)	218 (ms)	19.13%
API memory cost	142384 (KB)	142712 (KB)	0.23%
Verification run time	—	45 (ms)	—
Verification memory cost	—	74 (KB)	—

The Overhead of DAP Verification. The run time overhead of the online verification mainly comes from the signature verification and the search in the legal measurements (with the complexity of $O(nlogn)$), which is 45 ms in this case. The memory overhead mainly comes from the storage of legal measurements, which is 74 KB in this case. Such little overhead is mainly due to the optimization strategies used in DataAttest.

To sum up, DataAttest can be effectively applied to real-world cases to ensure the authenticity of the provided data. The modification to the data source system is lightweight, and the overhead of the DAP construction and verification is relatively low.

5 Discussion

The Integrity of Verification. To ensure the authenticity of off-chain data obtained by blockchain applications, it is also necessary to keep the integrity of the verification stage. When we put the verification stage in blockchian oracles, it can be done together with the data acquisition procedure which protected by the built-in security mechanisms of the oracles (e.g. the decentralized way [11], the TEE-based way [20]). In addition, the verification can also be placed in blockchain applications (i.e. in smart contracts) to take advantage of the security provided by blockchain platforms since the overhead of online verification is relatively low.

Privacy of the Data API Program. The program (e.g. binary file) of the data API is required for verifying the DAP, which may raise privacy concerns. To avoid this problem, we can leverage the privacy-preserving computation [16] when performing verification. For example, we can encrypt the program with the TEE public key and verify the DAP in TEE to make the program invisible to the verifier. Alternatively, the legal measurements can be calculated in a trusted and privacy-preserving way in advance, which prevent the original program from being exposed.

6 Related Work

6.1 Blockchain Oracle

Blockchain oracles collect and provide data to smart contracts, enabling them to interact with external data sources outside the blockchain [10]. Oracle researches focus on solving the security and trust problems in the process of off-chain data accessing.

Provable [6] provides a safe data-transport-layer for smart contracts to fetch external data from Web APIs by demonstrating that the data fetched from the original data source is genuine and untampered. This is accomplished by accompanying the returned data together with a document called authenticity proof. The authenticity proofs can build upon different technologies such as the

TLS-Notary [8] and auditable virtual machines. TownCrier [20] proposes a TEE-based oracle service to provide trusted data by performing data authentication in a trusted and secure execution environment. It supports collecting data from multiple data sources and performing secure data aggregation in the Intel SGX enclave. ChainLink [11] proposes a decentralized oracle network to enable trustworthy data feeds and connectivity between smart contracts and external data sources. It verifies data through the K-out-of-M threshold signature thus securely pushing the data between smart contracts and Web-API.

The difference between DataAttest and existing oracles is that DataAttest focus on the authenticity of the off-chain data itself while these oracles try to prove that the data providing to the blockchain application is what the data source provides. DataAttest can well combine with these oracles to further improve the security of off-chain data accessing.

6.2   Control-Flow Attestation

Control-Flow Attestation (CFA) is a dynamic remote attestation technique that allows the verifier to know if the instructions of a given program are executed in a specific expected order.

C-FLAT [9] proposed the first CFA scheme. It uses software tools and TEE to track the executed CFG path of the program, and calculates a cumulative hash to the ID of basic blocks in the path to obtain the attestation result. The verifier then compares the result to a set of pre-stored expected values to verify the integrity of the program execution. LO-FAT [13] uses hardware to improve the efficiency of C-FLAT. It utilizes the capabilities of existing processors to record CFG path in hardware without software instrumentation, thereby reducing the burden on the main processor and increasing parallel computing capabilities. ReCFA [21] proposes a resilient CFA strategy that does not require offline measurements of all legal CFA paths, improving the scalability of CFA. It focuses on condensing the runtime control-flow events, including filtering skippable call sites, folding program-structure related control-flow events and a greedy compression.

Different from the above work, DataAttest applies CFA to the attestation of data authenticity and proposes two optimization strategies to accelerate the verification and minimize the proving overhead, which are complementary to the strategies proposed in the above work.

7   Conclusion

Nowadays, many blockchain applications are threatened by the authenticity weakness of the off-chain data. To tackle this weakness, we draw on the idea of remote attestation and propose the DataAttest framework for proving that the data provided by the off-chain system is as it is. DataAttest constructs and verifies the DAP to attest the *code integrity*, *execution integrity* and *result integrity* during data fetching, thus guaranteeing the authenticity of the off-chain data itself. It also adopts the precise instrumentation strategy and the bypass strategy to accelerate DAP verification and minimize the overhead brought by DAP construction.

We implement DataAttest and evaluate it on a real-world data source system. The experimental results show that DataAttest can effectively detect data authenticity problems while the modification to the system is slight and the overhead of DAP construction and verification is relatively low.

Acknowledgments. This paper was supported by foundation items: The National Key RD Program of China (No. 2021YFF0901100), The National Science Fund for Distinguished Young Scholars, China (61725201).

References

1. Asm. https://asm.ow2.io/
2. Basic blocks. https://gcc.gnu.org/onlinedocs/gccint/Basic-Blocks.html
3. Blake2. https://www.blake2.net/
4. Hyperledger fabric. https://www.hyperledger.org/use/fabric
5. Intel software guard extensions (sgx). https://software.intel.com/content/www/us/en/develop/topics/software-guard-extensions.html
6. Provable documentation. https://docs.provable.xyz
7. Soot. https://soot-oss.github.io/soot/
8. Tls-notary. https://tlsnotary.org/
9. Abera, T., et al.: C-FLAT: control-flow attestation for embedded systems software. In: Proceedings of the 2016 ACM SIGSAC Conference on Computer and Communications Security, pp. 743–754 (2016)
10. Al-Breiki, H., Rehman, M.H.U., Salah, K., Svetinovic, D.: Trustworthy blockchain oracles: review, comparison, and open research challenges. IEEE Access **8**, 85675–85685 (2020)
11. Breidenbach, L., et al.: Chainlink 2.0: next steps in the evolution of decentralized oracle networks (2021)
12. Crosby, M., Pattanayak, P., Verma, S., Kalyanaraman, V., et al.: Blockchain technology: beyond bitcoin. Appl. Innov. **2**(6–10), 71 (2016)
13. Dessouky, G., et al.: LO-FAT: low-overhead control flow attestation in hardware. In: Proceedings of the 54th Annual Design Automation Conference 2017, pp. 1–6 (2017)
14. GlobalPlatform: Tee system architecture. http://www.globalplatform.org/specificationsdevice.asp
15. Trusted Computing Group: Trusted computing group: Tpm main - part 1 design principles - specification version 1.2 (2003). https://trustedcomputinggroup.org/resource/tpm-library-specification/
16. Kerschbaum, F.: Privacy-preserving computation. In: Preneel, B., Ikonomou, D. (eds.) APF 2012. LNCS, vol. 8319, pp. 41–54. Springer, Heidelberg (2014). https://doi.org/10.1007/978-3-642-54069-1_3
17. Peterson, J., Krug, J., Zoltu, M., Williams, A.K., Alexander, S.: Augur: a decentralized oracle and prediction market platform (v2. 0). Whitepaper (2019). https://augur.net/whitepaper.pdf

18. Stojanovski, N., Gusev, M., Gligoroski, D., Knapskog, S.J.: Bypassing data execution prevention on microsoftwindows XP SP2. In: The Second International Conference on Availability, Reliability and Security (ARES 2007), pp. 1222–1226. IEEE (2007)
19. Teixeira, A., Pérez, D., Sandberg, H., Johansson, K.H.: Attack models and scenarios for networked control systems. In: Proceedings of the 1st International Conference on High Confidence Networked Systems, pp. 55–64 (2012)
20. Zhang, F., Cecchetti, E., Croman, K., Juels, A., Shi, E.: Town crier: an authenticated data feed for smart contracts. In: Proceedings of the 2016 ACM SIGSAC Conference on Computer and Communications Security, pp. 270–282 (2016)
21. Zhang, Y., et al.: ReCFA: resilient control-flow attestation. In: Annual Computer Security Applications Conference, pp. 311–322 (2021)

Blockchain-Based Healthcare and Medicine Data Sharing and Service System

Xiaolian Yang[1] , Chaolei Wu[1] , Xingyu Yan[1] , and Fang Hu[1,2]($\boxtimes$)

[1] College of Information Engineering, Hubei University of Chinese Medicine,
Wuhan 430065, People's Republic of China
naomifang@hbtcm.edu.cn
[2] Department of Mathematics and Statistics, University of West Florida,
Pensacola 32514, USA

Abstract. As the remarkable development of blockchain technology, it attracts a considerable attentions and has a significant impact on various scientific domains, such as healthcare and medicine industry. However, in real-world scenarios of healthcare and medicine applications, data sharing and service are confronted with some challenges because the data has the characteristics of multi-source, heterogeneity, large-scale, etc. Moreover, security and management issues during the stages of data extraction, storage, transfer, access, etc., should be taken into account for healthcare and medicine data sharing and service. To provide a more flexible, reliable, and convenient service for healthcare and medicine, this paper proposes a data sharing and service system, termed HMChain, developed on blockchain technology. This system consists of three layers referring to a data extraction and storage layer for multi-source data integration and distributed data storage, a data management layer for data secure transfer and access, and a data application layer for various user-oriented services. Furthermore, several healthcare and medicine data sharing and service scenarios have been depicted in detail. Overall, this system can provide convenient services for healthcare management, clinical research, medicine traceability, neuroscience research, etc.

Keywords: Blockchain technology · Healthcare and medicine system · Data sharing and service · Electronic health record · Medicine traceability

1 Introduction

Blockchain technology is an integrated, reliable, distributed, and immutable innovative technology [1], which consists of decentralised peer-to-peer network (P2P) and storage [2], dynamic public key encryption algorithms [3], intelligent consensus mechanisms [4], transparent transactions [5], and programmable smart contracts [6]. It can be applied to construct a secure, reliable, and effective network system for data services [7]. Recently, blockchain technology plays a significant role in various research areas, including intelligent transportation, aeronautics and astronautics, healthcare monitoring, clinical data sharing, etc. [8–11].

© The Author(s), under exclusive license to Springer Nature Singapore Pte Ltd. 2022
D. Svetinovic et al. (Eds.): BlockSys 2022, CCIS 1679, pp. 79–90, 2022.
https://doi.org/10.1007/978-981-19-8043-5_6

In the applications of healthcare and medicine, blockchain is employed to realize the feasibility of healthcare and medicine data storage and transfer, which is developed and mainly focuses on improving the privacy of individuals' information [12], the integrity of various data from multiple sources, and the security of information interchange between patients and healthcare providers. The applications of blockchain will promote the scientific development of human healthcare and medicine [13].

Electronic medical record (EMR) is the significant clinical data source which consists of text, images, and video data generated during the processes of diagnosis, treatment, examination, test, etc. [14]. In order to realize collaboration and communication in healthcare and medicine data sharing process, it is crucially required to make data secure and convenient [15]. However, the existing systems cannot meet the overall requirements since they don't have consistent structures on the basis of access control strategies and security policies [16]. The EMR refers to the most private information of patients, if without the effective data security strategies, sensitive information is often leaked. Moreover, the healthcare and medicine data cannot be effectively shared and utilized because of data duplicates, non-standard data, data availability in heterogeneous networks [17].

Electronic health record (EHR) conserves the healthcare and medicine data during individual life circle including personal living conditions, individual activities, past and current medical history, family history, diagnosis and treatment, and physical examination results, etc. [18]. Because EHR also refers to a lot of private and sensitive data for individuals, the deficiency of EHR data sharing and service mechanism and lack of systematic infrastructure support for security will result in the delay or lost of information transfer and access [19]. Furthermore, if the patients' sensitive data are accessed by unlicensed users, their privacy will be leaked for some crimes [20]. By using the smart wearable devices, the personal healthcare record (PHR) data will be collected in real time and transferred to the healthcare management system. This kind of data includes daily activities, sleep exercise, heart rate, body fat, etc., which can be used for chronic disease monitoring, daily activity monitoring, etc. [21]. Furthermore, this real-time monitoring data will provide a basis of health activity analysis and disease prediction [22]. However, this individual data may be stored in different areas, different hospitals, or different medical insurance institutions, a fact that makes individual information cannot be effectively integrated and shared [23].

The greatest challenges in healthcare and medicine data sharing and service are summarized as follows:

- There exists a variety of mobile devices, systems, and platforms to share healthcare and medicine data. However, the data fusion from different sources and the data services in different scenarios cannot be effectively integrated and provided [24,25].
- The general data storing and transferring methods cannot satisfy the storage requirement of healthcare and medicine data with the features of heterogeneity, diversity, distribution, etc., and the transferring performance of security, real time, reliability, integrity, etc [26].

- For most of the data sharing and service systems, few data services have been provided for the public or specific user accesses, a fact that restricts the development of healthcare and medicine service [27].

To address these challenges, we develop a blockchain-based healthcare and medicine data sharing and service system (HMChain), which consists of data extraction and storage layer, data management layer, and data application layer. Using the characteristics of blockchain, this system realize a integrated, secure, reliable, effective data fusion, transferring, and access for healthcare and medicine applications. The contributions of HMChain are shown as follows:

- A blockchain-based healthcare and medicine data sharing and service system (HMChain) is presented to fuse the multi-source data, realize complicated data storing and transfer, and provide various user-oriented application services.
- This system realizes an effective data integration from various sources with multiple data structures. Then, the specific P2P network of blockchain, consensus mechanisms, smart contract, are constructed to guarantee the effective, secure, transparent, immutable, and reliable storage, transfer, and access for healthcare and medicine data.
- Based on this system, a wide range of user-oriented services are developed to extend the real-world applications. Referring to the clinical research, genetic engineering, biomedical development, medicine traceability, etc., this system can provide a variety of data services and promote the development of healthcare and medicine services.

The remainder organization of this paper is as follows. The architecture of HMChain is illustrated in Sect. 3. In Sect. 4, the data categories and storage mechanism are presented. We show the data management module in Sect. 5. In Sect. 6, the data application services and specific two application scenarios have been depicted. Finally, we give the conclusion and perspective in Sect. 7.

2 Related Work

In this section, we present the existing blockchain-based systems, platforms, and architectures referring to electronic healthcare record (EHR), electronic medicine record (EMR), medical image sharing, genomics research, prescription management, clinical trial research, etc. Based on blckchain, Hang et al. proposed a medical platform which uses a smart contract to ensure the EMR data security and provides a integrated medical information access for patients [16]. Tang et al. presented a blockchain-based system to achieve medical image sharing in a cross-organizational, cross-regional, supervisory, and trustworthy way [15]. Sultana et al. leveraged the zero trust principles, the immutability of blockchain, and the scalability of off chain data storage to propose a decentralized framework for the security, transfer, and storage of the medical data [28]. Bali et al. proposed a blockchain-based platform, termed BlockMedx, with the capability of secure prescription management. All the participators including physicians, patients, pharmacies, healthcare providers, etc., are involved in the platform and are connected to facilitate multiparty transactions [29]. Zhou et al. proposed MIStore, a medical insurance storage system based on blockchain, which can provide a high-credibility to users with small memory and CPU consumption [30].

Despite the aforementioned blockchain-based systems, platforms, and architectures can provide a good performance of data storage, security, transfer, access, etc., the multi-source and heterogeneous data sharing and collaboration in real-world healthcare and medicine scenarios is still facing some challenges. Therefore, we present a blockchain-based healthcare and medicine data sharing and collaboration system (HMChain) to fuse the multi-source data, realize complicated data storing and transfer, and provide various user-oriented application services.

3   HMChain Architecture

Figure 1 illustrates the architecture of blockchain-based healthcare and medicine data sharing and service system (HMchain), which consists of three layers, including data extraction and storage layer, data management layer, and data application layer. This system realizes cross-organizational, cross-regional, trustworthy, multi-level, effective, secure, and reliable healthcare and medicine data sharing and service.

– **Data Extraction and Storage Layer:** This layer consists of data extraction and storage, which provides the information fusion of clinical data, research data, individual behaviour data, payment and health insurance data,

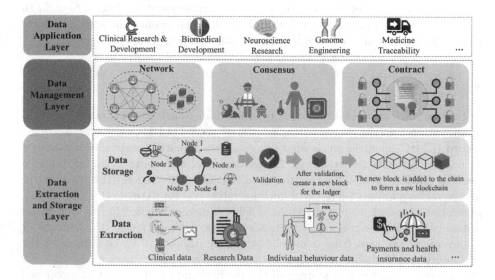

Fig. 1. HMChain architecture.

etc. The block generation and transaction mechanism have been presented for reliable data storage.

- **Data Management Layer:** The healthcare and medicine data is appended on an electronic ledger, which is distributed across a peer-to-peer network. Some consensus mechanisms are used to achieve agreement, trust, and security of network. Smart contract is applied to create a secure technical infrastructure.
- **Data Application Layer:** This layer provides user-oriented services referring to electronic health record, electronic medical record, clinical research and development, biomedical development, neuroscience research, genome market, medicine traceability, etc.

4   Data Extraction and Storage Layer

Healthcare and medicine data have the characteristics of multi-source, heterogeneity, variety, multi-relations, etc., which are extracted from various mobile devices, systems, platforms, etc. The data can be categorized as clinical data, research data, individual behaviour data, payment and health insurance data, etc. We also conduct the block and transaction mechanism designs in the data extraction and storage layer.

4.1   Data Extraction

This system mainly extracts four categories of data as follows:

1) Clinical Data: This data is extracted from hospital information system (HIS) covering various subsystems, such as outpatient/inpatient doctor stations, laboratory information system (LIS), picture archiving and communication system (PACS), pharmaceutical administration system, microbial experiments, pathological information system, etc. Focusing on the clinical diagnosis and treatment information in electronic medical record (EMR), textual data and image data referring to diagnosis, prescriptions, examination, testing data, etc., have been extracted.

2) Research Data: This kind of data referring to clinical trial data, medical data, gene sequence data, etc., mainly generated in the process of medical device research and development (r&d) enterprises, r&d outsourcing companies, genetic-testing companies, and scientific research institutions.

3) Individual Behaviour Data: Personal healthcare record (PHR) mainly refers to the individual behaviour data. The real-time data is obtained from individual behaviours perceived by smart wearable devices, such as smart bracelets, smart phones, etc., which monitor the personal daily activities, sleep exercise, heart rate. Some data is collected from various online medical platforms, physical examination system, etc. Most of this kind of information is stored in electronic health records (EHR).

4) Payment and Health Insurance Data: All records referring to the payment in audit and reimbursement, such as records of patient payment, reimbursement, audit, medical circulation, etc. In addition to the payment of patients, it also contains the expense data of medical services provided by the hospital, such as the expense data of drugs, equipment, and salaries of health personnel.

4.2 Data Storage

A healthcare and medicine blockchain is designed and generated for various data storing and sharing in a manner with distribution, transparency, and tamper resistance. Each block is composed of an index, time stamp, data, previous hash value, and current block hash value, and uses pointers to link with other blocks. Such sequence of blocks guarantee the data integrity and tamper resistance in the blockchain. A chain growth and data verification mechanism is designed to guarantee the stored data integrity. When new healthcare and medicine data is appended to the blockchain, one block or unit is created and linked to the free end to extend the blockchain. As the addition of more data, the sizes of blockchain will correspondingly grow. When one block is modified, cryptographic links will be broken and the whole blockchain will be disrupted. Furthermore, this blockchain permits the user to verify the data integrity.

It is a complex working sequence for blockchain to verify and validate transactions by using a distributed ledger network. Blockchain creates ledger technology which is immutable, secure, and consensus-based. Firstly, the network node of healthcare and medicine data requests the transaction, which broadcasts to peer nodes. This network then creates a unique hash via a algorithm such as the SHA-256 algorithm. Then, all hashes are linked by the previous hash and it makes a transactions' network, which is unbreakable and would be validated by the node or a smart contract, consensus. This immutable ledger can only be appended to the transaction of blocks. After the generation of a reliable and secure decentralized network, some confirmed transactions, such as encryption, contracts, clinical data, research data, individual behaviour data, and payment and health insurance data, can be verified.

5 Data Management Layer

The data management layer focuses on peer-to-peer (P2P) network, consensus mechanism, and smart contract.

5.1 Peer-to-Peer Network

We use the blockchain to manage the healthcare and medicine data, which is appended on a ledger distributed across a peer-to-peer (P2P) network. Concerned to this crucial enhancement, the nodes engaged in the blockchain are requested to agree on events in a P2P network manner by using various consensus mechanisms. Depending on a P2P network, the permissionless blockchain systems can propagate information among participating peers in the network. By using specific correct functions in the consensus mechanisms, all the peers in the network require knowledge of information consensus set is to be agreed on (e.g., blocks and transactions). In terms of the gossip or flooding protocols, the required information is propagated to all peers in the network. This converts the permissionless blockchain network to a unstructured P2P network.

5.2 Consensus Mechanism

The healthcare and medicine blockchain employs various consensus mechanisms including Proof of Work (PoW), Proof of Stake (PoS), Practical Byzantine Fault Tolerance (PBFT).

1) PoW: This consensus mechanism is always applied in the bitcoin network. In PoW, each node in a network calculates a hash value for the block header including a nonce, and the nodes will alter frequently to obtain various hash values. This consensus mechanism needs that the calculated value must be smaller than or equal to a specific given value. If one node comes up to a target value, it would broadcast this block to other nodes, and then all other nodes must interactively validate the correctness of the hash value. If a block is validated, other nodes will append this novel block to their blockchains.

2) PoS: It can save more energy and gives more effectiveness compared to PoW. Nodes in PoS have to prove the ownership of the currency amount. In general, people with more currencies will be less likely to attack the network. Based on account balance, the selection is quite unfair because the single richest person is bound to be dominant in a network. As a consequence, a number of solutions are presented combining with the stake sizes to determine which one to forge next block. This consensus mechanism relies on the node assets. The nodes just validate and confirm a novel block if the proportion of assets (wealth or stake), is higher than the blocks in a network. For the application perspective of cryptocurrency, the nodes are needed to predetermine a minimum amount of their asset value deposit.

3) PBFT: It is a replication algorithm to tolerate byzantine faults. PBFT has a key idea that all the nodes require to be predefined in a blockchain network. The process of PBFT consensus mechanism contains five phases: request, pre-prepare, prepare, commit, and reply events. A node in the blockchain network requires a maximum of two replica votes from all the connected nodes to be conducted throughout these phases. PBFT needs that each node is known to the blockchain network. The employment of PBFT consensus algorithm can greatly reduce the energy consumption and is more suitable for the existing structures of healthcare applications.

5.3 Smart Contract

As an improvement to blockchain technologies, smart contracts can be considered as the incorporation in the Hyperledger and Ethereum Blockchain. Smart contracts provide functions of eliminating intermediaries and supporting features, including auto-executing and self-executing, self-verification and immutability. The infrastructures of Ethereum blockchain can realize many decentralised applications in various scenarios by introducing smart contracts. The healthcare and medicine data operations and objects of smart contracts promote an application generation to communicate among blocks and provide the effective and convenient services to the users. In the research domains of healthcare and medicine, smart contracts in blockchain can be used to create a secure technology infrastructure to afford the data consistency of healthcare and medicine records that enhances the quality of services, coordination of users, and improves the diagnosis and treatment effectiveness.

6   Data Application Layer

This section presents the healthcare and medicine data application services, including electronic health record (EHR), electronic medical record (EMR), clinical research and development, biomedical development, neuroscience research, genome engineering, medicine traceability, etc. In terms of the service categories, this system is designed as a consortium blockchain, some pre-selected nodes are visible to the all users could take part in the consensus process, and the remainder nodes are permitted by specific users would be allowed to participate in it. Specifically, we focus on two representative scenarios, including the clinical research and development, and medicine traceability, to elaborately present the application services.

6.1   Clinical Research and Development

As shown in Fig. 2, the clinical data from EMR has been encrypted and stored in the blockchain of HMChain, which mainly contains the diagnosis, prescriptions, examination, testing data, etc. The clinical diagnosis and treatment activities refers to the various users, such as physician, patient, pharmacist, lab technician, radiologist, researchers, etc. Clinical information covering textual and image data can be authorized to transfer between the blockchain and user-oriented services. These activities of data request, approval, inspect, etc., realize the information communication. Through data access based on HMChain, the various users can obtain their customized services, such as clinical decision support for physician, lifestyle advice for patient, data-driven predictive analysis for researchers, etc.

6.2   Medicine Traceability

Based on the materials and pharmaceutical technology, the classes of medicine have be categorized as drug, Chinese patent medicine, herb, etc. Based on HMChain, we focus on the drug and herb traceability, which is applied to monitor the whole process management of medicine and improve the transparency, integrity, and reliability of medicine information. It can guarantee the medicine

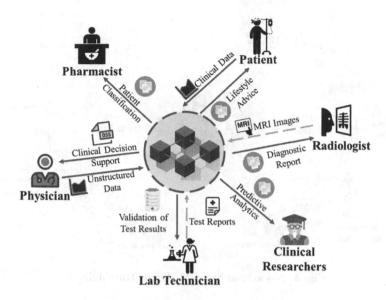

Fig. 2. Illustration of clinical application Services.

quality, prevent the circulation and sale of counterfeit medicine, etc. Depending on blockchain features of sharing, immutability, and encryption, etc., we present the herb and drug traceability of medicine whole process management in Fig. 3.

1) Herb Traceability. A safe and reliable herb traceability service is provided based on HMChain. As various requirements of herb materials with unique codes, the whole process management information referring to breeding, seedling cultivation, processing, packaging, circulation, transaction, and after-sale service, has encrypted and registered in the distributed nodes of blockchain. The Application layer provides the access interface for the breeding companies, field management, raw material factories, logistics companies, hospitals, pharmacies and consumers corresponded to the herb traceability service. When a accident occurs, this blochchain with data immutability can help to trace each process and find the accident cause and ascertain the responsibility.

2) Drug Traceability. Compared with the herb traceability blockchain, the drug blockchain removes the breeding and planting process information, and only requires the data generated in the production, processing, packaging, circulation, transaction, and after-sale services. Similarly, the immutable and encrypted storage characteristics of blockchain guarantee the authenticity and credibility in the whole process from drug production to after-sale services.

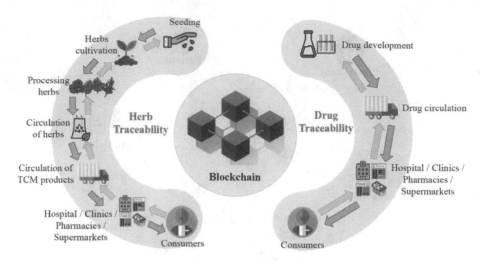

Fig. 3. Blockchain-based Medicine Traceability.

7   Conclusions

In this paper, we have investigated a blockchain-based system (HMChain) for healthcare and medicine data sharing and service. The proposed HMChain integrates multiple sources and realizes a distributed data storage through the data extraction and storage layer, utilizes the data management layer to guarantee the security of data transfer and access, provides user-oriented services by data application layer. Some application scenarios, such as clinical research and development, medicine traceability, have been presented in detail. One of our future research directions is proposing more effective algorithms applied in different sections of blockchain construction to enhance the efficiency and reliability of the real-time healthcare and medicine data storage, transfer, and access.

Acknowledgments. We acknowledge the funding support from the Key Research Project of Education Department of Hubei Province Under Grant D20212002.

References

1. Acharjamayum, I., Patgiri, R., Devi, D.: Blockchain: a tale of peer to peer security. In: 2018 IEEE Symposium Series on Computational Intelligence (SSCI), pp. 609–617. IEEE (2018)
2. Neudecker, T., Hartenstein, H.: Network layer aspects of permissionless blockchains. IEEE Commun. Surv. Tutor. **21**(1), 838–857 (2018)
3. Gao, S., Yu, T., Zhu, J., Cai, W.: T-PBFT: an EigenTrust-based practical byzantine fault tolerance consensus algorithm. China Commun. **16**(12), 111–123 (2019)
4. Nakamoto, S.: Bitcoin: a peer-to-peer electronic cash system. Decent. Bus. Rev., 21260 (2008)

5. Wang, Z., Jin, H., Dai, W., Choo, K.-K.R., Zou, D.: Ethereum smart contract security research: survey and future research opportunities. Front. Comput. Sci. **15**(2), 1–18 (2021)
6. Wu, L., Du, X., Wang, W., Lin, B.: An out-of-band authentication scheme for Internet of Things using blockchain technology. In: International Conference on Computing, Networking and Communications (ICNC), pp. 769–773. IEEE (2018)
7. Viriyasitavat, W., Da Xu, L., Bi, Z., Sapsomboon, A.: Blockchain-based business process management (BPM) framework for service composition in industry 4.0. J. Intell. Manuf. **31**(7), 1737–1748 (2020)
8. Chang, V., Baudier, P., Zhang, H., Xu, Q., Zhang, J., Arami, M.: How blockchain can impact financial services-the overview, challenges and recommendations from expert interviewees. Technol. Forecasting Soc. Change **158**, 120166 (2020)
9. Banerjee, M., Lee, J., Choo, K.-K.R.: A blockchain future for Internet of Things security: a position paper. Digit. Commun. Netw. **4**(3), 149–160 (2018)
10. Mollah, M.B., et al.: Blockchain for the internet of vehicles towards intelligent transportation systems: a survey. IEEE Internet Things J. **8**(6), 4157–4185 (2020)
11. Wang, Z.J., et al.: High-order CFD methods: current status and perspective. Int. J. Numer. Methods Fluids **72**(8), 811–845 (2013)
12. Alhadhrami, Z., Alghfeli, S., Alghfeli, M., Abedlla, J.A., Shuaib, K.: Introducing blockchains for healthcare. In: International Conference on Electrical and Computing Technologies and Applications (ICECTA), pp. 1–4. IEEE (2017)
13. Zhang, P., Walker, M.A., White, J., Schmidt, D.C., Lenz, G.: Metrics for assessing blockchain-based healthcare decentralized apps. In: IEEE 19th International Conference on E-health Networking, Applications and Services (Healthcom), pp. 1–4. IEEE (2017)
14. Ismail, L., Materwala, H., Zeadally, S.: Lightweight blockchain for healthcare. IEEE Access **7**, 149935–149951 (2019)
15. Tang, H., Tong, N., Ouyang, J.: Medical images sharing system based on blockchain and smart contract of credit scores. In: 2018 1st IEEE International Conference on Hot Information-Centric Networking (HotICN), pp. 240–241. IEEE (2018)
16. Hang, L., Choi, E., Kim, D.-H.: A novel EMR integrity management based on a medical blockchain platform in hospital. Electronics **8**(4), 467 (2019)
17. Shahnaz, A., Qamar, U., Khalid, A.: Using blockchain for electronic health records. IEEE Access **7**, 147782–147795 (2019)
18. Zhou, S., Sheng, H., Ma, J., Han, X.: Review of the application of blockchain technology in traditional Chinese medicine field. In: Proceedings of the 2020 International Symposium on Artificial Intelligence in Medical Sciences, pp. 225–230 (2020)
19. Dubovitskaya, A., et al.: ACTION-EHR: patient-centric blockchain-based electronic health record data management for cancer care. J. Med. Internet Res. **22**(8), e13598 (2020)
20. Shae, Z., Tsai, J.J.: On the design of a blockchain platform for clinical trial and precision medicine. In: IEEE 37th International Conference on Distributed Computing Systems (ICDCS), pp. 1972–1980. IEEE (2017)
21. Zhou, L., Wang, L., Sun, Y.: MIStore: a blockchain-based medical insurance storage system. J. Med. Syst. **42**(8), 1–17 (2018)
22. Long, Y., Chu, D., Wang, H., Fu, J., Yan, H.: Blockchain-based trace the source system for Chinese medicinal materials. In: 2022 14th International Conference on Measuring Technology and Mechatronics Automation (ICMTMA), pp. 1007–1010. IEEE (2022)

23. Skiba, D.J., et al.: The potential of blockchain in education and health care. Nurs. Educ. Perspect. **38**(4), 220–221 (2017)
24. Bodkhe, U., et al.: Blockchain for industry 4.0: a comprehensive review. IEEE Access **8**, 79764–79800 (2020)
25. Tanwar, S., Parekh, K., Evans, R.: Blockchain-based electronic healthcare record system for healthcare 4.0 applications. J. Inf. Secur. Appl. **50**, 102407 (2020)
26. Hussien, H.M., Yasin, S.M., Udzir, N.I., Ninggal, M.I.H., Salman, S.: Blockchain technology in the healthcare industry: trends and opportunities. J. Ind. Inf. Integr. **22**, 100217 (2021)
27. Zheng, Z., Xie, S., Dai, H., Chen, X., Wang, H.: An overview of blockchain technology: architecture, consensus, and future trends. In: IEEE International Congress on Big Data (BigData Congress), pp. 557–564. IEEE (2017)
28. Sultana, M., Hossain, A., Laila, F., Taher, K.A., Islam, M.N.: Towards developing a secure medical image sharing system based on zero trust principles and blockchain technology. BMC Med. Inform. Decis. Mak. **20**(1), 1–10 (2020)
29. Bali, V., Soni, P., Khanna, T., Gupta, S., Chauhan, S., Gupta, S.: Blockchain application design and algorithms for traceability in pharmaceutical supply chain. Int. J. Healthc. Inf. Syst. Inform. (IJHISI) **16**(4), 1–18 (2021)
30. Ravikumar, G., Venkatachalam, K., Masud, M., Abouhawwash, M.: Cost efficient scheduling using smart contract cognizant ethereum for IoMT. Intell. Autom. Soft Comput. **33**(2), 865–877 (2022)

BCSChain: Blockchain-Based Ceramic Supply Chain

Lingchao Kong[1]([✉]), Weili Chen[2], Huosheng Lv[1], Qiming Chen[1], Guoyou Lin[1], Shizhi Huang[1], and Weitao Deng[1]

[1] Foshan UCA Supply Chain Service Co., Ltd., Foshan, China
{konglc,lvhs,chenqm,lingy,huangsz,dengwt}@ucacc.com
[2] School of Information Science and Technology, Guangdong University of Foreign Studies, Guangzhou, China

Abstract. The ceramic supply chain is a complex network centered on ceramic products, encompassing business flow, logistics, information flow, and capital flow, and involving many participants and complex business processes. Currently, the key issues confronting the ceramic supply chain are lack of trust between different participants, financing difficulty for medium, small, and micro enterprises, inefficient transportation and distribution, and the inability to meet the diversified needs of customers. These pain points can be properly sloved by blockchain technology, with characteristics such as immutability and decentralization as well as the application of smart contracts. In this paper, a system architecture of **Blockchain-Based Ceramic Supply Chain (BCSChain)** is presented, and three applications of BCSChain in different scenarios are proposed, including logistics traceability, financing, and automatic trading. It is found that combing blockchain technology with ceramic supply chain can contribute to enable data sharing and information visualization, de-intermediation and data security, automated execution, as well as efficient collaboration.

Keywords: Blockchain · Ceramic supply chain · Applications

1 Introduction

Ceramic supply chains are becoming more and more complex as the number of participants and customers grows [22]. Non-transparent information, traceability difficulty and centralization are the problems that need to be solved immediately for ceramic supply chains [10].

Non-transparent information is one of the most serious problems in ceramic supply chains. In order to provide consumers with quality service at different stage, modern ceramic supply chains include a lot of different participants providing different services. However, the service providers are always geographically isolated, the transactional data and other information like contracts and logistics information are not interoperable. What's more, inefficient transactions, violations like fraud and pilferage make the problem even more acute. The issues

© The Author(s), under exclusive license to Springer Nature Singapore Pte Ltd. 2022
D. Svetinovic et al. (Eds.): BlockSys 2022, CCIS 1679, pp. 91–104, 2022.
https://doi.org/10.1007/978-981-19-8043-5_7

mentioned above has led to a serious trust shortage, inefficient cooperation and financing difficulty in ceramic supply chains.

Traceability difficulty is also a serious problem. In ceramic supply chains, traceability is an increasingly urgent requirement and a fundamental differentiator. In traditional case, the usual way to obtain the provenance of ceramic products is the paper certificates and receipts, which may be easily lost or altered, which leads to traceability difficulty in ceramic supply chains. Furthermore, the reliability and transparency of intermediaries and the cost of communication between participants has made this problem more complicate. It is hard for participants in supply chains or customers to verify and validate the true value of items.

The centralization of ceramic supply chains may also pose some problems [1]. Current ceramic supply chains rely heavily on centralized systems like enterprise resources planning systems. The reliance on centralized systems has the following disadvantages. First, participants in supply chains need to store their valuable and sensitive data in the centralized systems, which require significant trust in the systems. Second, if the centralized systems are prone to human mistake, hacking, attack, or corruption, the entire supply chain will suffer.

To solve these complicated problems, it is necessary to improve the transparency and security of the ceramic supply chains. One of the feasible solutions of these problems is blockchain technology [1,8].

Blockchain, the underlying technology of Bitcoin, has gotten a lot of attention from both industry and academia in recent years. Blockchain technology is a distributed ledger system, which records transactional data and other information without a trusted centralized third party. These information stored in the blockchain is extremely hard to alter, as well as traceable and auditable. Because blockchain technology ensures trust through its immutability, business activities can be completed in a cost-effective and timely manner. Because of the advantages mentioned above, blockchain has been used in a various of scenarios, such as decentralized finance, auctions, traceability, data management and so on.

Blockchain technology also enables smart contracts. In smart contracts, the clauses of contracts can automatically be executed though computer program when the preset conditions are met. Conventional contracts must be performed in a centralized manner by a trusted third party, which may lead to a long execution time and additional expense. In contrast, the execution of smart contracts is essentially based on transactions in distributed blockchain. Smart contracts bring us one step closer to the dream of "peer-to-peer ceramic supply chains".

Technological breakthroughs and new applications of blockchain technology make it more organizationally, technologically, and commercially viable for the improvement of ceramic supply chains transparency and security [7, 29]. With the characteristics of trustless decentralized database, blockchain technology facilitates ceramic supply chains for global-scale transactions and disintermediation and decentralization of process among different stakeholders.

In recent years, the problems in ceramic supply chains have received a lot of attention from industry. Foshan UCA Supply Chain Service Co., Ltd. (UCA), with the model of "Industry + Internet, Finance + Capital", commits to establishing a platform for the integration of the ceramic supply chain. UCA adopts the "four chains integration" general layout concept, which includes the industrial chain, supply chain, standard chain, and digital chain. UCA contributes significantly to the development of ceramic supply chains, for example, providing digital transformation solutions for the industry, constructing B2B information platforms for supply chain transactions, and providing information platforms for matching industrial logistics capacity, and so on. UCA has produced increased social, industrial, and business benefits after five years of exploration and practice.[1]

The purpose of this paper is to:

1. provide a ceramic supply chains system architecture based on blockchain BCSChain, to address the lack of transparency and security in the conventional ceramic supply chains.
2. introduce some specific applications based on blockchain in various scenarios in ceramic supply chains, such as logistics traceability and automatic trading.

The remainder of this paper is organized as follows. Section 2 introduces the situation of conventional ceramic supply chains, and explain blockchain and smart contracts in more detail. Some related work on the applications of blockchain in supply chains will also be mentioned in this section. Section 3 introduces the system architecture of BCSChain, and its advantages over conventional ceramic supply chains. Section 4 introduces some specific applications in various scenarios of ceramic supply chains. Section 5 provides a conclusion and discuss about the future research direction.

2   Background

2.1   Conventional Ceramic Supply Chains

Ceramic supply chain is a chain system which connects a variety of other stakeholders, like raw material suppliers, manufacturers, distributors, wholesalers, retailers, customers, financiers, logistics companies and so on. The common structure of conventional ceramic supply chains is shown in Fig. 1. The core of ceramic supply chains is ceramic products. In ceramic supply chains, raw material, product, capital, commercial information and other circulation elements are transferred between suppliers and consumers. The products will be delivered to customers, and the demands of customers are fed back to the production side, forming a closed loop.

Conventional ceramic supply chains, on the other hand, still have some significant issues.

---

[1] http://uca.ucacc.com/.

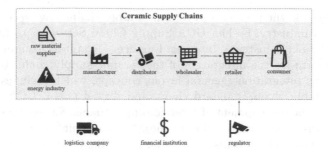

Fig. 1. The common structure of conventional ceramic supply chains.

Lack of Trust in Ceramic Supply Chains. There is a trust shortage among the participants in ceramic supply chains. Complex circulation model leads to the lengthening of circulation channels and an increase in the number of participants. However, the majority of ceramic supply chain participants are not willing to share information due to the protection for profit and information security. This results in a blockage of information flow and a lack of trust among the members in ceramic supply chains.

Financing Difficulties of Medium, Small and Micro Enterprises. In all stages of the ceramic supply chain, there are numerous medium, small, and micro enterprises (MSMEs). However, due to data silos and information mismatches among supply chains participants, it is difficult to transfer the credit from core enterprises to their associated upstream or downstream enterprises, which resulting in financing difficulty. Furthermore, opaque supply chain information transmission increases the cost of credit verification for financial institutions and regulators.

Inefficient Logistics Traceability and Distribution. In conventional ceramic supply chains, it is difficult to combine the storage, transportation and distribution of ceramic products, and the linkage between manufacturing, supply and marketing is insufficient. Due to technical issues, timely and accurate sharing of logistics information is difficult to achieve, potentially leading to counterfeit and shoddy issues during the logistics transfer process. As a result, ceramic products traceability is both expensive and ineffective.

2.2   Blockchain

Introduction to Blockchain. The concept of blockchain technology was first proposed in 2008 by a scholar called "Satoshi Nakamoto" in the bitcoin white paper [28]. As shown in Fig. 2, the blockchain mentioned in the bitcoin white paper is a chain structure of data blocks in chronological order [15]. Because of its specific data structure, blockchain can be viewed as a decentralized shared ledger which is guaranteed by cryptography and is nearly impossible to be tampered [11]. Blockchain has a number of appealing characteristics, including trustworthiness, decentralization, and distribution.

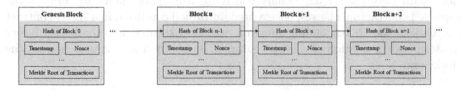

Fig. 2. The common blockchain structure.

Trustworthiness is traditional based on reputational history, professional knowledge and institutional status. However, in a blockchain-based system, trustworthiness is derived from mathematics and encryption [20]. Cryptography can be used to prove knowledge of confidential information without revealing it, as well as to prove the authenticity of information. And there is no opportunity to tamper the data stored in the blockchain because of the transparency and precision of mathematics.

Decentralization is another attractive element of blockchain. There is no authoritative blockchain or central server. The whole blockchain is managed through a predetermined set of rules encoded in program codes. Every node is able to get the comprehensive transaction history.

Distribution is also an attractive element. Reaching consensus is one of the most crucial aspects of constructing a distributed network. It is difficult due to the lack of trust among participants and every participant can be a malicious attacker. Therefore, consensus mechanism play an important role in overcoming this challenge, the following are common consensus algorithms: Proof of Work (PoW), Proof of Stake (PoS), Delegated Proof of Stake (DPoS), Practical Byzantine fault tolerance (PBFT), delegated Byzantine fault tolerance (DBFT), etc.

Evolution of Blockchain. Bitcoin, the first and the most well-known application of blockchain, was created to be a transaction protocol and payment system. In Bitcoin network, all transactions are visible to anyone, but only the owner of private key can unlock and spend the bitcoin he received previously.

Because Bitcoin was created only for the purpose of being a cryptocurrency, its scripting language is purposely limited: no loops or complicated features are available. The non-Turing-complete programing language ensures that scripts in Bitcoin network can only be executed in a limited complexity and predictable time. There is no script with infinite loops, which might cause the Bitcoin network to be blocked. However, this also means that it is impossible for bitcoin network to perform some powerful functions.

In order to extend the application scenario of blockchain technology, Ethereum was created. Ethereum is known as the second generation of blockchain because it expands on bitcoin's scripting language to create a fully functional, Turing-complete programming language, Solidity. What's more, Ethereum is constructed as a blockchain network capable of executing smart contracts.

Smart contracts can be viewed as the executable computer programs in blockchain network [17,32]. Smart contracts use logical flows to connect the approved contractual clauses, once a predetermined condition in a smart contract is satisfied, the corresponding function will be executed automatically. Every creation and invocation of a smart contract is recorded as a transaction on the blockchain.

2.3   Related Works

Most of current blockchain-related supply chains works is focused on agricultural food supply chains [9,12,14,19,26], and some of others involve supply chains of manufacturing. Some of the work focuses on developing a new blockchain-based architecture for data privacy preservation [30] and offering composition pattern-aware web services [25].

For agricultural food supply chains, [31] presents a system architecture with a multimode storage mechanism which combines chain storage. [4,16] and [27] present software frameworks enable Internet-of-Things devices to interface with a blockchain-based system for food traceability. [6] and [13] present architectures for food traceability with fully functional smart contracts. [18] presents a blockchain-based food safety traceability system with the management architecture of on-chain and off-chain data. [23] combines blockchain technology, machine learning and fuzzy logic traceability system for food shelf life management.

For manufacturing supply chains, [2] presents a blockchain-based framework for multitier textile and clothing traceability. [24] introduces a traceability framework for detecting operational disruptions or counterfeiting problems based on trade information and timestamped sensory data. [3] presents a Ethereum smart contract-based architecture to manage and trace transactions in the manufacturing process. [21] introduces a smartphone anticounterfeiting system based on an integrated approach of decentralized identifiers and verifiable claims. [5] proposes a steel quality traceability framework based on alliance chain as well as Internet-of-Things technology.

3   BCSChain: Blockchain-Based Ceramic Supply Chain

Blockchain is a decentralized, distributed digital ledger, which can be used to address problems such as privacy security protection, information traceability, transaction compliance, data authenticity and process processing efficiency. This addresses the challenges and pain points of the ceramic supply chain, demonstrating that blockchain technology has broad applicability and value in ceramic supply chain scenarios.

In this section, the system architecture of BCSChain will be presented, and the advantages of this architecture over conventional ceramic supply chain will be introduced at the same time.

3.1   System Architecture of BCSChain

Participants of ceramic supply chains includes raw material suppliers, manufacturers, distributors, wholesalers, retailers, and consumers. Additionally, supply chains may also interact with logistical companies, financial institutions, and regulators. According to the characteristics of ceramic supply chains, an architecture based on alliance chain is better suited to this scenario. The logical architecture of BCSChain is shown in the Fig. 3.

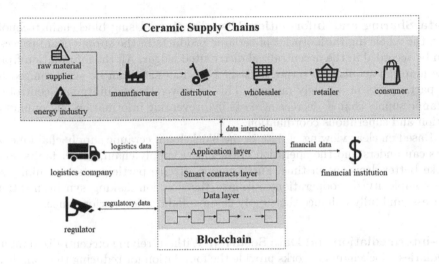

Fig. 3. The logical architecture of BCSChain.

How blockchain technology functions in ceramic supply chains can be summarized as follows:

First, the blockchain application layer enables participants in the ceramic supply chain to upload their data to the blockchain, which can be shared in real time using distributed ledger technology. It should be highlighted that the corresponding certifying documents or materials are required to be uploaded at the same time, ensuring data authenticity and validity, and avoiding the circumstance where fraudulent or erroneous data is stored on the blockchain.

Second, in the blockchain smart contracts layer, the authenticity and validity of data uploaded to the blockchain application layer can be verified. Verified data will be automatically classified and stored in the blockchain based on the particular criteria using smart contracts. Smart contracts can also encrypt or extract summaries of pertinent data, then send it to the logistics traceability platforms or financing platforms. All work on the blockchain smart contracts layer can be done according to predefined criteria in an automatically, accurately and timely manner.

Third, the blockchain application layer enables every participant to independently verify the data stored in the blockchain to confirm that it has not been tampered with. This can be achieved by means of hash verification, which implies that any tiny modification to the data in the blockchain will result in a huge and unpredictable change in the hash value.

3.2   Advantages of BCSChain

Compared to conventional ceramic supply chains, BCSChain has the following advantages:

Data Sharing and Information Visualization. Using blockchain technology, the whole digital footprint of ceramic products in the supply chain process can be recorded in the decentralized distributed ledger. All the information from raw material acquisition through finished product sales can be synchronized to all participants in a timely manner. This improves the visibility and control of ceramic supply chains, decreasing costs by preventing information miscommunication and superfluous coordination.

Based on clear viewing of data in the blockchain, ceramic supply chain members can understand the operation of the entire supply chain, detect faults, and make better decisions in time. Furthermore, diverse participants can minimize the complexity of cooperation, optimize the decision-making synchronization process, and fully enhance the supply chain collaboration performance.

De-intermediation and Data Security. Without relying on centralized intermediaries, blockchain networks provide the foundation for reducing the complexity of the middle ground: ensuring the integrity, consistency, authenticity, and availability of data. It can also considerably enhance the efficiency of the collaborative flow of information, funds, and products by eliminating the complex back-to-back transmission of paper documents as well as superfluous communication and other intermediate links.

Peer-to-peer data sharing is formed in real time between participants of ceramic supply chains, and the data in the blockchain is tamper-proof and manipulation-proof. The authenticity and accuracy of the data is guaranteed by the fact that each node server stores complete data. What's more, Smart contracts can assist in the digitization of paper documents, reducing the risks of data fabrication and document loss associated with paper documents.

Automated Execution and Efficient Collaboration Thanks to smart contracts, verification and execution of contract clauses can be performed in an automagical manner based on trusted public data in the blockchain rather than data controlled by a single participant. When new data is uploaded, it can automatically verify whether the relevant data meets the standard and whether the relevant terms or conditions are met. This improves the efficiency and credibility of the contract provisions' implementation and, as a result, the collaboration's efficiency.

It's also feasible to broaden the scope of smart contract applications. Incentives, performance of agreements, and risk metric assessments can all be translated into program codes of smart contracts by collaborative participants of ceramic supply chains. What's more, smart contracts may be used in conjunction with Internet of Things (IoT) and Artificial Intelligence (AI) technologies to intelligently track inventory, detect supply chain environment, estimate consumers' demand, and predict risk, resulting in increased efficiency and cost savings.

4   Application Scenarios of BCSChain

In this section, some applications in various scenarios of ceramic supply chains will be introduced, such as logistics traceability management, supply chains finance, and automatic trading.

4.1   Application in Logistics Traceability Management

To solve the problem of logistics traceability management, blockchain can be combined with IoT technology. This enables the demand for ceramic product traceability, such as anti-counterfeiting and circulation traceability, tracking and recall of problematic products, and query of ceramic product information.

As shown in Fig. 4, relevant information will be uploaded to the blockchain at each stage of the ceramic supply chain, including raw material information provided by raw material providers, ceramic product information provided by manufacturers, storage and sales information provided by distributors and retailers. Furthermore, logistics companies will upload the real-time logistical data to the blockchain. During the whole process of uploading data, IOT technology can be utilized to assure the validity and timeliness of data.

All this data will be verified at the blockchain smart contract layer, and then be aggregated and transferred to the blockchain-based logistics traceability platform. Consumers can check the anti-counterfeiting and logistics traceability information of ceramic products through the logistics traceability platform. Other logistics services, like return and exchange of problematic products can also be finished through the platform.

In contrast to the traditional situation, where it is difficult for customers to trace ceramic products and seek accountability, consumers' demands for product traceability and other logistics needs can be easily met through the logistics traceability platform. This may effectively minimize the cost and difficulty of product traceability, as well as give significant support for purifying the supply chain business environment and effectively protecting the rights and interests of customers.

The utilization of IoT technology can prevent errors caused by manual record-keeping, as well as falsification and misrepresentation. And the utilization of blockchain technology ensures that data cannot be tampered with, maintaining the legitimacy and reliability of traceability information.

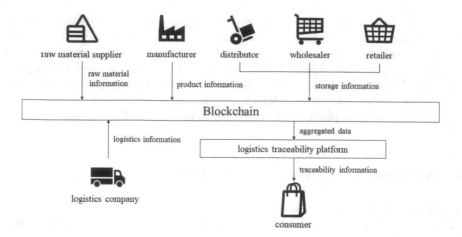

Fig. 4. Application in logistics traceability management.

Participants in ceramic supply chains also benefit greatly from real-time logistics traceability information. This information aids in the optimization of purchasing strategies and decisions, as well as the prompt adjustment of inventory levels, effective distribution and delivery, and product loss reduction. Furthermore, some functions can be accomplished through smart contracts, such as providing automatic warnings of long stay times in logistics or product quality issues.

4.2   Application in Supply Chains Finance

MSMEs in ceramic supply chains find it difficult to access credit through official channels because to their modest loan amounts, fragmented operations, and absence of credit status records. To address this problems, blockchain technology can be utilized to give banks and other financial institutions with the credit basis they require when financing MSMEs in the blockchain-based ceramic supply chain.

As shown in Fig. 5, the transaction information and credit information of the core enterprises in ceramic supply chains, as well as their upstream suppliers and downstream sellers at all levels, can be uploaded to the blockchain. The authenticity and tamper-evident nature of data can be guaranteed via blockchain technology.

Then, the aggregated and credible data will be transferred to the blockchain-based financing platform. Banks and other financial institutions can obtain reliable information on enterprises, allowing them to make the best financing decisions possible. Financial institutions can also track the utilization of the enterprise's funds through the financing platform in real time once the financing is completed, which can effectively mitigate risks.

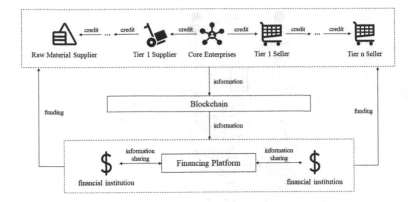

Fig. 5. Application in supply chains finance.

Information concerning accounts, storage assets, and notes may be digitized and uploaded to the blockchain by merging blockchain technology with ceramic supply chain financing. Blockchain technology ensures the authenticity of data, eliminate the risk of counterfeiting, and further enable the multi-level transmission of credit in ceramic supply chains.

MSMEs, core firms, and financial institutions all benefit from this blockchain-based application in supply chain finance. MSMEs can minimize the difficulty of obtaining funding, expand their financing options, and enhance their fund liquidity management. Core enterprises can lower the cost of capital for their upstream and downstream enterprises, allowing for greater collaboration and efficiency. Financial institutions can reduce the difficulty and cost of credit investigation and post-financing follow-up monitoring, as well as extend their customer base.

4.3 Application in Automatic Trading

Digital technology has had a significant impact on the business model of ceramic supply chains in recent years. That Efficient and secure automatic trading is a key aspect of the digitalization of supply chains. Smart contracts, which are program codes that are automatically executed on the blockchain, can assist in this endeavor.

As shown in Fig. 6, once the parties to a transaction have negotiated and signed a contract, the specific requirements, relevant terms and conditions of the contract can be translated into the form of a smart contract. In the process of contract execution, the buyer must lock the payment in the smart contract in advance, and the seller can take the payment locked in the smart contract after completing the delivery and sending the related proof to the smart contract for verification. It's worth noting that this entire process is executed in an automagical manner, and the nature of smart contracts ensures that contracts are executed correctly and on time.

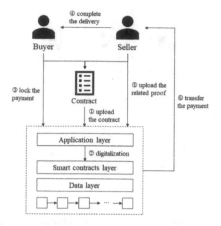

Fig. 6. Application in automatic trading.

In comparison to traditional trading models, the blockchain-based application can increase trade automation while reducing the risk of operational errors. There are numerous constraints on the use of paper documents in the past; there are hazards of data falsification, document loss, and so on. Smart contracts can implement a wide range of sophisticated terms and conditions in the form of code, which can effectively decrease costs and enhance efficiency.

Furthermore, the credit for normal execution of contract comes from the execution of the code, which can effectively avoid fraud or refusal to deliver by sellers, or default payment by buyers, this can reduce the cost of credit investigation by both parties to the transaction.

5   Conclusion

There are various problems in traditional ceramic supply chains, such as lack of trust between different participants, financing difficulty for medium, small, and micro enterprises, inefficient transportation and distribution, and the inability to meet the diverse needs of customers, and so on. Therefore, we present a system architecture for BCSChain, a blockchain-based ceramic supply chain since blockchain technology may be able to assist in tackling the difficulties described above. We discovered that embedding blockchain technology into the ceramic supply chain can help enable data sharing and information visualization, de-intermediation and data security, automated execution, as well as efficient collaboration. Then, we offer specific blockchain-based applications in various scenarios in ceramic supply chains, such as logistics traceability management, supply chain financing, and automatic trading.

References

1. Abeyratne, S.A., Monfared, R.P.: Blockchain ready manufacturing supply chain using distributed ledger. Int. J. Res. Eng. Technol. **5**(9), 1–10 (2016)

2. Agrawal, T.K., Kumar, V., Pal, R., Wang, L., Chen, Y.: Blockchain-based framework for supply chain traceability: a case example of textile and clothing industry. Comput. Ind. Eng. **154**, 107130 (2021)
3. Alkaabi, N., Salah, K., Jayaraman, R., Arshad, J., Omar, M., et al.: Blockchain-based traceability and management for additive manufacturing. IEEE Access **8**, 188363–188377 (2020)
4. Balamurugan, S., Ayyasamy, A., Joseph, K.S.: IoT-blockchain driven traceability techniques for improved safety measures in food supply chain. Int. J. Inf. Technol., 1–12 (2021)
5. Cao, Y., Jia, F., Manogaran, G.: Efficient traceability systems of steel products using blockchain-based industrial Internet of Things. IEEE Trans. Ind. Inform. **16**(9), 6004–6012 (2019)
6. Casino, F., et al.: Blockchain-based food supply chain traceability: a case study in the dairy sector. Int. J. Prod. Res. **59**(19), 5758–5770 (2021)
7. Cole, R., Stevenson, M., Aitken, J.: Blockchain technology: implications for operations and supply chain management. Supply Chain Manag. Int. J. (2019)
8. Crosby, M., Pattanayak, P., Verma, S., Kalyanaraman, V., et al.: Blockchain technology: beyond bitcoin. Appl. Innov. **2**(6–10), 71 (2016)
9. Dhaiouir, S., Assar, S.: A systematic literature review of blockchain-enabled smart contracts: platforms, languages, consensus, applications and choice criteria. In: Dalpiaz, F., Zdravkovic, J., Loucopoulos, P. (eds.) RCIS 2020. LNBIP, vol. 385, pp. 249–266. Springer, Cham (2020). https://doi.org/10.1007/978-3-030-50316-1_15
10. Dujak, D., Sajter, D.: Blockchain applications in supply chain. In: Kawa, A., Maryniak, A. (eds.) SMART Supply Network. EcoProduction, pp. 21–46. Springer, Cham (2019). https://doi.org/10.1007/978-3-319-91668-2_2
11. English, M., Auer, S., Domingue, J.: Block chain technologies & the semantic web: a framework for symbiotic development. In: Lehmann, J., Thakkar, H., Halilaj, L., Asmat, R. (eds.) Computer Science Conference for University of Bonn Students, pp. 47–61. sn (2016)
12. Feng, H., Wang, X., Duan, Y., Zhang, J., Zhang, X.: Applying blockchain technology to improve agri-food traceability: a review of development methods, benefits and challenges. J. Clean. Prod. **260**, 121031 (2020)
13. Ferdousi, T., Gruenbacher, D., Scoglio, C.M.: A permissioned distributed ledger for the us beef cattle supply chain. IEEE Access **8**, 154833–154847 (2020)
14. Galvez, J.F., Mejuto, J.C., Simal-Gandara, J.: Future challenges on the use of blockchain for food traceability analysis. TrAC Trends Anal. Chem. **107**, 222–232 (2018)
15. Gamage, H., Weerasinghe, H., Dias, N.: A survey on blockchain technology concepts, applications, and issues. SN Comput. Sci. **1**(2), 1–15 (2020)
16. Grecuccio, J., Giusto, E., Fiori, F., Rebaudengo, M.: Combining blockchain and IoT: food-chain traceability and beyond. Energies **13**(15), 3820 (2020)
17. Haiwu, H., An, Y., Zehua, C.: Survey of smart contract technology and application based on blockchain. J. Comput. Res. Dev. **55**(11), 2452 (2018)
18. Lin, Q., Wang, H., Pei, X., Wang, J.: Food safety traceability system based on blockchain and EPCIS. IEEE Access **7**, 20698–20707 (2019)
19. Lin, W., et al.: Blockchain technology in current agricultural systems: from techniques to applications. IEEE Access **8**, 143920–143937 (2020)
20. Nofer, M., Gomber, P., Hinz, O., Schiereck, D.: Blockchain. Bus. Inf. Syst. Eng. **59**(3), 183–187 (2017)

21. Omar, A.S., Basir, O.: Decentralized identifiers and verifiable credentials for smartphone anticounterfeiting and decentralized IMEI database. Can. J. Electr. Comput. Eng. **43**(3), 174–180 (2020)
22. Sarpong, S.: Traceability and supply chain complexity: confronting the issues and concerns. Eur. Bus. Rev. (2014)
23. Shahbazi, Z., Byun, Y.C.: A procedure for tracing supply chains for perishable food based on blockchain, machine learning and fuzzy logic. Electronics **10**(1), 41 (2020)
24. Suhail, S., Hussain, R., Khan, A., Hong, C.S.: Orchestrating product provenance story: when iota ecosystem meets electronics supply chain space. Comput. Ind. **123**, 103334 (2020)
25. Tang, B., Tang, M., Xia, Y., Hsieh, M.Y.: Composition pattern-aware web service recommendation based on depth factorisation machine. Connect. Sci. **33**(4), 870–890 (2021)
26. Tharatipyakul, A., Pongnumkul, S.: User interface of blockchain-based agri-food traceability applications: a review. IEEE Access **9**, 82909–82929 (2021)
27. Tsang, Y.P., Choy, K.L., Wu, C.H., Ho, G.T.S., Lam, H.Y.: Blockchain-driven IoT for food traceability with an integrated consensus mechanism. IEEE Access **7**, 129000–129017 (2019)
28. Vranken, H.: Sustainability of bitcoin and blockchains. Curr. Opin. Environ. Sustain. **28**, 1–9 (2017)
29. Wang, Y., Chen, C.H., Zghari-Sales, A.: Designing a blockchain enabled supply chain. Int. J. Prod. Res. **59**(5), 1450–1475 (2021)
30. Zhang, S., Yao, T., Arthur Sandor, V.K., Weng, T.H., Liang, W., Su, J.: A novel blockchain-based privacy-preserving framework for online social networks. Connect. Sci. **33**(3), 555–575 (2021)
31. Zhang, X., Sun, P., Xu, J., Wang, X., Yu, J., Zhao, Z., Dong, Y.: Blockchain-based safety management system for the grain supply chain. IEEE Access **8**, 36398–36410 (2020)
32. Zheng, Z., et al.: An overview on smart contracts: challenges, advances and platforms. Future Gener. Comput. Syst. **105**, 475–491 (2020)

Blockchain

A Highly Scalable Blockchain-Enabled DNS Architecture

Wenyu Dong[1](✉), Chenghong Lin[2], Min Li[1], Li Su[1], and Shen He[1]

[1] China Mobile Research Institute, Beijing 100032, China
{dongwenyu,liminqk,suli,heshen}@chinamobile.com
[2] China Mobile (Xiongan) Industry Research Institute, Beijing 100052, China
linchenghong@aliyun.com

Abstract. In future when de-centralized services become prosperous on Internet, the advantages brought by de-centralization might be compromised by traditional centralized DNS. Precedented de-centralized DNS-es are either not fully de-centralized or unable to satisfy objectives such as scalability.

In this paper, a new de-centralized DNS facility, HSD DNS, is proposed, featuring fully de-centralization and high scalability among other benefits. It adopts an on-demand manner to construct the index tree as the resolution skeleton, such that the overall lookup latency is highly optimized. Security issues are discussed before quantitative analysis on performance is given in the end.

Keywords: DNS · Blockchain · Scalability · De-centralization · Hash

1 Background

When de-centralized Internet services become popular in future, DNS facility shall be de-centralized accordingly. However, it is not ready.

For example, in a de-centralized Internet copyright infringement forensics service, a blockchain-based service acts as a trustworthy delegator to access pirate websites and record illegal usage of digital works. Due to trustworthiness conveyed by blockchain's DE-CENTRALIZATION, this service is eligible for lawsuit purpose. However, a client has to go through the traditional, CENTRALIZED DNS procedure to resolve the IP of blockchain's oracles as prerequisite, making the service vulnerable to DNS hijacking or other manipulation risks.

Thus, a de-centralized DNS facility, usually based on blockchain, is a must-have.

1.1 Challenges

A de-centralized DNS has to deal with four objectives: human readability, de-centralization, security and scalability. The first three come from Zooko's Triangle [4], i.e. no DNS can achieve more than two out of three fighting desirable objectives. The latter three come from Vitalik's Trilemma [1–3, 5], another impossible combination of objectives for blockchain technology, which is usually the underlying technology for de-centralized DNS.

D. Svetinovic et al. (Eds.): BlockSys 2022, CCIS 1679, pp. 107–121, 2022.
https://doi.org/10.1007/978-981-19-8043-5_8

- Human readability: Domain names shall be meaningful and memorable to humans.
- Decentralization: No centralized authority is needed to determine the availability of a name. The DNS service does not belong to any administration and is usually censorship-resistant.
- Security: There is exactly one, unique and specific entity to which a domain name maps. The client is not hijacked to a fake entity.
- Scalability: The naming service is able to process $O(n) > O(c)$ transactions, where c refers to the size of computational resources available to one node, and n refers to the size of (potential) workload within the ecosystem.

1.2 Related Work

Many precedented de-centralized DNS facilities do not fully satisfy the four objectives mentioned afore.

Namecoin [6] is the first de-centralized DNS, which is deployed on Bitcoin as the underlying blockchain platform. It successfully achieves de-centralization and human readability. However its scalability is quite limited due to Bitcoin's inherent performance bottleneck, typically up to 7 TPS.

Blockstack [7] inherits much from Namecoin with much improvement. It introduces a four-layer architecture, exploiting virtual chain and third-party storage to alleviate scalability limitation. However, its performance remains a serious concern, yet [8, 10].

FI-DNS [9] and Bitforest [10] sidestep the 'pure' de-centralization approach. They are designed to strengthen traditional centralized DNS with security or high-availability features enabled by de-centralized techniques. FI-DNS [9] exploits blockchain and IPFS to build a centralized domain name service. It intentionally remains compatible with traditional DNS, especially the centralized governance model under ICANN in order to ease early adoption and smooth deployment. Similarly, Bitforest [10] uses a hybrid architecture, combining a public blockchain with a minimally trusted centralized service. It purposely hires centralized management to deal with problems such as name-squatting and other abuse.

1.3 Contribution

This paper proposes HSD DNS, or Highly Scalable De-centralized DNS, a fully de-centralized DNS, meeting all four objectives in Sect. 1.1. It also features high scalability and optimized latency to accommodate de-centralized services from the entire Internet. The contribution in this paper includes:

- A new de-centralized DNS architecture is proposed, which uses a hash algorithm to covert a domain name into an integer, which is in turn used as an index onto a self-constructed tree to locate the proper addressing entity.
- High scalability is designed to accomodate vast amount of services from the entire Internet, and an on-demand spanning pattern is introduced to optimize lookup latency, which is a key performance perspect for DNS facility.
- Security merits are discussed including intra-node and inter-node security.
- Quantitative analysis on performance is given such as capacity and latency.

2 Architecture and Procedures

2.1 Design Principles

HSD DNS is designed to satisfy all four objectives mentioned in Sect. 1.1.

- Human readability. Human readability is prerequisite for both service owners and clients.
- Full de-centralization. The following procedures shall be free from authorities' censorship: (1) A service owner composes a name; (2) A service owner registrates and publishes its name-address bindings onto HSD DNS; (3) A client looks up a domain name from HSD DNS to find proper IP addresses.
- High scalability. HSD DNS' potential capacity is large enough to accommodate all services from entire Internet, even those emerging in years or decades. There are about 376 million domain names globally by 2021Q2, and the number is continuously increasing with an annual growth rate around 6.54% [12, 16]. HSD DNS shall be able to undertake workload of the same order of magnitude.
- Security. HSD DNS may adopt security measures proven by other precedented de-centralized DNS paradigmes, as well as security features that are infeasible in traditional DNS.

2.2 Architecture Overview

The skeleton of HSD DNS is an index tree, generated in a de-centralized way.

A well-known hash algorithm, for example SHA-256, is selected in advance to convert a domain name into an integer ranging in $[0, 2^p - 1]$ where integer $p > 1$. This algorithm shall be deterministic and publicly known such that anybody is able to perform the hash calculation and get the same result from the same domain name.

Then, the index tree is constructed based on the hashed values.

Each node in the tree represents a continous fraction of hash value range. The value range related to a descendent node is always a subset of its ancestors', and the value ranges related to sibling nodes in the same depth shall have no intersection.

Each node is a blockchain-enabled system. All non-leaf nodes, denoted as 'N-' nodes, are responbile to record and publish addresses of their immediate descendent nodes. All leaf nodes, denoted as 'R-' nodes, are responsible to record and publish name-address bindings for those de-centralized Internet services whose names' hash-values fall into the range related to this leaf node.

The addresses of descendent nodes and de-centralized Internet services are usually the URIs of the blockchains' oracles.

Suppose the tree is k-branch, d-depth, with t as the size of value range related to a leaf node, then we have:

$$k^{d-1} \times t = 2^p \tag{1}$$

In most cases, t takes the same value of k, thus

$$k^d = 2^p \tag{2}$$

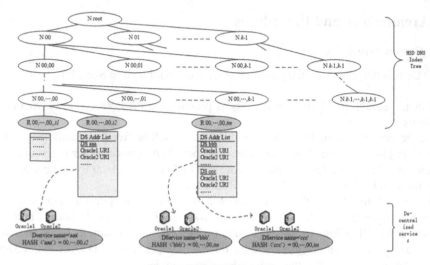

Fig. 1. HSD DNS index tree

In Fig. 1, for example:

(1) Suppose SHA-256 algorithm is used;
(2) Suppose $k = 256$, then $d = 32$;
(3) Exemplar non-leaf nodes and corresponding vlaue ranges are listed in Table 1;
(4) Exemplar leaf nodes and corresponding de-centralized Internet services may be:

Table 1. Exemplar nodes and relevant hash value ranges

Node	Hash value range	Note
Root	[0x00…00, 0xFF…FF]	$[0, 2^{256} - 1]$
<N 00>	[0x00 00…00, 0x00 FF…FF]	$[0, 2^{248} - 1]$
<N 00, 00>	[0x00 00 00…00, 0x00 00 FF…FF]	$[0, 2^{240} - 1]$
<N 00, 00, i_1>	[0x00 00 i_1 00…00, 0x00 00 i_1 FF…FF]	$[i_1 * 2^{232}, (i_1 + 1) * 2^{232} - 1]$, i_1 is an octect
<R 00,…, 00, i_2>	[0x00…00 i_2 00…00, 0x00…00 i_2 FF…FF]	i_2 is an octect

Leaf node <R 00,…,00,i_2> records and publishes name-address bindings for de-centralized Internet service 'aaa' since:

$$\text{Hash}('aaa') \in [0 \times 00\ldots00 i_2 00\ldots00, 0 \times 00\ldots00 i_2 FF\ldots FF] \tag{3}$$

Leaf node $<R\ 00,\ldots,00,i_m>$ records and publishes name-address bindings for decentralized Internet service 'bbb' and 'ccc' since:

$$\text{Hash}('bbb') \in [0 \times 00\ldots00i_m00\ldots00,\ 0 \times 00\ldots00i_m\text{FF}\ldots\text{FF}] \tag{4}$$

$$\text{Hash}('ccc') \in [0 \times 00\ldots00i_m00\ldots00,\ 0 \times 00\ldots00i_m\text{FF}\ldots\text{FF}] \tag{5}$$

Note that it is poosible a leaf node may contain more than one services' resolution entries since both their hash results fall in the hash value range of this leaf node.

2.3 Procedures

Main procedures are: (1) initialize index tree; (2) publish a domain name; (3) look up a domain name.

Initialize Index Tree
The main steps are:

(1) Prepare and announce the hash algorithm;
(2) Prepare and announce parameters for the index tree such as: k (branch number), d (depth), and t (size of value range of a leaf node);
(3) Compute hash-value range for each non-lead node as well as each leaf node;
(4) Prepare all nodes and deply them on the Internet. Each node is a blockchain-based system.
(5) Registrate each node's address information, usually the URIs of the blockchain's oracles, onto its immediate parent node, such that

    a) the value range related to a node is always a subset of its ancestors', and
    b) the value ranges related to sibling nodes in the same depth have no intersection.

(6) Perform step (5) iteratively, starting from leaf nodes and going upwards, until reaching the root node.

Publish a Domain Name
A serivce owner registrates the name-address bindings onto HSD DNS, requiring:

(1) The owner performs the hash algorithm against the domain name;
(2) The owner uses the hash result as a clue to search the index tree, starting from the root, until reaches a proper leaf node who owns the right hash value range;
(3) The owner submits the domain name-address bindings to the leaf node which then appends to its blockchian ledger and makes it accessible to the public.

Look-Up a Domain Name
When a client wants to access a de-cetranlized service via its domain name, he/she performs the hash algorithm against the domain name, and use the hash result as a clue to query the index tree. After loacting the proper leaf node, the client will find addresses of the domain name.

2.4 Data Structure

Each node comprises three types of data, namely the node's metadata, payload ledger and payload database. The payload database is the set of latest values of all variables in the payload ledger. The payload database is used to accelarate looking-up procedure as it can be verified against the payload ledger.

Metadata
AN example of node's metadata is depicted as follows (Table 2):

Table 2. An exemplar node's metadata

Field	Description	Example
NodeID	Node's ID	'N03', 'R03 00...A4'
NodeType	'Nonleaf' or 'Leaf'	'Nonleaf'
Version	For evolution purpose	'1.0.0'
HashLowest	The lowest value (included) of the hash range in this node	0x03 00...00
HashHighest	The highest value (included) of the hash range in this node	0x03 FF...FF

Payload Ledger and Database
The payload of a non-leaf node is the addresses of its direct child nodes, while the payload of a leaf node is the addresses of de-centralized services.

As each node is itself a blockchain-based system, its payload is a blockchain ledger. To faclitate looking-up, a payload database is introduced providing the lastest available addresses of child nodes (for non-leaf nodes) or addresses of de-centralized services (for leaf nodes).

The payload database of the non-leaf node 'N03' and the leaf node 'R03 01 02 03 AA BB CC DD' are as below (Tables 3 and 4).

Table 3. Payload database of a non-leaf node

Field	Sub field	Grand-sub field	Type	Count	Description	Example
Child			Object	1..n		
	ID		String	1	Child's ID	"N0301"
	HashLowest		Long	1	The lowest value (included) of the hash range in this child	0x03 01 00…00
	HashHighest		Long	1	The highest value (included) of the hash range in this child	0x03 01 FF…FF
	Addresses		Object	1..n		
		addr	String	1..n	The access addresses of this child node	"192.168.3.1"

Table 4. Payload database of a leaf node

Field	Sub field	Grand-sub field	Type	Count	Description	Example
DService			Object	1..n		
	Name		String	1	De-centralized Serive's name	"d-s001.ABCfirm.com.cn"
	Namehash		Long	1	Hash value of its name	0 × 03 01 02 03 AA BB CC DD 11 22 33 44…
	Addresses		Object	1..n		
		Addr	String	1..n	The access addresses of this service	"192.168.13.1"

3 Scalabiity

AS a worldwide facility, HSD DNS shall be as scalable as traditional DNS:

(1) Limitless capacity. There shall be no ceiling limit for the amount of de-centralized services that HSD DNS can serve.
(2) Reasonable latency. HSD DNS shall behave almost as well as, if not better than, traditional DNS in terms of latency.

3.1 Limitless Capacity

Commercial hash algorithms usually have enormous value ranges. For example, the value range of SHA-256 is 2^{256}, which is more than 2^{200} larger than the total amount of domain names in 2021 [12, 16]. The total amount can be even larger than the hash value range as one leafnode may accommdate more than one de-centralized services whose names have the same hash result, as depicted in Sect. 2.2 and 2.4.

3.2 Overload

In practice, HSD DNS can be regarded as overloaded if its leaf nodes are stuffed with too many domain-name entries, such that the lookup latency is unreasonably long or the performance of that leaf node becomes unstable or deteriorated. Overloading will take place sooner or later in either case:

(1) Even overload. All leaf nodes are overloaded with too many domain names.
(2) Skewed overload. Only partial leaf nodes are overloaded with too many domain names. Skewed overload may happen when quite a number of domain names generate hash values with the same leftmost bit string such that their resolution entries are located in the same leaf node.

3.3 Lookup Latency

In traditional DNS, the local DNS server repeatedly sends queries to the DNS root server, TLD servcr, SLD server and so on until it reaches the proper DNS server some levels below with the required name resolution data.

HSD DNS works similarly. The client's local DNS server has to iteratively send a series of lookup queries to HSD DNS index tree starting with the root, a level downwards with one round of query-response, until it reaches the proper lead node.

The total latency is the summary of latency of all query-response rounds, as depicted in Eq. (6), where d is the depth of HSD DNS index tree, LO_i is the lookup latency in the level i and RTT_i is the network transmitting time of the query-response packets in the level i.

$$LA = \sum_{i=1}^{d}(LO_i + RTT_i) \tag{6}$$

To simplify, LO and RTT are assumed to be the same for all levels, then:

$$LA = d \times (LO + RTT) \tag{7}$$

3.4 On-Demand Spanning

Rather than setting up a full-grown tree at the initial phase, HSD DNS may adopt an on-demand pattern to generate the index tree in order to shorten the latency, as inspired by dynamic resource allocation for imbalanced workload in blockchains [17, 18]. At the beginning when there are not many de-centralized services, the leaf nodes are unlikely to be overloaded even if they represent a large hash range. Thus, it is possible to use a 'shallow' index tree which offers the clients with less levels, and then less lookup query-response rounds. According to Eq. (7), if d, the tree depth, is decreased, the total latency LA will be optimized substantially.

Later when more de-centralized services emerge and a leaf node becomes overloaded, this leaf node can be replaced with a sub-tree. For example, if the leaf node $<R\,i, j>$ is overloaded, it sprouts a sub-tree with $<N\,i, j>$ as the root and $<R\,i.j, 00>,\dots, <R\,i, j, FF>$ as the leaf nodes. Then, all domain entries in previous $<R\,i, j>$ shall be re-distributed to $<R\,i, j, 00>,\dots, <R\,i, j, FF>$ according to hash-value-range rules depicted in Sect. 2.2 (Fig. 2).

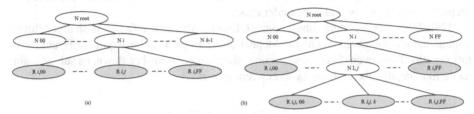

Fig. 2. Node $< R\,i, j >$ sprouts a new sub-tree rooted at $< N\,i, j >$ (a) Before (b) After

Blockchain splitting procedure in [13] provides more details. When a new sub-tree is generated, each leaf node, e.g. $<R\,i, j, k>$, may use the payload database of previous $<R\,i, j>$ as the initial transactions in the genesis block, and then new transactions only related to $<R\,i, j, k>$ are appended to the ledger of $<R\,i, j, k>$, and only domain names whose hash-values are related to $<R\,i, j, k>$ are maintained in the payload database.

3.5 Reasonable Lookup Latency

HSD DNS provides 'reasonable' lookup latency as:

- When there are not many de-centralized services, only limited rounds of lookup query-response are needed in a 'shallow' index tree, enabled by the on-demand spanning.
- Latency rises mildly when de-centralized services grow. It is easy to infer that the depth of index tree is a logarithmic function of the total amount of leaf nodes.

4 Security

HSD DNS architeture is open to deploy a wide range of security measures, proven by either traditional DNS or precedented de-centralized DNSes [14].

4.1 Intra-node Security

IN HSD DNS, the data stored in a node of the index tree are trustworthy and free from tampering, as each node itself is a blockchain system.

Other mechanisms, such as asymetric signature, proposed in [9] to verify the data authenticity are also applicable to HSD DNS with improvements accommodating to blockchain, for example, using de-centralized PKI rather than a centralized one.

4.2 Inter-node Security

Inter-node security ensures secure connections across different levels or different zones of domain name resolution.

In traditional DNS, resolution hierarchy is organized according to the naming pattern. If a domain, for example 'abc.com.cn', is attacked, its child domain/zones, for example 'dept01.abc.com.cn', will also be under attack.

HSD DNS brings a more robust context. Due to avalanche effect of hash algorithms, domain names like 'abc.com.cn' and 'dept01.abc.com.cn' may have quite different resolution paths. Thus, even if the domain name 'abc.com.cn' is broken down, its sub-domain name like 'dept01.abc.com.cn' probably remains intact.

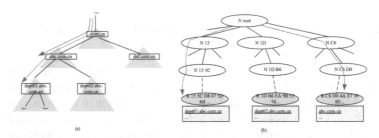

Fig. 3. Resolution path in traditional DNS (a) and HSD DNS (b) (Color figure online)

As shown in Fig. 3, the resolution paths of 'abc.com.cn' (in blue) and 'dept01.abc.com.cn' (in red) share a long common beginning in traditional DNS, while they two diverge from the second level in HSD DNS.

Note that SHA-256 ('abc.com.cn') = 0xC6D04AE7398E45F92..., and SHA-256('dept01.abc.com.cn') = 0x155CD8075D8B5D3210F9....

5 Assessment

Quantitative analysis is needed to determine parameters' values for performance purposes. In HSD DNS context, key paramenters include LA, d, LO, k, RTT and TN where TN is the total amount of de-centralized services. Bearing in mind that on-demand spanning model is adopted, quantative analysis needs to cover the process from the beginning to scaling-up.

LA, the overall looking-up latency, is the main performance index, and is determined by d, LO and RTT according to Eq. (7).

LO is affected by k since a larger k means each non-leaf node has to maintain more entries of nodes from downwards and then generates a larger LO. So does in leaf nodes.

Suppose SHA-256 is used, then $k^d = 2^{256}$. According to Eq. (2), d and k are reversly related, thus quantitative analysis is needed to find a decent balance.

5.1 Lookup-Latency (LO) and Branch Number (k)

LO is fundamentally the reading latency of blockchain system in each node in the index tree. Although blockchain is notorious for its writing throughput, its reading performance is much better as only a local copy of ledger is accessed and can be highly optimized. In addition, the payload database like Hyperledger Fabric 'world-state database' offers extra help. The experiment in section III.E [15] shows that reading latency remains 1 ms for reading queries up to a quite high arriving rate.

However, the K-V store capacity suggests a clue of performance ceiling. The experiment in section IV.B [15] shows that reading latency is relatively constant for the key-value store size up until 100 million entries, but at 1 billion entries, read latency suddenly becomes more than twice higher and the disk utility goes higher than a linear pattern. It is reasonable to redeem this as a deterioration singlarity and a strating point of overloading.

Thus, we set 100 milion as the ceiling of k.

LO takes the value of 1 ms, the reading latency on K-V stores no more than 100 million entries as in section IV.B [15].

5.2 Amount of De-centralized Services (TN) and TREE'S Depth (D)

As K-V store in each node cannot exceed k entries, it is obvious that

$$d = \log_k^{TN} \tag{8}$$

5.3 Round-Trip Time (RTT)

RTT is mainly determined by geographical distance and bandwith. In practice, we use Ping RTT as rough estimation, which happens between a client and the root DNS server, rather than between local DNS server and the root, TLD or SLD DNS servers. Network Pinger is used to test Ping RTT between a home-located client in Beijing and a well-known DNS server 8.8.8.8 for 25 times, and the average is 111.08 ms (Fig. 4).

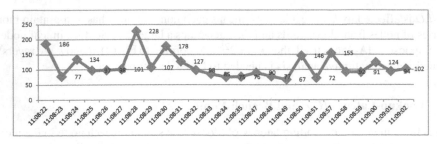

Fig. 4. Ping *RTT* (ms)

5.4 Total Latency (*LA*)

LA and its trend can be speculated based on the following assumption:

(1) On-demand spanning pattern is used;
(2) Eq. (7) is used to compute *LA*, and Eq. (8) is used to compute *d*;
(3) Parameters are set as: $LO = 1$ ms; $RTT = 111.08$ ms; $k = 100$ million entries; *TN* starts as 10 million, and annual increase rate is 6.54%.

According to [16], the average annual increase rate of domain names from 2010 to 2019 is 6.54%. 2020 and 2021 are excluded due to abnormality cause by Covid-19.

Table 5 depicts typical values for *d* and *LA*. From the year when there are 10 million de-centralized services, a 1-level index tree, i.e. only the root node, is capable to serve complete HSD DNS for 37 years, and *LA* remains 112.08 ms. A 2-level index tree is capable until the 329th year.

Table 5. Speculation of d and *LA* ($k = 100$ million)

Years coming	1	38	329	619	910	1201
TN (million)	10.0	104.2	1.06E + 10	1.01E + 18	1.02E + 26	1.04E + 34
d	1	1-> 2	2-> 3	3-> 4	4-> 5	5-> 6
LA (ms)	112.08	224.16	336.24	448.32	560.4	672.48

In Fig. 5, *LA* versus years coming is speculated for $k = 100$ million (noted as *LA1* in red) and $k = 10$ million (noted as *LA2* in green). The latter is added in case a 'smaller' K-V store is preferred.

It can be seen that the growth patterns are similar for different k, and the lookup latency increases mildly while the de-centralized services increase exponentially.

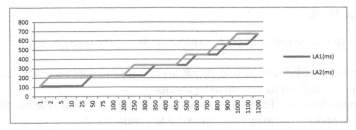

Fig. 5. Speculation of *LA* vs years coming

6 Discussion

Discussion is given here on four aspects: human readable, de-centralized, secure and scalable.

6.1 Merits

Human readability is satisfied in HSD DNS. Any naming pattern meaningful and memorable can be used, even those other than traditional DNS pattern.

HSD DNS is fully de-centralized throughout DNS life cycle including name composition, name registration-publishing, and name looking-up. No centralized administration is needed.

Security of HSD DNS is discussed in Sect. 4. Firstly, blockchain technology ensures trustworthiness of the data storage within a tree node. In addition, the avalanche effect of hash algorithms generates robust resolution paths for domain names in the same organization, avoiding domain-name-zone-wide unavailability caused by failure of a company's root domain name. Finally, security measures proven in other de-centralized DNS like FI-DNS [9] can also be exploited to ensure trustwothiness across parent-child nodes in the index tree.

Scalability is examined in Sect. 3. While HSD DNS has limitless capacity, the lookup latency can also be highly optimized as HSD DNS adopts an on-demand spanning pattern and fewer query-response rounds are needed.

6.2 Further Discussion

IT seems that HSD DNS has realized Zooko's Triangle [4] and solved Vitalik's Trilemma [1–3, 5]. Acutally, this is enabled by expedient measures.

Human readibility is enabled by hash algorithms, mapping human readble names into unmemorable hash results which are in turn used as the lookup clues. This is enabled by computation facility on the clients and is transparent to human users.

Scalability is achieved by setting an index tree comprising of multiple nodes, each of which is a blockchain-based system, while other blockchain-based DNS facilities like Namecoin [6], Blockstack [7] and FI-DNS [9] use one single blockchain system.

6.3 Future Work

More research is required in future to explore the following questions:

- Cache policy. Cache is needed in clients and local DNS servers, and plocily details like caching and flushing remain to be specified.
- Operating technology. Technology needs to be set up to maintain the healthiness and coordinate nodes so as to realize a sustainable development.

7 Conclusion

IN this paper, a highly scalable, de-centralized DNS facility, HSD DNS, is proposed, conveying merits including human readability, de-centralization, security and scalability. The fundamental philosophy is to use a hash algorithm to convert domain names into has values, which are in turn used as clues to determine the resolution path in an index tree. Its lookup latency is highly optimized due to the on-demand spanning policy and it takes only one looking-up round-trip to find the access entry in the initial decades. Also it provides robustness to prevent a zone-wide domain name failure.

References

1. Bez, M., Fornari, G., Vardanega, T.: The scalability challenge of ethereum: an initial quantitative analysis. In: 2019 IEEE International Conference on Service-Oriented System Engineering (SOSE), pp. 167–176 (2019). https://doi.org/10.1109/SOSE.2019.00031
2. Ethereum Whitepaper. https://ethereum.org/en/whitepaper/. Accessed 04 Feb 2022
3. Ometoruwa, T.: Solving the Blockchain Trilemma: Decentralization, Security & Scalability. https://www.coinbureau.com/analysis/solving-blockchain-trilemma/. Accessed 04 Feb 2022
4. Li, Y., Xu, S.: Design and implementation of a scalable distributed DNS system. In: 2021 IEEE 6th International Conference on Computer and Communication Systems (ICCCS), pp. 528–535 (2021). https://doi.org/10.1109/ICCCS52626.2021.9449106
5. Zooko's Triangle. https://wiki.p2pfoundation.net/Zooko's_Triangle. Accessed 04 Feb2022
6. Namecoin. https://www.namecoin.org/. Accessed 04 Feb 2022
7. Ali, M., Nelson, J., Shea, R., Freedman, M.J.: Blockstack: a global naming and storage system secured by blockchains. In: USENIX ATC 2016. https://www.usenix.org/conference/atc16/technical-sessions/presentation/ali. Accessed 04 Feb 2022
8. Wang, X., Li, K., Li, H., Li, Y., Liang, Z.: ConsortiumDNS: a distributed domain name service based on consortium chain. In: 2017 IEEE 19th International Conference on High Performance Computing and Communications; IEEE 15th International Conference on Smart City; IEEE 3rd International Conference on Data Science and Systems (HPCC/SmartCity/DSS), pp. 617–620 (2017). https://doi.org/10.1109/HPCC-SmartCity-DSS.2017.83
9. Liu, W., Zhang, Y., Liu, L., Liu, S., Zhang, H., Fang, B.:A secure domain name resolution and management architecture based on blockchain. In: 2020 IEEE Symposium on Computers and Communications (ISCC), pp. 1–7 (2020). https://doi.org/10.1109/ISCC50000.2020.9219632
10. Dong, Y., Kim, W., Boutaba, R.: Bitforest: a portable and efficient blockchain-based naming system. In: 2018 14th International Conference on Network and Service Management (CNSM), pp. 226–232 (2018)

11. Kalodner, H.A., Carlsten, M., Ellenbogen, P., Bonneau, J., Narayanan, A.: An empirical study of namecoin and lessons for decentralized namespace design. In: WEIS (2015). https://www. cs.princeton.edu/~arvindn/publications/namespaces.pdf. Accessed 04 Feb 2022

12. China Academy of Information and Communications Technology (CAICT). Internet Domain Name Industry Report (2021 Edition). (in Chinese). http://www.caict.ac.cn/kxyj/qwfb/ztbg/202107/P020210721569896835962.pdf. Accessed 04 Feb 2022

13. Yu, L., Jin, Y.: Research on splitting technology of blockchain data. Chin. High Technol. Lett. **27** (2017). (in Chinese), https://doi.org/10.3772/j.issn.1002-0470

14. Ramdas, A., Muthukrishnan, R.: A survey on DNS security issues and mitigation techniques. In: 2019 International Conference on Intelligent Computing and Control Systems (ICCS), pp. 781–784 (2019). https://doi.org/10.1109/ICCS45141.2019.9065354

15. Baliga, A., Solanki, N., Verekar, S., Pednekar, A., Kamat, P., Chatterjee, S.: Performance characterization of hyperledger fabric. In: 2018 Crypto Valley Conference on Blockchain Technology (CVCBT), pp. 65–74 (2018). https://doi.org/10.1109/CVCBT.2018.00013

16. The Verisign Domain Name Industry Brief Archive. https://www.verisign.com/en_US/domain-names/dnib/domain-name-industry-brief-reports/index.xhtml#2021. Accessed 04 Feb 2022

17. Huang, H., et al.: Brokerchain: a cross-shard blockchain protocol for account/balance-based state sharding. INFOCOM, May 2022. https://www.researchgate.net/requests/r99816816. Accessed 04 Feb 2022

18. Huang, H., et al.: Elastic resource allocation against imbalanced transaction assignments in sharding-based permissioned blockchains. IEEE Trans. Parallel Distrib. Syst. (TPDS) **33**(10), 2372–2385 (2022). https://www.henrylab.net/wp-content/uploads/2022/03/Elastic_Resource_Allocation_Against_Imbalanced_Transaction_Assignments_in_Sharding-Based_Permissioned_Blockchains.pdf. Accessed 04 Feb 2022

Traceable Ring Signature Schemes Based on SM2 Digital Signature Algorithm and Its Applications in the Evidence-Storage System

Yongxin Zhang[1], Qinghao Wang[1,2], Ning Lu[2,3], Wenbo Shi[2], and Hong Lei[1,4(✉)]

[1] SSC Holding Company Ltd., Chengmai 571924, China
{yongxin,qinghao}@oxhainan.org, leiluono1@163.com
[2] The College of Computer Science and Engineering, Northeastern University,
Shenyang 110819, China
{luning,shiwb}@neuq.edu.cn
[3] The School of Computer Science and Technology, Xidian University,
Xi'an 710071, China
[4] The School of Cyberspace Security, Hainan University, Haikou 570228, China

Abstract. A high-quality evidence-storage service is crucial for many existing applications. For example, judicial or arbitral authorities need to guarantee that their systems are available and trustworthy to conduct the arbitration. Such a system should protect witnesses' privacy from potential adversary threats. Ring signatures can be employed in blockchain-based systems to conceal the witness's identity among a group of persons while guaranteeing the availability and trustworthy of evidence. However, the strong anonymity of ring signature makes regulation tough and shields criminals. The traceable ring signature (TRS) is a de-anonymization mechanism that, unlike group signatures, does not rely on centralized trust, making it suitable for the blockchain system. Unfortunately, no SM2-based designs could be discovered in the TRS public literature. To fill the gap, this paper proposes a traceable ring signature scheme based on SM2 digital signature algorithm. It is shown that SM2 traceable ring signature (STRS) satisfies integrity, unforgeability, anonymity, and traceability. Moreover, we present an STRS-based blockchain evidence-storage system, in which users upload evidence with traceable ring signature generated by themselves, and regulators can learn the true identity of the signer if necessary.

Keywords: Blockchain · Evidence-storage system · SM2 · Traceable ring signature · Traceability

1 Introduction

Ring signatures, introduced by Kalai, Rivest, and Shamir in [1], allow a participant to sign a message anonymously on behalf of a group, named "ring". The

D. Svetinovic et al. (Eds.): BlockSys 2022, CCIS 1679, pp. 122–133, 2022.
https://doi.org/10.1007/978-981-19-8043-5_9

verifier can check the validity of the signature but cannot determine the identity of signer within the ring; this attribute is also possessed by group signature. However, the major difference between ring signatures and group signatures [2] is that there is no centralized manager who generates the keys, manages the group, and de-anonymizes the signer if required. This type of digital signature, which ensures anonymity without a centralized manager, is therefore appropriate for a decentralized system, and there are existing uses for it as a building block. For example, each transaction in blockchain clearly shows the input and output accounts (public keys) of funds, hence, we can determine the flow direction of funds. Monero requires user's key and other public keys to form a ring as the input account to construct the transaction, preventing the external observers from learning which possible signer in the ring is the real input account, thus realizing untraceability [3–5].

However, the lack of manager in ring signatures enables members to abuse their anonymity. In the example of Monero [6], the strong anonymity provides shelter for illegal acts, such as money laundering [7]. Due to the anonymity guarantees, the regulators cannot distinguish whether this transaction is signed by which one.

To address the uncontrolled anonymity guaranteed by ring signatures, Fujisaki and Suzuki proposed traceable ring signatures (TRS) in [8], in which each message is attached with a one-time random number, named ISSUE. TRS contains an algorithm Trace that can detect the signer in the ring. In detail, if Alice signed two messages m and m' to get traceable ring signatures σ and σ' with the same ISSUE, the Trace will expose the public key of Alice. It should be noted that if the message $m = m'$, it just finds the same signer but cannot tell who signed them, which is known as linkability [9].

Fujisaki [10] presented a sub-linear traceable ring signature with the trusted common reference string (CRS). Ho Au et al. in [11] build the traceable ring signatures based on bilinear maps. Scafuro et al. [12] proposed the one-time traceable ring signatures, where a member can sign anonymously only one message. Fan et al. [13] presented a ring signature with SM2 algorithm, where SM2 (Shangyong Mima) is proposed by the State Password Administration of China. Peng et al. [14] constructed the ring signature with SM9 algorithm. Although TRS has several variants, no scheme has yet been developed that is based on SM2, the Chinese cryptographic public key algorithm standard [15]. To balance the privacy and regulation of signers, we propose a traceable ring signature scheme based on the SM2 signature algorithm in this paper. In our proposed scheme, the signer can generate a valid ring signature that can be verified efficiently in a manner of privacy-preserving. Moreover, all signers can combine to trace back to the signer of a certain signature without revealing the identities of the rest.

1.1 Application Case

Regulated Anonymous Evidence-Storage System. Born with open, transparent, and tamper-proof qualities, blockchain technology is ideal for the evidence-storage system to provide the solidification and permanent maintenance of data [16–18]. In the case of a disagreement, users, judicial or arbitration institutions can access proof from any node of the blockchain, eliminating the requirement for a third-party institution to give proof and thereby increasing the efficiency of related work. It is a challenge to settle out how evidence submitters can maintain their identity privacy for safe while yet proving their identification to the judiciary when necessary without alerting a third party.

Based on our scheme, the user first generates the ring signature for the evidence, after which others may check it and discover it is signed in a ring. Upon receiving the trace requirements, the user resigns a new message. Finally, the regulator can determine who the true signer of the signature is.

1.2   Our Contributions

To protect the user's privacy, we propose a novel traceable ring signature scheme based on SM2 signature algorithm, which yields privacy and traceability. Our key contributions in this paper are as follow:

- We design a traceable ring signature scheme based on SM2 signature algorithm.
- We prove that our scheme can satisfy the property of privacy-preserving and traceability.
- We construct a blockchain evidence-storage scheme based on our algorithm and design a traceable data structure used in the tracing process, proving the feasibility of proposed scheme.

1.3   Layout

The rest of this paper is organized as follows. In Sect. 2, we give the preliminaries in this paper. In Sect. 3, we show the construction of the proposed SM2 traceable ring signature (STRS). In Sect. 4, we analyze the cost of STRS. In Sect. 5, we propose a blockchain evidence-storage system (SBES) based on STRS. In Sect. 6, we analyze the properties of SBES. We then present the conclusion in the last section.

2   Preliminaries

2.1   Notions

In this paper, we set λ represents the security parameter, ε denotes negligible function, $\mathcal{PPT}$ represents the probability polynomial time, H represent the hash algorithm, e.g., SM3 cryptographic hash algorithm [19]. Also, $\mathbb{G}$ is an elliptic curve point group of order q, G is the generator of $\mathbb{G}$.

2.2   SM2 Signature Algorithm

SM2 is a public key encryption standard adopted by the People's Republic of China. SM2 Public key cryptography algorithms based on elliptic curve mainly include a trio of parts: digital signature algorithm, key exchange protocol and public key encryption.

In this section, we briefly review the SM2 digital signature algorithm, which includes a set of algorithms: Setup, Key Generation, Signature Generation and Verification, defined below:

1. Setup. Given the security parameter 1^λ, the algorithm outputs an elliptic curve point group $\mathbb{G}$ of order q, where G is the generator of $\mathbb{G}$ and a hash function $H_1 : \{0,1\}^* \to \mathbb{Z}_q^*$.
2. Key Generation. A user U randomly chooses $d_A \in \mathbb{Z}_q^*$ as the private key, sets the public key $P_A = d_A \cdot G$. The algorithm outputs the key pair (pk, sk).
3. Signature Generation. Given a user's private key d_A, a message m, the user A first computes $e = H_1(m)$, then randomly chooses $k \in \mathbb{Z}_q^*$, then calculates $(x_1, y_1) = k \cdot G$, computes $r = (x_1 + e) \bmod q$ and $s = ((1 + d_A)^{-1} \cdot (k - r \cdot d_A)) \bmod q$. Finally, the algorithm outputs the signature $\sigma = (r, s)$.
4. Verification. Given a user's private key d_A, a message m, a signature (r, s), the verifier first checks whether $r, s \notin \mathbb{Z}_q^*$, then computes the hash value $e = H_1(m)$, lets $t = (r + s) \bmod q$, calculates $(x_1, y_1) = s \cdot G + t \cdot P_A$, sets $R = (e + x_1) \bmod q$. If $R = r$, the algorithm outputs 1, which means the signature is valid; otherwise outputs 0.

3   The Proposed SM2 Traceable Ring Signature

In this section, we put forward the SM2 traceable ring signature (STRS). Generally speaking, a traceable ring signature works as follows: Each user U_i generates its own key pair (pk_i, sk_i). They register their own public key P_i with the public key infrastructure. The user U_i randomly chooses $(n - 1)$ users' public keys, adds his own public key, constructs the list LIST $= \{pk_1, pk_2, ..., pk_n\}$. For a topic ISSUE, the user forms a tag TAG $= \{$ISSUE, LIST$\}$, he can sign a message m with his private key and the tag. If the signer outputs two message/signature pairs (i, m, σ), (i', m', σ'), if $i \neq i'$, everyone can know that the two signatures are independent; else if $i = i', m = m'$, we can link the two signatures; otherwise, we can trace the identity of the real signature.

3.1   Definition

A traceable ring signature scheme [8] Σ is a quartet of algorithms {KeyGen, Sign, Verify, Trace} defined as follows.

- KeyGen. It is a probabilistic polynomial-time algorithm, which takes as input the security parameter 1^λ, outputs a key pair (pk, sk).

- Sign. It is a probabilistic polynomial-time algorithm, which takes as input a private key sk_i where $i \in [1, n]$, a tag TAG $= \{$ISSUE, LIST$\}$ where LIST $= \{pk_1, pk_2, ..., pk_n\}$, and a message m, outputs a signature σ.
- Verify. It is a deterministic polynomial-time algorithm, which takes as input a tag TAG $= \{$ISSUE, LIST$\}$ where LIST $= \{pk_1, pk_2, ..., pk_n\}$, a message m, and a signature σ, outputs a bit b. If $b = 1$, the signature is valid; otherwise, not.
- Trace. It is a deterministic polynomial-time algorithm, which takes as input a tag TAG $= \{$ISSUE, LIST$\}$, two message/signature pairs $\{(m, \sigma), (m', \sigma')\}$, outputs the following string: "indep", "linked" or pk_i, where $pk_i \in$ LIST.

Public Traceability. The output of the Trace algorithm looks confusing, which we discuss in detail here. For any ISSUE, any message m, m', any $i, i' \in [1, n]$, we have $(pk, sk) \leftarrow$ KeyGen, $\sigma \leftarrow$ Sign(sk, TAG, m), $\sigma' \leftarrow$ Sign(sk, TAG, m), it holds with an overwhelming probability that the following statement holds.

$$\mathsf{Trace}(\mathsf{TAG}, m, \sigma, m', \sigma') = \begin{cases} \text{"indep"}, & \textit{if } i \neq i' \\ \text{"linked"}, & \textit{else if } i = i', \ m = m' \\ pk_i, & \textit{otherwise.} \end{cases}$$

Correctness. We define the correctness of a traceable ring signature scheme as follows. For any ISSUE, any message m, any $i \in [1, n]$, we have $(pk, sk) \leftarrow$ KeyGen, $\sigma \leftarrow$ Sign(sk, TAG, m), it holds with an overwhelming probability Verify(TAG, m, σ)=1.

3.2   Constructions

In this section, we first appoint the notions that will be used. $H_1 : \{0,1\}^* \to G$, $H_2 : \{0,1\}^* \to G$ and $H_3 : \{0,1\}^* \to \mathbb{Z}_q^*$ denote hash functions, $\parallel$ denotes the concatenation of bit string, $\perp$ denotes abort, $\emptyset$ denotes an empty set. $\#$ denotes the number of members in a set. We use the same elliptic curve point group $\mathbb{G}$ of order q as the SM2 digital signature standard, where G is the generator of $\mathbb{G}$.

Here, we give the detailed constructions of our SM2 traceable ring signature.

1. KeyGen. Each user runs this algorithm, gets their key pairs.
   (a) Each user U_i randomly chooses $d_{A_i} \in \mathbb{Z}_q^*$ as the private key, sets the public key $P_i = d_i \cdot G$.
   (b) The algorithm outputs the key pair (pk_i, sk_i), $pk_i = P_i, sk_i = d_i$.
2. Sign. Given the private key sk_i, the tag TAG $= \{$ISSUE, LIST$\}$, and the message m, the user runs this algorithm to output a signature σ.
   (a) The user A_i randomly chooses $(n-1)$ users' public keys, adds his own public key, constructs the list LIST $= \{pk_1, pk_2, ..., pk_n\}$, Let TAG $= \{$ISSUE, LIST$\}$.
   (b) Calculate the hash value $W = H_1($TAG$)$.
   (c) Compute $\sigma_i = d_i \cdot W$.
   (d) Compute $A_0 = H_2($TAG$, m)$ and $A_1 = (\sigma_i / A_0)^{1/i}$.

(e) For all $j \neq i$, compute $\sigma_j = A_0 A_1{}^j \in \mathbb{G}$.

(f) Randomly choose $k_i \in Z_q^*$, set $c_{i+1} = H_3\left(\mathsf{TAG}, A_0, A_1, k_i \cdot G, k_i \cdot W\right)$.

(g) For $j = i+1, \ldots, n, 1, \ldots, i-1$, the user A_i chooses $s_j \in Z_q^*$, computes $T_j = s_j \cdot G + (s_j + c_j) \cdot P_j$, $Y_j = s_j \cdot W + (s_j + c_j) \cdot \sigma_i$, then computes $c_{j+1} = H_3\left(\mathsf{TAG}, A_0, A_1, T_j, Y_j\right)$, lets $c_1 = c_{n+1}$.

(h) Compute $s_i = \left((1+d_i)^{-1} \cdot (k_i - c_i \cdot d_i)\right) \bmod q$.

(i) Output the traceable ring signature value $\sigma = (A_1, c_1, s_1, s_2, \ldots, s_n)$ on message m.

3. Verify. Given the tag $\mathsf{TAG} = \{\mathsf{ISSUE}, \mathsf{LIST}\}$, the message m, and the signature σ, the verifier runs this algorithm to output a bit.

   (a) If $c_1, s_1, s_2, \ldots, s_n \notin Z_q^*$, return $\perp$.

   (b) For $i = 1, 2, \ldots, n$, compute $A_0 = H_2\left(\mathsf{TAG}, m\right)$ and $\sigma_i = A_0 A_1{}^i$.

   (c) Calculate the hash value $W = H_1(\mathsf{TAG})$.

   (d) For $i = 1, 2, \ldots, n$, compute $T_j = s_j \cdot G + (s_j + c_j) \cdot P_j$, $Y_j = s_j \cdot W + (s_j + c_j) \cdot \sigma_i$, then compute $c_{j+1} = H_3\left(\mathsf{TAG}, A_0, A_1, T_j, Y_j\right)$.

   (e) If $c_1 = c_{n+1}$, then outputs $b = 1$; otherwise $b = 0$.

4. Trace. Given the tag $\mathsf{TAG} = \{\mathsf{ISSUE}, \mathsf{LIST}\}$, two message/signature pairs $\{(m, \sigma), (m', \sigma')\}$, everyone can run this algorithm.

   (a) Calculate the hash value $W = H_1(\mathsf{TAG})$.

   (b) For $i = 1, 2, \ldots, n$, compute $A_0 = H_2\left(\mathsf{TAG}, m\right)$ and $\sigma_i = A_0 A_1{}^i$.

   (c) Similarly, for $i = 1, 2, \ldots, n$, compute $A_0 = H_2\left(\mathsf{TAG}, m'\right)$ and $\sigma_i' = A_0 A_1{}^i$.

   (d) For $i = 1, 2, \ldots, n$, if $\sigma_i = \sigma_i'$, store P_i on TLIST, TLIST is an empty list initially.

   (e) Finally, perform the following steps:

     – If the public key P is the only entry in TLIST, output P;

     – If $\mathsf{TLIST} = \mathsf{LIST}$, output "link";

     – If $\mathsf{TLIST} = \emptyset$ or $1 < \#\mathsf{TLIST} < n$, output "indep".

3.3 Discussion

This scheme realizes the generation of traceable ring signature based on SM2 digital signature algorithm. The signer hides his identity in the signature group by collecting the users' public keys, and generates a signature label at the same time, which protects the signer's privacy, avoids the abuse of signature, and realizes the tracking of the signer by means of a secondary signature. The invention ensures the integrity, unforgeability, anonymity and traceability of the signature.

– **Integrity.** In signature phase, the signature $\sigma = (A_1, c_1, s_1, s_2, \ldots, s_n)$, where $A_1 = (\sigma_i/A_0)^{1/i}$ and $A_0 = H_2\left(\mathsf{TAG}, m\right)$. In verification phase, the verifier should calculate the $A_0 = H_2\left(\mathsf{TAG}, m\right)$ to verify the signature. Consequently, the signature σ is generated via original data m. Once the data is tampered with, it cannot pass the verification phase, so as to ensure the integrity of data.

– **Unforgeability.** In our construction, the signature $\sigma = (A_1, c_1, s_1, s_2, \ldots, s_n)$, where $A_1 = (\sigma_i/A_0)^{1/i}$ and $\sigma_i = d_i \cdot W$. The private key d_i is only known by the signer U_i, so it is impossible for others to forge the signature without private key.

- **Anonymity.** In verification phase, the verifier uses $\mathsf{LIST} = \{pk_1, pk_2, ..., pk_n\}$ to verify the signature σ. Besides, the auxiliary parameters $c_1, ...c_n$ are generated with users' public keys rather than the signer's public key. As a result, the probability that adversary can identify the real signer is less than $1/n$, where n is the number of users.
- **Traceability.** In trace phase, all users in the ring should resign data m' with the same tag TAG. Recall that $\sigma_i = A_0 A_1{}^i = d_i \cdot W = d_i \cdot H_1(\mathsf{TAG})$. If the old signature σ is equal to new σ', it means that they are generated by the single private key d_i. Hence, we catch the signer.

4   Evaluation and Analysis

In this section we evaluate the performance of STRS from communication cost and computation cost.

4.1   Communication Cost

Let $|q|$ be the bits of order q, $|\mathbb{G}|$ be the bits of group $\mathbb{G}$. In STRS, the Sign generates signatures $\sigma = (A_1, c_1, s_1, s_2, \ldots, s_n)$, where $A_1 \in \mathbb{G}$ and $c_1, s_1, s_2, \ldots, s_n \in \mathbb{Z}_q^*$. Consequently, the communication cost of STRS are $(n+1)|q| + |\mathbb{G}|$.

4.2   Computation Cost

This paper focus the computation cost in algorithms includes Sign, Verify and Trace. Suppose that the number of ring member is n, T_{add} is the additive operation on group $\mathbb{G}$, T_{mul} denotes the multiplication operation on group $\mathbb{G}$, T_{exp} is the exponentiation operation on $\mathbb{G}$, T_H is the hash function for $\{0,1\}^* \rightarrow G$ (*e.g.*, the H_1 and H_2), and $T_{H'}$ represents the hash function for $\{0,1\}^* \rightarrow \mathbb{Z}_q^*$ (*e.g.*, the H_3). In addition, T_{ZA} denotes the inverse operation on group $\mathbb{Z}_q^*$.

We analyze and compare STRS and other SM2-related ring signature work, the results are shown in Table 1.

Table 1. Computation cost for SM2 ring signature schemes.

Schemes	Sign	Verify	Trace
STRS	$2T_H + nT_{H'} + T_{ZA} + (2n-2)T_{add} + (5n-1)T_{mul} + (n+1)T_{exp}$	$2T_H + (n-1)T_{H'} + (2n-2)T_{add} + (5n-4)T_{mul} + nT_{exp}$	$3T_H + 2nT_{mul} + 2nT_{exp}$
SRS [13]	$nT_H + T_{ZA} + (n-1)T_{add} + (2n-1)T_{mul}$	$nT_H + nT_{add} + 2nT_{mul}$	–
SLRS [13]	$T_H + nT_{H'} + T_{ZA} + (2n-2)T_{add} + (4n-1)T_{mul}$	$nT_{H'} + T_{ZA} + 2nT_{add} + 4nT_{mul}$	–

5 STRS-Based Blockchain Evidence-Storage System

As a decentralized trust platform, all nodes adopt full backup mechanism to ensure availability, causing the huge storage overhead. Generally, to reduce the storage pressure of blockchain, massive data is often stored in the remote cloud, and a handful of critical proof is stored in the trusted blockchain that is used to ensure the trustworthy of the data in the cloud. Typically, to achieve traceable evidence storage, we present SBES, a blockchain-based evidence-storage system that employs STRS to secure users' privacy while also tracing the target signer. Moreover, a traceable data structure is introduced for the traceability of evidence.

5.1 System Model

Figure 1 shows the system model of SBES, which involves four entities:

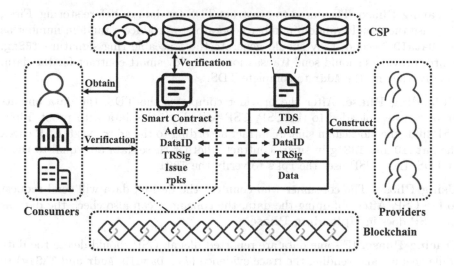

Fig. 1. System model.

- **Consumers.** They prefer to request data from cloud storage providers and evidence from blockchain for arbitration or other actions.
- **Providers.** They are in form of group to provide evidence via cloud storage providers due to limited storage capacity.
- **Blockchain.** Blockchain runs on nodes distributed all over the world, with the characteristics of decentralization, tamper-proof and supporting smart contract execution. It is accessible to everyone and responsible for storing the evidence for the data in CSP.
- **Cloud storage provider (CSP).** They are typically commercial entities, which offer users on-demand network access to a large, shared pool of storage resources.

Additionally, we design a traceable data structure for evidence-storage, named TDS, as shown in Fig. 1, consisting of data identity `DataID`, smart contract address `Addr`, traceable ring signature `TRSig` and data itself. Correspondingly, we also require the smart contract to trustfully record the above information, including topic `issue` (i.e., the ISSUE in proposed scheme) and providers' public keys `rpks=` $\{P_i, i \in n\}$. Note that the data can be in the form of encryption or others, it's out of our scope.

5.2   Our Protocol

Our protocol is defined by a collection of phases as follow:

Setup Phase. In this phase, n data providers generate their cryptographic parameters. First, all providers generate their STRS parameters, i.e., P_i and d_i. Next, they should generate blockchain account parameters, i.e., pk_i, sk_i. Here, we suppose that the blockchain runs safely and smoothly.

Creating Phase. They need to construct TDS for data m before storing. First, they use the pseudo random number generator to produce a random number as the `DataID`. Second, they should generate the traceable ring signature `TRSig`. Third, providers should send transaction to deploy smart contract for the data. Finally, they fill the `Addr` to complete TDS.

Uploading Phase. After the provider completes the TDS, the data and its proof can be uploaded to the CSP. CSP will check the data with proof. First, CSP finds the blockchain smart contract according to the `Addr`. Next, CSP check the `DataID` and `TRSig` in smart contract whether these data are equal to those in TDS. Last, CSP uses the `rpks` to verify the `TRSig`.

Using Phase. The consumer who counters the desired data will send request to the CSP. After obtaining the data, the consumer can also check the data as the CSP does in **Uploading Phase**.

Tracing Phase. IF some data are reported illegal, CSP should delete the data while keeping and sending the trace evidence (i.e., `DataID`, `Addr` and `TRSig`) to providers for accountability. Providers should execute the trace algorithm with parameters in blockchain (i.e., `issue`) to disclose the malicious.

6   Security Analysis

In this section, we analyze the following security features of our scheme, namely: privacy-preserving, integrity, and traceability.

Theorem 1 (Privacy-Preserving). *For the purpose of protecting the providers' privacy, SBES is able to restrict the following behaviors of the consumers: (1) obtain the identity of provider with the off-chain data. (2) get the identity of provider with the on-chain data. (3) obtain the identity of providers while tracing.*

Proof. For the purpose (1), we use the traceable ring signature σ to replace the traditional signature that will reveal the signer. As explained in Sect. 3.3, the STRS provides anonymity for providers. The consumer can only use the public key $\{P_i, i \in n\}$ in the group to verify the signature. Hence, the consumer cannot judge which provider signed the data. For the purpose (2), the blockchain, such as Bitcoin [20] and Ethereum [21], provides pseudonyms to protect identity. Although some studies [22,23] have been proposed to realize de-anonymity, the success rate and accuracy rate are still very low. For the purpose (3), as shown in the Trace algorithm, only the provider whose $\sigma_i' = \sigma$ will be pushed into **TList** and be revealed. The rest providers are still protected by SBES.   □

Theorem 2 (Integrity). *SBES is able to ensure the data integrity in the evidence-storage process.*

Proof. As explained in Sect. 3.3, the STRS provides integrity for providers with signature σ. The signature σ is generated via original data m. Once the data m is replaced by m', the $A_0 = H_2(\mathsf{TAG}, m')$, resulting the $c_1 \neq c_{n+1}$. As a result, it cannot pass the verification phase, so as to ensure the integrity of data.

Theorem 3 (Traceability). *In SBES, any provider who violates the protocol would be exposed.*

Proof. As the blockchain is maintained by all nodes via the consensus mechanism, the data in blockchain smart contract is reliable. When one provider violates the protocol, the group can execute the Trace algorithm with the data in blockchain (*i.e.*, issue). They first compute the hash $W = H_2(\mathsf{TAG})$ with issue. Second, all providers compute the $\sigma_i' = A_0 A_1{}^i$, where $A_0 = H_2(\mathsf{TAG}, m')$, m' is a string of arbitrary length. Third, if $\sigma_i = \sigma_i'$, the public key P_i is pushed into **TList**. Finally, the **TList** records all the malicious providers.

7   Conclusion

Traceable ring signature (TRS) scheme has a wide range of applications, such as an evidence-storage system. On the one hand, it has the complete anonymity and unforgeability of ring signatures. On the other hand, it effectively avoids the problem of regulation faced by traditional ring signatures. Researchers have proposed many TRS algorithms with different forms and characteristics, but there is no TRS based on SM2 digital signature algorithm. To promote the application of SM2 digital signature algorithm in these fields, a traceable ring signature based on SM2 digital signature algorithm, named STRS, is proposed in this paper. Furthermore, we describe an STRS-based blockchain evidence-storage system (SBES) in which users submit evidence with a signature generated by STRS, and the regulator can figure out the identity of the signer.

Acknowledgments. This work was supported in part by the Finance Science and Technology Project of Hainan Province (No. ZDKJ2020009); in part by the National Key R&D Program of China (No. 2021YFB2700601); in part by the National Natural Science Foundation of China (Nos. 62163011, 62072092, 62072093 and U1708262); in part by the Fundamental Research Funds for the Central Universities (No. N2023020); in part by the Natural Science Foundation of Hebei Province (No. F2020501013); in part by the China Postdoctoral Science Foundation (No. 2019 M653568); and in part by the Key Research and Development Project of Hebei Province (No. 20310702D).

References

1. Rivest, R.L., Shamir, A., Tauman, Y.: How to leak a secret. In: Boyd, C. (ed.) ASIACRYPT 2001. LNCS, vol. 2248, pp. 552–565. Springer, Heidelberg (2001). https://doi.org/10.1007/3-540-45682-1_32
2. Chaum, D., van Heyst, E.: Group signatures. In: Davies, D.W. (ed.) EUROCRYPT 1991. LNCS, vol. 547, pp. 257–265. Springer, Heidelberg (1991). https://doi.org/10.1007/3-540-46416-6_22
3. Sun, S.-F., Au, M.H., Liu, J.K., Yuen, T.H.: RingCT 2.0: a compact accumulator-based (linkable ring signature) protocol for blockchain cryptocurrency Monero. In: Foley, S.N., Gollmann, D., Snekkenes, E. (eds.) ESORICS 2017. LNCS, vol. 10493, pp. 456–474. Springer, Cham (2017). https://doi.org/10.1007/978-3-319-66399-9_25
4. Yuen, T.H., et al.: RingCT 3.0 for blockchain confidential transaction: shorter size and stronger security. In: Bonneau, J., Heninger, N. (eds.) FC 2020. LNCS, vol. 12059, pp. 464–483. Springer, Cham (2020). https://doi.org/10.1007/978-3-030-51280-4_25
5. Zhang, F., Huang, N.N., Gao, S.: Privacy data authentication schemes based on Borromean ring signature. J. Cryptol. Res. **5**(5), 529–537 (2018). https://doi.org/10.13868/j.cnki.jcr.000262
6. Monero: About Monero. https://getmonero.org/knowledge-base/about. Accessed 4 Mar 2022
7. Kolachala, K., et al.: SoK: money laundering in cryptocurrencies. In: The 16th International Conference on Availability, Reliability and Security, Vienna, Austria, pp. 5:1–5:10 (2021). https://doi.org/10.1145/3465481.3465774
8. Fujisaki, E., Suzuki, K.: Traceable ring signature. In: Okamoto, T., Wang, X. (eds.) PKC 2007. LNCS, vol. 4450, pp. 181–200. Springer, Heidelberg (2007). https://doi.org/10.1007/978-3-540-71677-8_13
9. Liu, J.K., Wei, V.K., Wong, D.S.: Linkable spontaneous anonymous group signature for ad hoc groups. In: Wang, H., Pieprzyk, J., Varadharajan, V. (eds.) ACISP 2004. LNCS, vol. 3108, pp. 325–335. Springer, Heidelberg (2004). https://doi.org/10.1007/978-3-540-27800-9_28
10. Fujisaki, E.: Sub-linear size traceable ring signatures without random oracles. In: Kiayias, A. (ed.) CT-RSA 2011. LNCS, vol. 6558, pp. 393–415. Springer, Heidelberg (2011). https://doi.org/10.1007/978-3-642-19074-2_25
11. Au, M.H., et al.: Secure ID-based linkable and revocable-iff-linked ring signature with constant-size construction. Theor. Comput. Sci. **469**, 1–14 (2013). https://doi.org/10.1016/j.tcs.2012.10.031
12. Scafuro, A., Zhang, B.: One-time traceable ring signatures. In: Bertino, E., Shulman, H., Waidner, M. (eds.) ESORICS 2021. LNCS, vol. 12973, pp. 481–500. Springer, Cham (2021). https://doi.org/10.1007/978-3-030-88428-4_24

13. Fan, Q., He, D.B., Luo, M., Huang, X.Y., Li, D.W.: Ring signature schemes based on SM2 digital signature algorithm. J. Cryptol. Res. **8**(4), 710–723 (2021). https://doi.org/10.13868/j.cnki.jcr.000472

14. Peng, C., He, D.B., Luo, M., Huang, X.Y., Li, D.W.: An identity-based ring signature scheme for SM9 algorithm. J. Cryptol. Res. **8**(4), 724–734 (2021). https://doi.org/10.13868/j.cnki.jcr.000473

15. State Cryptography Administration: Public key crypto graphical algorithm SM2 based on elliptic curves - Part 2: digital signature algorithm (2010). http://www.sca.gov.cn/sca/xwdt/2010-12/17/1002386/files/b791a9f908bb48038 75ab6aeeb7b4e03.pdf

16. Su, Z., et al.: LVBS: lightweight vehicular blockchain for secure data sharing in disaster rescue. IEEE Trans. Depend. Secur. Comput. **19**(1), 19–32 (2020). https://doi.org/10.1109/TDSC.2020.2980255

17. Li, T., et al.: Synchronized provable data possession based on blockchain for digital twin. IEEE Trans. Inf. Forensics Secur. **17**, 472–485 (2022). https://doi.org/10.1109/TIFS.2022.3144869

18. Cui, L., et al.: A blockchain-based containerized edge computing platform for the internet of vehicles. IEEE Internet Things J. **8**(4), 2395–2408 (2021). https://doi.org/10.1109/JIOT.2020.3027700

19. Kircanski, A., Shen, Y., Wang, G., Youssef, A.M.: Boomerang and slide-rotational analysis of the SM3 hash function. In: Knudsen, L.R., Wu, H. (eds.) SAC 2012. LNCS, vol. 7707, pp. 304–320. Springer, Heidelberg (2013). https://doi.org/10.1007/978-3-642-35999-6_20

20. Nakamoto S.: Bitcoin: a peer-to-peer electronic cash system. Decent. Bus. Rev. 21260 (2008). https://www.debr.io/article/21260.pdf

21. Wood, G., et al.: Ethereum: a secure decentralised generalised transaction ledger. Ethereum Project Yellow Paper, 151(2014), pp. 1–32 (2014). https://files.gitter.im/ethereum/yellowpaper/VIyt/Paper.pdf

22. Kappos, G., et al.: An empirical analysis of anonymity in Zcash. In: 27th USENIX Security Symposium (USENIX Security 2018), Baltimore, MD, USA, pp. 463–477 (2018). https://www.usenix.org/conference/usenixsecurity18/presentation/kappos

23. Biryukov, A., Tikhomirov, S.: Deanonymization and linkability of cryptocurrency transactions based on network analysis. In: 2019 IEEE European symposium on security and privacy (EuroS&P), Stockholm, Sweden, pp. 172–184 (2019). https://doi.org/10.1109/EuroSP.2019.00022

Blockchain-Enabled Techniques for Energy Internet of Things: A Review

Qiulin He[1], Mingzhe Liu[1(✉)], Jianping Wang[2], and Runxi Liu[3]

[1] College of Computer Science and Cyber Security, Chengdu University of Technology, Chengdu 610059, China
liumz@cdut.edu.cn

[2] Petrochina Southwest Oil and Gas Field Company Northeast Sichuan Gas District, Chengdu 610059, China

[3] Dipont King's College School, Chengdu 610059, China

Abstract. The Internet of Things (IoT) technology involved in applications such as microgrids, new energy vehicles, smart charging piles, smart home and other intelligent equipment with function of energy prosumer is called the Energy Internet of Things (EIoT), which aims to create a better environment to manage energy data as well as to enhance efficiency of the information exchange. EIoT has become a vital role in the energy field. However, a challenge facing the widespread adoption of EIoT is the issue of data leakage caused by nontransparent and untrusted energy market. Blockchain technology has the characteristics of decentralization, traceability, and no need for a third-party trust mechanism. It can be synergistic and complementary with EIoT to improve its security. This paper aims to study the integration of blockchain and EIoT. We present the typical applications of blockchain in the EIoT field from the three technical dimensions of smart contract, consensus protocol, and cross-chain communication. In addition, we summarize the performance evaluation methods of the blockchain-based EIoT scheme. Furthermore, we discuss the challenges associated with blockchain technology in the field of EIoT, and also presented the state-of-the-art research works addressing these challenges.

Keywords: Energy Internet of Things · Blockchain · Smart contract · Consensus mechanism · Cross-chain technology

1 Introduction

The clean energy industry has become an important force in promoting energy transformation and has made outstanding contributions to the construction of a pollution-free, low-carbon energy system. A variety of IoT devices are involved in the collection and transaction of clean energy, such as wind turbines that collect wind energy, smart charging piles for new energy vehicles, photovoltaic generators, on-board networks, and smart meters. Through the advanced technology of the IoT, different forms of energy data are sensed to realize the interconnection

D. Svetinovic et al. (Eds.): BlockSys 2022, CCIS 1679, pp. 134–146, 2022.
https://doi.org/10.1007/978-981-19-8043-5_10

of energy systems, which is called Energy Internet of Things (EIoT) [1]. In the traditional energy market, decentralized clean energy is collected by the energy control center and sold on a centralized platform. This method will increase the storage pressure of the platform, and data security will not be guaranteed well. The EIoT which has the natural decentralization advantage of equal and decentralized decision-making by various energy subjects will change this centralized and inefficient traditional energy consumption way.

The peer-to-peer (P2P) communication mechanism in the EIoT can avoid the disadvantages of centralized transactions due to its decentralized nature. However, in terms of trust between the two parties in communication, there is a lack of authority mechanism to maintain the privacy and security of the participants. The traditional communication mode usually requires a trusted intermediary to punish the misbehaviors of participants. However, this brings new centralization problems: When a third party is attacked, it is difficult to maintain a fair judgment, and even indirectly leads to data loss and privacy leakage during the peer-to-peer communication process of participants [2].

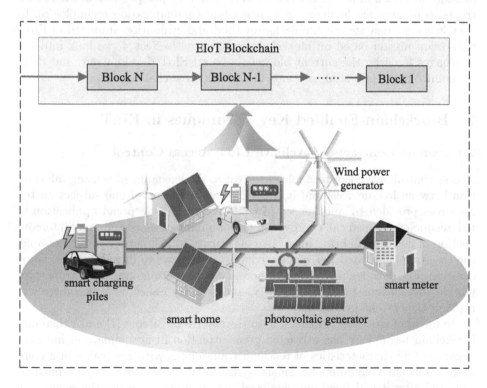

Fig. 1. Systematical diagram of the blockchain-based EIoT.

Blockchain technology has the characteristics of data immutability, traceability, decentralization, and a trust mechanism that does not require a third party [3]. The EIoT network based on blockchain technology can protect the privacy and integrity of data, and it has the following advantages: (1) The decentralized decision-making feature of EIoT is similar to the accounting function of blockchain nodes, which does not require centralized transaction processing and overcomes single points of failure; (2) The blockchain data structure ensures that each energy transaction record cannot be tampered with, which is conducive to data traceability and evidence collection; (3) Blockchain consensus mechanism and digital signature verification ensure the security of EIoT data sharing. As a result, blockchain technology can provide a secure and distributed ecosystem for IoT applications, and is a reliable choice for EIoT networks to ensure data security and privacy [4]. Figure 1 shows a graphic example of the blockchain-based EIoT system.

In this paper, we focus on the techniques of blockchain in EIoT and investigate the application of blockchain-based EIoT that have been presented in different research works. The remainder of this paper is structured as follows. In Sect. 2, we introduce the technical feasibility of blockchain in the EIoT, which include the review of previous research works from the perspectives of smart contracts, consensus mechanisms, and cross-chain communication technologies. In Sect. 3, we summarize the simulation method and evaluation standard of EIoT data transmission based on blockchain technology. In Sect. 4, we look into the challenges faced by the current blockchain-based EIoT development, and then, we point out the potential solutions to address these challenges.

2   Blockchain-Enabled Key Techniques in EIoT

2.1   Smart Contracts to Achieve EIoT Access Control

Access control is the key technology to realize the exchange of sensing information between IoT devices, and it is the limited operation of one subject on the resources provided by another subject [5]. With the widespread application of IoT technology in medical, energy, and urban buildings, more and more interconnection of devices will bring huge risks of security to IoT networks, for example, the case of [6] exploited IoT connectivity security flaws to illegally access home cameras. IoT data transmission and access control permissions lack strong protection mechanisms to ensure security, and security issues have become a hot topic in the current IoT areas.

In terms of trust mechanism, due to the success of Bitcoin [7] and Ethereum, blockchain technology has attracted great attention in academia and industry because of its characteristics of reaching transactions with real value in a completely untrusted environment. Smart contracts (it is a logical code that must be executed after it is defined and deployed) can be used to ensure the security of IoT device data exchange. [8] designed a smart contract system on the Ethereum platform to achieve secure and distributed control access between the Internet of Things, the process of access control is implemented in turn by three smart contracts which includes registration, error judgment, and device interaction.

In the area of EIoT, it is inevitable to face the sharing of data resources between distributed energy producers and consumers. Using smart contracts to implement EIoT access control is a feasible way to realize the point-to-point secure interaction between devices. A wide range of research works about access control are exploring to adopt the blockchain technology especially smart contract by taking benefits of its unmodified and executable properties. Jiang et al. [9] designed smart contracts to complete wireless energy transmission in order to avoid additional power consumption caused by malicious node attacks. Yang et al. [10] designed a transactive energy management which adopts blockchain to realize horizontal transactions between IoT-aided smart homes and vertical transactions between IoT smart homes and local power grids, and then, they solve the problems of low transaction efficiency and privacy leakage by using smart contracts to implement a distributed transactive energy management (TEM) algorithm. Guo et al. [11] used smart contracts of blockchain and a credit-based consensus mechanism to realize peer-to-peer energy transactions in smart cities. The paper [12] proposed a price-sensitive game theory model and a smart contract mechanism to ensure the balance of supply and demand, which not only realizes the automatic management of energy distribution, but also improves the security of energy P2P transactions.

2.2 Consensus Protocol in EIoT Network

In the energy transaction process supported by blockchain technology, the most important thing is how to enable each distributed energy entities to agree on a single version of a transaction, so as to ensure the stability and attack resistance in the process of node interaction in untrusted environment. In traditional blockchain research, data consistency agreement is completed according to consensus mechanism which is a key part of blockchain technology to ensure the integrity and security of distributed systems. A number of consensus have been proposed, some of notable consensus algorithms include: Proof of Work Algorithm (PoW) [7], Proof of Stake (PoS) [13], Delegated Proof of Stake (DPoS), Byzantine Fault Tolerant (BFT) and Practical Byzantine Fault Tolerant (PBFT) [14]. The characteristics of each consensus algorithm are shown in Fig. 2. However, traditional consensus algorithms cannot be directly applied to the field of EIoT since the computing resources of energy IoT devices are originally limited. Using traditional algorithms to solve the consensus problem of a large number of energy entities will consume a lot of computing resources and cause unnecessary communication delay.

Most of the existing research works on the transaction process of EIoT supported by blockchain are improved on the traditional consensus algorithm to meet the needs of specific EIoT scenarios. The schematic diagram of variant consensus algorithm is shown in Fig. 3. Wang et al. [15] used the Random Practical Byzantine Fault Tolerance (RPBFT) algorithm to enable participants in distributed energy market to quickly reach a consensus on the cost sharing result, the algorithm obtains an unpredictable random number from the hash value of the block header of each round of consensus, only the master node whose node

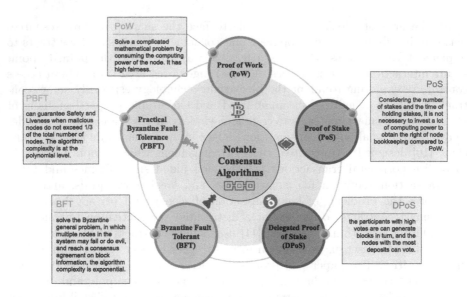

Fig. 2. The characteristics of notable consensus algorithms.

number equal to the random number is selected to participate in the process of PBFT consensus, adapting to the situation of a large number of nodes participating in the consensus. In [9], a lightweight share consensus mechanism based on DPoS is designed to shorten the transaction confirmation time and reduce the attack possibility from malicious nodes. [16] adopted genetic algorithm to optimize the configuration parameters of the Kafka algorithm in Hyperledger such as block size, confirmation time, and longest confirmation time, so as to improve the transaction confirmation efficiency of the IoT authorization system using this architecture. [17] proposed a lightweight proof of block and trade (PoBT) consensus algorithm that provide a double-check mechanism to reduce the difficulty of solving a computationally complicated math puzzle and solve the problems of poor expansion and low efficiency of PoW due to the high cost of calculation in IoT. Guo et al. [11] combined the stake quantification of nodes in the transaction process into trust scores to improve the efficiency of grid transactions, which avoid the disadvantage of high latency in traditional PoW. Sheikh et al. [18] in order to solve the problem that the charging pile of electric vehicles is vulnerable to be attacked during peak hours, they realized the energy transaction of electric vehicles and distribution network under the framework of Byzantine consensus algorithm. They analyzed the possible network attacks on nodes under different operations, so as to verify the effectiveness of blockchain application. Liu et al. [19] presented a fast adaptive consensus algorithm in order to ensure security access on wlan mesh network, which effectively protect voters' privacy as well as reduce cost of vote. N. Pradhan et al. [20] adopted blockchain technology to implement the point-to-point energy transaction, and used Istanbul Byzantine fault tolerance (ibft) to realize a flexible authorization scheme.

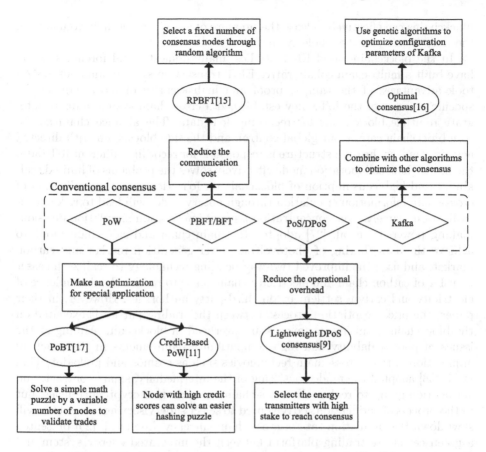

Fig. 3. The schematic diagram of variant consensus algorithm.

2.3 Cross-Chain Communication in Distributed Energy Transactions

Cross-chain technology can realize value transfer between different blockchains [21]. Common cross-chain technologies include: notary mechanism, hash locking mechanism, side chain mechanism, and relay chain. The notary mechanism can support blockchain interactions with different structures, and hash locking uses atomic swaps to transfer information. The side chain technology uses two-way pedding to achieve equal value transfer in the side chain and the main chain to lock assets [22]. The relay chain is a fusion extension of notary and profile. Notable cross-chain projects that have been formed now include Polkadot [23], Cosmos [24], and Plasma [25]. To cope with issues of complex energy businesses, it is necessary to classify energy businesses, and adopt multiple blockchains to correspond to different types of energy producers and consumers, so as to realize the diversion of different businesses. The cooperation between different blockchains can effectively release the pressure of a single blockchain to maintain the data security of the whole system.

In the blockchain-based EIoT studies, many domestic and foreign scholars have built a multi-chain collaborative EIoT transaction system. Jiang et al. [26] took advantages of the tamper proof and high security of blockchain in the specific scenario of the IoT, they established a cross-chain system aims to integrate multiple blockchains for recording IoT data. The alliance chain as the core blockchain carries out global control, and the side blockchain with directed acyclic graph as the data structure is responsible for recording different IoT data, the multi-chain collaboration mode effectively solves the problems of limited scalability and high consumption of blockchain on IoT. However, the realization of cross-chain information circulation through notary nodes will lead to risk of centralization, namely, over concentration issue of information circulation decision-making power. He et al. [27] adopted the main chain and side chain mode to achieve the data sharing of photovoltaic power generation market and carbon market, and used the improved two-way pedding technology to realize the asset transfer of carbon chain and electricity chain, so as to reduce the dependence of electricity and carbon settlement on third-party authorities. However, in their paper, the price negotiation process between the trading parties is executed on the blockchain, resulting in unnecessary overhead in blockchain. Aiming at the issues of poor scalability and high compatibility requirements in the practical application of relay cross-chain technologies such as cosmos and polkadot, Tian et al. [28] adopted the mode consisting of the intermediary, smart contract, and verification group to realize the cross-chain circulation of cryptocurrencies, but in the process of verification, PoW is used to select supervisory agents, which will slow down the circulation rate of cross-chain currency. Luo et al. [29] presented a green certificate trading platform between the integrated energy system and new energy power generation, and realized the cross chain circulation of green certificates among different subjects by utilizing the relay chain technology. However, the blockchain technology is only used as an energy circulation efficiency optimization means in this mode, and the details of the blockchain transaction in this scheme need to be further explored.

3   Performance Evaluation Methods of Blockchain-Based EIoT

In the research on the integration of blockchain technology and EIoT, how to conduct simulation experiments and what indicators are used to evaluate the effectiveness of the model are important issues that researchers are concerned about. However, the current blockchain-based EIoT research works focus on the process of adopting blockchain to solve data security and privacy, they do not introduce more about the test environment and model performance evaluation details. Therefore, this paper will summarize the test schemes and evaluation criteria used in various researches at present for reference in subsequent research simulations.

Table 1. Summary of testbeds and performance metrics used in the EIoT system.

Paper	Year	Test method	Performance metric	Topic
Zhang et al. [8]	2019	– Geth – Remix – Raspberry Pi	– Gas cost of smart contract	Smart contracts enable IoT access control
He et al. [27]	2020	– IEEE 33 bus system – Ropsten	– Transaction confirmation time	Cross-chain technology realizes photovoltaic electricity and carbon transaction
Sheikh et al. [18]	2020	– IEEE 33 bus system	– Probability of attack	Blockchain ensures the safety of charging and discharging transactions of electric vehicle charging stations
Yang et al. [12]	2020	– Game theory	– Power supply – Load demand	Smart contract realizes local electric energy security P2P transaction
Li et al. [30]	2021	– Ethereum – Fisco Bcos – Ropsten	– Gas cost of smart contract – Communication overhead	Smart contracts enable cross-chain communication between two blockchains and interactions between IoT devices
Yang et al. [10]	2021	– Quorum – Raspberry Pi – Matlab	– CPU time – The delay of transaction	smart contract used in IoT smart home
Yang et al. [31]	2021	– Hyperledger fabric – Raspberry Pi	– Time cost of trading	Blockchain encryption technology enables secure controlled access to smart grids
Pradhan et al. [20]	2021	– Ethereum – Hyperledger fabric – Remix – Metamask	– Block time – Block behind time – Throughput – Success rate – Fail rate – Memory used	Blockchain enables P2P energy trading

Blockchain-based EIoT testing methods are divided into two categories according to existing research: (1) theoretical analysis methods (game theory); (2) test platforms (Hyperledger fabric, Fisco Bcos [32], Ethereum, other environments). Figure 4 presents the classification of the performance methods in blockchain-based EIoT networks. Li et al. [33] established a credit-based payment method and proposed a credit loan pricing strategy based on the Stacklberg game to maximize the benefits of credit banks. Reference [15] uses matlab to simulate the PBFT and RPBFT consensus algorithms, and compare the fault tolerance performance of the two. The IEEE bus 33 is used to verify the security of the blockchain framework based on the Byzantine problem in [18], they uses virtual data to evaluate the possible network attacks of energy information data exchanges in the system.

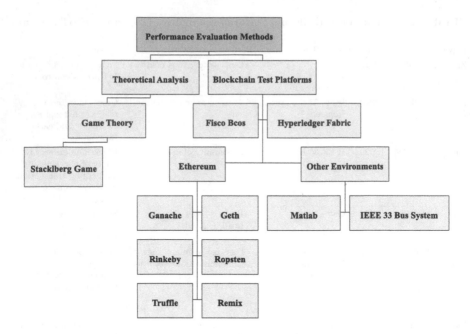

Fig. 4. Classification of performance evaluation methods in blockchain-based EIoT.

As shown in the Table 1, we enumerate comparisons on research testbeds and performance metrics in different EIoT network. It can be seen that most of the researches use the Ethereum and Hyperledger fbric test platforms with mature technology and good scalability for simulation experiments. In terms of performance indicators, the evaluation focus of each paper is different. The indicator considered in the application of smart contract research is usually gas cost consumed by deployment contract, such as [8,30]. The indexes that focus on improving consensus algorithm are mostly Lantency, Throughput, computational storage, communication cost, etc. [10,20]. When it comes to evaluating network performance by simulating IoT nodes, Raspberry Pi is mostly used in studies: In [31], Raspberry Pi is used to simulate lightweight IoT device nodes, and the system validity is verified on Hyperledger Fabric platform. The experimental performance is compared with the time cost of previous research on blockchain data sharing.

4   Challenges and Future Research Opportunities

Blockchain technology has great development potential in the field of EIoT. Literature [34] has built a demonstration site of bilateral green certificate security trading platform based on blockchain technology in Zhuhai. However, blockchain-based EIoT network is still in the exploratory stage in reality. As an auxiliary way to maintain network security in the energy system, it has not become the mainstream technology of energy application, and there are some challenging issues related to utilizing blockchain in EIoT, such as resource consumption, storage pressure and security loophole.

(1) It is hard to deploy the EIoT network based on blockchain in reality. In terms of the computing cost, the implementation of blockchain on the EIoT requires strong computing power support. However, the computing ability of the ordinary IoT devices cannot be comparable to that required by blockchain nodes, especially in the scenario of processing large-scale energy transaction data. In terms of the storage, incorporating blockchain into EIoT may require the capability of storing a large number of information within a highly frequent environment of energy circulation, this is a limitation that blockchain can accommodate directly into EIoT in current. On the one hand, energy IoT devices play the roles of energy producer and consumer, and their storage capacity of data is limited. On the other hand, if the data is stored on the blockchain, it will increase transaction processing time and reduce the efficiency, which violates the principle of efficient and economical energy blockchain application.

(2) The privacy and security of EIoT network based on blockchain still faces challenges. The blockchain adopts hash encryption algorithm to ensure the data privacy of transaction information, which can improve the security of the whole network, but the energy market is monopolized, and the more data the relevant industries have, the more possibility it is that users' privacy will be compromised. Reference [35] can analyze the relationship between users and transactions through address information and electricity consumption data. Due to the particularity of the energy system, most of the energy data needs to be collected and processed in local equipment, while the blockchain technology can only guarantee the reliability of the contents (transactions or records) on the chain, and it cannot directly guarantee the privacy and security of data (devices' information) off the chain. Relying on blockchain technology cannot fully guarantee the security and privacy of EIoT networks.

A number of hot research works have been introduced to deal with the aforesaid challenges. In the future area of blockchain-based EIoT, researching smart devices with edge computing capabilities and functions of blockchain node is a key step in realizing the expansion of blockchain computing in the energy field, which will provide intelligent hardware support for collection and storage of energy data. In order to reduce the high computing cost of EIoT based on blockchain, we propose to rely on cloud computing and fog computing knowledge to move the computing process of EIoT to cloud server, these methods have been used to reduce the computational overhead of system in [36–38]. The Inter Planetary File System (IPFS) [39] provides a solution to relieve the pressure of blockchain storage. The technology adopts distributed point-to-point transmission and storage. The more nodes, the higher the access efficiency. The energy data can be stored on the IPFS network in shards, and all decentralized hash value of the data address is merged into a new encrypted data, which is placed in the block to store, thereby establishing a storage collaboration mode on the chain and off the chain to reduce overhead of block storage. For security, a series of modern cryptographic techniques such as differential privacy [40] and verifiable random function [41] can be combined with blockchain technology to improve the data security of the entire energy system. Zhao et al. [42] used the chaotic restricted Boltzmann machine in combination with blockchain, which is proved more secure than traditional encryption algorithms in digital image by various numerical experiments.

5   Conclusion

This paper has presented a comprehensive review on the integration of blockchain and EIoT. The key issues in the blockchain-based EIoT are how to ensure the deterministic execution of energy business, how to ensure the authenticity of energy data, and how to realize the reliable circulation of energy data among multiple participants. The underlying technologies of blockchain: smart contract, consensus mechanism and cross-chain technology can solve these problems well. So we have started with describing the typical applications of EIoT system maintained by blockchain technology from three perspectives of smart contract, consensus algorithm and cross-chain communication. In view of the difficulties in the recent experiment of blockchain-based EIoT system, we have presented the systematic investigations on different research and experimental methods in this direction and have summarized the performance evaluation parameters. Finally, we have discussed the challenges faced by blockchain technology in the field of EIoT, and have highlighted the future research opportunities addressing these challenges. We hope this article can provide reference for follow-up research works in this area to move forward.

References

1. Energy IoT - how Internet of Things is transforming the energy industry. https://codibly.com/news-insights/energy-iot-how-internet-of-things-transforms-energy/. Accessed 6 Mar 2022
2. Aitzhan, N.Z., Svetinovic, D.: Security and privacy in decentralized energy trading through multi-signatures, blockchain and anonymous messaging streams. IEEE Trans. Depend. Secur. Comput. **15**(5), 840–852 (2016)
3. Xiao, Y., Zhang, N., Lou, W., Hou, Y.T.: A survey of distributed consensus protocols for blockchain networks. IEEE Commun. Surv. Tutor. **22**(2), 1432–1465 (2020)
4. Alam, T.: Blockchain and its role in the Internet of Things (IoT). Int. J. Sci. Res. Comput. Sci. Eng. Inf. Technol. **5**(1) (2019)
5. Hussein, D., Bertin, E., Frey, V.: Access control in IoT: from requirements to a candidate vision. In: 2017 20th Conference on Innovations in Clouds, Internet and Networks (ICIN), pp. 328–330. IEEE (2017)
6. CheckPoint: Checkpoint joins forces with LG to secure their smart home devices. https://www.checkpoint.com/press/2017/check-point-joins-forces-lg-secure-smart-home-devices/. Accessed 10 Mar 2022

7. Nakamoto, S.: Bitcoin: a peer-to-peer electronic cash system. Bitcoin.org (2009). https://bitcoin.org/en/bitcoin-paper
8. Zhang, Y., Kasahara, S., Shen, Y., Jiang, X., Wan, J.: Smart contract-based access control for the Internet of Things. IEEE Internet Things J. **6**(2), 1594–1605 (2018)
9. Jiang, L., Xie, S., Maharjan, S., Zhang, Y.: Blockchain empowered wireless power transfer for green and secure Internet of Things. IEEE Netw. **33**(6), 164–171 (2019)
10. Yang, Q., Wang, H.: Privacy-preserving transactive energy management for IoT-aided smart homes via blockchain. IEEE Internet Things J. **8**(14), 11463–11475 (2021)
11. Guo, J., Ding, X., Wu, W.: A blockchain-enabled ecosystem for distributed electricity trading in smart city. IEEE Internet Things J. **8**(3), 2040–2050 (2020)
12. Yang, X., Wang, G., He, H., Lu, J., Zhang, Y.: Automated demand response framework in ELNs: decentralized scheduling and smart contract. IEEE Trans. Syst. Man Cybern. Syst. **50**(1), 58–72 (2019)
13. Mechanic, Q.: Poof of stake. https://bitcointalk.org/index.php?topic=27787.0. Accessed 1 Apr 2022
14. Castro, M., Liskov, B., et al.: Practical byzantine fault tolerance. In: OsDI, vol. 99, pp. 173–186 (1999)
15. Wang, Q., et al.: A multiblockchain-oriented decentralized market framework for frequency regulation service. IEEE Trans. Ind. Inform. **17**(12), 8219–8229 (2021)
16. Klaokliang, N., Teawtim, P., Aimtongkham, P., So-In, C., Niruntasukrat, A.: A novel IoT authorization architecture on hyperledger fabric with optimal consensus using genetic algorithm. In: 2018 Seventh ICT International Student Project Conference (ICT-ISPC), pp. 1–5. IEEE (2018)
17. Biswas, S., Sharif, K., Li, F., Maharjan, S., Mohanty, S.P., Wang, Y.: PoBT: a lightweight consensus algorithm for scalable IoT business blockchain. IEEE Internet Things J. **7**(3), 2343–2355 (2019)
18. Sheikh, A., Kamuni, V., Urooj, A., Wagh, S., Singh, N., Patel, D.: Secured energy trading using byzantine-based blockchain consensus. IEEE Access **8**, 8554–8571 (2019)
19. Liu, M., Jiang, X., Zhao, F., Feng, X., Wang, R.: A fast adaptive blockchain consensus algorithm via WLAN mesh network. J. Internet Technol. **21**, 523–533 (2020)
20. Pradhan, N.R., Singh, A.P., Kumar, N., Hassan, M., Roy, D.: A flexible permission ascription (FPA) based blockchain framework for peer-to-peer energy trading with performance evaluation. IEEE Trans. Ind. Inform. **18**, 2465–2475 (2021)
21. Robinson, P.: Survey of crosschain communications protocols. Comput. Netw. **200**, 108488 (2021)
22. Back, A., et al.: Enabling blockchain innovations with pegged sidechains, 72 (2014). http://www.opensciencereview.com/papers/123/enablingblockchain-innovations-with-pegged-sidechains
23. Wood, G.: Polkadot: vision for a heterogeneous multi-chain framework. White Paper 21, pp. 2327–4662 (2016)
24. Kwon, J., Buchman, E.: Cosmos: a network of distributed ledgers (2016). https://cosmos.network/whitepaper
25. Poon, J., Buterin, V.: Plasma: scalable autonomous smart contracts. White Paper, pp. 1–47 (2017)
26. Jiang, Y., Wang, C., Wang, Y., Gao, L.: A cross-chain solution to integrating multiple blockchains for iot data management. Sensors **19**(9), 2042 (2019)
27. He, H., et al.: Joint operation mechanism of distributed photovoltaic power generation market and carbon market based on cross-chain trading technology. IEEE Access **8**, 66116–66130 (2020)

28. Tian, H., et al.: Enabling cross-chain transactions: a decentralized cryptocurrency exchange protocol. IEEE Trans. Inf. Forensics Secur. **16**, 3928–3941 (2021)

29. Luo, Z., Qin, J., Liang, J., Zhao, M., Wang, H., Liu, K.: Operation optimization of integrated energy system with green certificate cross-chain transaction. Power Syst. Technol. **2**, 1–11 (2021)

30. Li, Z., Hao, J., Liu, J., Wang, H., Xian, M.: An IoT-applicable access control model under double-layer blockchain. IEEE Trans. Circuits Syst. II Express Briefs **68**(6), 2102–2106 (2020)

31. Yang, W., Guan, Z., Wu, L., Du, X., Guizani, M.: Secure data access control with fair accountability in smart grid data sharing: an edge blockchain approach. IEEE Internet Things J. **8**(10), 8632–8643 (2020)

32. The building block of open consortium chain. https://www.fisco-bcos.org/. Accessed 1 Apr 2022

33. Li, Z., Kang, J., Yu, R., Ye, D., Deng, Q., Zhang, Y.: Consortium blockchain for secure energy trading in industrial Internet of Things. IEEE Trans. Ind. Inform. **14**(8), 3690–3700 (2017)

34. Cai, Y., Gu, Y., Luo, G., Zhang, X., Chen, Q.: Blockchain based trading platform of green power certificate: concept and practice. Autom. Electr. Power Syst. **44**(15), 1–12 (2020)

35. Zyskind, G., Nathan, O., et al.: Decentralizing privacy: using blockchain to protect personal data. In: 2015 IEEE Security and Privacy Workshops, pp. 180–184. IEEE (2015)

36. Wen, M., Chen, S., Lu, R., Li, B., Chen, S.: Security and efficiency enhanced revocable access control for fog-based smart grid system. IEEE Access **7**, 137968–137981 (2019)

37. Lu, R.: A new communication-efficient privacy-preserving range query scheme in fog-enhanced IoT. IEEE Internet Things J. **6**(2), 2497–2505 (2018)

38. Alkadi, O., Moustafa, N., Turnbull, B., Choo, K.K.R.: A deep blockchain framework-enabled collaborative intrusion detection for protecting IoT and cloud networks. IEEE Internet Things J. **8**(12), 9463–9472 (2020)

39. IPFS powers the distributed web. https://github.com/ipfs/ipfs. Accessed 16 Mar 2022

40. Hassan, M.U., Rehmani, M.H., Chen, J.: Differential privacy techniques for cyber physical systems: a survey. IEEE Commun. Surv. Tutor. **22**(1), 746–789 (2019)

41. Goldberg, S., Vcelak, J., Papadopoulos, D., Reyzin, L.: Verifiable random functions (VRFs) (2018)

42. Feixiang, Z., Mingzhe, L., Kun, W., Hong, Z.: Color image encryption via Hénon-zigzag map and chaotic restricted Boltzmann machine over blockchain. Opt. Laser Technol. **135**, 106610 (2021)

Blockchain-Based Social Network Access Control Mechanism

Minjun Dai[1], Yongsheng Li[2(✉)], Yong Wen[2], Dongyu Liu[2], and Honglin Chen[2]

[1] College of Electronic Information, Guangxi Minzu University, Nanning Guangxi 530006, China

[2] School of Artificial Intelligence, Guangxi Minzu University, Nanning Guangxi 530006, China
lyshlh@163.com

Abstract. With the development of society and the rapid increase of social networks, access control has become a big challenge. The current mainstream centralized access control methods have shortcomings such as single point of failure, low scalability, low availability and low non-repudiation. When using blockchain technology for access control, it is necessary to consider how to use the characteristics of blockchain to solve the problem of centralized access control and improve the performance limitations of the blockchain itself. Therefore, this paper proposes a blockchain-based social network access control mechanism, which uses feature extraction to simplify roles, and uses voting to allow users to participate in the authorization process of personal information. User identity authentication is more complete, and the process of information data circulation is effectively achieved. Transparent. Simulation experiments show that the scheme can provide a fast, comprehensive and scalable access control mechanism.

Keywords: Blockchain · Role access · Access control · Smart contract · Social network

1 Introduction

In life, people need registration information to use software, log in to various websites, use system services, etc., and often need to register as users of these centralized companies before they can use them. This information is stored in these centralized databases, and users cannot see it, can't operate it, and don't know whether the data is still in a safe place. Especially in recent years, there have been frequent information leakage incidents. In 2011, more than 6 million registered email accounts and passwords of CSDN users were leaked; in 2018, more than 50 million user information of FaceBook was leaked. If the leaked data is used by some criminals, it will not only harm individuals but also threaten the society. It can be seen that the consequences of unauthorized sharing of data are extraordinary. How to ensure data security and how to ensure authorization under the user's own wishes, access control is a very important part.

Traditional access control includes discretionary access control (DAC), mandatory access control (MAC), attribute-based access control (ABAC) and role-based access

D. Svetinovic et al. (Eds.): BlockSys 2022, CCIS 1679, pp. 147–164, 2022.
https://doi.org/10.1007/978-981-19-8043-5_11

control (RBAC) [1, 2]. Traditional access control often has shortcomings such as single point of failure, access policy tampering, and denial. From the perspective of social networks, more and more people use social networks, and there are various social applications, but the user information of various social applications is stored separately, and users need to register similar information many times, which also causes user information is centrally stored in the databases of major centers. Although these social service providers are committed to protecting user information, the premise is that users maintain a trust relationship with these service providers. In fact, from the news we frequently see information leaks, a crisis of confidence has already occurred. The emergence of blockchain [3] and smart contracts [4] has allowed many scholars to see the advantages of blockchain. The blockchain solves the problem of trust establishment between nodes in a decentralized system by deeply integrating various technologies such as P2P networks, cryptography, consensus algorithms, and smart contracts. In view of the characteristics of the blockchain, using it in access control can bring the following benefits: (1) The bottom layer of the blockchain is a P2P network, a distributed system, so that data is no longer centralized. (2) The access policy on the blockchain cannot be maliciously tampered with. (3) The blockchain uses encryption technology to make data secure and immutable. (4) The introduction of smart contracts takes into account the needs of different parties in access control. Of course, the blockchain also brings some problems, such as access control response time. With the improvement of the blockchain itself, the time efficiency problem will continue to be improved.

A part of the literature studies the access control of centralized systems. Although these methods have low implementation complexity and low time efficiency of access verification, they have single point of failure, low scalability, low availability and low non-repudiation and other issues [5]. There are two main types of blockchain technology for access control, one of which is to store the blockchain as an access control rule, and the other to use smart contracts to implement the blockchain as a decision point.

Many literatures store blockchain as access control rules. This type of method effectively improves the problems of non-repudiation and unchangeable rules of centralized access control, but there is still a single point of failure problem. Among them, [6] proposes an ABAC mechanism in which the owner of an object can define access rules and store them in the blockchain. In an access request, the owner sends an authorization token to the requester only if the requester satisfies the conditions defined in the access control policy. Reference [7] proposes a CapBAC mechanism, in which smart contracts are used to store access control matrices. Each node interacts with the smart contract through the provided contract address and remote procedure call interface. Reference [8] proposes another CapBAC scheme, where the blockchain stores users' capability sets and access logs. Reference [9] proposes another ABAC approach for cloud computing, where a central authority (CA) is responsible for managing the security of the entire system. First, the CA issues the attribute key to the user and adds the validity period of the key in the smart contract.

There is also a lot of literature using blockchain in the access management process, where blockchain is not only used as a database, but also as a decision point. This means that the rules are stored in the blockchain and access decisions can be done using smart contracts. Although these approaches are slightly more complex to implement and slightly less time efficient than centralized solutions, they can provide high scalability (in terms of number of users), availability, fault tolerance, immutability of rules and decisions, non-repudiation, and debacle listening [10]. Reference [11] proposes a policy chain, where policies and access logs are stored in the blockchain, and access control is done by smart contracts. Reference [12] designed a scheme that uses smart contracts and blockchain to provide a secure data sharing and access environment, which to a certain extent solves the problem of centrally providing users with web services to manage their own data, allowing users to truly have control over their own data, right. Reference [13] proposes an attribute-based access control solution by leveraging the blockchain to share the resources of network providers and service providers, enabling service providers to outsource their access control procedures without the need for a trusted third party tripartite.

In terms of role-based access control using blockchain, literature [14] based on the ABAC model, proposed a blockchain-based big data access control mechanism, using the form of transactions in the blockchain to manage access control policies. Reference [15] proposed a role delegation access control scheme based on blockchain technology. Reference [16] presents an automatic review method for a role-based multi-level access control model, which depicts the generalized feature expression of the access control by sampling the temporal and spatial features of the existing correct and incorrect authorizations. So that the existing access control model can still give correct judgment in the new situation under the migration environment.

The contributions of this paper are: (1) The access control of users and social service providers (companies) is actively mastered by users, which is a new business model. Users do not need to register information every time they use software products, and more importantly, users fully know the flow and direction of their own information, which effectively protects user privacy information. (2) For social service providers, there is no need to spend a lot of time and cost in user access control, but only need to obtain information on the chain according to the user's authorization. (3) Role-based access control, the policy is published on the chain by the resource owner (user), and the resource owner can adjust the policy at any time, which improves the flexibility of the system. (4) Use smart contracts to handle access control without the need for a central authority. Smart contracts can also make this process completely secure, immutable and automatic. In the design of smart contracts, more flexible designs can be added, such as the number of users that the company can accept in its current state, and the expectations of users for the company.

2 Preliminaries

2.1 Blockchain and Smart Contract

The concept of blockchain was introduced by Satoshi Nakamoto in 2008 and implemented by Bitcoin in 2009 [3]. It is a peer-to-peer network environment, based on transparent and trusted consensus mechanism rules, and stores data blocks in a chain as a specific data structure in chronological order, and cryptographically ensures that it cannot be tampered with and cannot be forged, can be traced back to [17]. A smart contract [4] is a script that is stored on the blockchain and can run automatically on distributed network nodes. It is a computer protocol designed to spread, verify or execute contracts in an information-based manner. Smart contracts allow for trusted transactions without third parties that are traceable and irreversible. The subsequent Ethereum [18] proposed to provide a Turing-complete virtual machine for the blockchain. Since then, the blockchain can be used as a "world state machine" to execute smart contracts running on it, and through a distributed consensus algorithm Ensure data consistency on the blockchain. Blockchain technology can bring profound changes to various fields such as finance, economy, science and technology, and even government affairs [19].

2.2 Role-Based Access Control

Access control is a security technique that dictates who or what (i.e. subjects) can perform what operations on resources (i.e. objects) [20]. In traditional access control, there is a trusted central authority that manages user requests (see Fig. 1). There are a variety of access control mechanisms for different purposes. Role-based access control is a traditional access control model [21]. The basic idea is that various permissions for system operations are not directly granted to specific users, but are a role set is established between the user set and the permission set. Each role corresponds to a corresponding set of permissions. Once a user is assigned the appropriate role, the user has all the operational permissions for that role. The advantage of this is that it is not necessary to assign permissions every time a user is created, as long as the user is assigned the corresponding role, and the permissions of the role are changed much less than the permissions of the user. The scenario set in this paper is a social network. The access policy that users make for their uploaded resources has many similar permission settings. Generally, after we determine to use a social service, our permissions will not be updated frequently and the access time will be relatively long. For these reasons, this article chooses role-based access control (Fig. 2).

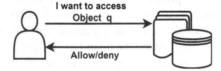

Fig. 1. Centralized systems

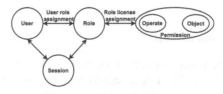

Fig. 2. Role-based access control

3 General Process and Design Model of Blockchain-Based Social Network Access Control Mechanism

Aiming at the problems of role-based access control in practical applications, this section proposes a blockchain-based access control mechanism. This mechanism deploys the access control strategy on the blockchain in the form of a smart contract, and evaluates the access request of the subject by executing the distributed smart contract on the blockchain, realizing the non-centralized access authorization management. At the same time, using the advantages of blockchain transparency and immutability, the access authorization process is recorded on the blockchain to achieve transparency and traceability of the access control process.

3.1 Procedure of Blockchain-Based Social Network Access Control

Taking the use of this solution in the social network blockchain as an example, the general process is shown in Fig. 3. According to different operations performed in the process, it assumes different identity roles. The same user can have different identities at the same time, for example, as the authorizer of his own information, the access initiator of access to other people's information. When the system authenticates everyone, the attributes of the company and a single user are different, and the operation of the system is the same. Blockchain and smart contracts, as carriers, have the ability to store announcement parameters, ciphertext, and perform basic queries and user registration. The specific process is as follows.

(1) Premise: All users or companies can obtain data on the blockchain, and publicly upload the public key generated by initialization, encrypted ciphertext, etc. to the blockchain.
(2) User registration on the blockchain: The user (including companies and other organizations) selects the global identification ID and performs initialization, selects the user attribute when performing authentication, and uploads the generated user or attribute to the chain.
(3) The user authorizes the personal information uploaded by himself: The user uploads data to the data server, and selects relative permissions, such as hobbies and reading, and eating habits are prohibited from viewing. The system provides several roles with assigned permissions, and users can also set permissions by themselves.
(4) Select the permission feature set by the user: When the number of users is large, the permission interaction between users will consume a lot, so the feature extraction of the permission settings made by the user is carried out. For example, a large number of users have set hobbies. Read, Eating Habits forbid to consult, make this encapsulation a character.
(5) User application role: Users with company attributes can apply to the system for roles or any other user to apply for operations. When applying for a role directly to the system, the system will initiate a vote on whether the user is willing to grant the operation authority corresponding to this role to the applicant.

(6) The role granted by the user: Users can judge whether the application (or vote) is approved by the applicant. If it is approved, the corresponding secret parameters are returned. The applicant calculates the attribute private key according to the secret parameters and saves it. If the vote is passed, the role will be added to the applicant's attributes.

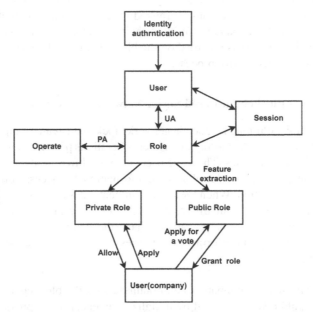

Fig. 3. Blockchain-based social network access control mechanism flowchart

3.2 Design Model of Social Network Access Control Based on Blockchain

The blockchain-based social network access control design model includes four stages: user authentication, uploading resources, access authorization, and access data acquisition (see Fig. 4). The first stage is user identity authentication. The main steps are as follows.

Step1. Before entering the blockchain, first perform identity authentication. The identity authentication of the blockchain itself is a pair of public and private keys. First, obtain the public and private keys, that is, the account password.

Step2. If there is only one pair of public and private keys for identity authentication, the authentication system is very thin. After obtaining the public and private keys, the user adds some attributes, including global identification ID, registered social platforms.

The second stage is uploading resources. The main steps are as follows.

Step3. The resource owner (user) uploads his own data to the data server, and the address where the data is stored on the chain.

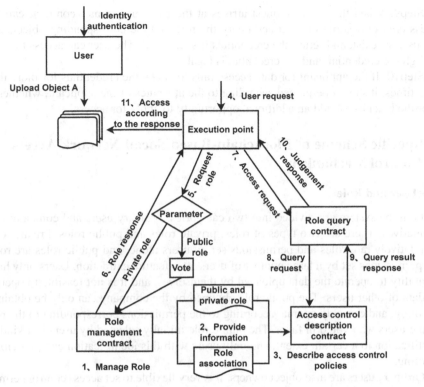

Fig. 4. Design model of social network access control mechanism based on blockchain

Step4. The resource owner sets permissions on the resource, generates an access policy, stores the access policy on the chain, and presents it in the form of a smart contract.

Step5. Perform feature extraction on the permissions written by users, and set the same permissions role for a large number of users to encapsulate it into a public role on the chain and write it into the role management contract.

The third stage is the access authorization stage, and the main steps are as follows.

Step6. When applying to access data, users with company attributes generate a role request, and the role request should have a judgment parameter. The role request arrives in the role management smart contract. If it is a role application for a large number of users, you can initiate an off-chain vote in the delegation system to obtain the public role on the chain, thereby obtaining the data access control authority for the relevant users. If it is a role application for a single user, the role is obtained through the session between users.

Step7. The role management contract responds to the role, and then generates an access request based on the role and role association.

Step8. If a malicious applicant is to be authenticated, the operation on the chain requires cost. This prevents malicious applicants from operating.

The fourth stage is the data access stage, and the main steps are as follows.

Step9. When the access request arrives at the role query smart contract, call the access control description contract, query the role and the corresponding objects and permissions exist, and return the credentials if successful. The user can access the data through the credential, and the credential is legal.

Step10. If the applicant for data access fails to check the credentials for more than three times, it should be judged according to the attributes of the applicant, whether to enter the blacklist or add an additional opportunity to apply for access.

4 Specific Scheme of Blockchain-Based Social Network Access Control Mechanism

4.1 User and Role

Users in the system are divided into two categories: ordinary users and company representatives. There are two types of roles: private roles and public roles. Private roles are relatively rare roles and permissions set by users alone, and public roles are roles and permissions set by a large number of users after feature extraction. Users only have the ability to operate the data uploaded by themselves, and it is not feasible to operate the data of other users. The public role obtained by the company can only be obtained by voting, and can only operate according to the permissions corresponding to the role for the users who voted in favor. The public role initially selected by users is a kind of identification to a certain extent, and only users with this identification can participate in voting.

Ordinary users are also object owners. It is very flexible to set access control permissions. Different from the pure role-based access control mechanism, although each user will generate more roles, they will be integrated at temporary role management points, and features The number of roles extracted and finally written into the role management contract is reasonable. As users continue to grow, subsequent users can continue to set arbitrary permissions, and at the same time, the system will also provide some roles that are more suitable for most people's habits (see Table 1).

Table 1. Initial roles

Role	Operate
A	View name, registered social platform
B	A + View basic info + View hobbies
C	B + Change the hobby + Change the registered platform
D	C + Change the address + Change the personal basic information

4.2 Upload Data

New users send transactions to the chain and call smart contracts on the chain. After user identity authentication, they can upload information to the data server, and the data server returns the address and summary to the user. In the process of uploading data, it is necessary to ensure that it is a legitimate user on the chain, and the data server will verify the user's identity. Only users who have completed the authentication can upload. Doing so can prevent other users from uploading a large amount of malicious data, causing the server to crash, or forging fake data. Figure 5 shows the specific operations of identity authentication and uploading data.

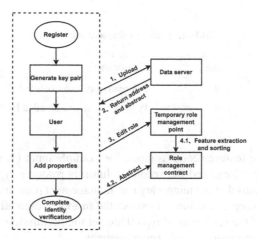

Fig. 5. Upload data flowchart

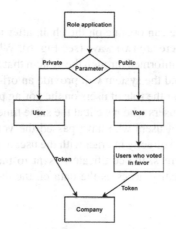

Fig. 6. Role application flowchart

4.3 The Public Role of Feature Extraction

When users set permissions for the information data uploaded by themselves, if they are directly uploaded to the chain, a large amount of access data and response data will be generated on the chain. Therefore, a temporary role management point is set up, and some access features can be extracted according to the necessary elements of the set permissions, and then written into the role management contract. For example, a large number of users have set hobbies to read, and eating habits are prohibited from viewing, making this package a role. Some noteworthy features are listed in this paper, which is certainly not limited to those listed in this paper. The feature extraction in this paper is mainly to solve the problem of system crash caused by too many characters (see Table 2).

Table 2. Feature value and meaning

Feature	Value	Significance
Operate	1–9	1–3 readable, 4–6 executed, 7–9 writable
Resource type	1–9	Type of resource uploaded by the user

Taking the above feature vector as input, for example input (1, 9), the first column is readable by permissions, and the second column is resource type 9. Convert each permission setting record of the temporary role management point into the above vector, and the result of feature extraction is to select the most representative vectors, such as (1,9), a large part of the resources of type 9 are set the permissions are all 1 readable, convert it to a role, and write the role smart contract.

4.4 Role Application

The company representative can operate on the chain after identity verification. When the company needs data, there are two ways (see Fig. 6). When a large amount of user data is needed, users can be informed through the system that an existing company needs data from multiple users, and the system will provide an off-chain platform for voting. Company users can apply for the role of users on the voting platform. Behind each role, there are a large number of users who have it at the same time. After obtaining this role, they can operate the data of users who have passed the vote. Another way to obtain permission for user data is to directly interact with the user and initiate a role application for the user. If the user agrees, the certificate is sent to the company representative, and the company representative accesses the data on the data server according to the certificate.

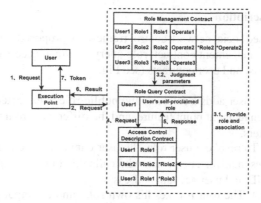

Fig. 7. Main contract

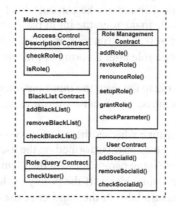

Fig. 8. Functions in smart contracts

5 Realization of Social Network Access Control Based on Smart Contracts

The blockchain-based social network control architecture proposed in this paper is mainly implemented by three smart contracts: role management contract, role query contract, and access control description contract (see Fig. 7). The role management contract defines all roles and their corresponding permissions required for system access control. These roles or permissions are extracted from temporary role points and private to users. As shown in the figure above, in the role management smart contract, the roles and permissions marked with * are private to the user. When the access request arrives at the role query contract, the access control contract is called for other contract to check whether the user's self-proclaimed role or permission is true. The content of the access control description contract is provided by the role management contract.

5.1 Contract Description

The blockchain-based social network control framework proposed in this paper is mainly composed of role management contract, role query contract, access control description contract, and blacklist and user contracts (see Fig. 8).

1. addRole(). The user adds a role, and the public role is extracted through the temporary role management point feature, and the difference from the private role lies in the parameters.
2. revokeRole(). To revoke a user role, the user cannot revoke the public role of the company representative. The person who calls this function is the role owner, just enter the role ID and user account address.
3. renounceRole(). The user revokes his own role, and the input parameters are the role identifier and the user account address. The function requires that the caller must be the same as the input user account address. If the user's identity is stolen or encounters some critical situations, he can call this function to revoke his role.
4. setupRole(). Grant the role to the user, the input parameters are the role's identifier and the user account address. This function is called when the company representative is granted the public role after a voting application is made by the company representative.
5. grantRole(). Grant the role to the user, the input parameters are the role's identifier and the user account address. The function requires the caller to be the owner of the private role.
6. checkParameter(). Determine whether the role is private or public.
7. checkUser(). A policy evaluation is performed on the user to check whether the user has the role he claims, the input parameters are the identifier of the role claimed by the user and the user account address. If the policy evaluation is successful, it will return true, otherwise, return false. If the number of user failures is equal to 3, first call the user smart contract to query the user's attribute completeness. Users with low identity attribute completeness are directly added to the blacklist.
8. checkRole(). This function is used to verify that the role and user are the same, the input is the role identifier and the address of the user account.
9. isRole(). Verify whether the role exists, the input is the identifier of the role.
10. addBlackList(). This function is called when the access policy evaluation fails, and the user is added to the blacklist.
11. removeBlackList(). Remove user from blacklist.
12. checkBlackList(). To determine whether it is a user in the blacklist, enter the user account.
13. addSocialid(). When users improve their identity system, they add existing social IDs, and after voting for company representatives, add the company's ID.
14. removeSoicalid(). When the user deletes the social ID, the corresponding company will no longer have the permission to operate the user's data.
15. checkSocialid(). To query the user's social ID, enter the user account.

5.2 Access Control Algorithm

Algorithm 1 (see Fig. 9) is an algorithm for access control, the algorithm receives the user account address and role identifier, and returns the access result.

Input: bytes32 role,address account;Output: bytes32 role,address account
if user want to access data
    if isBlackList() → false
        access directly.
        if the number to access ≤ 2
            if checkUser() → true (1)
                give this user the data's address and token
                addSocialid(the social software)
            else
                ++ the number to access
            end if
        else if the number to access = 3
            if checkSocialid() → true
                goto (1)
            else
                addBlackList(the user's account)
            end if
        else
            end the access
        end if
    else
        end the access
end if

Fig. 9. Algorithm 1

6   Verification of Social Network Access Control Mechanism Scheme Based on Blockchain

6.1   Experimental Environment

This paper uses the Ethereum platform to implement the access control framework proposed in this paper. Ethereum is an open blockchain platform that allows the deployment of smart contracts. The language of smart contracts is solidity. There are many tools for deploying smart contracts in Ethereum. This article chooses Hardhat, which is a development environment for compiling, deploying, testing and debugging Ethereum applications. Hardhat has the Hardhat network built into it, a native Ethereum network designed for development. It allows you to deploy contracts, run tests and debug code. According to the description in this article, those who have Hardhat network accounts can be regarded as the users proposed in this article. Using a laptop, where users upload data to a database, multiple Hardhat accounts represent developers, users, and company representatives.

6.2 Experimental Details

Based on the access control mechanism of the smart contract, the test plan mainly calls the method in the smart contract, and other logical problems can be realized in the front end.

Call the function grantRole(), enter the ID of the role bytes32, the parameters to determine whether the role is public or private, and the address of the authorized user 0x976ea74026e726554db657fa54763abd0c3a0aa9, the result is shown in Fig. 10.

Fig. 10. Result of calling grantRole()

Call the function checkUser() to determine whether the user's role is consistent with its own identity, and return true, otherwise it returns false. Enter an unauthorized address 0x3c44cdddb6a900fa2b585dd299e03d12fa4293bc, checkUser() returns false (see Fig. 11).

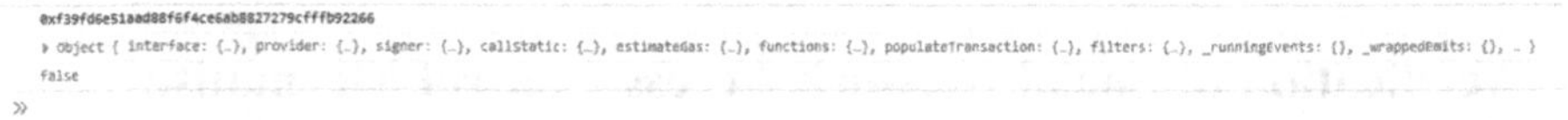

Fig. 11. Result of calling checkUser() when the address is not authorized

Call the function addBlackLlist() to add illegal users to the blacklist, enter 0x15d34aaf54267db7d7c367839aaf71a00a2c6a65.

Call the function checkBlackList() to determine whether the user is in the blacklist, and return true if the user is in the blacklist, enter address 0x15d34aaf54267db7d7c367839aaf71a00a2c6a65.

Call the function addSocialid(), users who agree to authorize private data to the company are added with this company ID.

The specific data of the test smart contract is shown in Table 3:

Table 3. Smart contract function test data

Serial number	Function	Input	Output
1	grantRole()	Role: the ID of the role bytes32 User: 0x976ea74026e726554db657fa54763abd0c3a0aa9 Parameter: true	A successful transaction
2	addBlackList()	User: 0x15d34aaf54267db7d7c367839aaf71a00a2c6a65	A successful transaction
3	addSocialid()	User: 0x976ea74026e726554db657fa54763abd0c3a0aa9 company ID: 3001	A successful transaction
4	addRole()	Role: the ID of the role bytes32 Parameter: true	A successful transaction
5	revokeRole()	Role: the ID of the role bytes32 User: 0x976ea74026e726554db657fa54763abd0c3a0aa9	True
6	checkUser()	User: 0x3c44cdddb6a900fa2b585dd299e03d12fa4293bc	False (unauthorized)
		User: 0x976ea74026e726554db657fa54763abd0c3a0aa9	True (authorized)
7	checkBlackList()	User: 0x15d34aaf54267db7d7c367839aaf71a00a2c6a65	True

6.3 Interpretation of Result

It is analyzed from two aspects, one is the cost problem, and the other is the time-consuming problem. GAS is the fee a sender must pay when submitting a transaction to the Ethereum network. The fee mentioned in this section is the cost of sending a contract's transaction to the Ethereum blockchain (i.e. transaction cost). This paper and experiments are based on the Hardhat network, which is the test network of Ethereum. The cost of calling functions (grantRole(), addBlackList(), addSocialid(), addRole(), revokeRole(), checkUser() and checkBlackList()) is as follows shown in Table 4. On the private chain, these operations are free, and the costs on different chains are inconsistent.

As can be seen from Table 4, the cost of common function calls is within the acceptable range. Since the experiments in this paper are built in the Ethereum tool Hardhat, the costs here are not incurred in the production environment. Nonetheless, the data presented here are valuable for demonstrating the mechanism proposed in this paper.

Table 4. The cost of calling function

Serial number	Function	Gas
1	grantRole()	0.00003649ETH
2	addBlackList()	0.00004744ETH
3	addSocialid()	0.00008211ETH
4	addRole()	0.00004078ETH
5	revokeRole()	0.00003268ETH
6	checkUser()	0
7	checkBlackList()	0

In terms of time-consuming, the process of completing the entire access control process is a combination of operations both on-chain and off-chain. The time consumed by these operations needs to be viewed from different dimensions. In the off-chain process, feature extraction is to extract the largest features of user permissions from temporary management points and generate roles. The quality of the feature extraction algorithm and the number of users are directly related to the time of role generation. This can set a processing interval for temporary management points in the system. In actual scenarios, when we register a social application, we need to fill in a series of messages and verify the mobile phone number to complete the registration. Some social applications even require many steps to complete the identity information. Although the scheme extracted in this paper takes some time (acceptable level) before the role is generated, registration will become very convenient for a large number of social applications after the role is generated. There is also a voting link under the chain, which is also an authorization process. This solution is to facilitate the authorization of social service providers (companies) and multiple users. The time-consuming of uploading off-chain data to the chain, writing roles and querying strategies through smart contracts, the time-consuming here is related to the consensus algorithm of the blockchain, the synchronization between blocks, and the on-chain and off-chain interactions.

As can be seen from Fig. 12, these functions do not take much time, and the policy judgment function checkUser() takes 131 ms, which is acceptable for the scenario proposed in this paper. It can be concluded that the blockchain-based access mechanism proposed in this paper is feasible in terms of cost and time-consuming, and also solves the problem of user information centralization.

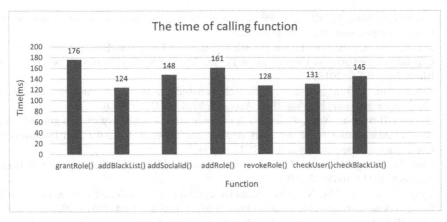

Fig. 12. The time of calling function

7 Conclusion

This paper adopts blockchain-based role access and proposes a blockchain-based social network access mechanism. The main features of this framework are uploading a large number of users' private data, feature extraction when setting role permissions, and voting when applying for roles. In order to verify the feasibility of this scheme, tests and analysis are carried out in the Hardhat network, and the results confirm that this scheme can become the future development direction of social networks. In addition to further improving and perfecting the scheme proposed in this paper, issues such as data upload speed, security, performance, and more complex scenarios should also be considered. This is the next step.

Acknowledgement. This work was supported by National Natural Science Foundation of China (No. 61862007, No. 61866003).

References

1. Rosic, D., Novak, U., Vukmirovic, S.: Role-based access control model supporting regional division in smart grid system. In: 2013 Fifth International Conference on Computational Intelligence, Communication Systems and Networks, pp. 197–201 (2013). https://doi.org/10.1109/CICSYN.2013.59
2. Figueroa-Lorenzo, S., Añorga, J., Arrizabalaga, S.: A role-based access control model in modbus SCADA systems. A centralized model approach. Sens. (Basel) **19**(20), 4455 (2019)
3. Nakamoto, S.: Bitcoin: a peer-to-peer electronic cash system. Decent. Bus. Rev., 21260 (2008)
4. Larrucea, X., Pautasso, C.: Blockchain and smart contract engineering. IEEE Softw. **37**(5), 23–29 (2020)
5. Ali, G., et al.: xDBAuth: blockchain based cross domain authentication and authorization framework for Internet of Things. IEEE Access **8**, 58800–58816 (2020). https://doi.org/10.1109/ACCESS.2020.2982542

6. Shafeeq, S., Alam, M., Khan, A.: Privacy aware decentralized access control system. Future Gener. Comput. Syst. **101**, 420–433 (2019)

7. Xu, R., Yu, C., Blasch, E., et al.: BlendCAC: a BLockchain-ENabled Decentralized Capability-based Access Control for IoTs. In: The 2018 IEEE Internal Conference on Blockchain. IEEE (2018)

8. Tan, L., Shi, N., Yang, C., et al.: A blockchain-based access control framework for cyber-physical-social system big data. IEEE Access **8**, 77215–77226 (2020)

9. Qin, X., Huang, Y., Yang, Z., et al.: An access control scheme with fine-grained time constrained attributes based on smart contract and trapdoor. In: 2019 26th International Conference on Telecommunications (ICT) (2019)

10. Zhou, Q., Huang, H., Zheng, Z., et al.: Solutions to scalability of blockchain: a survey. IEEE Access **8**, 16440–16455 (2020)

11. Yang, C., Tan, L., Shi, N., et al.: AuthPrivacyChain: a blockchain-based access control framework with privacy protection in cloud. IEEE Access **8**, 70604–70615 (2020)

12. Chiu, W.Y., Meng, W., Jensen, C.D.: My data, my control: a secure data sharing and access scheme over blockchain. J. Inf. Secur. Appl. **63**, 103020 (2021)

13. Ghaffari, F., Bertin, E., Crespi, N., et al.: A novel access control method via smart contracts for internet-based service provisioning. IEEE Access **9**, 81253–81273 (2021)

14. Liu, A., Du, X., Wang, N., Li, S.: Big data access control mechanism based on blockchain. J. Softw. **30**(09), 2636–2654 (2019)

15. Guo, X., Wang, Y., Feng, T., Cao, L., Jiang, Y., Zhang, D.: A role delegation access control mechanism for industrial control system based on blockchain. Comput. Sci. **48**(09), 306–316 (2021)

16. Huang, M., Ou, B., He, S.: An access control method based on feature extraction. Comput. Sci. **46**(02), 109–114 (2019)

17. Zhu, J., Gao, S., Duan, M., et al.: Blockchain Technology and Application. Machinery Industry Society, Beijing (2018)

18. Zyskind, G., Nathan, O.: Decentralizing privacy: using blockchain to protect personal data. In: 2015 IEEE Security and Privacy Workshops, pp. 180–184. IEEE (2015)

19. Wang, C., Cheng, J., Sang, X., et al.: Blockchain data privacy protection: research status and prospects. Comput. Res. Dev. **58**(10), 21 (2021)

20. Ferraiolo, D., Chandramouli, R., Kuhn, D.R., et al.: Role-Based Access Control, 2nd edn. Artech House, Inc., Norwood (2007)

21. Xiong, H., Chen, X., Zhang, B., Du, X.: Scalable access control model based on two-layer roles and organizations. J. Electron. Inf. **37**(07), 1612–1619 (2015)

Latency Analysis for Raft Consensus on Hyperledger Fabric

Xuefeng Piao[1], Mingxin Li[1], Fanchao Meng[1(✉)], and Huihui Song[2]

[1] School of Computer Science and Engineering, Harbin Institute of Technology,
Weihai 264209, China
{hbpark,fcmeng}@hit.edu.cn, 181110506@stu.hit.edu.cn
[2] School of New Energy, Harbin Institute of Technology, Weihai 264209, China
songhh@hitwh.edu.cn

Abstract. As a permissioned blockchain system, Hyperledger Fabric is getting increasing attention from enterprises, however, the current Hyperledger Fabric system is difficult to meet the real-time application requirements of enterprises. This paper focus on the Raft consensus latency that is time consumption of consensus, we provide a theoretical model of the Raft consensus latency. Subsequently, we analyze the effect of consensus latency on the transaction latency and the effect of a block size on consensus latency by extensive experiments. The experimental result shows that the proportion of consensus latency in the entire transaction latency is relatively small, while the block size has more greater effect on the consensus latency.

Keywords: Blockchain · Raft consensus · Consensus latency · Transaction latency · Hyperledger fabric

1 Introduction

Blockchain is a distributed ledger technology in the form of a distributed transactional database, which consists of a chain of data blocks that contains hashed information about a set of transactions. Due to the decentralization, immutability, transparency and auditability features, the blockchain technology can be applied to many fields such as financial services, social services, healthcare facilities and electrical power systems.

The blockchain system can be categorized as permissionless blockchain and permissioned blockchain according to access rights [1]. In the permissionless blockchain systems such as Bitcoin and Ethereum, any node can participate in the process of consensus without any specific identity, it has complexity in reaching consensus among participants [2]. On the contrary, in the permissioned blockchain systems such as Hyperledger Fabric, only authenticated node can participate in the process of consensus, it enforce strict membership. Therefore, different consensus algorithms are used for different blockchain systems in order to reach consensus more efficiently. For example, the Bitcoin system employs the

D. Svetinovic et al. (Eds.): BlockSys 2022, CCIS 1679, pp. 165–176, 2022.
https://doi.org/10.1007/978-981-19-8043-5_12

PoW consensus algorithm [3] and the Hyperledger Fabric system employs the Raft consensus algorithm [2].

Furthermore, the time taken to reach consensus in the system of permissionless blockchain is longer than that of permissioned blockchain since tampering with data should be prevented from malicious nodes in the permissionless blockchain systems. Obviously, relative to the permissionless blockchain, the permissioned blockchain is generally more suitable for enterprise applications, where a group of companies collaborate to use the blockchain technology to share data and improve business processes. However, most of permissioned blockchain systems cannot be meet the real-time requirement of the latency sensitive applications. For example, in smart grids, the entire system is a real-time network that requires timely relaying of messages and quick response to large amounts of data, otherwise the system may collapse resulting in considerable damage [4].

The Hyperledger Fabric is one of the most popular permissioned blockchain system, its performance is gradually recognized by the industry [5]. The system network consists of three types of nodes including peer nodes, ordering nodes and client nodes, and may have multiple blockchains by multiple channels. A peer node can maintain a replicated blockchain and a current world state for each channel, be responsible to endorse transaction, execute chaincode, validate and commit block. Where the endorsing peer nodes simulate execution of transaction and send back a result to the client node. The ordering nodes are responsible to establish an order for the transactions and package the transactions to a block according to certain rules.

When each endorsing peer node receives a transaction request from a client node, the endorsing peer node simulates processing the transaction request based on the own state database and sends back its endorsement result to client node. After the client has gathered enough endorsements, the client submits the transaction with its endorsements to the ordering node. The ordering node receives transactions containing endorsed transaction responses from many clients, orders the transactions into blocks and distributes to all peer nodes on the channel. Each peer node verifies the transactions in the block and commits them to the ledger independently, but the process is guaranteed to be identical to every other peer node on the channel use consensus algorithms such as Solo, Kafka and Raft consensus algorithms. It is worth mentioning that a good consensus algorithm is very important to the stable and efficient operation of a blockchain system [6].

This paper focus on the Raft consensus in Hyperledger Fabric, with the aim of providing a better reference and more rigorous analysis for designers in production environment, our contributions are as follows: (1) We provide a theoretical model for latency of the Raft consensus by analyzing the process of the ordering service. (2) We conduct a series of experiments to analyze the consensus process of Raft in Hyperledger Fabric.

The rest of this paper is organized as follows. Section 2 surveys some related work and Sect. 3 present a theoretical modeling of the Raft consensus in the Hyperledger Fabric system. The experimental results and analysis is provided in Sect. 4, and we conclude our work in Sect. 5.

2   Related Work

On performance evaluation, most researches presented performance metrics by modeling transaction flow in blockchain systems. Wai et al. [7] presented the performance metrics for ordering service in Hyperledger Fabric by using an M/D/1 queueing model therefore the number of orderer nodes can be decided based on the proposed model in real systems. Meng et al. [8] proposed an analytical framework for consortium blockchain consistency using a queuing network model. The framework can evaluate the performance of three phases in blockchain consensus, including execution phase, ordering phase and validation phase. They argued that the ordering phase can be modeled as an M/M/1 queue node, whether applied consensus algorithm is the Solo, Raft or Kafka algorithms. Xu et al. [9] proposed a novel theoretical model to calculate transaction latency for the Hyperledger Fabric system. They indicated that configuration parameters have a significant impact on the transaction latency of three phases, especially for the ordering phase. They performed a quantitative latency analysis for the Solo and PBFT consensus algorithms, and argued that the ordering service is a performance bottleneck in the Hyperledger Fabric system.

Moreover, stochastic petri net based approaches are also proposed. Sukhwani et al. [10] proposed a performance model for the Hyperledger Fabric v1.0 by using stochastic reward net to compute throughput, utilization and mean queue length at various peers. They indicated that the endorsement policy and the number of peers have a significant impact on transaction latency in endorsing phase. The performance bottleneck of ordering service and ledger write can be mitigated using a larger block size albeit with increase in latency, latency of validation check using VSCC can be mitigated by parallel computing in committing phase. Yuan et al. [11] proposed a performance model for the Hyperledger Fabric v1.2 by using generalized stochastic petri nets. They indicated performance bottleneck for the different configurations of ordering service and proposed a configuration selection approach to determine configuration parameters in order to achieve the maximum throughput.

In addition, Thakkar et al. [12] conducted a comprehensive empirical study for the Hyperledger Fabric system by varying the configuration parameters, such as block size, endorsement policy, channel, resource allocation, and state database. As a result of the study, endorsement policy verification, sequential policy validation, state validation and commit are the three major bottlenecks in the system. Furthermore, optimized approaches are proposed in order to resolve the bottleneck problem. Wang et al. [13] studied the performance characteristics of execution phase, ordering phase and validation phase while they conducted a performance comparison between the Solo, Kafaka and Raft consensus algorithm. They found that the execution phase exhibited a good scalability under the OR endorsement policy but not with the AND endorsement policy, and there are no significant performance difference between the three consensus algorithms.

On consensus algorithm, there are some researches since the consensus process is an import link in transaction process and bring a significant impact on blockchain system [14]. Sukhwani et al. [15] modeled the PBFT consensus process by using stochastic reward nets to get the mean time to complete consensus, and indicated that the PBFT could be a performance bottleneck for networks with the large number of peer nodes. Huang et al. [16] studied the performance of the Raft consensus algorithm in networks with non-negligible packet loss rate. They concentrated on analyzing the network split probability of the Raft, and presented the network split probability as a function of the network size, the packet loss rate, and the election timeout period. Hao et al. [17] proposed a method to evaluate the performance of consensus algorithm in private blockchain platforms. By extensive experiments and analysis, they presented that consensus mechanism may induce performance bottleneck, and indicated the PBFT outperforms the PoW in terms of latency and throughput under the varying workloads.

On the other hand, some researches proposed novel consensus mechanisms to improve performance. Wang et al. [18] proposed a Kademlia-Raft which is Raft-like consensus algorithm with high throughput and high scalability. It optimized leader election and consensus process in the Raft algorithm by using Kbucket formed in the Kademlia protocol. They demonstrated the proposed consensus algorithm has better performance in transaction throughput than the Raft consensus algorithm by simulation. Fu et al. [19] proposed an AdRaft consensus algorithm that optimized the Raft consensus algorithm in terms of log replication and leader election. Improvement of the log replication is achieved by reducing communication complexity of leader node, and improvement of the leader election is achieved by changing vote affiliation of peer node.

3   Theoretical Modeling

In this section, we theoretically model the time taken by Raft consensus algorithm to reach consensus among ordering nodes in the Hyperledger Fabric system. For this purpose, size of a transaction block was analyzed, since a consensus is reached between orderers with a block as the basic unit, and we derived the time taken to reach consensus for a transaction block. For the modeling methods for block size and Raft consensus latency, we reference the analytical latency model proposed by Xu et al. [9].

3.1   A Transaction Block Size Modeling

Throughout a transaction process, a client generates a transaction request when enough endorsements are collected, which is then broadcast into blockchain network. A transaction request contains information including a transaction proposal, multiple endorsements from endorsing nodes, and a client signature. The client can construct a valid transaction request if the number of collected endorsement is more than the minimum number of endorsements required which is defined in endorsement policy. It is assumed that N^e number of endorsements are collected by a client, the packet size of a transaction proposal is α bits, the packet size of an endorsement is β bits, and the size of a signature is γ bits, then the packet size of a transaction request can be represented as $\alpha + N^e \cdot \beta + \gamma$ [9].

In the Raft consensus, multiple ordering nodes are cooperated to reach a consensus, in which one node is a leader and other nodes are followers, and all transaction requests will be handed over to the leader ultimately. When the leader receives the transaction requests from clients, it constructs these transactions as a transaction block only if one of the following conditions is met [9]. A newly constructed block containing several transaction requests will be recognized by consensus among the ordering nodes.

(1) The number of pending transaction(waiting to construct into a block) reaches the maximum block size which is permitted in the system.
(2) The waiting time interval from the last block was constructed to reaching the maximum waiting time which is permitted in the system.

The permitted maximum number of transactions in a block is defined as a channel configuration parameter `BatchSize`, and the permitted maximum waiting time is defined as a channel configuration parameter `BatchTimeout` respectively. A transaction block will be constructed when either the `BatchSize` or the `BatchTimeout` is reached earlier. We denote the number of transaction requests reach the maximum block size by $N^b_{\max}$, and denote the permitted maximum waiting time by $N^t_{\max}$. It is assumed that the arrival process of transaction requests follows a Poisson process, which means the arrival interval follows negative exponential distribution, and the average transaction arrival rate is λ [9]. Then the actual number of transaction requests is $\lambda \cdot N^t_{\max}$ when the above condition (1) is satisfied, or is $N^b_{\max}$ when the above condition (2) is satisfied. Combining Xu et al. [9] and our analysis, the actual number of transaction request, denoted by N^b, as the following Eq. (1).

$$N^b = \max\{N^b_{\max}, \ \lambda \cdot N^t_{\max}\} \tag{1}$$

Meanwhile, the packet size of a transaction block, denoted by S_{block}, can be derived as the following Eq. (2).

$$S_{block} = \max\{N^b_{\max}, \ \lambda \cdot N^t_{\max}\} \cdot (\alpha + N^e \cdot \beta + \gamma) \tag{2}$$

3.2   Raft Consensus Latency Modeling

Raft consensus works on the basis of leader-follower protocol [20]. As mentioned above, a cluster consensus service consists of one leader and multiple followers. They maintains the replication via `AppendEntries` message, and the empty `AppendEntries` message is used for the heartbeat. Notice that, a transaction block is in uncommitted state at the beginning of consensus. When the leader completes construction of a transaction block, it sends an `AppendEntries` request message with the block to the followers, the follower will then use an `AppendEntries` reply message to give a feedback to the leader as shown in the following Fig. 1.

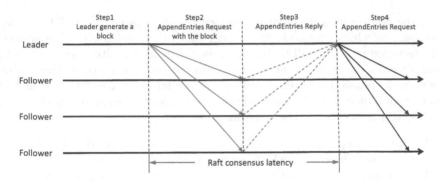

Fig. 1. `AppendEntries` message interaction flow.

The block state of leader will be updated to be committed when the received confirmation responses is more than half of the number of followers. For the block state of the followers, it will be updated to be committed when it receives the next heartbeat from the leader.

For theoretical analysis, it is assumed that the bottleneck link bandwidth of blockchain network is B, the average propagation delay is D, the size of data other than block in `AppendEntries` request is $S_{request}$, and the packet size of `AppendEntries` reply is S_{reply}. Then, the latency of `AppendEntries` request, denoted by $L_{request}$, can be derived as the following Eq. (3) from the Eq. (2).

$$L_{request} = \frac{\max\{N_{max}^b, \ \lambda \cdot N_{max}^t\} \cdot (\alpha + N^e \cdot \beta + \gamma) + S_{request}}{B} + D \quad (3)$$

And, the latency of `AppendEntries` reply, denoted by L_{reply}, can be defined as the following Eq.(4).

$$L_{reply} = \frac{S_{reply}}{B} + D \quad (4)$$

It is clear that the latency to reach consensus for a block, i.e., the consensus latency, denoted by L, can be represented as $L = L_{request} + L_{reply}$ therefore we can obtain the following Eq. (5).

$$L = \frac{\max\{N_{max}^b, \ \lambda \cdot N_{max}^t\} \cdot (\alpha + N^e \cdot \beta + \gamma) + S_{request} + S_{reply}}{B} + 2D \quad (5)$$

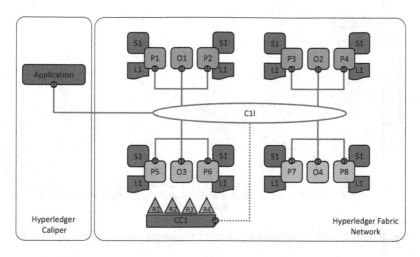

Fig. 2. Network topology of our simulation.

4 Experiments and Analysis

Our experiment was conducted on the Hyperledger Fabric v2.0 system. To evaluate the performance of Raft consensus, we deployed a single channel fabric network on 4 physical servers in an isolated LAN with 1,000 MB/s network bandwidth. The hardware configuration of each server is 2.2 GHz 4-Core CPU, 32 GB main memory, and 500 GB magnetic disk, and each server is installed Ubuntu Linux 16.04 64 bits operating system. We simulated two peers belonging to the same organization with an orderer on each server using docker container as shown in Fig. 2.

In our experiments, the time interval from the time point a leader node sends out a `Append-Entries` request to it receives the corresponding `AppendEntries` reply from majority of followers is regarded as the consensus latency. The sum of time consumption in the three phases including execution phase, ordering phase and validation phase is regarded as the transaction latency. The time consumption of execution phase is the time interval from the time point the client node sends a transaction request to the endorsing node to the time point it sends the transaction to the ordering service. The time consumption of ordering phase is the time interval from the time point the ordering node received a transaction from client node to the time point the peer node received the block. The time consumption of validation phase is the time taken to validate transactions and commit transactions and block on peer nodes. It should be noted that the transaction latency in our experiment is less than the latency of a transaction which is observed from the client side since each record of time consumption is conducted on the corresponding node.

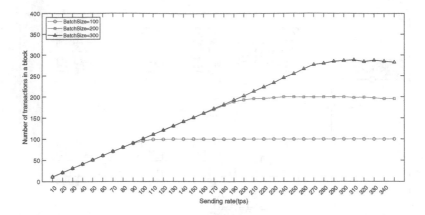

Fig. 3. Relationship between number of transactions and the sending rate.

We wrote a script program based on the Hyperledger Caliper [21] to send transaction requests to the fabric network which follows the Poisson process according to the set time series. The Hyperledger Caliper is open source benchmarking tool of blockchain performance evaluation. In our experiment, the configuration parameter `BatchSize` is set to 100, 200, and 300 respectively. The configuration parameter `BatchTimeout` is set to 1 second. The sending rate ranges from 10 tps(transactions per second) to 350 tps with a 10 tps interval. Notice that, a block cannot be constructed within 1 second. In other words, if the sending rate is less than the `BatchSize`, the construction of a block have to wait the `BatchTimeout` according to the Eq. 2.

Figure 3 shows the relationship between the number of transactions in a block and the sending rate when the `BatchTimeout` is 1 second in our experiment environment. For the case the `BatchSize` is 100, from the point that the sending rate reaches 100, the number of transactions in a block is fixed to 100 since the sending rate is larger than the `BatchSize`. In the same way, the fixed point is 200 and 300 for the cases `BatchSize` = 200 and `BatchSize` = 300 respectively.

The experiments were performed for the different batch size mentioned above with increasing the sending rate of transaction request from a client node in the same local network. Figure 4 shows the experimental result of the Raft consensus latency that the higher transaction sending rate has the longer consensus latency on all the case of batch size because as the sending rate increases the size of a block also increase. However, it's worth noting that the increasing of consensus latency is modest when the sending rate ranges from about 100 tps to 200 tps with the batch size is 100, and from the start of the sending rate reaches 200 tps, the consensus latency still increases substantially as the sending rate increase regardless of the batch size, but the curve grows relatively flat compared to the other two. The increasing of consensus latency with batch size is 200 is also slower than that with batch size is 300 after the sending rate exceeds 200 tps. Figure 5 shows the experimental results of the transaction latency that the higher transaction sending rate has the longer transaction latency for the cases the batch size is 300, but for the case the batch size is 100 and 200, the transaction latency decreases as the sending rate increases within a certain range.

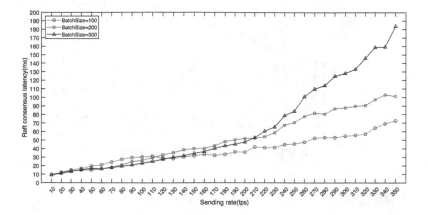

Fig. 4. Raft consensus latency.

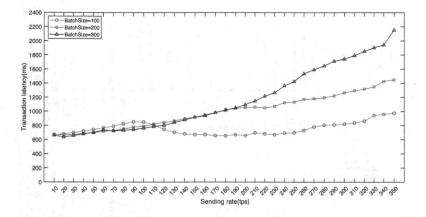

Fig. 5. Transaction latency.

For convenience of analysis, we combine the experimental results of Raft consensus latency and that of transaction latency together as shown in Fig. 6. The transaction latency is an order of magnitude larger compared with the consensus latency, as well as the consensus latency accounted for less than 10% of the overall transaction latency. This indicates that the Raft consensus latency has a small proportion of the transaction latency, such that the impact of Raft consensus algorithm on the performance of transaction processing is not much. However, we found that the proportion of consensus latency in transaction latency increases as the sending rate increases, regardless of whether the overall transaction latency increases or decreases when the sending rate ranges from 10 tps to about 250 tps.

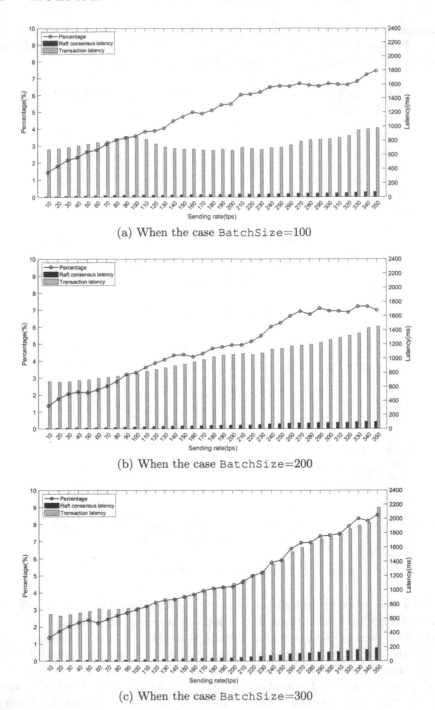

(a) When the case BatchSize=100

(b) When the case BatchSize=200

(c) When the case BatchSize=300

Fig. 6. The ratio of consensus latency to transaction latency for the cases that the BatchSize is 100, 200, 300 respectively.

The obvious reason is that the `AppendEntries` message exchanged during the consensus process contains a transaction block, and the larger block size takes the longer time to reach consensus. As a result, we can determine that the sending rate is a factor that affects the performance of Raft consensus, i.e., the block size is an important impact factor for the consensus latency.

5   Conclusion

This paper studied the latency performance of Raft consensus on the Hyperledger Fabric. We presented a theoretical model of consensus latency by analyzing the process of ordering service using the Raft consensus. The experiments were conducted on the Hyperledger Fabric v2.0 network deployed in our university cloud platform. The results shows that the Raft consensus latency is much lower compared to transaction latency, although as the sending rate increases, the proportion of Raft consensus latency tends to increase. Furthermore, it is determined that as one of configuration parameters in blockchain that directly affect the consensus latency, the size of a block results in the longer Raft consensus latency.

Acknowledgments. This work was supported by the Natural Science Foundation of Shandong Province in China under grant ZR2020MF032.

References

1. Zheng, Z., Xie, S., Dai, H.N., Chen, X., Wang, H.: Blockchain challenges and opportunities: a survey. Int. J. WebGrid Serv. **14**(4), 352–375 (2018)
2. Hyperledger fabric (2020). https://hyperledger-fabric.readthedocs.io/
3. Nakamoto, S.: Bitcoin: a peer-to-peer electronic cash system. Decentralized Business Review, p. 21260 (2008)
4. Khan, M.W., Zeeshan, M., Farid, A., Usman, M.: Qos-aware traffic scheduling framework in cognitive radio based smart grids using multi-objective optimization of latency and throughput. Ad Hoc Networks **97**(2), 102020 (2020)
5. Zhou, E., Sun, H., Pi, B., Sun, J., Yamashita, K., Nomura, Y.: Ledgerdata refiner: a powerful ledger data query platform for hyperledger fabric. In: 6th International Conference on Internet of Things: Systems. Management and Security (IOTSMS), pp. 433–440. IEEE, Granada, Spain (2019)
6. Javaid, H., et al.: Blockchain machine: a network-attached hardware accelerator for hyperledger fabric. Distributed, Parallel, and Cluster Computing, CoRR arXiv:2104.06968 (2021)
7. Su Wai, K.S., Htoon, E.C., Myint Thein, N.N.: Performance evaluation of m/d/1 queuing model on hyperledger fabric. In: International Conference on Advanced Information Technologies (ICAIT), pp. 36–41. IEEE, Yangon, Myanmar (2020)
8. Meng, T., Zhao, Y., Wolter, K., Xu, C.Z.: On consortium blockchain consistency: a queueing network model approach. IEEE Trans. Parallel Distrib. Syst. **32**(6), 1369–1382 (2021)
9. Xu, X., Sun, G., Luo, L., Cao, H., Yu, H., Vasilakos, A.V.: Latency performance modeling and analysis for hyperledger fabric blockchain network. Inform. Process. Manage. **58**(1), 102436 (2021)

10. Sukhwani, H., Wang, N., Trivedi, K.S., Rindos, A.: Performance modeling of hyperledger fabric (permissioned blockchain network). In: 17th International Symposium on Network Computing and Applications (NCA), p. 8548070. IEEE, Cambridge, MA, United states (2018)
11. Yuan, P., Zheng, K., Xiong, X., Zhang, K., Lei, L.: Performance modeling and analysis of a hyperledger-based system using GSPN. Comput. Commun. **153**(3), 117–124 (2020)
12. Thakkar, P., Nathan, S., Viswanathan, B.: Performance benchmarking and optimizing hyperledger fabric blockchain platform. In: 26th International Symposium on Modeling. Analysis, and Simulation of Computer and Telecommunication Systems (MASCOTS), pp. 264–276. IEEE, Milwaukee, Wisconsin (2018)
13. Wang, C., Chu, X.: Performance characterization and bottleneck analysis of hyperledger fabric. In: 40th International Conference on Distributed Computing Systems (ICDCS), pp. 1281–1286. IEEE, Singapore (2020)
14. Du, M.: Ma, X, Zhang, Z., Wang, X., Chen, Q.: A review on consensus algorithm of blockchain. In: International Conference on Systems. Man, and Cybernetics (SMC), pp. 2567–2572. IEEE, Banff, AB, Canada (2017)
15. Sukhwani, H., Martínez, J.M., Chang, X., Trivedi, K.S., Rindos, A.: Performance modeling of PBFT consensus process for permissioned blockchain network (hyperledger fabric). In: 36th Symposium on Reliable Distributed Systems (SRDS), pp. 253–255. IEEE, Hong Kong, China (2017)
16. Huang, D., Ma, X., Zhang, S.: Performance analysis of the raft consensus algorithm for private blockchains. IEEE Trans. Syst. Man Cybern. Syst. **50**(1), 172–181 (2020)
17. Hao, Y., Li, Y., Dong, X., Fang, L., Chen, P.: Performance analysis of consensus algorithm in private blockchain. In: Intelligent Vehicles Symposium(IV), pp. 280–285. IEEE, Changshu, Suzhou, China (2018)
18. Wang, R., Zhang, L., Xu, Q., Zhou, H.: K-bucket based raft-like consensus algorithm for permissioned blockchain. In: 25th International Conference on Parallel and Distributed Systems (ICPADS), pp. 996–999. IEEE, Tianjin, China (2019)
19. Fu, W., Wei, X., Tong, S.: An improved blockchain consensus algorithm based on Raft. Arabian J. Sci. Eng. **46**, 8137–8149 (2021)
20. Ongaro, D., Ousterhout, J.: In search of an understandable consensus algorithm. In: Proceedings of the 2014 USENIX Conference on USENIX Annual Technical Conference. p. 305–320. USENIX ATC 2014, USENIX Association, USA (2014)
21. Hyperledger Caliper (2020). https://hyperledger.github.io/caliper/

A Survey of Blockchain-Based Stablecoin: Cryptocurrencies and Central Bank Digital Currencies

Jin Zhu[1], Jun Zou[2], Yingxia Jing[3], Weiwei Yao[3], Yifan Mo[4(✉)],
and Zibin Zheng[4]

[1] Guangzhou Municipal Local Financial Supervision and Administration,
Guangzhou 510000, China
gzjrj@gz.gov.cn
[2] GRGBanking Blockchain Express Inc. Pty., Guangzhou 510000, China
[3] Guangzhou Digital Finance Association, Guangzhou 510000, China
[4] School of Software Engineering, Sun Yat-sen University, Zhuhai 519082, China
moyifan@inpluslab.com

Abstract. With the development of blockchain technology and regulation, blockchain-based stablecoins have explosive growth recently. Our study provides an overview of the applications and regulations of blockchain-based stablecoins, which not only provides a clear view of current development but also has important referential value for guiding regulatory strategies. We begin with a new categorization perspective based on the legal position, the stability mechanism, target user, and decentralization. Then, we investigate the technical application of real-world projects and analysis it comparatively. Further, we explore the different regulations technologies and policies of blockchain-based stablecoins. Finally, several unresolved difficulties and prospective future are discussed.

Keywords: Blockchain · Stablecoins · Central bank digital
currencies · Cryptocurrencies · Regulation

1 Introduction

Ongoing digitalization has changed the way we live and communicate and affected our usage of money. Rapid advancements in computer processing, data storage, and internet connectivity have led to new technologies to transfer value that may change the traditional currency systems. Recently, a new type of digital currency, called blockchain-based stablecoin, has attracted numerous attention. This kind of stablecoin is exchanged using blockchain technology [1]. A blockchain-based stablecoin can be issued by a private or public organization. Private issuers claimed that the blockchain-based stablecoin in cryptocurrencies are value-stable because they are backed by safe and liquid assets. At the same time, many central banks across the globe are currently working on a public alternative: CBDC [2]. CBDC is regarded as money in its digital version, which has the same legal position as banknotes and central bank reserves. The design of CBDC may or may not include blockchain according to the specific situation of the project. [3]. More than 88% of CBDC projects, in the pilot or production phase, use blockchain as the underlying technology due to the benefits of Integrated platforms, smart contract programmability, transparent audit trails, and configurable confidentiality [4].

Compared with traditional stablecoins, significant advantages of blockchain-based stablecoins include faster and cheaper payments, less friction associated with traditional banking, and stronger resilience against cyberattacks on vulnerable traditional systems. [5]. However, it is still controversial on adoption of blockchain-based stablecoins design because of the existing challenges of blockchain technology, such as security and scalability issues. Besides, considering the blockchain-based stablecoins have the potential to be adopted as a global scale payment method, the risks related to dominance and stability should be taken into account in advance.

This paper conducts a systematic overview of application and regulation in blockchain-based stablecoins. Contributions of this paper are highlighted as following:

- A new categorization perspective of blockchain-based stablecoins is provided.
- Detailed introductions and comparisons of typical blockchain-based stablecoins projects are made.
- Diverse regulatory technologies and policies of blockchain-based stablecoins are summarized.
- Open issues and futures directions blockchain-based stablecoins of are discussed.

The paper is organized as follows. Section 2 introduces introduce the background of blockchain technology and blockchain-based stablecoins. Section 3 is a project review on blockchain-based stablecoins. Section 5 discusses the challenges and open issues on blockchain-based stablecoins, and Sect. 6 concludes the paper. Commonly used acronyms in this paper are listed in Table 1.

2   Background

2.1   Blockchain Technology

Blockchain is a distributed software system that enables the processing of transactions without the involvement of a trusted third party [6]. The blockchain is composed of a sequence of blocks, which holds a complete list of the transactions like a conventional ledger. Distributed ledger technology (DLT) guarantees that transactions is shared across all blockchain network and that only transactions verified by all participants are recorded [7]. With cryptographic techniques and consensus algorithms, blockchain can guarantee that data recorded on the ledger cannot tamper.

Transactions on blockchain can be automatically executed via smart contracts, which is a program run on the blockchain [8]. Smart contracts consisting

Table 1. Acronym table.

Terms	Acronyms
Central Bank Digital Currentcy	CBDC
Decentralized Finance	DeFi
United States Dollar	USD
Chinese Yuan	CNY
European Monetary Unit	EUR
Singapore Dollar	SGD
Enterprise Operation System	EOS
Tether United States Dollar	USDT
United States Dollar Coin	USDC
synthetic United States Dollar in Synthetix Protocol	sUSD
Ampleforth token	AMPL
Terra United States Dollar	UST
Know Your Custome	KYC
Anti-Money Laundering	AML

of transactions are essentially stored, replicated, and updated on distributed blockchains. The integration of blockchain technology with smart contracts has obvious advantages in reducing risks, cutting down on administration and service costs, and improving the efficiency of business processes. Conventional contracts, on the other hand, require a trusted third party to complete them in a centralized way, which takes a long time and more costs.

Current blockchain systems are categorized roughly into three types: public blockchain, consortium blockchain, and private blockchain. Public blockchain is permissionless and anyone can participate in the blockchain, but it has some drawbacks such as performance, privacy, and security. Consortium blockchain is permissioned and built by consortia with several organizations. Each organization is one node of the chain. If other organizations want to join, authorization from other nodes is necessary. Private blockchains are managed by a single entity, which controls who may join, how consensus is carried out, and how the shared ledger is maintained. Table 2 is a detailed comparison of these three kinds of blockchain. In cryptocurrency, stablecoins are usually based on public blockchain. But stablecoins are usually based on private or consortium blockchain in CBDC.

2.2   Blockchain-Based Stablecoins

A blockchain-based stablecoin is a kind of digital token on a blockchain. Stablecoin is intended to reduce on-chain asset price volatility in relation to a fiat currency. Most blockchain-based stablecoins are pegged to fiat currencies such as USD and CNY. A few others are pegged to precious metals or a basket of assets.

Table 2. Comparison of three kinds of blockchain.

Property	Public blockchain	Consortium blockchain	Private blockchain
Consensus determination	All miners	Selected nodes of set	One organization
Consensus process	Permissionless	Permissioned	Permissioned
Efficiency	Low	Medium	High
Scalability	Low	Medium	High
Openness	High	Medium	Low
Decentralization	High	Medium	Low
Example	Bitcoin, Ethereum	Fabric, Corda	–

Blockchain-based stablecoins are fledgling with diversified definitions, which have the ability to take on a variety of forms. We summarize it from legal position, stability mechanism, target user, and decentralization. And then we categorize it in Table 3. It has broad application in CBDC and cryptocurrencies.

Stablecoins in CBDC. Stablecoins in CBDC are backed by the credit of the central bank and have the same legal status as the banknote. According to the usage scenarios, CBDC can be categorized as wholesale and retail CBDC [9]. Retail CBDC [10] is a digital version of cash and is mainly used for payments among individuals and businesses. It can be directly held by citizens and corporates. Wholesale CBDC [11] is restricted to financial institutions. It can help to reduce the credit risk of cross-border payments, inter-bank transfers, and financial settlements.

Stablecoins in Cryptocurrencies. Stablecoins in cryptocurrencies are crypto assets with extremely low volatility and are usually pegged to a fiat currency like USD. Its stability is usually weaker than CBDC because it does not have the central bank's credit backing. Broadly speaking, it can be categorized by stability mechanism as asset-backed stablecoins and algorithmic stablecoins. Asset-backed stablecoins are collateralized by fiat or crypto assets. It links the stablecoins circulated on the blockchain with assets held in reserve. Algorithmic stablecoins rely on a seigniorage share system and an algorithm mechanism to keep their peg. It automatically change the number of coins in circulation-based on the algorithm without having to use the collateralized assets.

Use Cases. Numerous use cases are driving the blockchain-based stablecoins in a variety of forms. We summarize the use cases as follows:

- Payments. Stablecoins can be used to facilitate fast peer-to-peer, cross-border payments, and programmable money [12].
- Internal transfer and settlement. Stablecoins act as a store of value and a medium of exchange in the wholesale market. It can facilitate internal transfer and settlement.

- Digital markets. Stablecoins are used to exchange digital assets and serve as a gateway currency between fiat money and crypto assets.
- DeFi. The programmability and composability of stablecoins enable the development of decentralized, blockchain-based cryptocurrency markets and services. Protocols run in smart contracts enable market-making, lending, derivatives, and asset management to take place on blockchain.

Table 3. Blockchain-based stablecoins categorization.

Type	Legal position	Stability mechanism	Target user	Decentralization
Wholesale CBDC	CBDC	The Credit of Central Bank	Financial Institutions	Low
Retail CBDC	CBDC	The Credit of Central Bank	Permitted Citizens and Corporates	Low
Fiat Asset-backed	Cryptocurrencies	Over Collateralized Fiat Asset	Every People	Medium
Crypto Asset-backed	Cryptocurrencies	Over Collateralized Crypto Asset	Every People	Medium High
Algorithmic	Cryptocurrencies	Auto Adjust by Algorithm	Every People	High

3 Project Review on Blockchain-Based Stablecoins

Blockchain is one of the fundamental technologies of digital cryptocurrencies. Central banks around the world are actively researching and exploring potential applications of blockchain in CBDC. Besides, some asset-backed and algorithmic stablecoin projects have been explored and developed on the blockchain. In this section, we present a project review on blockchain-based stablecoins from central banks and research communities, as shown in Table 4.

3.1 Wholesale CBDC Stablecoins

Wholesale CBDC is issued for use only by financial institutions and clearing-houses for more efficient inter-bank payments. The followings are some projects in prototype or application.

Inthanon-LionRock [13]. Inthanon-LionRock is a joint study between the Hong Kong Monetary Authority and the Bank of Thailand with the objective of developing a software prototype for cross-border settlement in the CBDC. A blockchain tunnel network is used to connect LionRock and Inthanon, two blockchain-based CBDCs. In comparison to traditional cross-border payments, LionRock-Inthanon enables real-time cross-border payments, significantly increasing efficiency and lowering the cost of cross-border payments. Later, The UAE and Chinese mainland joined the project in early January 2021.

Jasper [14]. In 2016, the Bank of Canada launched Project Jasper, developed a proof-of-concept payment system for high-amount inter-bank payments. In 2017, the central bank of Canada extended Project Jasper and developed a blockchain-based CBDC prototype. The scope of this work included improvements to the platform of increasing efficiency and reducing costs. When applied to high-value inter-bank payment and settlement processes, blockchain technology has the potential to revolutionize the project.

Khokha [15]. In 2018, the South African Reserve Bank launched Project Khokha as a proof-of-concept inter-bank payment and settlement system based on Quorum blockchain. Results showed that the typical daily volume of the South African payments system could be processed in less than two hours with full confidentiality of transactions and settlement finality. South Africa's financial regulators say that people in the industry will be able to buy the debentures with a wholesale CBDC and a wholesale digital settlement token. The project is moving forward to integrate with the wholesale system and evaluate supporting frameworks.

Table 4. A summary of blockchain-based stablecoins projects.

Stablecoin or project name	Type	Blockchain	Blockchain type	Use cases	Regions
Inthanon-LionRock	Wholesale CBDC	Corda, Hyperledger	Consortium	Payments	Thailand, Hong Kong, Chinese mainland, UAE
Jasper	Wholesale CBDC	Corda	Consortium	Internal Transfer and Settlement	Canada
Khokha	Wholesale CBDC	Quorum	Consortium	Internal Transfer and Settlement	South African
Stella	Wholesale CBDC	–	Consortium	Internal Transfer and Settlement	Europe, Japan
Ubin	Wholesale CBDC	Corda, Fabric, Quorum	Consortium	Internal Transfer and Settlement	Singapore
Bakong	Retail CBDC	–	Private	Payments	Cambodia
DC/EP	Retail CBDC	–	Private	Payments	China
E-krona	Retail CBDC	Corda	Consortium	Payments	Swedish
Sand Dollar	Retail CBDC	–	Private	Payments	Bahamas
Diem	Fiat Asset-backed	Diem Blockchain	Consortium	Payments	Community
USDT	Fiat Asset-backed	Bitcoin, Ethereum, Tron, Algorand	Public	Digital Markets	Community
USDC	Fiat Asset-backed	Ethereum, Stellar, Algorand, Solana	Public	Digital Markets	Community
Dai	Crypto Asset-backed	Ethereum	Public	DeFi	Community
sUSD	Crypto Asset-backed	Ethereum	Public	DeFi	Community
AMPL	Algorithmic	Ethereum	Public	DeFi	Community
Basis	Algorithmic	Ethereum	Public	DeFi	Community
UST	Algorithmic	Ethereum, Luna	Public	DeFi, Payments	Community

Stella [16]. Project Stella is launched by the European Central Bank and the Bank of Japan. There are 4 phases to this project. The first phase evaluates the feasibility of using blockchain to process large-value payments. The second phase compares security delivery to payment via blockchain. The third phase assesses the utility of blockchain in improving cross-border payments. The fourth phase examines how to strike a balance between privacy and auditability in a distributed ledger environment.

Ubin [17]. In 2016, the Monetary Authority of Singapore launched a blockchain-based CBDC, Project Ubin, to explore the use of blockchain for clearing and settlement of payments and securities. Five-phase experiments demonstrated that blockchain technology is applicable to CBDC. Ethereum is used in phase 1 to facilitate inter-bank payments. In phase 2, Corda, Fabric, and Quorum are used in phase 2 to investigate decentralized inter-bank payments. Smart contracts are used in phase 3 to investigate delivery versus payment. Phase 4 conducts experiments with blockchain-based cross-border settlement payments. As a continuation of phase 4, phase 5 employs blockchain technology and the CBDC to facilitate cross-border payments and to investigate the development of a multi-currency payment model. The network plans to start in Singapore and then spread to other places.

Inthanon-LionRock connects different CBDC systems to achieve cross-border payments by the blockchain tunnel network. Jasper and Khokha try to improve the inter-bank payment and settlement system via blockchain technology. Stella applies blockchain technology to improve privacy and auditability in a distributed ledger environment. Ubin utilizes blockchain technology to support multi-currency cross-border payment.

3.2   Retail CBDC Stablecoins

Retail CBDC is issued for general use of payments such as person-to-person or person-to-businesses. There are some projects in prototype and application in the following.

Bakong [18]. Bakong's mission is to improve financial inclusion in a nation where the majority of residents are unfamiliar with bank accounts yet have a high level of mobile phone use. Additionally, it facilitates inter-bank electronic transactions in real-time and encourages transactions in Cambodian riels. It currently links 11 domestic commercial banks with payment processors and has also started experimenting with digital wallets for cross border transactions with Maybank, a Malaysian-based bank.

DC/EP [19]. In 2014, China began developing a retail CBDC named Digital Currency Electronic Payment (DC/EP). Its design features suggest that it could eventually replace M1 (circulating cash currency, such as coins and banknotes), and it could be used both online and offline. Blockchain technology is used in DC/EP to facilitate the right confirmation of registration and to enhance security. Central banks and commercial banks collaborate to create a decentralized ledger that can be used to query other parties regarding CBDC ownership. The regulator claims that it won't entirely substitute for long-term bank deposits. In April 2020, China became the world's first major economy to pilot a digital currency. Pilot programs in four of the country's largest cities in China have demonstrated that the DC/EP can be used to retail payment.

E-Krona [20]. In 2018, the Swedish central bank proposed E-krona, a CBDC built on the Corda blockchain. E-krona is a two-tier model based on a private blockchain. The first tier is controlled by the central bank, which controls the private blockchain network and has the authority to approve and add new participants to the network. Additionally, the central bank is in charge of issuing and withdrawing ekronor. Through the second tier, participants in the E-krona network distribute e-kronor to end users, who can then use it for a variety of purposes. E-kronor is a domestic currency, with the majority of application scenarios centered on retail payments, such as payments between individuals.

Sand Dollar [21]. Sand Dollar is a digital counterpart to the Bahamian Dollar, and launched in October 2020. A digital wallet can be used on a smartphone app or with a physical payment card. The records gathered during daily operations, such as income and expenditure data, can be used to support microloan applications. The project's objectives are to decrease cash usage and costs, and improve accessibility to financial services throughout the Bahamas. Additionally, it seeks to bolster controls over AML activities.

Bakong is aimed to solve the problem of the low usage rate of bank accounts. DCEP is designed to replace cash in circulation and improve the supervision capacity of the financial system. E-Krona is the digital strategy to overcome declining cash usage for the central bank. Sand Dollar provides access to financial services for residents.

3.3   Fiat Asset-Backed Stablecoins

Fiat asset-backed stablecoins are collateralized by assets in reserve. When amounts of stablecoins are minted on the blockchain, the assets of the corresponding value must be deposited in reserves. Fiat asset-backed stablecoins are issued by intermediaries who serve as custodians of cash-equivalent assets and offer redemption of their stablecoin liabilities. The intermediaries can be companies, private banks, Decentralized Autonomous Organization (DAO) and so on. Fiat assets can be fiduciary deposits, cash, reserve repo notes, and treasury bills.

USDT [22]. USDT is originally launched in July 2014 as a second-layer cryptocurrency token built on Bitcoin's blockchain through the Omni platform. It is later updated to work on the Ethereum [23], EOS [24], Tron [25], Algorand [26] blockchains and so on. USDT is issued by the Hong Kong-based company Tether. In order to keep it pegged to the USD, it holds in reserve fiduciary deposits, cash, reserve repo notes, and treasury bills that are equal to the amount of USDT on the blockchain.

USDC [27]. USDC is a token on the Stellar blockchain network [28] pegged to the USD and originally launched in September 2018. USDC is issued by the Centre consortium, which is formed by Coinbase and Circle. Each unit of USDC is backed by a reserve of one USD, which is stored in a combination of cash and short-term US Treasury bonds. It is qualified to comply with a variety of regulations, including AML audits and Financial Action Task Force compliance. The Center asserts that an important aspect of USDC is that it is audited by a reputable independent company (Grant Thornton LLP) and regulated in the United States.

Diem [29]. Diem is developed by the Diem Association (previously called the Libra Association) and cofounded by the social networking giant Meta (previously called Facebook). Unlike the USD-pegged USDC and USDT, the original Project Libra has moved forward with the addition of single-currency stablecoins from their proposed currency basket (e.g., USD, EUR, and SGD) to their platform. It will instead be a composite of single-currency stablecoins with defined weights. Regulatory uncertainty about Libra's classification, in addition to other regulatory concerns such as fraud prevention, received regulatory backlash. Consequently, the project has made various changes to the whitepaper and plans to launch at the end of 2020. Diem abandoned the goal of a diversified currency basket in favor of pegging to the USD. The team wants to work with regulators, banks, and financial institutions to add more types of pegged assets to their platform.

USDT and USDC are only aimed to peg USD and issued in public blockchain. USDT have more token in circulation. USDC have better Compliance. Diem is aimed to peg the proposed currency basket and issued in consortium blockchain.

3.4   Crypto Asset-Backed Stablecoins

Crypto asset-backed stablecoins is collateralized by crypto asset on blockchain, such as bitcoin token, ether token and ERC20 token.

Dai [30]. Dai is issued by the Maker Protocol, which is one of the largest DeFi applications on Ethereum. It is issued without a central authority and not backed by fiat assets. Dai is generated when a user locks the accepted crypto asset as collateral in the smart contract called Maker Vaults. The collateral provider will get a stability fee as a reward. The stability fee functions similarly to an interest rate and is a key aspect of Dai's stability mechanism. The reduced stability fee encourages users to open more vaults and borrow Dai, increasing the quantity of Dai in circulation and decreasing the price when the market price of Dai is higher than 1 USD. Similarly, a higher stability fee encourages users to seal vaults, removing Dai from circulation and driving up the price when the market price of Dai is less than the goal price. The collateralization ratio must be set above the liquidation ratio to prevent collateral becomes too hazardous throughout this procedure. When a vault becomes too hazardous, it is immediately liquidated and sold using internal market-based auction procedures, beginning with collateral auctions.

sUSD [31]. sUSD is issued by Synthetix, a decentralized synthetic asset Protocol. The Synthetix Network Token (SNX) serves as collateral for sUSD. When collateral is deposited in the smart contract, the user gets SNX to issue synthetic assets (Synths). Exchange rates are allocated to synths by price feeds given by an oracle. This pooled collateral mechanism enables users to make Synth-to-Synth conversions directly via the smart contract, eliminating the need for counterparties. This results in limitless liquidity up to the value of the system's collateral, zero slippage, and permissionless on-chain trading. Holders of SNX tokens are rewarded for staking them in exchange for exchange rewards. Synths are now collateralized at 400%, this may be increased or decreased in the future by community governance.

The above projects represent direct and indirect models. Dai uses the direct model, that the stablecoins are directly collateralized by crypto-assets. But sUSD adopts the indirect model, that the stablecoins are collateralized by synthetic tokens and synthetic tokens are collateralized by original crypto-assets.

3.5   Algorithmic Stablecoins

Algorithmic stablecoins aim to automate the process of minting and withdrawing coins. The process utilizes smart contracts driven by external price feeds.

AMPL [32]. AMPL is a purely algorithmic stablecoin issued by the Ampleforth platform to reduce cryptocurrency volatility. AMPL is elastically and directly supplied due to an algorithmic rebasing mechanism that exerts countercyclical pressure on the market's fluctuations. If the market price of AMPL surpasses the goal price plus the price threshold, the algorithm adjusts the price downward by increasing the supply of tokens. Whereas, if the market price of AMPL goes below the goal price minus the price threshold, the algorithm decreases the supply by withdrawing tokens from user accounts directly and automatically, thereby boosting the AMPL price. In addition, changes to supply targets that are determined by an algorithm are graded over a certain amount of time to make sure that they are spread out evenly during this time.

Basis [33]. The Basis protocol expands and contracts the supply of bonds to indirectly stabilize the peg. It featured a three-token system, with Basis Cash (BAC), Basis Bond (BAB) and Basis Share (BAS) tokens: BAC is the stablecoin pegged to the USD; BAB can exchange equal BAC from the treasury; BAS holders can receive minted BAC if the treasury is sufficiently full. If the price of BAC falls below 1 USD, the protocol will issue and auction BAB to users, therefore eliminating BAC from circulation. In the event that the price of BAC exceeds 1 USD, fresh BAB would be issued to increase supply and bring the price down to the peg. Unfortunately, Basis was unable to launch owing to regulatory concerns over bond and share tokens, and investors were refunded.

UST [34]. UST (Terra USD) is a stable digital currency that was created as a payment method and value storage to complete the existing fiat and cryptocurrency. The Terra protocol dynamically adjusts UST supply in response to changes in demand in order to maintain a stable price. This is accomplished through the use of Luna, a mining token on the LUNA blockchain whose stable rewards are designed to withstand the volatility associated with changing economic cycles. It can transfer the volatility of UST to LUNA. Terra has partnered with a number of payment platforms, most notably in the Asia-Pacific region. Terra announced a partnership with Chai, a South Korean mobile payments application. In July 2019, Terra processed purchases made through the Chai application on e-commerce platforms using the blockchain network.

The above projects are different from the algorithm for adjusting stablecoin supply. AMPL directly adjusts the stablecoin supply according to the market price. Basis indirectly adjusts the stablecoin supply from the perspective of seigniorage. UST transfers the volatility from stablecoins to other tokens.

4   Regulation Towards Blockchain-Based Stablecoins

4.1   Regulation Towards Stablecoins in CBDC

Blockchain technology offers new opportunities for the development of CBDC. However, due to the rapid development and changes of blockchain-based stablecoins in CBDC, there is no unified consensus on indicators and methods of regulatory compliance. Most countries do not have clear policies and plans for the regulation of it yet. Researchers and practitioners are actively exploring possible technology solution to regulate it and giving advice for regulators to make policies. The followings are some regulatory frameworks.

Ledger Design Regulatory Framework. Due to the different positioning and authority control of central banks and participants in CBDC, researchers utilize different transaction ledger design for regulators. Arthur et al. [35] proposed a framework that identified nine fundamental technical dimensions for the regulation of CBDC. Ben et al. [36] proposed a framework for determining whether a central bank should consider creating a digital currency and improving the retail payment system's efficiency. Kahn and Wong [37] proposed a custodians and intermediaries CBDC schemas. Han et al. [38] proposed the three-layered CBDC framework including a supervisory layer.

Legal Assessment Regulatory Framework. Since blockchain-based stablecoin in CBDC is a new form of currency, it is not perfectly compatible with the traditional currency system in law. There are papers offer frameworks for central banks and regulators to assess legal risks from blockchain, such as risks to legal settlement finality, issues with a management and protection of data, connectivity with legacy systems, standards development [39] and suitability for KYC compliance [40].

Decentralized Regulatory Framework. Traditional regulatory manifestations are often dominated by centralized institutions. Since decentralized regulation has certain advantages in fairness, researchers have made an attempt to decentralize the regulatory framework. Hayes [41] provided a conceptual framework for a workable decentralised central bank to perform functionality of a "technocratic, rules-following monetary authority".

Transaction Report Regulatory Framwork. Transfer is the most basic and common operation of blockchain, making the supervision of it essential. Kavassalis et al. [42] presented an innovative framework for a consistent technological approach to financial transactions and risk reporting. This framework is based on distributed computing, decentralised data management technologies such as blockchain, distributed storage, algorithmic financial contract standards, automated legal text and document engineering methods and techniques.

4.2   Regulation Towards Cryptocurrencies Stablecoins

In the past few years, Blockchain technology is widely recognized as having significant potential for improving public service functions, especially the cost and complexity of burdensome processes [55]. Blockchain-based stablecoins in circulation have seen explosive growth. It has prompted several countries like Switzerland to market themselves as crypto-friendly jurisdictions to attract investment [56].

However, many countries have negative sentiments about blockchain-based stablecoins. One of the key arguments is that the blockchain technology is yet too immature to risk implementing critical large-scale payment systems. Although the performance does not seem to match or exceed that of settlement systems of many countries, it would inject unknown risks, such as sustainability of the blockchain industry and excessive decentralization [57,58]. There is scepticism about the current potential of blockchain technology for economic applications. Some have even raised concerns about a bubble situation in blockchain investment and finance, with speculation, market manipulation and suggested conduct in breach of law and regulation are widespread [59].

There are various policy responses of blockchain-based stablecoins in cryptocurrencies. Many countries state that it is not considered legal tender and ban to the offering of it and the exchanges used to trade it. Some countries takes the position that it is too risky and issued a warning to investors about the dangers of investment but has since declined to take a position on regulation. Some countries take position is that it should be viewed as a financial asset for tax purposes. The Table 5 summarises some public policy responses.

Table 5. Regulation of blockchain-based stablecoins in cryptocurrencies.

Policy	Regions
Ban	Chinese mainland [46], Poland [47], Slovakia [48]
Warning	Slovenia [51], Lithuania [49], Sweden [50]
Regulate as financial assets	Switzerland [53], Singapore [52], Israel [54]

5   Discussions

Blockchain technology can bring unique advantages to stablecoin and financial systems. Characters like auditability and immutability make blockchain ideal to meet requirements of stablecoin. Besides, blockchain-based stablecoin model has an advantage of regulation and can help to reduce cost and improve payment efficiency. Even though some central banks have already confirmed that they are working on blockchain-based CBDC, it is still controversial on adoption of Blockchain.

5.1   Regulation Issues

Tax. Blockchain-based stablecoins may facilitate the tax avoidance or weaken domestic oversight. This can occur if domestic authorities have only a limited overview of holdings or transactions by residents in a foreign CBDC. A further potential concern is undesired volatility in exchange rates, for instance, if flows between domestic currency and a foreign CBDC were to be disorderly. Finally, there could be complications in macroeconomic management and in foreign economic cooperation from the perspective of the issuing central bank.

Privacy. A large amount of user information is bound to be stored on distributed ledgers, and the central bank holds all user information, including identity information, transaction information, and property information. The problem of how to balance the relationship between transaction transparency and user information privacy in the context of decentralization has become a major problem. User privacy with personal private information and account property as the main content will be leaked if the user's privacy is breached. This will not only violate individual rights and property rights, but also cause a great currency credit crisis, which will cause price fluctuations of stablecoins and regional financial turmoil.

Credit Policy. The regulation of credit policies become more difficult. The rapid circulation of stablecoins requires timely adjustment of government credit policies according to the real-time dynamics of stablecoins. Otherwise, problems such as restricting the development of enterprises and citizens' consumption due to too small credit scales or inflation and economic bubbles due to excessive credit scales will occur. This will destroy the stability of the monetary system, trigger financial panic, and hinder the orderly development of various industries and the economy as a whole.

5.2   Technology Issues

Smart Contract Audit. Blockchain-based Stablecoins' circulation relies on the smart contract. Due to the distributed nature of the blockchain, once the contract is deployed, the code cannot be modified. Smart contract vulnerabilities are fatal to blockchain-based stablecoins. Therefore, the smart contract audit is an important way to keep blockchain-based stablecoins safe.

Performance and Scalability. Performance and scalability are two significant constraints for blockchain-based stablecoins. In 2019, FastFabric [61] is proposed as an extension of Hyperledger Fabric, which increases transaction throughput from 3000 to 20,000 TPS (transactions per second). However, Alipay can process over 80,000 transactions per second. The performance of the current blockchain system is still lower than traditional centralized systems. And the blockchain should have good scalability to deal with increasing transactions. However, there are no perfect solutions to resolve these issues in blockchain.

Cross-Chain Interoperability. Different regions and projects may utilize different blockchains. For example, Corda is used in Project Jasper and E-krona, and Quorum is adopted in Project Khokha. As for cross-border trans-actions, these different blockchain-based CBDC networks need to communicate and exchange data. However, different blockchains may use different encryption algorithms, consensus algorithms, digital signature schemes, hash algorithms, transaction structures, and block sizes. Cross-chain interoperability among different blockchains is a big challenge for both the blockchain and blockchain-based CBDC schemes. If only domestic payments are the focus of CBDC, cross-chain interoperability may not be on the list of things to think about.

5.3 Stability Issues

Liquidity. Due to the extreme volatility of the collateral value in the case of crypto asset-backed stablecoins, loans may not be completely recovered in the event of failure. Additionally, tokens with numerous on-chain collaterals have correlation risk, which means the diversification advantage will be diminished if the volatility of the collaterals is highly correlated. Increasing one's exposure to a certain form of collateral may entail comparable risks. Crypto asset-backed stablecoins additionally need greater attention in their design owing to the risk of liquidity concerns and the necessity to account for human variables such as incentives for creating and closing collateralized deposits.

Algorithmic. Algorithmic stablecoins are quite sophisticated. Users may not completely comprehend the elements affecting issuance and stability. Because they lack collateral, pure-algorithmic stablecoins are particularly susceptible to market collapses and "death spirals." Algorithmic stablecoins rely more heavily on the purchasing and selling activity of users with reasonable economic incentives to ensure stability. The peg cannot be maintained if the participants lose rationality in purchasing and selling.

6 Conclusion

In recent years, blockchain-based stablecoins have seen explosive growth in both CBDC and cryptocurrencies. Blockchain-based stablecoins have shown its potential for transforming the traditional industry with its key characteristics of decentralization, persistency, anonymity, and auditability. We present a survey classifying and describing the many different kinds of blockchain-based stablecoins that are being researched and developed. It includes wholesale CBDC, retail CBDC, fiat asset-backed, crypto asset-backed, and algorithmic stablecoins, as well as the closely related efforts of developing digital currencies. Besides, the ledger design regulatory framework, legal assessment regulatory framework, decentralized regulatory framework, and transaction report regulatory framework in CBDC are also being investigated. For the regulatory policy of cryptocurrencies, there are 3 types: ban, warning, and regulate as financial assets.

Considering most projects are at a relatively early stage with a lot of open questions, particularly related to regulation, technology, and stability, significant further research is necessary to address these challenges.

Acknowledgments. The work described in this paper is supported by the Special fund (Financial Development) project of Guangdong Province for Promoting High-Quality Economic Development in 2022, as a deliverable of the project of E-CNY Payment Judicial Evidence Preservision System for the Characteristic Application Scenarios in Guangdong-Hong Kong-Macao Greater Bay Area. The authors are key members of the project working group.

References

1. Carapella, F., Flemming, J.: A literature review, Central bank digital currency (2020)
2. John, C., Liao, G.Y.: Stablecoins: growth Potential and Impact on Banking. No. 1334. Board of Governors of the Federal Reserve System (US) (2022)
3. Ayten, K., Krishnamachari, B., Yun, S.: Reducing the Volatility of Cryptocurrencies-A Survey of Stablecoins. arXiv preprint (2021)
4. PwC CBDC global index 2021 (2021). https://www.pwc.com/gx/en/industries/financial-services/assets/pwc-cbdc-global-index-1st-edition-april-2021.pdf
5. Cœuré, B.: Investigating the impact of global stablecoins. Bank for International Settlements, Basel (2019)
6. Zheng, Z., et al.: An overview of blockchain technology: architecture, consensus, and future trends. In: 2017 IEEE International Congress on Big Data (2017)
7. Zheng, Z., et al.: Blockchain challenges and opportunities: a survey. Int. J. Web Grid Serv. **14** (2018)
8. Zheng, Z., et al.: An overview on smart contracts: challenges, advances and platforms. Future Gener. Comput. Syst. **105**, 475–491 (2020)
9. Raphael, A., Cornelli, G., Frost, J.: Rise of the central bank digital currencies: drivers, approaches and technologies (2020)
10. John, K., et al.: A Survey of Research on Retail Central Bank Digital Currency. IMF Working Papers (2020)
11. Edwin, A.O., Kim, K.: Design Practices for Wholesale Central Bank Digital Currencies from the World. Symposium on Cryptography and Information Security (2020)
12. Alexander, L.: What is Programmable Money? Board of Governors of the Federal Reserve System (US) (2021)
13. Project Inthanon-LionRock (2020). https://www.hkma.gov.hk/eng/news-and-media/press-releases/2020/01/20200122-4/
14. James, C., et al.: Project jasper: are distributed wholesale payment systems feasible yet. Finan. Syst. **59** (2017)
15. Project khokha (2022). https://consensys.net/blockchain-use-cases/finance/project-khokha/
16. Project Stella (2020). https://www.ecb.europa.eu/paym/intro/publications/pdf/ecb.miptopical200212_01.en.pdf?4362b9bc33cd54ed51c86825b1
17. Project Ubin (2019). https://www.mas.gov.sg/schemes-and-initiatives/Project Ubin
18. Project Bakong (2022). https://bakong.nbc.org.kh/

19. Yao, Q.: Experimental study on prototype system of central bank digital currency. J. Softw. **29** (2018). https://doi.org/10.13328/j.cnki.jos.005595. (in Chinese)
20. Hanna, A., et al.: The e-krona and the macroeconomy. Sveriges Riksbank Economic Review (2018)
21. Project Sand Dollar (2022). https://www.sanddollar.bs/
22. USDT white paper (2016). https://tether.to/wp-content/uploads/2016/06/TetherWhitePaper.pdf
23. Ethereum white paper (2022). https://ethereum.org/en/whitepaper/
24. EOS white paper (2018). https://github.com/EOSIO/Documentation/blob/master/TechnicalWhitePaper.md
25. Tron white paper (2018). https://developers.tron.network/docs
26. Algorand white paper (2019). https://www.algorand.com/technology/white-papers
27. USDC white paper (2018). https://f.hubspotusercontent30.net/hubfs/9304636/PDF/centre-whitepaper.pdf
28. Marta, L., et al.: Fast and secure global payments with stellar. In: Proceedings of the 27th ACM Symposium on Operating Systems Principles (2019)
29. Diem white paper (2020). https://www.diem.com/en-us/
30. MakerDAO white paper (2020). https://makerdao.com/en/whitepaper/
31. Synthetix white paper (2022). https://docs.synthetix.io/
32. Evan, K., Brandon, I., Cruz, M.R.: A New Synthetic Commodity, Ampleforth (2019)
33. Nader, A.-N., Chen, J., Diao, L.: Basis: a price-stable cryptocurrency with an algorithmic central bank (2017)
34. UST white paper (2019). https://assets.website-files.com/611153e7af981472d8da1 99c/618b02d13e938ae1f8ad1e45_Terra_White_paper.pdf
35. Macherel, A., Treccani, A., Moyano, J.P.: A 9-dimension grid for the evaluation of central bank digital currencies. University of Zurich Working Paper (2018)
36. Ben, S.C.F., Halaburda, H.: Central bank digital currencies: a framework for assessing why and how. SSRN 2994052 (2016)
37. Charles, M.K., Rivadeneyra, F., Wong, T.-N.: Should the central bank issue e-money?. Money **2019**, 01–18 (2019)
38. Xuan, H., Yuan, Y., Wang, F.-Y.: A blockchain-based framework for central bank digital currency. In: International Conference on Service Operations and Logistics, and Informatics (SOLI) (2019)
39. David, C.M., et al.: Distributed ledger technology in payments, clearing, and settlement (2016)
40. Shah, T., Jani, S.: Applications of blockchain technology in banking and finance (2018)
41. Hayes, A.: Decentralized banking: monetary technocracy in the digital age. In: Tasca, P., Aste, T., Pelizzon, L., Perony, N. (eds.) Banking Beyond Banks and Money. NEW, pp. 121–131. Springer, Cham (2016). https://doi.org/10.1007/978-3-319-42448-4_7
42. Petros, K., et al.: An innovative RegTech approach to financial risk monitoring and supervisory reporting. J. Risk Finan. **19** (2018)
43. Codruta, B., Holden, H., Wadsworth, A.: Impending arrival-a sequel to the survey on central bank digital currency. BIS paper 107 (2020)
44. Rizk, A.: Central Bank Digital Currency: Legal and Regulatory Issues. University of Westminster, Diss (2022)

45. Blackstone, B.: Switzerland wants to be the world capital of cryptocurrency. Wall Street J. (2018). www.wsj.com/articles/switzerland-wants-to-be-the-world-capital-of-cryptocurrency-1524942058
46. Notice On Preventing The Financing Risk Of The Issuing Of Tokens. Sept. 4 (2017). http://www.cbrc.gov.cn/Chinese/home/docView/BE5842392CFF4BD98B0F3DC9C2A4C540.html
47. Nat'l Bank Of Pol. & Pol. Fin. Supervision Auth., Announcement Of The National Bank Of Poland And The Polish Financial Supervision Authority Regarding Virtual Currencies. July 7 (2017). https://www.knf.gov.pl/knf/en/komponenty/img/Statement_by_NBP_and_KNF_on_virtual_currencies_7_07_2017_57364.pdf
48. National Bank Of Slovakia: Several Considerations On The Virtual Currency Bitcoin (2018). http://www.nbs.sk/_img/Documents/_PUBLIK_NBS_FSR/Biatec/Rok2013/08-2013/06_biatec13-8_nadasky.pdf
49. Bank Of Lithuania: Position Of The Bank Of Lithuania On Virtual Currencies And Initial Coin Offering (2017). https://www.lb.lt/uploads/documents/files/PozicijosdelvirtualiuvaliutuirVVzetonuplatinimoEN.pdf
50. Finansinspektionen: Warning For Risks With Initial Coin Offerings (ICO) (2017). url http://www.fi.se/sv/publicerat/nyheter/2017/varning-for-risker-med-initial-coin-offerings
51. Bank Of Slovenia: Financial Stability Board Warning (2017). https://www.bsi.si/en/media/1138/financial-stability-board-warning
52. Monetary Authority of Singapore Media Release: MAS clarifies regulatory position on the offer of digital tokens in Singapore (2017). http://www.mas.gov.sg/News-and-Publications/Media-Releases/2017/MAS-clarifies-regulatory-position-on-the-offer-of-digital-tokens-in-Singapore.aspx
53. Swiss Fin. Mkt. Supervisory Auth. Guidelines For Enquiries Regarding The Regulatory Framework For Initial Coin Offerings (ICOS) (2018). https://www.finma.ch/en/~/media/finma/dokumente/dokumentencenter/myfinma/1bewilligung/fintech/wegleitung-ico.pdf
54. Nadine Baudot-Trajtenberg, Bank of Israel Deputy Governor, Activity and Use of Virtual Currencies, remarks at the Knesset Finance Committee Meeting on Activity and Use of Virtual Currencies (2018). http://www.boi.org.il/en/NewsAndPublications/PressReleases/Pages/8-1-18-DeputyGove.aspx
55. Diego, C., et al.: Blockchain for public services: a systematic literature review. IEEE Access 9 (2021)
56. Mikayla, N.: Crypto-friendliness: understanding blockchain public policy. J. Entrepreneurship Public Policy 9 (2019)
57. Pasquale, G., et al.: Current trends in sustainability of bitcoins and related blockchain technology. Sustainability 9 (2017)
58. Shangrong, J., et al.: Policy assessments for the carbon emission flows and sustainability of Bitcoin blockchain operation in China. Nat. Commun. 12 (2021)
59. Douglas, W.A., Auer, R., Frost, J.: Stablecoins: risks, potential and regulation. Financial Stability Review (2020)
60. Xuemei, B., Zhong, L.: Legal Protection of Blockchain from the Perspective of the Cybersecurity Law: Legislation and Practice of China. In: International Conference on Blockchain and Trustworthy Systems (2021)
61. Gorenflo, C.: Scaling hyperledger fabric to 20,000 transactions per second. arXiv preprint (2019)

Collusion Attack Analysis and Detection
of DPoS Consensus Mechanism

Xinxin Qi[1], Xiaodong Fu[1,2(✉)], Fei Dai[3], Li Liu[1,2], Lijun Liu[1,2], Jiaman Ding[1,2], and Wei Peng[1,2]

[1] Yunnan Provincial Key Laboratory of Computer Technology Application, Kunming 650500,
China
xiaodong_fu@hotmail.com
[2] Faculty of Information Engineering and Automation, Kunming University of Science and
Technology, Kunming 650500, China
[3] College of Big Data and Intelligent Engineering, South Forestry University, Kunming 650224,
China

Abstract. With the development of blockchain technology, the increasing safety
accidents result in huge economic losses in blockchain systems. Delegated Proof
of Stake (DPoS) selects the witness nodes to produce blocks by voting, leading
to the quick confirmation of transactions. As one of the widely used consensus
mechanisms in public blockchain, DPoS is still threatened by attacks. In this
paper, an analysis method for collusion attacks of DPoS consensus mechanism is
proposed. Meanwhile, we analyze the behavioral motivations of malicious nodes
and detect the attacks that exist in the voting process of DPoS. First, the coalitional
game is the basic form of cooperative game, which can be used to analyze the
structure, strategy and benefits of cooperative game. We build a coalitional game
model to analyze motivations of DPoS nodes that launched collusion attacks.
And then we use the Shapley-Shubik power index and Banzhaf power index in
weighted voting games of DPoS, which calculated different values that DPoS
suffered attacks during the voting phase. Experimental results show that collusion
attacks in DPoS can be effectively detected by this method. In addition, the analysis
results can further contribute to the security of the DPoS blockchain system.

Keywords: Blockchain · Consensus mechanism · DPoS · Collusion attack ·
Coalitional game · Weighted voting game

1 Introduction

Bitcoin is a cryptocurrency proposed by Satoshi Nakamoto in 2008 in the form of peer-to-
peer (P2P) [1]. Since then, people gradually pay more attention to blockchain technology
used in Bitcoin. Blockchain is widely used in finance, the Internet of Things, transportation and other fields because of its characteristics of decentralization, non-tamper ability,
collective maintenance, etc. Generally speaking, the consensus mechanism, as an important part of the blockchain, undertakes the consistency and security of blockchain's data.
The performance of the consensus mechanism directly affects the security, transaction

D. Svetinovic et al. (Eds.): BlockSys 2022, CCIS 1679, pp. 194–206, 2022.
https://doi.org/10.1007/978-981-19-8043-5_14

processing capabilities, and scalability of blockchain systems. However, due to the complexity of the blockchain technology structure and the lack of security control, attacks on blockchain systems are increasing rapidly. For example, on January 5–8, 2019, due to the decline in ETC's market capitalization and subsequent decline in network computing power, malicious attackers used network computing power to carry out at least 15 suspected double-spend attacks on the ETC blockchain. This resulted in 219,500 ETC attacks, or about $1.1 million. However, the cost of this attack was only about $20,000, and the malicious attacker benefited 50 times.

Currently, there are several common consensus mechanisms in blockchain. Among them, Proof-of-Work (PoW) is the consensus mechanism used in Bitcoin system. Principle of PoW is that nodes compete through computing power to decide who can produce blocks and get rewards. This process is also called mining. Although this process is simple and easy to achieve, the process of achieving consensus through "mining" creates waste of resources. In order to solve the problem of resource wasting in PoS [2], Sunny King, the founder of Peercoin, proposed proof of stake (PoS) in the white paper. And PoS is attracted widespread attention as soon as it was proposed. PoS avoids the waste of resources, but the process of reaching consensus is easy to produce monopolies. There are also various risks of being attacked in PoS. Subsequently, in April 2014, Dan Larimer (BM), the lead developer of Bitshares, proposed the Delegated proof of stake (DPoS) [3]. DPoS is now used on platforms such as Ethereum, EOS, etc.

In DPoS consensus mechanism, each node has voting rights. Then, some delegates, or super-nodes are elected based on the vote. These super-nodes have complete equal rights to each other. In the end, they take turns producing blocks. If delegates fail to perform their duties (such as failing to generate blocks when it's their turn), they are removed and the network chooses new super-nodes to replace them. Although, in the process, nodes reach consensus very quickly, in other words, nodes produce blocks quickly, the process still creates some problems. For example, whether there is bad behavior or whether there are various attacks in voting between nodes. That is, whether there are malicious nodes manipulating the results of voting. This also raises the question of how to measure the power of different participants in a cooperative environment. Because, in voting games, the player's weight does not fully reflect the player's actual power over an alliance decision. The power here can be understood as the prior probability that the player will play a key role in the game. The power index [4] is a measure of a player's ability to influence the outcome of a game in the context of a weighted voting game. Two most common power indices are Shapley-Shubik power index and Banzhaf power index.

In order to effectively analyze and detect collusion attacks in DPoS, this paper uses cooperative game theory as the theoretical basis [5], analyzes the malicious nodes conspiring with other nodes in election of DPoS. Meanwhile, we get comparative experimental data through the Shapley-Shubik power index and the Banzhaf power index. In order to show the effectiveness of this proposed method, we compare our method with the literature [6] by Pearson correlation coefficient. The results of experiment obtained by this method show that the attacker can increase his power in election through collusion, and manipulate the election results in the end. At the same time, detecting attacks is more effective than [6].

The contribution of this paper can be summarized as follows.

- We analyze the collusion attack in DPoS consensus mechanism by using game theory and Shapley-Shubik power index and Banzhaf power index, and the attacker's behavioral motivation can be effectively analyzed through experiments.
- We detect collusion attacks in DPoS through the coalitional game model and the magnitude of changes in two power indices. In order to highlight the superiority of our method, we compare with other experiments by using Pearson correlation coefficient.

The remainder of paper is organized as follows. Section 2 reviews related work. Section 3 introduces the related background knowledge. Section 4 shows the coalitional model of DPoS in game theory and definition of various methods and indicators. The experimental results are shown in Sect. 5. Section 6 concludes and discuss the future work.

2 Related Work

In order to alleviate the 51% attack in PoW, Yang et al. [7] proposed a scheme to combine history weighted information of miners with total calculation difficulty. And for long range attack in PoS, AlMallohi et al. [8] put forward to a new strategy for implementing checkpoints in blockchain technology, which could mitigate long range attacks. In the weighted voting game on DPoS, collusion attacks aim at forming a collusive coalition. They can select delegated nodes to participate in the final consensus phase of DPoS by this way. The delegated nodes selected by malicious attackers can interfere with the final consensus result, in consensus phase of DPoS. Finally, they benefit themselves by causing massive damage to the blockchain system. Up to now, some scholars have conducted relevant research on the above issues. We divide the types of research into two categories, one is theoretical and strategic analysis, the other is improvement of consensus mechanism.

1. Theoretical and strategic analysis. W. lei et al. [9] proposed a game analysis method on DPoS, which could well theoretically analyze to show that there are malicious attacks. In 2021, Tian and Hu [10] have compiled various attacks and defense methods against blockchain systems that are already known. Wei et al. [11] introduced blockchain technology, reviewing the security risks in blockchain. Secondly, the security issues in this paper are classified and summarized. Finally, they looked forward to the current research hotspots and development trends of blockchain security.
2. Improvement of consensus mechanism. Y. Luo et al. [12] in 2018 proposed a new election algorithm for the DPoS consensus mechanism to strengthen the characteristics of decentralization. Xu et al. [13] put forward a kind of vague set to improve DPoS. At the same time, this article improves the security and fairness of the blockchain. Y. Yao et al. [14] improved the security of the blockchain network by using the fish swarm algorithm during the voting stage of DPoS.

At present, there are endless attacks on the consensus process of DPoS. If we don't analyze these attacks, blockchain systems still face significant risks and even huge losses. What's more, given the peculiarities of DPoS consensus, scholars have not yet analyzed the attacks encountered during the node voting process in the original DPoS.

3 Preliminaries

3.1 DPoS: Delegated Proof of Stake

The consensus mechanism emerged, because of "Byzantine Generals Problem" in blockchain. In order to solve this problem, Miguel Castro and Barbara Liskov proposed the Byzantine fault-tolerant algorithm [15] in 1999. Currently, more common than other consensus mechanisms are proof of work (PoW), proof of stake (PoS), and delegate proof of stake (DPoS).

To better understand the principles of DPoS, we we consider the more common case of 21 delegate nodes. The voting nodes of DPoS participating in elections are defined as a finite set $N = \{n_1, n_2, n_3, \ldots\}$, and because the voting weight of DPoS nodes is proportional to their stake. Their stake or voting weight is defined as a finite set $W = \{w_1, w_2, w_3, \ldots\}$. During the voting phase of DPoS, the voting nodes N elect 21 delegate nodes according to voting weight W. These nodes take turns producing blocks for a given amount of time, and the remaining members validate and, eventually reach consensus. This is a visual description of the DPoS (Delegated Proof of Stake) consensus mechanism (Fig. 1).

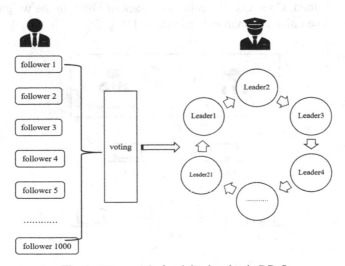

Fig. 1. The model of weighted voting in DPoS

3.2 Weighted Voting Games

Under the well-known majority voting, every voter has the same power. However, the power of all voters cannot be always equal. In parliamentary elections, each party has different seats, and when voting on whether a bill passes, each party has different power. Besides, in the process of consensus among the nodes of DPoS, the nodes vote according to their stake, and the stake of each node are different. This form of voting games called weighted voting games. During the voting process of DPoS, the nodes form different coalitions, and when a coalition meets or exceeds the prescribed quota, it becomes the winning coalition. The quota mentioned here is defined as q. A weighted voting game in DPoS is defined as $G = (N, W, q)$.

3.3 Collusion Attack

Collusion is a secret cooperation between two or more parities that restricts open competition by deceiving, misleading, or deceiving another person's legal right. In the study of economics, collusion occurs within the industry when companies cooperate for mutual benefit. For example, it was revealed that both companies agreed not to hire each other's employees to stop wage increases, in a 2015 case of collusion between Google and Apple for employee poaching.

During the voting process, malicious nodes collude with other nodes to form an alliance through various means to manipulate the election results. Usually, this kind of attack is called a collusion attack [16]. Such as, in 2018 Venezuelan presidential election, reports of vote purchases were common during the presidential campaign. Hungry Venezuelans were forced to vote for Maduro as the government bribed potential supporters with food. Consequently, collusion attack of DPoS in the weighted voting process need to be rationally analyzed and detected (Fig. 2).

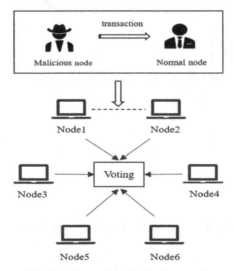

Fig. 2. The model of collusion attack

4 Model and Definitions

In order to analyze collusion attacks in DPoS, we use the coalitional game model and two power indices as analytical methods and tools. At the same time, we use the Pearson correlation coefficient as an indicator of the effectiveness and superiority of detecting attack. For defending against attacks, we also consider using saturation activation functions to constrain the behavioral motivations of the attack nodes. The above research models and methods are defined in the following definition.

4.1 Coalitional Games in DPoS

In a cooperative game, when agents form alliances for the same goal, we can model the system as a coalitional game. A coalitional game $C = (N, v)$, consist of [17]:

- a finite set $N = (1, 2, 3 \ldots n)$, of nodes participating in voting and
- a function $v : 2^N \rightarrow R$. In a simple coalitional game, we say v only takes values in $\{0, 1\}$. We say a coalition $S \subseteq P$ wins if $v(S) = 1$, otherwise loses.

The weighted voting game is a well-known model of cooperative game in the field of voting. At the same time, the weighted voting game in DPoS is a simple coalitional game that can be described as a non-negative weight vector W and a positive quota q. Moreover, when the weight of a coalition S meets and exceeds the quota (i.e., $\sum_{i \in S} w_i \geq q$), it will win (i.e., $v(S) = 1$). We can also use $G = (C, W, q) = (N, W, q, v)$ denotes the weighted voting game in DPoS.

Given a weighted voting game G in DPoS, a voting node $i \in S$ is pivotal in the winning coalition S, if S becomes a losing coalition after the voting node i leaves coalition S(i.e. $v(S) = 1$ and $v(S \backslash i) = 0$). Since the influence of individual voting node on the game is obvious and related to the indicator of measuring power, we need to make accurate calculations of the voting nodes in DPoS by using two power indices. The following two power indices are described in detail.

4.2 SSI: Shapley-Shubik Power Index

The Shapley value [18] reflects the average marginal contribution or expected marginal contribution of the participants. Usually, when it's applied to the voting games, the Shapley value of nodes is the Shapley-Shubik power index. Since elections in DPoS are also voting games, we can calculate the Shapley-Shubik power index of voting nodes. The Shapley-Shubik power index is given by $SSI(G) = SSI(N, W, q, v) = (SSI_1(N, W, q, v), SSI_2(N, W, q, v), \ldots, SSI_n(N, W, q, v))$ where the Shapley-Shubik power index of node i:

$$v(S) = \begin{cases} 1 & \sum_{i \in S} w_i \geq q \\ 0 & otherwise \end{cases} \tag{1}$$

$$SSI_i(N, v) = \sum_{S \subseteq N | i \in S} \frac{(|S|-1)!(n-|S|)!}{n!} [v(S) - v(S \backslash \{i\})] \tag{2}$$

The formula calculates the contribution of node i to all coalitions and adds them up. $\frac{(|S|-1)!(n-|S|)!}{n!}$ represents the probability that node i joined the coalition $S - \{i\}$. Its denominator represents the number of permutations of n nodes, and the numerator represents the number of permutations with the coalition $S - \{i\}$, then node i enters the coalition $S - \{i\}$, and finally multiplied by the number of permutations with the others. $[v(S) - v(S\backslash\{i\})]$ is the value that node i contributed to the coalition S.

4.3 PBI: Banzhaf Power Index or Penrose Index

The Banzhaf power index [19], refers to the power of a voter in the fact that he(she) can make a winner by joining a coalition that supposed to lose, which also means he can make it lose by turning his back on a coalition that meant to be won. That said, he is a "key joiner" to the coalition. In this paper, we deem that the voting nodes' Banzhaf power index is the number of winning coalitions when it is a "key joiner". The Banzhaf power index is given by $PBI(G) = PBI(N, W, q, v) = (PBI_1(N, W, q, v), PBI_2(N, W, q, v), \ldots, PBI_n(N, W, q, v))$ where the Banzhaf power index of node i:

$$PBI_i(N, v) = \frac{1}{2^{n-1}} \sum_{S\subseteq N | i \in S} [v(S) - v(S\backslash\{i\})] \tag{3}$$

4.4 The Weighted Voting Game in DPoS

Detection of Collusion Attacks in DPoS. Since, the nodes of weighted voting game in DPoS select n delegate nodes participating in the production of blocks according to the majority criterion, given a set of weighted voting game $\overline{G} = [G_1, G_2, \ldots, G_k, \ldots]$. Based on the Banzhaf power index and Shapley-Shubik power index, we can analyze the difference of two power indices before and after collusion attack in DPoS. We can judge whether there was a collusion attack, based on the magnitude of the change in the minimal power index before and after the formation of coalition in the n weighted voting sets.

Let M_k be a magnitude of the change in the k-th voting partition. Let $\widetilde{SSI}(G_k)$ and $\widetilde{PBI}(G_k)$ be the smallest Shapley-Shubik and Banzhaf power index after the formation of the coalition. Let $\widetilde{SSI}(G_k)$ and $\widetilde{PBI}(G_k)$ be the smallest power indices before the formation of the coalition. Then we write:

$$M_k = \frac{1}{2}\left(\frac{\widetilde{SSI}(G_k)}{\widetilde{SSI}(G_k)} + \frac{\widetilde{PBI}(G_k)}{\widetilde{PBI}(G_k)}\right) \tag{4}$$

For a more rational analysis, we classify the types of attackers in the attack, let M_k^l and M_k^h is the lowest and highest magnitude of variation in collusion attacks. At the same time, let $D_k(M_k)$ denote the result of whether there is an attack on the k-th weighted voting game partition in $\overline{G}$. That is to say,

$$D_k(M_k) = \begin{cases} 1 & M_k^l \leq M_k \leq M_k^h \text{ for every } G_k \in \overline{G} \\ 0 & \text{otherwise} \end{cases} \tag{5}$$

To demonstrate the effectiveness of the method, we refer to Pearson correlation coefficient. Let A is a set of m-dimensional vectors that set the number of collusion attacks. Let $\overline{A}$ is average of A-vector elements. Let D be a set of calculated m-dimensional vectors, let $\overline{D}$ is average of D-vector elements, where:

$$\begin{cases} D = \left(D_1, D_2, \ldots D_j, \ldots D_m\right) \\ D_j = \sum_{i=1}^{n} D_k(M_k) \end{cases} \tag{6}$$

According to the definition of Pearson correlation coefficient, the following formula can be obtained:

$$Pcc(A, D) = \frac{\sum_{j=1}^{m}\left(\left(A_j - \overline{A}\right) \times \left(D_j - \overline{D}\right)\right)}{\sqrt{\sum_{j=1}^{m}\left(\left(A_j - \overline{A}\right)\right)^2} \times \sqrt{\sum_{j=1}^{m}\left(\left(D_j - \overline{D}\right)\right)^2}} \tag{7}$$

5 Experiment and Analysis

In order to analyze the collusion attack on the weighted voting process among nodes in DPoS, this paper performs simulation experiments from the public X-Block dataset. The dataset contains tagged privacy data as well as transaction data for some Ethereum blockchain nodes. At the same time, all experiments were conducted on a PC with Intel Core i7-11700k 3.6 GHz CPU and 16 GB RAM. The programs are implemented in PyCharm 2021.3. In our next work, we use Shapley-Shubik and Banzhaf power index to analyze collusion attackers in DPoS. And, we highlight the effectiveness of the power index-based detection through the Pearson correlation coefficient.

5.1 Analysis of Collusion Attack in DPoS

To be able to simulate a simple and realistic DPoS voting process, we ony consider the situation when $k = 21$. That is, we set up 21 weighted voting games in DPoS. According to the particularity of weighted voting in DPoS. The tagged privacy data of Ethereum nodes is divided into 21 weighted voting games. And the 21 partitions simulate the difficulty of selecting the 21 delegate nodes with the most votes in the DPoS blockchain in the order of increasing total weights. In order to get effective analysis results, we selected attackers with the same weight in 21 weighted voting game, and divide the attackers who participate in the weighted vote into two types with larger weights and smaller weights, and conducted experiments separately.

First, according to the above model and definition, we need to experiment with the values of two power indices before and after the collusion attack of malicious nodes in DPoS. The experimental results are divided into Fig. 3 and Fig. 4. The black and red lines in Fig. 3 and Fig. 4 represent the magnitude of changes in two power indices of the attacker before and after the launch of collusion attack, respectively.

We then use the squares to represent the specific values of the attacker's power index before and after the collusion attack when the attacker has a larger weight. For the case when the attacker has a small weight, we use a diamond shape to represent the specific value of the attacker.

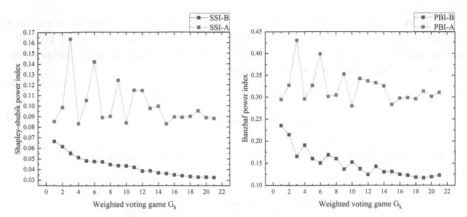

Fig. 3. Two power indices values before and after the collusion attack, when the attacker has a larger weight

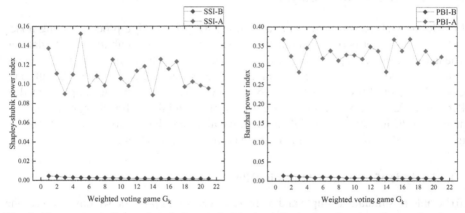

Fig. 4. Two power indices values before and after the collusion attack, when the attacker has a lower weight

Based on the above results (Fig. 3 and 4), regardless of the type of malicious node that launched the collusion attack, its two power indices will increase. That is to say, the attackers will be motivated to launch this attack by increasing their power in weighted voting game.

Furthermore, Fig. 3 is more pronounced than Fig. 4, proving that the Shapley-Shubik power index is monotonic [20] before the launch of collusion attack. In other words, it's cheaper for an attacker to manipulate a lower-ranked election through the collusion attack than a top-ranked election. For the Banzhaf power index, Fig. 3 also shows more clearly than Fig. 4 that there is no regular change in the value of PBI of the same weight in different weighted votes.

All in all, these two power indices can help us analyze the attacker's motives for evil from the individual rationality of game theory. And we can use this as an entry point to further look for collusion attacks in different weighted voting games.

5.2 Detection of Collusion Attack in DPoS

In order to show the effectiveness and superiority of the detection method of this paper, we divide the comparative experiment into two categories: self-comparison and method comparison.

Muti-group Detection. Let's first assume that the vector containing the voting partition where there is a collusion attack. Since, in DPoS, 21 delegate nodes are selected, then let a five-dimensional vector (3, 6, 9, 12, 16) represents the number of partitions with the attack.

Figure 5 visually shows the comparison of setpoints and analytical values. The horizontal axis representing the elemental ordinal number of the vector and the vertical axis representing the number of partitions which contain the attack in the weighted voting game G_i. Although, it is shown that the detection value is not much different from the set value, we still need to compare with more specific metrics.

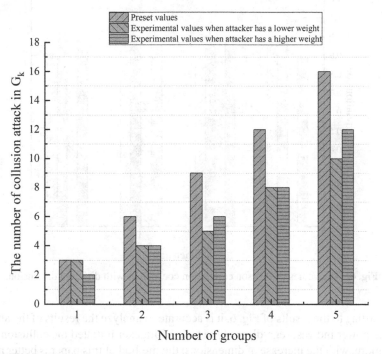

Fig. 5. The results of collusion attack analysis compared with the set value.

Comparison of Detection Effects. Similarity algorithms are often used in recommended environments. In this way, we can calculate the similarity between users by using the preferences of individual or all users for the whole items as vector. In this article, we measure the quality of the analysis method by the similarity between the set-point and the detected value. Since the Pearson correlation coefficient is more reflective in trend of movement between vectors than Euclidean distance, And it can compensate for the lack of dimensions compared to Cosine similarity. Besides, it can be used here to judge the effectiveness of the detection method. To highlight the effectiveness of this method, we compare this article with an anomaly detection algorithm mentioned in literature. The experimental data of literature will be obtained through the historical transaction data of some Ethereum blockchain nodes.

First of all, based on the nature of Pearson's correlation coefficient, we can know that the closer the value is to 1, the more positively correlated the two vectors are. The horizontal axis of Fig. 6 represents the dimensions of the vector and the vertical axis represents the Pearson correlation coefficient. That's to say, we analyze it by different experimental dimensions. Furthermore, we define the detection method in this article as PI, and the detection method of supporting vector machines in the literature as OSVM.

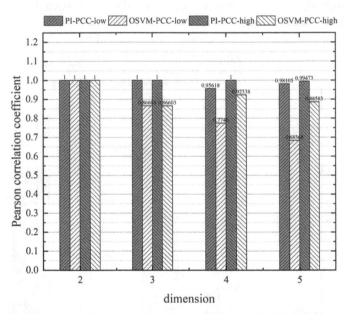

Fig. 6. The values of Pearson correlation coefficient with different dimension.

According to the results of Fig. 6, it is accurate to analyze the results of the attack by using the power indices, regardless of the type of attacker initiated the collusion attack. Furthermore, with the increase of dimensions, the method of this paper is better than the anomaly detection algorithm which is based support vector machine.

6   Conclusion

IN this paper, we presented an analysis method, which can detect the collusion attack in DPoS. We use the Shapley-Shubik power index and Banzhaf power index to analyze the motives for the attackers. At the same time, two power indices are used to effectively detect collusion attacks in DPoS. In order to highlight the superiority of the proposed method, we demonstrate the detection effect by Pearson correlation coefficient.

Although, we effectively analyze and detect collusion attacks in DPoS, how to prevent such attack is still a problem that needs to be solved. What's more, in order to ensure the security of blockchain systems, we still urgently need to establish effective and general prevention models for different consensus mechanisms. And in the next step, we can also consider whether we can apply this method to other similar consensus mechanisms to analyze whether similar attacks with the collusion attack exist. Then we can test the effectiveness of this method.

Acknowledgement. This work was partially supported by the National Natural Science Foundation of China (Grand No. 61962030, 61862036), the Yunnan Provincial Foundation for Leaders of Disciplines in Science and Technology (201905C160046). The Dou Wanchun Expert Workstation of Yunnan Province (202105AF150013).

References

1. Nakamoto, S.: Bitcoin: a peer-to-peer electronic cash system (2008). https://bitcoin.org/bit coin.pdf
2. Ometov, A., et al.: An overview on blockchain for smartphones: state-of-the-art, consensus, implementation challenges and future trends. IEEE Access **8**, 103994–104015 (2020). https://doi.org/10.1109/ACCESS.2020.2998951
3. Larimer, D.: Delegated proof-of-stake white paper (2014). http://www.bts.hk/dpos-baipishu.html
4. Lucas, W.F.: Measuring power in weighted voting systems. In: Brams, S.J., Lucas, W.F., Straffin, P.D. (eds.) Political and Related Models, pp. 183–238. Springer, New York (1983). https://doi.org/10.1007/978-1-4612-5430-0_9
5. Peleg, B., Sudhölter, P.: Introduction to the Theory of Cooperative Games. Springer, Heidelberg (2007). https://doi.org/10.1007/978-3-540-72945-7
6. Wei, Y., Liang, L., Zhou, B., Feng, X.: A modified blockchain DPoS consensus algorithm based on anomaly detection and reward-punishment. In: 2021 13th International Conference on Communication Software and Networks (ICCSN), Chongqing, China, pp. 283–288. IEEE (2021)
7. Yang, X., Chen, Y., Chen, X.: Effective scheme against 51% attack on proof-of-work blockchain with history weighted information. In: 2019 IEEE International Conference on Blockchain (Blockchain), pp. 261–265 (2019). https://doi.org/10.1109/Blockchain.2019.00041
8. AlMallohi, I.A.I., Alotaibi, A.S.M., Alghafees, R., Azam, F., Khan, Z.S.: Multivariable based checkpoints to mitigate the long range attack in proof-of-stake based blockchains. In: Proceedings of the 3rd International Conference on High Performance Compilation, Computing and Communications, pp. 118–122. Association for Computing Machinery, New York (2019). https://doi.org/10.1145/3318265.3318289
9. Lei, W., Qinghua, Z., Baozhen, L.: Extensive game analysis and improvement strategy of DPOS consensus mechanism. J. China Univ. Posts Telecommun. **28**, 27–35 (2021). https://doi.org/10.19682/j.cnki.1005-8885.2021.0030
10. Guo-Hua, T., Yun-Han, H.U., Xiao-Feng, C.: Research progress on attack and defense techniques in block-chain system. J. Softw. **32**, 1495–1525 (2021)

11. Song-Jie, W.E.I., Wei-Long, L., Sha-Sha, L.I.: Overview on typical security problems in public blockchain applications. J. Softw. **33**, 324–355 (2021)
12. Luo, Y., Chen, Y., Chen, Q., Liang, Q.: A new election algorithm for DPos consensus mechanism in blockchain. In: 2018 7th International Conference on Digital Home (ICDH), Guilin, China, pp. 116–120. IEEE (2018)
13. Xu, G., Liu, Y., Khan, P.W.: Improvement of the DPoS consensus mechanism in blockchain based on vague sets. IEEE Trans. Ind. Inf. **16**, 4252–4259 (2020)
14. Yao, Y., Tian, F., Zhang, C.: The research of an improved blockchain consensus mechanism. In: 2020 2nd International Conference on Applied Machine Learning (ICAML), pp. 305–310 (2020). https://doi.org/10.1109/ICAML51583.2020.00069
15. Wang, H., Guo, K.: Byzantine fault tolerant algorithm based on vote. In: 2019 International Conference on Cyber-Enabled Distributed Computing and Knowledge Discovery (CyberC), pp. 190–196 (2019). https://doi.org/10.1109/CyberC.2019.00041
16. Araujo, F., Farinha, J., Domingues, P., Silaghi, G.C., Kondo, D.: A maximum independent set approach for collusion detection in voting pools. J. Parallel Distrib. Comput. **71**, 1356–1366 (2011). https://doi.org/10.1016/j.jpdc.2011.06.004
17. Saad, W., Han, Z., Debbah, M., Hjorungnes, A., Basar, T.: Coalitional game theory for communication networks. IEEE Sig. Process. Mag. **26**, 77–97 (2009)
18. Hart, S.: Shapley value. In: Eatwell, J., Milgate, M., Newman, P. (eds.) Game Theory, London, UK, pp. 210–216. Palgrave Macmillan (1989). https://doi.org/10.1007/978-1-349-20181-5_25
19. Banzhaf, J.F.I.: Weighted voting doesn't work: a mathematical analysis. Rutgers Law Rev. **19**, 317 (1964)
20. Turnovec, F.: Monotonicity of power indices. In: Stewart, T.J., van den Honert, R.C. (eds.) Trends in Multicriteria Decision Making, pp. 199–214. Springer Berlin Heidelberg, Berlin, Heidelberg (1998). https://doi.org/10.1007/978-3-642-45772-2_17

Decentralized Blockchain Transaction Scheme Based on Digital Commitment

Yang Li[1,2]([✉]), Hongyu Wan[1,2], Mengmeng Wang[1,2], Jianming Zhu[1,2], and Xiuli Wang[1,2]

[1] School of Information, Central University of Finance and Economics, Beijing 100081, China
liyang@cufe.edu.cn
[2] Engineering Research Center of State Financial Security, Ministry of Education, Central University of Finance and Economics, Beijing 102206, China

Abstract. As a framework based on data transaction between blocks, blockchain has a high degree of transparency and decentralization. Zhang et al. proposed a transaction framework that combines digital commitment and cryptographic algorithm, which can hide the transaction amount during transaction process. However, there are two problems we should consider: the transactions recording on ledger are operated by trusted full-functional accounting nodes, so the decentralization of the blockchain cannot be realized completely; there is also a risk of data leakage during transaction process as the transaction parameters and transaction amounts are required to be transmitted multiple times. In order to solve the above problems, this paper proposes a multi-key homomorphic encryption transaction scheme based on digital commitment with every node records transaction data. The transaction amount hidden in the commitment can be directly updated in the encrypted state and relevant parameters do not need to be transported multiple times. The transaction scheme proposed in this paper is with better efficiency and provable security, which provides a novel idea for the secure transaction framework in the blockchain.

Keywords: Blockchain · Digital commitment · Homomorphic encryption · Multi-keys

1 Introduction

As a transaction framework that has been emphasized in the 21st century, the blockchain represents a new transaction concept, which is essentially a transaction method of encrypting currency. The blockchain originated from bitcoin [1], which is a digital encrypted currency system proposed by S Nakamoto. It's essentially an open distributed dispersion database. A typical feature of the blockchain transaction is decentralization, and the transaction between the blocks does not require trusted third parties. Transaction data in the block chain is broad casting to network. The powerful dissemination of the blockchain will achieve the rapid transaction. For example, Fan et al. [2] researched the information communication of the 5G era, proposed a high-efficiency sharing scheme based on the blockchain.

If there is a criminal, the user's personal information is illegally stealing or leaked, and it may bring difficult to estimate losses. Therefore, the fairness of the transaction and data security have become an urgent point for users who use the blockchain. In recent years, researchers have used improved encryption mechanisms in blockchain transactions, and the transactions between nodes are usually transmitted after being encrypted. Jemel and Serhrouchni [3] use the idea of attribute-based encryption (ABE) to implement fine-grained access control on the blockchain, and propose a dispersed access control mechanism.

Some transaction mechanisms use fully homomorphic encryption (FHE) [4] to encrypt transaction data, which can resist post quantum attack to ensure the security of the transaction data during transmission. According to the transformation mechanism of identity-based multi-identity homomorphic encryption scheme proposed by Clear et al. [5] in 2015, Tu et al. [6] and Bai et al. [7] achieves the homomorphic operation between ciphertexts of different identity, which can directly calculate the encryption data of the transaction multiple parties.

In order to ensure that ciphertext is not crackd or rewritten by disconnect, we need a safe verification solution to ensure the correctness of the encryption mechanism. Some transactions introduced a trusted third part to verify the correctness of encryption, Zhang et al. [8] proposes a secure transaction scheme based on digital commitment, which performs a function of recording transactions by a trusted full-featured accounting node. According to the digital commitment agreement, you can use a commitment to hide the transaction amount. However, But there are some problems with Zhang's transaction program: 1) Each time the transaction, it is necessary to transfer relavent parameters and key data in the blockchain, which increases the risk of intercepting the restrained by other users; 2) The full-featured accounting nodes leading to the loss of the democratization characteristics of the blockchain transaction. At the same time, there have been a problem to verify the authority of the central node, increasing the danger of concentrated attack on the full-featured accounting node; 3) The real transaction data is recorded, and the data privacy of nodes in the blockchain cannot be guaranteed.

According to the secret verification method of blockchain transaction amount based on digital commitment by Zhang [8], combined with the method of multi-key homomorphic encryption, this paper realizes the verification method of decentralized blockchain transaction based on digital commitment to solves the above three problems: 1) This study modifies the transaction scheme of digital commitment and establishes a decentralized transaction model using homomorphic encryption. When users conduct transactions, they no longer need an authoritative central certification node, and they do not need to send relevant parameters in the transaction process to the central node. 2) This study combines digital commitment with zero knowledge proof to establish a transaction verification scheme that can perform verification without obtaining real transaction data. To ensure the verification of the correctness and rationality of the transaction in the hidden state of the transaction amount.; 3) This research implements the ledger update scheme based on homomorphic encryption, which ensures the security of transaction data transmission in the network.

2 Preliminaries

The privacy model in this paper is mainly based on digital commitment, multi-key fully homomorphic encryptionand and zero-knowledge proof to realize decentralized blockchain transaction in blockchain.

2.1 Digital Commitment

Digital commitment [9, 10] is a method to ensure the method of trusted data transactions between communication between communication, as a result, the real data can't be decrypted by unrelated nodes in the process of transmission. It is a cryptographic protocol that mainly includes two phases, and is done between the committer and the receiver. The first phase is a promise phase: the committer encrypts data by using a key or random number before transmitting data, and only the encrypted data or keyword is transmitted to the receiver. The receiver cannot view real data or keywords, which can not make judgments on the authenticity of the relevant data. The committer has passed the real data to the receiver in encryption, and the receiver saves the encrypted data to verify the authentication of data authenticity later. The second phase is the open phase: the committer will send the key and the true plaintext data used in the previous phase to the receiver. Only at this phase, the receiver can read and obtain real data, and the receiver will use the received key to operate plaintext. If the calculation result is consistent with the encrypted data accepted during the commitment phase, it can be proved that the received data is not tampered.

Taking perdersen commitment as an example, the digital commitment include the two stages of commitment phase and open phase:

1) Commitment Phase
    The committer selects a multiplicative group G with order p, and p is a large prime. Selects two generators g and f in multiplication group G to make $log_g f$ cannot be known by both parties. That is, $g, f \in G$. Then, the committer selects the random number $r \in Z_p$. m is defined as the plaintext symbol, and y is defined as the commitment symbol. According to Formula

$$y = g^m f^r \bmod p \tag{1}$$

    The corresponding commitment value y is calculated. The committer sends the commitment to the receiver and discloses the parameters (g, f, p). The receiver accepts the ciphertext sent by the committer, but cannot decrypt the commitment value to obtain the plaintext m only according to the public parameters (g, f, p).
2) Open Phase
    When The receiver needs to obtain the real data sent by the committer, the committer will send the real plaintext data m' and the random number r to the receiver. At this time, the receiver needs to verify the authenticity of the plaintext sent by the committer. The ciphertext y' corresponding to the plaintext data m' can be calculated according to the formula $y' = g^{m'} f^r \bmod p$. If the formula below

$$y = g^m f^r \bmod p == y' = g^{m'} f^r \bmod p \tag{2}$$

is satisfied, it can be proved that the plaintext data sent by the committer twice are consistent, and the tamperability of plaintext data can be proved.

2.2 Homomorphic Encryption

Homomorphic encryption (HE) means that the result of directly calculating the encrypted ciphertext is the same as that of encrypting the plaintext before encryption. In 1978, Rivest et al. [11] first proposed the concept of privacy homomorphism to construct an encryption mechanism supporting ciphertext retrieval. It is assumed that the plaintext group is $m = \{m_1, m_2 \ldots m_n\}$ and the encrypted ciphertext group of the plaintext group is $c = \{c_1, c_2 \ldots c_n\} = \{E_k(m_1), E_k(m_2) \ldots E_k(m_n)\}$. $E_k()$ is defined as encryption operation, and $D_k()$ is defined as decryption operation. k is the key used in the encryption and decryption process. Two basic operations u and v are defined, which can operate plaintext group m and ciphertext group c. If the encryption operation satisfies the formula

$$E_k\{u\{m_1, m_2 \ldots m_n\}\} == v\{E_k(m_1), E_k(m_2) \ldots E_k(m_n)\} \tag{3}$$

It indicates that the encryption operation is homomorphic. HE includes additive homomorphism and multiplicative homomorphism. Additive homomorphism refers to replacing the basic operation in formula (3) with addition operation, that is, the formula below is satisfied.

$$E_k\left\{\sum_{i=1}^{n} m_i\right\} == \sum_{i=1}^{n} E_k(m_i) \tag{4}$$

Multiplicative homomorphism refers to replacing the basic operation in formula (3) with multiplication operation, that is, the formula below is satisfied.

$$E_k\left\{\prod_{i=1}^{n} m_i\right\} == \prod_{i=1}^{n} E_k(m_i) \tag{5}$$

If the encryption scheme satisfies both additive homomorphism and multiplicative homomorphism, it is called HE. he is mainly divided into four parts: key generation algorithm, encryption algorithm, decryption algorithm and ciphertext calculation algorithm.

2.3 Multi-key Fully Homomorphic Encryption

Multi key homomorphic encryption [12, 13] (MKFHE) is an improvement based on HE, which can encrypt the same data for multiple users. Each user generates a key that can uniquely represent itself according to its own attributes, which can ensure the traceability of the encryption process and the preciseness of the encryption process. The ciphertext encrypted by multiple keys can participate in homomorphic operation together, so as to realize the purpose of multi-user operating the same ciphertext. Homomorphic operation of encrypted ciphertext can realize rewriting or correctness verification of data on the premise of ensuring the confidentiality of plaintext. After the operation, the joint key can be calculated by a specific algorithm which combines the key of all user together, so as to decrypt the ciphertext and obtain the corresponding plaintext. At present, MKFHE is mainly divided into three categories:

1) A MKFHE scheme based on NTRU encryption mechanism proposed by López et al.;
2) A MKFHE scheme based on Gentry-Sahai-Waters (GSW) proposed by clear et al.;
3) A MKFHE scheme based on Brakerski-Gentry-Vaikuntanathan (BGV) proposed by Chen et al.

MKFHE schemes usually include four algorithms: key generation algorithm *KeyGen* encryption algorithm *Enc* decryption algorithm *Dec* and joint key generation algorithm *Eval* In this paper, homomorphic operation can be realized by re-encrypting both sides of communication. After homomorphic encryption, the balance quantity of both parties can be homomorphic, so that the balance data of different users can be compared after encryption.The algorithms required by the MKFHE scheme used in this paper can be roughly described as follows:

1) Key Generation Algorithm *KeyGen*()
   Each user selects a random number λ_i as a security parameter, which is the only parameter that each user is unique. λ_i is the input value of this function which eneratesthe public key pk_i and private key sk_i of each user.
2) Encryption Algorithm *Enc*()
   According to the public key pk_i disclosed in each user, the public key group $pk = \{pk_1, pk_2 \ldots pk_n\}$ can be obtained. The data group that needs to be encrypted is a plaintext group $m = \{m_1, m_2 \ldots m_n\}$. This function uses the public key group pk and ciphertext m as input to generate encrypted ciphertext group $c = \{c_1, c_2 \ldots c_n\}$.
3) Joint Key Generation Algorithm *Eval*()
   The Ciphertext in the ciphertext group encrypted by multiple users can perform an operating operation.

2.4 Zero-Knowledge Proof

Zero-knowledge proof [14, 15] refers to the verification of the transaction or calculation correctness in the case where the proof is not directly acquired but obtains relevant data. It guarantees that real data is not certified to directly know, thereby ensuring confidentiality and security in real data during transmission verification.

For example, if there is a transactor A and transactor B. Both sides need to send a transaction amount to the other party (assuming the transaction amount is the value of the balance change). It is clear that the transaction can be established only when the absolute value of the transaction amount sent by both parties is equal. But both sides don't want the other party to know the specific number of transactions that they send, and only want the transaction amount on the other party's account as the encrypted data. So how should we verify the correctness of the transaction?

Then we can introduce a zero-knowledge proof. We suppose the number of account balances of transactor A before the transaction is C_A, and after the transaction is C'_A. The number of account balances of transactor B before the transaction is C_B, and after the transaction is C'_B. Then these four data meet the following formula:

$$C_A + C_B == C'_A + C'_B \tag{6}$$

The correct value of the transaction is performed without knowing the exact number of the transaction amount sent by the other party. Of course, the premise of this assumption is that the two sides cannot get the number of transaction amounts of the other party by calculating the difference in account balance before and after the transaction.

3   Blockchain Transaction Scheme Based on Digital Commitment

3.1   Transaction Scene

It is assumed that there is a scene as shown in Fig. 1, and two nodes in the blockchain want to make a transaction. The transactor A wants to transfer out the transaction amount with quantity $T_{A \to B}$ to transactor B, therefore, transactor B wants to accept the transaction amount of $T_{B \to A}$ from transactor A. After obtaining the transaction amount sent by the other party, both parties need to verify the transaction. After the verification is successful, both sides will issue the correctness certificate of the transaction to the whole network. The transaction process is broadcast by transactor A and transactor B in the blockchain. Any user within the broadcast range can listen to the transaction process and record the transaction. However, there are several problems in this transaction: 1) The transaction is based on a completely decentralized transaction framework, and the public accounting node no longer exists. So what accounting method should be adopted to achieve a completely decentralized accounting behavior. 2) How to ensure that the transaction amount sent by both parties is not obtained by users other than the sender. Of course, this "user other than the sender" also includes the receiver of transaction amount data. 3) Last but not least, what verification methods should be adopted to verify the consistency of transaction amount and the legitimacy of transaction when the transaction amount data is confidential.

In order to solve these three problems, this paper proposes a decentralized blockchain transaction scheme based on digital commitment. The core of the transaction scheme is to update the book in each node locally. No public accounting nodes are required, and no need to consider the reliability of public nodes. Each node does not need to transfer relevant parameters in the encryption process to the public node, reducing the storage pressure of the central node in the blockchain. All nodes in the network generate private keys according to their own attributes. Before the transaction, the community sends the transaction amount encrypted by its own private key. After confirming the correctness of the transaction, each node performs the update of the account, and records the encrypted transaction amount corresponding to the transaction. Therefore, any user in the network can record the transaction amount after the transaction encryption. However, in addition to the transactors, other nodes cannot decrypt ciphertext or acquire the real transaction amount proposed by the transaction.

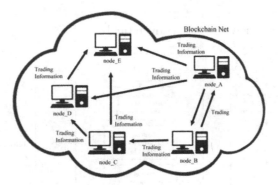

Fig. 1. Transaction scene

3.2 Scheme Design

The scheme is a decentralized blockchain network within the communication range, which does not require an authoritative center certificate node. When the mode is transaction, it is not necessary to send a public parameter that needs to be used during the encryption process to the central node. Assuming that two nodes in the present blockchain want to make a transaction of the transaction amount T, division of transactions is the transactor A and the transactor B. The transaction occurs between the two modes in the blockchain network, which does not consider the transaction behavior between multiple nodes.

In the transaction scheme of this article, the transaction amount is hidden in the digital commitment, and Transaction two sides mutual commitment party and commitment receiver. Take the transactor A and the transactor B as an example, in the promise phase, the committer (the transactor A) send the encrypted transaction amount $E_{k_A}\{T_{A \to B}\}$ to the receiver (the transactor B). The receiver retains and stores this data, but it is not possible to verify the correctness of the transaction. In the same way, the transactor B will send the encrypted transaction amount $E_{k_B}\{T_{B \to A}\}$ to transactor A, and the receiver retains and stores this data. In the open phase, the two sides need to use their own key to reprroun the received encrypted data, that is, the transactor A calculates to get $E_{k_A}\{E_{k_B}\{T_{B \to A}\}\}$, the transactor B calculates to get $E_{k_B}\{E_{k_A}\{T_{A \to B}\}\}$. The two sides will send the results to each other. The two sides are each verified locally. If the formula $E_{k_A}\{E_{k_B}\{T_{B \to A}\}\} == E_{k_B}\{E_{k_A}\{T_{A \to B}\}\}$ is established, the correctness of the transaction can be proved. The other nodes in the network can make bills. Due to all the encryption method mentioned above is HE, each node can directly operate the account balance of a node during accounting, and update the account balance data of each node. According to Fig. 2, we can see the specific process of the transaction scheme in this study.

3.2.1 Initialization Phase

The initialization phase takes place before the transaction, when the node in the blockchain is executed to perform the book update process. M_A is defined as the account balance of the transactor A, K_A is defined as the public key, and k_A is defined as the private key. The transactor A selects a random number r_A that can only identify the identity

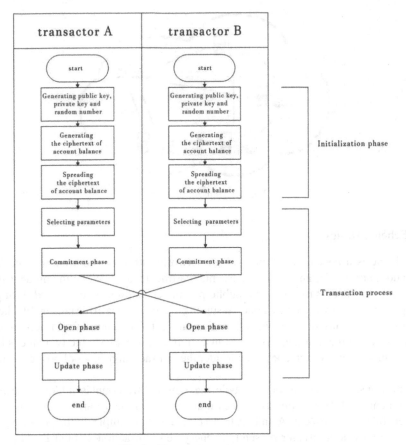

Fig. 2. Transaction scheme process

according to its own attribute. Then the HE algorithm $Enc()$ use an input of account balance M_A, public key K_A, and random number r_A to generate the encrypted account balance of the transactor A, which is $C_A = Enc(M_A, r_A)$. The transactor A will broadcast the encrypted account balance to the blockchain network. Other nodes in the network acquire ciphertext, updating the account balance data of the transactor A in this node. In this kind, all nodes in the blockchain send their account balances in encrypted state to the network, then these datas will be accepted and stored by all nodes in the network. After a round of update, the accounts in all nodes in the blockchain have been updated, storing the ciphertext of the account balances of all nodes in the current blockchain.

3.2.2 Transaction Process

The transaction process is divided into parameter selection phase, commitment phase, open phase, and account update phase.

1) Parameter Selection Phase

We define $hash()$ as a safe hash function, random selection l, t, s_1, s_2 as security parameters, and select a large prime number p, q satisfing $p = 2q+1$. Z_p^* is a positive integer set p. For $\forall x \in Z_p^*$, it satisfy $\left\{ |hash(x)| == |p| - 1 \right\} \cap \left\{ hash(x) \in Z_p^* \right\}$. The transactor A selects the random number $u \in Z_p^*$, and defines the generation formulas of g_A and f_A as follows, g_A and f_A are not 1 and the orders are q.

$$g_A = hash(u_A)^{\frac{p-1}{q}} = hash(u_A)^2 \bmod p \tag{7}$$

$$f_A = hash(g_A)^2 \bmod p \tag{8}$$

The transactor B selects the random number $u_B \in Z_p^*$, and defines the generation formulas of g_B and f_B as follows, g_B and f_B are not 1 and the orders are q.

$$g_B = hash(u_B)^{\frac{p-1}{q}} = hash(u_B)^2 \bmod p \tag{9}$$

$$f_B = hash(g_B)^2 \bmod p \tag{10}$$

2) Commitment Phase

The transactor A selects the random number $r_A \in \left[-2^{s_1}q + 1, 2^{s_1}q - 1 \right]$. The commitment algorithm $y_A()$ uses r_A, g_A, f_A, p and the transaction amount $T_{A \rightarrow B}$ as the input to calculate the transaction amount y_A hidden by the transactor A in the commitment form:

$$y_A = y_A(T_{A \rightarrow B}, r_A) = g^{T_{A \rightarrow B}} f^{r_A} \bmod p \tag{11}$$

The encryption algorithm $Enc_A()$ uses r_A and transaction amount $T_{A \rightarrow B}$ as input to calculate $c_A = Enc_A(T_{A \rightarrow B}, r_A)$, and obtain ciphertext c_A of the transaction amount of the transactor A.

The transactor B selects the random number $r_B \in \left[-2^{s_2}q + 1, 2^{s_2}q - 1 \right]$. The commitment algorithm $y_B()$ uses r_B, g_B, f_B, p and the transaction amount $T_{B \rightarrow A}$ as the input to calculate the transaction amount y_B hidden by the transactor B in the commitment form:

$$y_B = y_B(T_{B \rightarrow A}, r_B) = g^{T_{B \rightarrow A}} f^{r_B} \bmod p \tag{12}$$

The encryption algorithm $Enc_B()$ uses r_B and transaction amount $T_{B \rightarrow A}$ as input to calculate $c_B = Enc_B(T_{B \rightarrow A}, r_B)$, and obtain ciphertext c_B of the transaction amount of the transactor B.

The transactor A uses the public key E_{K_B} to encrypt the commitment y_A to get $E_{K_B}(y_A)$, uploads this combination $\left\{ E_{K_B}(y_A), c_A \right\}$ to the blockchain network and broadcasts this combination in the network. The transactor B accepts and stores c_A, using the private key k_B to decrypt $E_{K_B}(y_A)$ to get the commitment value y_A. At this time, the transactor B cannot verify the authenticity of c_A, and cannot update directly the account of the transactor A. In the same way, the transactor B uploads this combination $\{E_{K_A}(y_B), c_B\}$ to the blockchain network and broadcasts this combination in the network. The transactor A accepts and stores c_B, using the private key k_A to decrypt $E_{K_A}(y_B)$ to get the commitment value y_B. In the commitment phase, the transaction only stores ciphertext of the transaction amount sent by the other party, but cannot verify that the transaction amount of the two parties is consistent. Therefore, it is impossible to confirm the rationality of the transaction, and it is impossible to determine if the transaction is required.

3) Open Phase

In the open phase, the transaction amount value received during the commitment phase is reprressed by the other transactor. The transactor A re-encrypts y_B to get commitment value y_{BA}; The transactor B re-encryptes $y_A y_B$ to get commitment value y_{AB}.

$$
\begin{aligned}
y_{BA} &= y_B * f^{r_A} \\
&= g^{T_{B \to A}} f^{r_B} mod p * f^{r_A} \\
&= g^{T_{B \to A}} f^{r_B + r_A} mod p
\end{aligned}
\tag{13}
$$

$$
\begin{aligned}
y_{AB} &= y_A * f^{r_B} \\
&= g^{T_{A \to B}} f^{r_A} mod p * f^{r_B} \\
&= g^{T_{A \to B}} f^{r_A + r_B} mod p
\end{aligned}
\tag{14}
$$

The transactor A encrypts y_{BA} using uses the public key E_{K_B} of the transactor B to generate $E_{K_B}(y_{BA})$ and sends it to the transactor B; The transactor B encrypts y_{AB} using the public key E_{K_A} of the transactor A to generate $E_{K_A}(y_{AB})$ and sends it to the transactor A. The two parties of the transaction use their own private key to decrypt ciphertext, which has received the ciphertext of the other party's commitment value, and constructs zero-knowledge proof:

$$
y_{BA} = g^{T_{B \to A}} f^{r_B + r_A} mod p == g^{T_{A \to B}} f^{r_A + r_B} mod p = y_{AB}
\tag{15}
$$

4) Update Phase

If the Eq. (15) is established, the transaction amount proposed by the transaction is the same, and the correctness of the transaction can be proved. The two sides sends a transaction license in the blockchain network, and each node in the blockchain performs an update operation of the book. Taking the account balance of the trander A as an example, the following calculation is performed in all nodes in the blockchain network:

$$
C'_A = C_A - c_A
\tag{16}
$$

All nodes get the ciphertext of the account balance of the transactor A after the transaction, and update the account of the transactor A.

4 Scheme Analysis

4.1 Positive Analysis

4.1.1 Verifing the Correctness of the Transaction

The transaction scheme can determine whether the number of transaction amounts proposed by the trading party A and the transaction B B is consistent. The transaction is hidden in the digital commitment, and the zero knowledge of the formula (15) can be constructed to compare the transaction amount proposed by the Eq. (15) based on the normal creativity of the commitment algorithm:

$$y_{BA} = g^{T_{B \to A}} f^{r_B + r_A} \bmod p == g^{T_{A \to B}} f^{r_A + r_B} \bmod p = y_{AB}$$

If the number of transaction amounts proposed by both parties are the same, the zero knowledge proof is established, which can prove the correctness of the transaction, and the transaction is sent to the network correct signal, and the various nodes in the network are updated. If the number of transactions proposed by both parties is different, the zero knowledge certificate is not established, the transaction fails, the transaction is sent to the network to send the transaction failed, and the various nodes do not perform a book update.

4.1.2 The Correctness of the Account Updating

Each node in the block chain records the account balance of each node on the chain, and the account balance of each node is saved with the key generated by the own attribute. Whenever a transaction is performed, a ciphertext that receives and stores the transaction amount transmitted by the transaction is used, and the transaction part is used as an example, and the balance text of the transaction party is updated according to the formula (16).

$$C'_A = C_A - c_A$$

Only when a transaction is established, each node performs the homogeneous calculation of the account balance of the transaction, otherwise the transaction fails, and the account will not be updated. Since the account balance and transaction amount of each node use the same state-of-the-state encryption mechanism, the data obtained after ciphertext decryption of the account balance updated to a node is the real account balance of the node. When the node needs to get your own account balance data, you can use your own private key k_A calculation to get a real account balance $m = Dec(C'_A)$.

4.2 Security Analysis

4.2.1 Verifing the Security of the Commitment

When there is a transaction, the commitment is transmitted between the transactors after encrypted by the public key of receiver, so only the committer can decrypt the encrypted commitment. When the commitment is re-encrypted during the commitment phase and the open phase, the random numbers r can be generated, which has a unique identification. The security of Perdersen commitment is based on the issue of discrete logarithms. And the digital commitment in this paper can prove the security of the commitment algorithm according to the elliptic curve discrete logarithm problem. The most efficient algorithm that can crack the discrete logarithmic difficult problem based on P-step programs requires approximately $O(\sqrt{p-1})$ times. It is proven to be expressed in the same difficulty in its commitment y_1 and y_2 to the formula as:

$$PK(y_1, y_2, p) = \{\exists t, r_1, r_2 : y_1 = g^t f^{r_1} mod p \land y_2 = g^t f^{r_1} mod p \qquad (17)$$

Therefore, it can be proved that only the only m can be calculated to get y, any $m' \neq m$ cannot obtain $y == y'$. In the case of y and p, non-correlated people cannot decipher the m and r value. It is guaranteed that the commitment is security during the transmission process and the commitment process, and cannot be could not be cracked.

4.2.2   The Security of the Account Updating

In the transaction scenario in this paper, the account balance data is transmitted or stored in a state in which the encryption algorithm is encrypted. Based on a limited domain of elliptic curve and complex elliptic curve discrete pair problem, the encryption program has proven security and cannot be cracked. Some and only the transaction can decrypt using a private key, and other nodes cannot obtain the real account balances and transaction amounts of nodes.

4.3   Performance Analysis

This paper solves some of the deficiencies in the safety trading program proposed by Zhang et al. [8], and also improves in efficiency. Li et al. [16] and WANG et al. [17] combined with Paillier algorithm and zero knowledge certification to realize the security verification function of the transaction. Zhang et al. [8] class combined with the nominal encryption algorithm and zero knowledge certificate based on the elliptic curve to realize the security verification and account update of the transaction. This paper combines the elliptical encryption algorithm and zero knowledge certificate based on the elliptic curve to achieve complete decentralized transactions. Security verification and account update.

During the commitment verification process of this paper, four encrypted operations were performed, and two state-made encryption operations were performed during the book update. It is assumed that in the multiplication group G of the step p, p is a large number of calculation complexity, and the calculation complexity of the transaction process of this paper is $36 + 24 \log p$. The homogeneous encryption scheme based on the elliptic curve is smaller than the key generated by the RSA encryption algorithm, so the speed of the key generated is very fast, and has an absolute efficiency advantage during the generation of the key and initialization. Therefore, we can ignore the overhead of the key generation and initialization, and you can get the performance analysis results of Table 1:

Table 1. Performance analysis results

Transaction scheme	Computational complexity	Decentralization	Hidden function
Li et al. [16]'s scheme	$9\log^3 p$	–	$\checkmark$
WANG et al. [17]'s scheme	$3\log^3 p$	–	$\checkmark$
Zhang et al. [8]'s scheme	$36 + 66\log p$	$\times$	$\checkmark$
Scheme in this paper	$36 + 24\log p$	$\checkmark$	$\checkmark$

The trading scheme proposed in this paper may be a certain advantage over other algorithms, according to Table 1.

5 Conclusion

With the increasing maturation of blockchain, the privacy of users' personal information is increasingly valued. The technical defect of blockchain have gradually appeared, and powerful data mining and analysis technology gives personal privacy potential threat. As a result, the event of the security attack occurs frequently. Unsafe problem in the blockchain transaction have become a problem that needs to be solved as soon as possible. This paper establishes a decentralized blockchain transaction scheme based on digital commitment, without an authoritative center certificate node. When there is a transaction, transactors do not need to send the relevant parameters to the central node during the transaction process. This scheme combines the digital commitment with MKFHE to support the privacy. It implements the correctness and rationality of the transaction, supporting the accounts in encryption form in each node. This paper proposed a improved scheme based on decentralized blockchain transaction scheme, providing new ideas for security transactions in the blockchain.

While placing high hopes on the transaction scheme based on blockchain, we also need to pay attention to the loopholes in it. We need to improve the correctness of authentication and optimize the limitation of computing cost. It should be noted that although the continuous improvement of the encryption algorithm will bring higher computing efficiency and security, the encryption algorithm is not always perfect. For example, the homomorphic encryption based on NTRU in this study, although it has high computational efficiency and is very consistent with the transaction scheme of this study, it still has the risk of decryption failure with a very small probability. Therefore, this study can find the relevant parameters more suitable for this scheme, adjust the target range of decryption operation, improve the success rate of decryption, and achieve a more accurate transaction model.

Acknowledgment. This work is supported by the Emerging Interdisciplinary Project of CUFE, the National Natural Science Foundation of China (No. 61906220) and Ministry of education of Humanities and Social Science project (No. 19YJCZH178).

References

1. Nakamoto, S.: Bitcoin: a peer-to-peer electronic cash system (2008). https://bitcoin.org/bit coin.pdf
2. Fan, K., Ren, Y., Wang, Y., Li, H., Yang, Y.: Blockchain-based efficient privacy preserving and data sharing scheme of content-centric network in 5G. IET Commun. **12**(5), 527–532 (2017)
3. Jemel, M., Serhrouchni, A.: Decentralized access control mechanism with temporal dimension based on blockchain. In: 2017 IEEE 14th International Conference on e-Business Engineering (ICEBE), Shanghai, pp. 177–182. IEEE Press (2017)
4. Gentry, C.: Fully homomorphic encryption using ideal lattices. In: Proceedings of the 41st Annual ACM Symposium on Theory of Computing (STOC 2009), Bethesda, pp. 169–178 (2009)
5. Clear, M., McGoldrick, C.: Multi-identity and multi-key leveled FHE from learning with errors. In: Gennaro, R., Robshaw, M. (eds.) CRYPTO 2015. LNCS, vol. 9216, pp. 630–656. Springer, Heidelberg (2015). https://doi.org/10.1007/978-3-662-48000-7_31
6. Guangsheng, T.U., Xiaoyuan, Y.A.N.G., Tanping, Z.H.O.U.: Efficient identi-ty-based multi-identity fully homomorphic encryption scheme. J. Comput. Appl. **39**(03), 750–755 (2019)
7. Bai, P., Zhang, W.: Fully homomorphic encryption scheme based on learning with errors under multi-attribute environment. J. Comput. Appl. **38**(05), 1377–1382 (2018)
8. Zhang, X., Li, Q., Fu, F.: Secret verification method of blockchain transaction amount based on digital commitment. Comput. Sci. **7**(2), 1–9 (2021). http://kns.cnki.net/kcms/detail/50.1075.TP.20210209.0955.008.html
9. Pedersen, T.P.: Non-interactive and information-theoretic secure verifiable secret sharing. In: Feigenbaum, J. (ed.) CRYPTO 1991. LNCS, vol. 576, pp. 129–140. Springer, Heidelberg (1992). https://doi.org/10.1007/3-540-46766-1_9
10. Dong, G.S., Chen, Y.X., Fan, J., et al.: Research on privacy protection strategy in blockchain application. Comput. Sci. **46**(5), 29–35 (2019)
11. Rivest, R.L., Adleman, L., Dertouzos, M.L.: On data banks and privacy homomorphisms. Found. Secure Comput. **4**(11), 169–180 (1978)
12. López, A.A., Tromer, E., Vaikuntanathan, V.: On-the-fly mul-tiparty computation on the cloud via multikey fully homomorphic encryption. In: Proceedings of the 44st Annual ACM Symposium on Theory of Computing (STOC 2012), pp. 1219–1234. ACM (2012)
13. Rui-Qi, L.I., Chun-Fu, J.I.A.: A multi-key homomorphic encryption scheme based on NTRU. J. Cryptol. Res. **7**(5), 683–697 (2020)
14. Feige, U., Fiat, A., Shamir, A.: Zero-knowledge proofs of identity. J. Cryptol. **1**(2), 77–94 (1988). https://doi.org/10.1007/BF02351717
15. Schnorr, C.P.: Efficient signature generation by smart cards. J. Cryptol. **4**(3), 161–174 (1991). https://doi.org/10.1007/BF00196725

Private Computing

Research on Abnormal Transaction Detection Method for Blockchain

Hualong Han[1], Ranran Wang[1], Yvpeng Chen[1], Kang Xie[2], and Ke Zhang[1(✉)]

[1] School of Information and Communication Engineering, University of Electronic Science and Technology of China, Chengdu, China
zhangke@uestc.edu.cn
[2] Key Lab of Information Network Security, Ministry of Public Security, Beijing, China

Abstract. Blockchain has become a hot topic in current academic research due to its decentralization, imtamability and anonymity. However it also makes blockchain a tool for money laundering, fraud, extortion and other illegal activities. Therefore, it is particularly important to supervise and detect abnormal transactions on blockchain. In our paper, graph data structure is used to express blockchain node transactions. Aiming at the problem of too few abnormal transaction samples of block chain, k-rate sampling and feature similarity are used to solve the problem of unbalanced data. Further more, we select some features for feature preprocessing according to the distribution of multiple features of blockchain transactions. Finally, the blockchain transaction topology is used for multi-graph convolutional neural network machine learning methods to train the blockchain transaction data. So the abnormal nodes and non-abnormal nodes classification model is obtained. And the abnormal transactions of blockchain is detected by using the classification model. Experimental results show that compared with traditional algorithms such as logistic regression (LR), multi-layer perceptron (MLP) and linear regression (LR), the anomaly detection algorithm based on sample equalization and feature engineering has significantly improved recall rate. This provides a theoretical and practical basis for our next work – tracing abnormal nodes of blockchain, which has a good prospect for industrial application.

Keywords: Blockchain anomaly detection · Sample equalization · Feature engineering · Graph convolutional neural network

1 Introduction

In recent years, due to the imperfect legal system, unclear legal provisions, weak execution of anti-money laundering regulatory measures and insufficient effectiveness of anti-money laundering measures in the field of blockchain transaction, blockchain has become one of the tools for criminals to get away with crimes and evade sanctions. In the case of Bitcoin, $10.1 billion flowed out of China via blockchain in 2017, $17.9 billion in 2018, and $11.4 billion in 2019. The three-year outflow amounts are more than 1% of China's $3 trillion in foreign exchange reserves. It is urgent to supervise the blockchain technology and detect abnormal transactions on the blockchain.

The abnormal behaviors on blockchain have attracted the attention of various governments and become a hot issue in academic research. A large number of scholars have found money laundering, fraud, Ponzi scheme and other abnormal behaviors on the blockchain after studying the real transaction data of the blockchain. With further analysis of blockchain transaction data, scholars at home and abroad have found blockchain's more little-known abnormal behaviors, such as base-pseudo-spam transactions, dark web transactions, market manipulation and so on. However, previous studies often found abnormal behaviors by manually analyzing token flow direction after constructing blockchain transaction topology, and the research method used was not applicable to industry. What's more, it's poor for the first generation of blockchain without the application of smart contract (Bitcoin blockchain) to analysis the opcode of the smart contract code to determine the attributes of transactions initiated by the smart contract on the blockchain. Moreover, the blockchain transaction network has the following problems:

- Unknown and complex transaction features: In blockchain transaction data, transaction amount, time, people and other features are involved, but the physical meaning of specific features in the actual data set is unknown. Traditional recognition methods are cumbersome and difficult, and the effect is not good. It is an unsolved problem to mine the features with strong model expression ability from these features so as to improve the identification ability of abnormal transaction model of blockchain.
- Large blockchain transactions and unbalanced positive and negative samples: There is a large amount of data in the blockchain transaction network, and the number of negative samples (abnormal behavior data) is much smaller than the number of positive samples in the huge transaction network dataset, so the traditional detection method is not good. However, there are many transactions with unknown attributes in these transaction data. How to use this part of the transaction data to reduce the impact caused by unbalanced samples is also a problem to be solved in this paper.

Therefore, this paper introduces feature engineering and sample equalization into abnormal transaction detection in blockchain network. In view of the imbalance of abnormal transaction categories in blockchain, we first mark random samples k% of unknown attribute transactions as abnormal samples, and the rest (100%–k%) as normal transactions to be add to the dataset, so as to increase the proportion of abnormal samples in training. Furthermore, in order to better associate the unknown attribute transactions with the known attribute transactions, we calculate the feature similarity of the two transactions according to the values of transactions' features so as to better mark the unknown attribute transactions. At the same time, the weighted cross entropy loss method is used to train the neural network model to give higher importance to illegal samples. In view of the diversified characteristics of blockchain transactions, we statistically and visually analyze the distribution of related features, and encode some discrete features and continuous features respectively and divide them into discrete boxes. Finally, the blockchain transaction network dataset (Elliptic) is composed, which is decomposed into 49 time steps for the computation of graph neural network. In order to further explore the application effect of blockchain trading network and multiple graph convolutional neural network in block chain trading network, and improve the accuracy of abnormal recognition scenes in block chain trading network, this paper realizes feature extraction and mining of block chain trading network by constructing GNN-FiLM and other kinds of graph neural network.Our main contributions are as follows:

- Proposed the viewpoint of improving abnormal transaction detection of blockchain based on feature engineering, which is that the expression ability of key features of blockchain transaction is fully extracted and utilized by feature engineering method.
- Proposed the idea of improving abnormal transaction detection of blockchain based on sample equilibrium, and the proportion of abnormal transaction is increased by k-rate sampling and feature similarity respectively, making full use of unknown transaction attribute data.
- Proposed blockchain abnormal transaction detection point of view based on data driven, and designed a complete solution from the blockchain transaction data to the blockchain abnormal transaction detection,which adopts multigraph convolution neural networks like GNN-FiLM to extract and mining blockchain transaction network characteristics. Finally we verify the validity of the proposed method on Elliptic datasets. It provides reference and choice direction for follow-up researchers.

2   Related Work

The proposal of blockchain is undoubtedly a great success. However, due to the lack of regulatory mechanism, many abnormal transactions have been derived. Therefore, literature [1] uses k-means clustering, Mahalanobis distance and SVM for the user graph and transaction graph generated according to bitcoin network respectively, so as to detect abnormal transactions in blockchain. Literature [2] for the first time took users and transactions as data features, and adopted unsupervised learning to detect abnormal transaction behaviors through the topology structure of transaction graphs. Weber et al. [3] used logistic regression, random forest, and MLP to detect abnormal transactions on blockchain.

However, since the topology of blockchain transaction network can be considered as an infinite dimensional dataset, the processing of such non-European data is also a big research problem. Traditional machine learning methods have poor research effect on the graph network of such non-European data. Therefore, with the rise of graph convolutional neural network, graph convolutional neural represented by GCN also shines in blockchain anomaly detection. Convolution neural network graph is by Bruce based on graph theory and takes the lead in putting forward convolution theorem. Due to the high cost of time and space, subsequent appeared by convolution kernels parametric optimization figure greatly reduces the cost of time and space after the graph convolutional neural network (GCN). GCN uses graph convolution operator as the core to extract information aggregation of graph data in spatial structure to complete feature extraction. GCN [3] was first applied to the abnormal recognition of blockchain, but the experimental results were not good because the number of negative samples (criminal behavior data) was much smaller than the number of positive samples in the huge dataset of transaction networks. Aldo et al. [4] improved on GCN and proposed EvolveGCN. EvolveGCN uses RNN to Evolve GCN for dynamic capture of neural network parameters. The experimental results showed that EvolveGCN performed better than GCN.

In recent years, with the good application effect of graph convolutional neural networks in graph data structure, a number of improved graph convolutional neural networks based on GCN have been proposed. Veličković P et al. [5] introduced the attention mechanism into graph convolutional neural network, calculated the hidden features of each node in the graph by taking care of adjacent nodes, and proposed GAT graph neural network. Du [6] used K graph convolution kernels to extract local features of different sizes, and reserved K (the receptive fields of K convolution kernels were 1 to K respectively) as hyperparameters to propose TAGCN, which avoided the previous defect of incomplete and sufficient graph information extraction due to the approximation of the convolution kernels, and improved the expression ability of the model. Many GNNS propagate information along the edge of the graph, so only the source representation information of the edge can be calculated. For this, Brockschmidt [7] uses the target node representation of an edge to calculate the transformation that can be used for all incoming information and proposes GNN-FiLM, which uses the feature module based on past information. In addition, literature [8–16] proposed a variety of graph neural networks, which have a good application effect in the classification of open source datasets. Blockchain abnormal transaction detection is essentially a binary classification problem, so it can be used for data mining and analysis of blockchain abnormal transaction topology.

To sum up, starting from the topology of blockchain network, different blockchains can be covered, anomalies of more types of blockchain can be detected, and the application scope is wider. At the same time, the graph convolutional neural network solves the non-European data set problem and shows excellent performance in the field of graph deep learning. However, the application of graph neural network to blockchain abnormal transaction detection lacks attention to block chain transaction data, does not well apply the rich characteristics of blockchain transaction nodes, and ignores the problem of less abnormal transaction data in blockchain, which results in unsatisfactory final detection results. Therefore, from the perspective of blockchain transaction topology, this paper uses a variety of graph convolutional neural network to detect anomaly transactions in blockchain. At the same time, in order to better improve the training effect of the model, this paper further processes the transaction features of blockchain, discretizes some continuous features and conducts one-hot encoding of discrete features. Furthermore, the transaction nodes with unknown attributes of blockchain are treated with sample equalization to improve the detection ability of the model.

3   Model

3.1   System Model

The blockchain abnormal transaction detection model architecture proposed in this paper is shown in Fig. 1, which is divided into three functional modules, namely, transaction data collection module, transaction topology building module and abnormal transaction detection module.

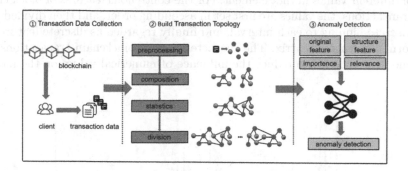

Fig. 1. Blockchain abnormal transaction detection model architecture

The transaction data collection module collects and collates the transaction information on the blockchain through the client. The authenticity of the transaction data on the blockchain can be guaranteed as much as possible due to its immutable characteristics. After obtaining the blockchain transaction data, the transaction data is input into the building transaction topology module for composition, so as to be input into the graph neural network for calculation.

3.2   Building Transaction Topology

3.2.1   Feature Preprocessing

In the real blockchain transaction data, there are rich features such as time step, in-and-out-degree of nodes, transaction fees required by exchanges, etc. It is necessary to screen out features that can improve the anomaly detection of blockchain from these features. To this end, we do the relevant feature preprocessing before the block chain transaction data composition. Feature preprocessing is mainly divided into two parts.

(1) The binning of blockchain transaction continuous feature: As shown in Fig. 2, blockchain transactions are distributed in some characteristic value of the long tail, and mostly focused on the near zero value. Therefore, equidistant binning processing was carried out for the 12 features similar to the long-tail distribution. After several experiments, the optimal binning number was determined. The features after binning processing were focused on the numerical range rather than the specific size, so as to reduce the influence of abnormal data and noise on model training. We will present our experimental results in chapter 4.

(2) Discrete feature encoding processing of blockchain transactions: Specifically, we use one-hot encoding to process data features according to the following rules: For discrete feature of blockchain transactions, each different state value is extended to a new feature column and a feature matrix is formed. In addition, the number of columns for each element is equal to the number of different values in that element. For the continuous features of block chain transactions, the values are first set in ascending order, and then divided into discrete binning to each interval, and finally regarded as discrete features to form the feature matrix. The characteristics of blockchain transactions are one-heat encoded to reduce the influence of numerical values on the model.

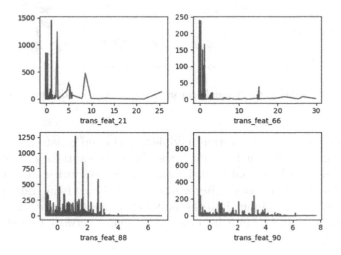

Fig. 2. Distribution of characteristics of certain blockchain transactions

3.2.2   Sample Equalization

The data set used in this paper is Elliptic dataset. In the whole Elliptic dataset, there are 203,769 transactions, including 42019 normal transactions (21%) and 4545 abnormal transactions (2%). Most of the remaining transaction attributes are unknown. The proportion of abnormal transactions is very small, and abnormal transaction nodes are very sparse after composition, which is not conducive to graph convolutional neural network extracting structural features of abnormal nodes from the transaction topology. At the same time, in other studies, transaction attribute in the experiment of the unknown node will be masked off. You can see that the transaction attributes of the unknown is accounted for most of the time, so masking off these nodes are bound to have great deal for the whole blockchain topology change, which makes whole blockchain topology nodes more sparse, and further weakens the graph convolutional neural network learning ability. Therefore, it is bound to reuse transactions with unknown blockchain transaction attributes to reduce the impact of abnormal sample imbalance.

- For this reason, k-rate sampling is used in the study to reduce the impact of sample imbalance caused by too few anomaly samples. More precisely, we randomly sample a certain proportion of unknown attribute transactions marked as abnormal transactions.We assume that this part accounts for k% of the total location attribute nodes (k is a decimal between 0 and 1), and the rest (1–k%) nodes participate in the construction of the blockchain transaction topology as normal transactions.
- The above k-rate sampling method may be a bit abrupt. Random sampling of unlabeled transaction data is not so "fair" for those transactions with abnormal labels. After all, no transaction is willing to be supervised and investigated. Therefore, we design a second sample equalization method based on the feature similarity between transaction nodes. The labeling process of unlabeled transaction nodes through feature similarity is as follows:

$$O_{normal} = normal(|P| \times |Q|^T) \tag{1}$$

$$Z = O_{normal} \times F \tag{2}$$

$$if \begin{cases} Z_i > thr \quad label(Z_i) = normal \\ Z_i < thr \quad label(Z_i) = abnormal \end{cases} \tag{3}$$

where, $|P|_{|A| \times d}$ represents the characteristic matrix of unlabeled nodes. A is the set of unlabeled trading nodes. $|Q|_{|B| \times d}$ denotes the characteristic matrix of labeled nodes, where B is the set of labeled nodes. $normal$ indicates the normalized operation. F is a vector of a labeled node label of $|Q| \times 1$ dimension.

The pre-processed blockchain transactions contain a richer variety of features while reducing the imbalance between positive and negative samples. In composition, the blockchain trading data within the same time step are marked as a graph, Where nodes represent transactions and edges represent the next transaction of Bitcoin from a transaction process. In this way, 49 graphs were constructed. In the actual experiment, the first 34 graphs were divided into training sets and the last 15 into test sets. Finally, the constructedblock chain transaction topology is transferred to the third module – abnormal recognition module for abnormal transaction detection.

4   Blockchain Anomaly Detection Based on GNN-FiLM

We introduce a new graph convolutional neural network (GNN-FiLM) to block chain anomaly detection, and propose a graph convolutional neural network blockchain anomaly detection model based on feature linear modulation. In the model, the target nodes on the edges represent transformations that can be applied to all incoming messages, allowing for characteristic modulation of the transmitted information, which better fits the characteristics of the rich and diverse features of blockchain nodes.

Assume that within the time step T, the blockchain transaction graph network $G(V, \varepsilon)$ has V nodes and directed edge $\varepsilon \subseteq (V \times L \times U)$, where $(v \times l \times u) \in \varepsilon$ denotes the directed edge from node V to node u, written as $u \xrightarrow{l} v$. In this paper, node V represents blockchain transactions, while edge ε represents the flow direction of blockchain transactions. Each node is associated with 166 features, and several features are screened out from these features for binning processing and one-hot encoding representation, which are input to GNN-FiLM together with the previous 166 features for abnormal transaction detection. The specific detection process of GNN-FiLM is as follows:

1. First, generate weights of GNN-FiLM using a supernetwork:

$$\beta_{l,v}^{(t)}, \gamma_{l,v}^{(t)} = g(h_v^{(t)}, \theta_{g,l}) \tag{4}$$

where $h_v^{(t)}$ is the characteristic representation of transaction node v at $t.h_v^{(0)} = X$ represents the initial characteristics input to GNN-FiLM.θ represents neuron parameters and G is the function used to learn weights, which is represented by linear layers in real experiments. $\beta_{l,v}^{(t)}, \gamma_{l,v}^{(t)}$ is the scale and translation parameters of the obtained radial transformation, and also the weight factor learned by the supernetwork to update the graph convolutional neural network.

2. Then, according to the weight update graph convolutional neural network obtained from the hypernet:

$$h_v^{(t+1)} = \sigma(\sum_{u \xrightarrow{l} v \in \varepsilon} \gamma_{l,v}^{(t)} \odot W_l h_v^{(t)} + \beta_{l,v}^{(t)}) \tag{5}$$

3. Finally, linear operation is added to obtain the input of T +1 layer GNN-FiLM:

$$h_v^{(t+1)} = l(\sigma(\sum_{u \xrightarrow{l} v \in \varepsilon} \gamma_{l,v}^{(t)} \odot W_l h_v^{(t)} + \beta_{l,v}^{(t)}); \theta_l) \tag{6}$$

The input of the first layer of GNN-FiLM is the characteristic matrix of nodes within T time step, and each row of this matrix is the n-dimensional feature vector of each node. After the GNN-FiLM convolution of the first layer, the output vector of each time slice aggregates the node's neighborhood information. In the real experiment, in order to fully mine the information of blockchain transaction network and avoid overfitting, we used double-layer GNN-FiLM to complete abnormal detection of blockchain transaction.

5   Experiment

5.1   Method Comparison

The following table shows the experimental results of convolutional neural networks of different graphs, as well as traditional algorithms such as logistic regression, multi-layer perceptron and linear regression for comparative experiments (Table 1).

Table 1. Method comparison

Method	Illicit			MicroAVG
	Precision	Recall	F1	F1
Logistic Regression	0.453	0.632	0.528	0.937
MLP	0.749	0.598	0.665	0.962
Linear regression	0.506	0.171	0.256	0.928
GAT	0.763	0.619	0.684	0.962
GCN	0.8241	0.4109	0.5484	0.9584
TAGCN	0.9527	0.4275	0.5902	0.9614
GNN-FiLM	0.9520	0.5679	0.7114	0.9701
GraphSAGE	0.9115	0.5993	0.7231	0.9702
GraphConv	0.8172	0.6150	0.7018	0.9660
TransformerConv	0.8195	0.5282	0.6423	0.9618
SGConv	0.7682	0.5660	0.6518	0.9607
LEConv	0.7854	0.5679	0.6592	0.9618
ARMAConv	0.8088	0.6288	0.7075	0.9662
MFConv	0.8142	0.5300	0.6421	0.9616
ClusterGCNConv	0.8607	0.6334	0.7298	0.9695
SuperGATConv	0.7557	0.5199	0.6160	0.9579

As can be seen from the above experimental results, traditional algorithms based on logistic regression, multi-layer perceptron and linear regression have poor results in abnormal transaction detection of blockchain, especially logistic regression and linear regression. This is because linear regression usually calculates an appropriate "line" for a series of data point predictions, and then maps new data points to this line to make predictions. On the basis of logistic regression, logistic regression adds a layer of sigmoid function mapping from feature to result, but it is still linear regression in essence. Compared with logistic regression and linear regression, multilayer perceptron has relatively good results in abnormal transaction detection of blockchain. This is because the multi-layer perceptron adds activation functions to the hidden layer neurons of each layer and introduces nonlinear factors to the neurons, so that the neural network can approach any nonlinear function and better fit the prediction curve of abnormal transactions of blockchain. Therefore, it is shown that the complex network of block chain transaction needs to conduct nonlinear modeling from the association relationship of complex objects, and the topology network structure is formed by the intricate relationship between nodes and nodes (relationships between entities), so as to realize the detection of abnormal transactions on block chain from the global network perspective.

Compared with the traditional method, graph convolutional neural network has a good effect on the block chain abnormal transaction detection. The bitcoin transaction topology structure formed by elliptic data set corresponds to a kind of non-European data. Traditional discrete convolution cannot maintain translation and deformation on this data structure, so it cannot be directly used. And GCN has made good progress in solving this problem. Specifically, a GCN is composed of multi-layer graph convolution, which is similar to a multi-layer perceptron. The difference is that GCN transforms topology structure from spatial domain to frequency domain through Fourier transform, and additionally uses neighborhood aggregation step driven by frequency domain convolution, which can effectively extract topology features. GAT adds the graph attention mechanism on the basis of GCN. When updating the feature vector of a transaction node, it first calculates the attention score of all neighbors, and then multiply the attention score by the corresponding adjacent features, which together is the updated feature of the node. TAGCN imitates CNN and uses K graph convolution kernels at each layer to extract local features of different sizes respectively, avoiding the previous defect of incomplete and sufficient graph information extraction due to the approximation of the convolution kernels, and improving the expression ability of the model. However, in GNN-FiLM, more attention is paid to the feature transformation of nodes. Many GCN and its variants only calculate the message idea based on the representation of each edge source, so as to spread information along the edge of the graph. Gnn-FiLM uses the representation of the target node of the edge to calculate the transformation that can be applied to all incoming messages. The hypernetwork allows feature modulation of the transmitted information, so that the feature information of graph nodes can be fully extracted and the detection results of the model can be improved (Figs. 3, 4 and 5).

5.2   Feature Preprocessing and Sample Equalization

From figure there you can see, with the unknown attribute trading on sampling rate increased, for the detection of abnormal transactions both precision and recall, have significantly increased, and this is obviously, after dealing with the abnormal samples equalization of samples with more data nodes, means that the model can learn from these data better parameters, At the same time, after abnormal sample equalization, the model will also assign more weight to abnormal samples during training, so as to improve the detection results of abnormal transactions. It can be seen from the graph in Fig. 6 that with the increase of

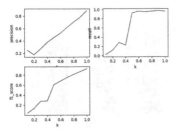

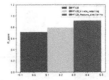

Fig. 3. Sample equilibrium evaluation index curve

Fig. 4. Loss curve

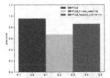

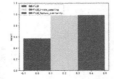

Fig. 5. Precision histogram   **Fig. 6.** Recall histogram   **Fig. 7.** F1_score histogram

k value, the three evaluation criteria have an obvious upward trend. In particular, when k value rises from 0.4 to 0.5, the Recall curve rises sharply. It can be predicted that when all unknown transaction attributes are treated as abnormal transactions, the detection result of the model is the best, but this is obviously not consistent with the real transaction situation of the blockchain, after all, this part of the transaction contains both abnormal transactions and normal transactions. In order to be more consistent with the real blockchain transactions and reduce the impact of random sampling on the precision of anomaly detection as much as possible, we suggest that the unknown transactions in the blockchain be mixed sampled at a ratio of 4:1 to improve the expression ability of the model. Figure 7 shows the loss curve of verification set after k-rate random sampling and equalization of feature similarity samples. It can be seen that, with the increase of training rounds, the whole loss function is decreasing on the whole and finally tends to be stable, and the feature similarity sample equilibrium has a smaller loss than k-rate sampling. Figure 8, Fig. 9 and Fig. 10 are k-rate random sampling and feature similarity sample equalization evaluation indexes respectively. It can be seen that after K-rate random sampling, recall and $F1_score$ increase significantly, but precision also decreases significantly. After feature similarity is used for sample equalization, Recall and $F1_score$ have significantly increased, while precision has slightly decreased, which verifies the effectiveness of using sample equalization to improve abnormal transaction detection of blockchain (Figs. 11 and 12).

234 H. Han et al.

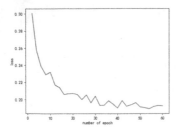

Fig. 8. Discrete feature independent thermal coding loss curve

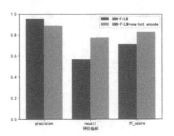

Fig. 9. Evaluation index before and after discrete feature one-hot encoding

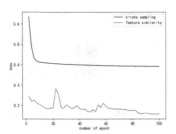

Fig. 10. Final loss curve

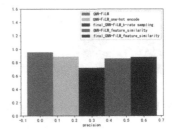

Fig. 11. Final Precision histogram

It can be seen from Fig. 13 that after the discrete features of elliptic data set are independently coded, the abnormal transaction detection ability of the model is greatly improved, indicating the effectiveness of feature engineering in abnormal transaction detection of blockchain. It can be seen from Figure 14 to Figure 17 that the precision of blockchain anomaly detection after feature engineering and data balancing has slightly decreased, but recall and $F1_score$ have greatly improved, which is of great significance for correctly detecting abnormal transactions from hundreds of millions of transaction data. In addition, in elliptic data set, the physical meaning of most original features and aggregate features is unknown, so how to screen out useful features from these features will be a problem worth discussing.

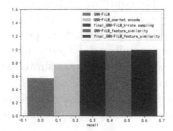

Fig. 12. Final Recall histogram

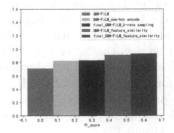

Fig. 13. Final $F1_score$ histogram

6   Conclusion

In view of the abnormal behavior of blockchain, we systematically explore the abnormal detection scheme under the unique scenario of blockchain transaction network. Based on the real transaction data of blockchain, sample equalization and feature engineering are integrated into abnormal transaction identification of blockchain, and the proportion of abnormal transactions is increased by random sampling of unknown attribute transactions, and part of discrete features and continuous features are encoded and divided into discrete boxes, respectively, to improve the model detection ability. Starting from the block chain transaction topology, we constructed the block chain transaction network topology with graph structure data, and trained the block chain transaction topology data with GNN-FiLM and other graph convolutional neural network machine learning methods, and obtained the classification model of block chain anomaly detection. The experimental results show that the GNN-FiLM graph neural network has excellent performance in the abnormal detection and classification of blockchain, which is superior to the relevant methods. This paves the way for our next work – traceability of abnormal nodes of blockchain.

Acknowledgement. This work is supported in part by the National Key R&D Program of China (No. 2020YFB1006002), in part by the National Natural Science Foundation of China under Grant 62071092, and in part by Key Lab of Information Network Security, Ministry of Public Security under Grant C19603.

References

1. Pham, T., Lee, S.: Anomaly detection in bitcoin network using unsupervised learning methods. arXiv preprint arXiv:1611.03941 (2016)
2. Chen, W., Zheng, Z., Cui, J., et al.: Detecting ponzi schemes on ethereum: towards healthier blockchain technology. In: Proceedings of the 2018 World Wide Web Conference. pp. 1409–1418 (2018)
3. Weber, M., Domeniconi, G., Chen, J., et al.: Anti-money laundering in bitcoin: experimenting with graph convolutional networks for financial forensics. arXiv preprint arXiv:1908.02591 (2019)
4. Pareja, A., Domeniconi, G., Chen, J., et al.: Evolvegcn: evolving graph convolutional networks for dynamic graphs. In: Proceedings of the AAAI Conference on Artificial Intelligence, vol. 34(04), pp. 5363–5370 (2020)
5. Veličković, P., Cucurull, G., Casanova, A., et al.: Graph attention networks. arXiv preprint arXiv:1710.10903 (2017)
6. Du, J., Zhang, S., Wu, G., et al.: Topology adaptive graph convolutional networks. arXiv preprint arXiv:1710.10370 (2017)
7. Brockschmidt, M.: GNN-film: graph neural networks with feature-wise linear modulation. In: International Conference on Machine Learning. PMLR, pp. 1144–1152 (2020)
8. Hamilton, W.L., Ying, R., Leskovec, J.: Inductive representation learning on large graphs. In: Proceedings of the 31st International Conference on Neural Information Processing Systems, pp. 1025–1035 (2017)

9. Morris, C., Ritzert, M., Fey,. M, et al.: Weisfeiler and leman go neural: higher-order graph neural networks. In: Proceedings of the AAAI Conference on Artificial Intelligence, vol. 33(01), pp. 4602–4609 (2019)

10. Wu, F., Souza, A., Zhang, T., et al.: Simplifying graph convolutional networks. In: International Conference on Machine Learning. PMLR, pp. 6861–6871 (2019)

11. Ranjan, E., Sanyal, S., Talukdar, P.: Asap: adaptive structure aware pooling for learning hierarchical graph representations. In: Proceedings of the AAAI Conference on Artificial Intelligence, vol. 34(04), 5470–5477 (2020)

12. Bianchi, F.M., Grattarola, D., Livi, L., et al.: Graph neural networks with convolutional arma filters. IEEE Trans. Pattern Anal. Mach. Intell. **44** (2021)

13. Duvenaud, D., Maclaurin, D., Aguilera-Iparraguirre, J., et al.: Convolutional networks on graphs for learning molecular fingerprints. arXiv preprint arXiv:1509.09292 (2015)

14. Chiang, W.L., Liu, X., Si, S., et al.: Cluster-GCN: an efficient algorithm for training deep and large graph convolutional networks. In: Proceedings of the 25th ACM SIGKDD International Conference on Knowledge Discovery & Data Mining, pp. 257–266 (2019)

15. Xu, Q. Song, Z., Goh, R.S.M., Li, Y.: Building an ethereum and IPFS-based decentralized social network system. In: 2018 IEEE 24th International Conference on Parallel and Distributed Systems (ICPADS) (2018)

16. Kim, D., Oh, A.: How to find your friendly neighborhood: Graph attention design with self-supervision. In: International Conference on Learning Representations (2020)

Cross Cryptocurrency Relationship Mining for Bitcoin Price Prediction

Panpan Li[1,2], Shengbo Gong[1,2], Shaocong Xu[1,2], Jiajun Zhou[1,2(✉)], Shanqing Yu[1,2], and Qi Xuan[1,2,3,4]

[1] Institute of Cyberspace Security, Zhejiang University of Technology, Hangzhou 310023, China
jjzhou@zjut.edu.cn
[2] College of Information Engineering, Zhejiang University of Technology, Hangzhou 310023, China
[3] Peng Cheng Laboratory, PCL Research Center of Networks and Communications, Shenzhen 518000, China
[4] Utron Technology Co., Ltd., Hangzhou 310056, China

Abstract. Blockchain finance has become a part of the world financial system, most typically manifested in the attention to the price of Bitcoin. However, a great deal of work is still limited to using technical indicators to capture Bitcoin price fluctuation, with little consideration of historical relationships and interactions between related cryptocurrencies. In this work, we propose a generic Cross-Cryptocurrency Relationship Mining module, named C^2RM, which can effectively capture the synchronous and asynchronous impact factors between Bitcoin and related Altcoins. Specifically, we utilize the Dynamic Time Warping algorithm to extract the lead-lag relationship, yielding Lead-lag Variance Kernel, which will be used for aggregating the information of Altcoins to form relational impact factors. Comprehensive experimental results demonstrate that our C^2RM can help existing price prediction methods achieve significant performance improvement, suggesting the effectiveness of Cross-Cryptocurrency interactions on benefitting Bitcoin price prediction.

Keywords: Blockchain · Bitcoin · Price prediction · Time series · Lead-lag relationship

1 Introduction

Bitcoin is the first cryptocurrency based on blockchain technology [1] and is characterized by high price fluctuation [2,3]. Since its launch in 2009, the price of Bitcoin has been in a trend of short-term fluctuation and long-term upward, and rose to nearly $20,000 in December 2017, which consolidated its position in the mainstream market, catching the attention of investors and governments. Meanwhile, new progress has been made in key technologies such as distributed storage, consensus mechanisms, smart contracts and encryption algorithms, laying the foundation for blockchain finance and promoting its integration into the

D. Svetinovic et al. (Eds.): BlockSys 2022, CCIS 1679, pp. 237–250, 2022.
https://doi.org/10.1007/978-981-19-8043-5_17

international financial system. In such phenomenon, more and more researchers are devoted to analyzing the trend of Bitcoin price, yielding *Bitcoin price prediction*, which can help investors better deal with the changing cryptocurrency market [4–6].

Due to the transparency of cryptocurrency transactions, researchers consider using transaction information such as overall trends and cyclical changes to predict cryptocurrency prices. The most common practices [7,8] are to use time series data of Bitcoin for price prediction, which predicts future prices using historical price information. Meanwhile, other work [9,10] considers incorporating external information such as relevant policy news and Google Trends into prediction models. In addition, several work [11] considers Bitcoin price prediction as a classification problem to reduce the task difficulty, i.e., transforming the regression problem of predicting specific price values into a classification problem of predicting price fluctuation. However, existing price prediction methods suffer from several shortcomings and challenges. First, historical price information is usually misleading in short-term forecasts, e.g. even a well-designed LSTM model with minimal error may not beat the naive strategy—predicting that the price of the next day is equal to the previous day. Second, external information is complex, and the impact on price fluctuation is difficult to quantify. Third, existing price prediction models have a poor scalability or generalization, failing in transferring to new data or scenarios.

In blockchain finance market, the price fluctuation of cryptocurrencies depend not only on their historical records, but also on other economic factors and external events [12]. In other words, the signals contained in the price fluctuation can reflect the influence of internal and external factors. The signals are embedded in the price fluctuation of each cryptocurrency, which inspires us to use the price information of various cryptocurrencies and their interaction relationship to predict the price of another cryptocurrency. Such practices are already present in stock price prediction. Li et al. [13] considered that companies of different scales have different reaction speeds to market information, and simulates the asynchronous lead-lag relationship between stocks to predict stock trends. Similarly, there is also a lead-lag relationship between mainstream cryptocurrencies and Altcoins [14]. Most Altcoins are modeled after Bitcoin, they are based on the same consensus mechanism as it, and even completely copy its code. Compared with Altcoins, mainstream cryptocurrencies such as Bitcoin will be more difficult to reach Nash equilibrium due to the constraints of many parties, so the price will be reflected later.

In this paper, we consider improving the performance of traditional time series prediction models for Bitcoin price prediction and propose C^2RM, a generic Cross-Cryptocurrency Relationship Mining method that can be regarded as an auxiliary module to enhance price prediction. C^2RM can extract the synchronous and asynchronous relationship between Bitcoin and related Altcoins. Specifically, we use Dynamic Time Warping (DTW) algorithm to extract the lead-lag relationship between Bitcoin and related Altcoins, yielding Lead-lag Variance Kernel (LVK), which will further be used for aggregating the information of Altcoins to form relational impact factors. The relational impact factors will replace the original price series as the input of the downstream models. Our proposed module allows for improving the performance of existing time series prediction methods for Bitcoin price prediction through cross cryptocurrency relationship extraction without adjusting them.

The main contributions of this paper are summarized as follows:

- To the best of our knowledge, this is the first work to utilize the price information of various cryptocurrencies and their synchronous and asynchronous relationship to predict the price of Bitcoin.
- We propose a generic cross-cryptocurrency relationship mining module, called C^2RM, which allows for extracting and aggregating the synchronous and asynchronous relationship features between Bitcoin and related Altcoins, further improving the performance of existing time series prediction methods for Bitcoin price prediction.
- Experimental results show the effectiveness of C^2RM module on improving the performance of existing time series prediction methods for Bitcoin price prediction. We study the advancement of Altcoins over Bitcoin in response to external information when Nash equilibrium is reached. We also find that using short- and medium-term time series data (24 time series intervals) to predict short-term time series data (3 time series intervals) can achieve optimal investment benefits.

The remainder of this paper is organized as follows. In Sect. 2, we discuss related work. In Sect. 3, we describe the details of how our C^2RM module works. In Sect. 4, we introduce the dataset and experimental settings, and discuss the experimental results. In Sect. 5, we conclude this work and present future research.

2 Related Work

Recently, the popularity of Bitcoin in the financial market has spawned a lot of research on blockchain cryptocurrencies, especially for Bitcoin price prediction, of which the related work mainly concentrates on external factors, machine learning methods and graph analytics.

2.1 External Factors

The earliest studies [15] of Bitcoin aimed to trace transactions to locate the circulation of Bitcoin used for illegal activities such as money laundering and extortion. Ladislav [16] studied the relationship between Bitcoin and search terms on Google Trends and Wikipedia, and confirmed that the fluctuation of Bitcoin prices is almost positively correlated with the number of search terms. Bin et al. [17] also studied the comments on Twitter and found that comments, especially positive ones, have a very large impact on the Bitcoin price. Karalevicius et al. [18] collected and studied the database of Bitcoin-related news and blogs, and the results show that there is an interaction between media sentiment and Bitcoin price. Gurrib [19] used linear discriminant analysis (LDA) and sentiment analysis to predict the trend of Bitcoin price fluctuation, and the results show that the LDA (SVM) model that considers both news sentiment and Bitcoin price information as input features achieves relatively good results. These studies have shown that external information is an important factor affecting the prediction of Bitcoin price.

2.2 Machine Learning Methods

For Bitcoin price prediction, early work attempted to use time series data for trend prediction. Azari [7] used the autoregressive moving average (ARIMA) model for Bitcoin price prediction, and proved that the traditional ARIMA performs better on short-term time series data than long-term ones. Sean et al. [8] used Bayesian optimized Recurrent Neural Network (RNN) and Long Short-Term Memory (LSTM) network to predict Bitcoin price, proving that nonlinear deep learning methods outperform ARIMA. Stefano [20] proposed a Bitcoin trend prediction method based on one-dimensional convolutional neural network and introduced a new trading strategy, and experimental results show that the method and its strategy can more accurately predict Bitcoin trends when compared with the traditional LSTM model.

2.3 Graph Analytics

Akcora et al. [21] studied the impact of local topology on Bitcoin price fluctuation, and combined the "chain" of Bitcoin transaction network with statistical models to predict Bitcoin price. Abay et al. [4] found that the graph-related topological features show high utility in predicting Bitcoin price fluctuation. Crowcroft et al. [22] considered the concept of a trusted transaction graph and proposed a set of features at a single-day time granularity. They applied the principle of autoregressive distribution lags linear regression to evaluate the intensity and duration of the changes in the features to affect the exchange rate.

3 Methodology

This section outlines our data processing approach based on the DTW algorithm for extracting information from short-term price fluctuation of seven Altcoins, as well as the overall framework for Bitcoin price prediction. Our task is to use the historical prices of multiple Altcoins, and the fluctuation differences relative to Bitcoin within the time window, to predict the price of Bitcoin over the next few days. To reveal information about fluctuation in Altcoins prices, we propose two methods for computing time series, in a synchronous and asynchronous manner, respectively. Both methods are based on the DTW algorithm, and Fig. 1 illustrates the synchronous method used to adjust the input sequence weights and Fig. 2 explains the method of extracting asynchronous information and aggregating the input sequences.

3.1 Data Preprocessing

Normalization. The prices of these Altcoins differ by orders of magnitude from each other, according to the market's assessment of their value. In order to preserve their absolute impact on Bitcoin, instead of normalizing the prices of these Altcoins individually, we perform min-max normalization on them. We observe that the lower the price base, the greater the relative fluctuation, so lower-priced Altcoins will gain a greater DTW distance from Bitcoin over the entire time span.

Time Series Segmentation. Let $\mathcal{A} = \{a_1, a_2, \cdots, a_m\}$ represent the set of Altcoins considered in this paper, and b represent the Bitcoin. We represent the normalized prices of Altcoin a at timestep t_i as p_i^a. In this paper, we make one timestep equal to 4 hours, and take the price sequences of the past 24 timesteps (96 hours) as input, and the future 3 timesteps as the label to be predicted. For an input time window $T_w = [t_1, t_2, \cdots, t_{24}]$, the price sequences of Altcoin a and Bitcoin b can be represented as

$$
\begin{aligned}
\mathbf{P}_{T_w}^a &= [p_1^a, p_2^a, \cdots, p_{24}^a], \\
\mathbf{P}_{T_w}^b &= [p_1^b, p_2^b, \cdots, p_{24}^b].
\end{aligned}
\tag{1}
$$

The input time window size (here 24 timesteps) and the output time window size (here 3 timesteps) are a pair of hyperparameters that can be tuned. The input time window is slid by 24 timesteps each time, that is, the input data will not be repeated. Using more timesteps in input time window can generate LVKs with more elements, which can characterize more complex interaction relationships. Using more timesteps in output time window means a more difficult price prediction task.

3.2 Lead-Lag Variance Kernel

DTW Distance Measure. DTW is a method for determining the similarity of two time series that vary in different speed. For two price curves, similar fluctuation results in a shorter DTW distance, even if there is a time shift between the two curves. The DTW algorithm first calculates the Euclidean distance between arbitrary two timesteps on two sequences and forms a matrix. Then it uses a dynamic programming algorithm to find the shortest path from the bottom right corner of the matrix to the top left corner, whose length is the sum of the matrix elements it contains.

Influenced by the entire cryptocurrency market, the prices of different currencies often fluctuate in concert. Our method will capture the fluctuation variance directly through DTW distance calculation.

Synchronous Method. Our synchronization method start from the DTW distance calculation between Altcoins price sequence in specific time window and Bitcoin price sequence in the same one. For the price sequences of Altcoin

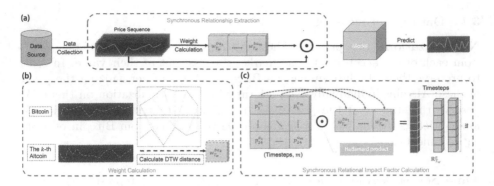

Fig. 1. Illustration of synchronization method, where (a) is the overview, (b) is the process of synchronous weight calculation via DTW algorithm, and (c) is the process of aggregating Altcoin information to generate synchronous relational impact factors.

a and Bitcoin b in the time window T_w, we define the weight from Bitcoin to Altcoin as follows:

$$w_{T_w}^{ba} = \mathrm{DTW}\left(\mathbf{P}_{T_w}^b, \mathbf{P}_{T_w}^a\right). \tag{2}$$

The $w_{T_w}^{ba}$ is treated as a weight, which will be multiplied to the corresponding price sequence, yielding the synchronous relational impact factor:

$$\mathbf{R}_{T_w}^a = w_{T_w}^{ba} \cdot \mathbf{P}_{T_w}^a. \tag{3}$$

Asynchronous Method. Unlike the synchronous method, asynchronous method captures the asynchronous impact of leading-lag relationship between Altcoin and Bitcoin, yielding Lead-lag Variance Kernel (LVK). Specifically, for two input price sequences of Bitcoin and one Altcoin, the input time windows are first divided into n subwindows which contain $\frac{24}{n}$ timesteps:

$$T_w = [t_{sw}^1, t_{sw}^2, \cdots, t_{sw}^n]. \tag{4}$$

We then calculate the DTW distance between arbitrary two subwindows between the two sequences. Due to time causality, only the earlier subwindow will affect the later ones, the final distance of Bitcoin to a certain Altcoin form the lower triangular matrix.

$$w_{ij}^{ba} = \begin{cases} \mathrm{DTW}\left(\mathbf{P}_{t_{sw}^i}^b, \mathbf{P}_{t_{sw}^j}^a\right) & \text{for } i \geq j \\ 0 & \text{for } i < j \end{cases} \tag{5}$$

where $i, j \in \{1, \cdots, n\}$, and $\mathbf{W}^{ba} = \{w_{ij}^{ba_k}\}_{m \times n \times n}$ is the LVK of Bitcoin relative to Altcoins. The LVK will be flattened to $\bar{\mathbf{W}}^{ba} \in \mathbb{R}^{m \times n^2}$ and multiplied with the price sequences, yielding the asynchronous relational impact factor:

$$\mathbf{R}_{T_w}^{ba} = \mathbf{P}_{T_w} \times \bar{\mathbf{W}}^{ba}. \tag{6}$$

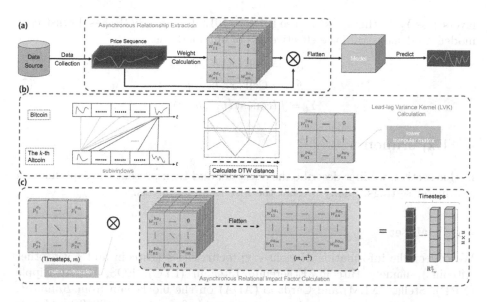

Fig. 2. Illustration of asynchronous method, where (a) is the overview, (b) is the process of generating the Lead-lag Variance Kernel (LVK) via DTW algorithm, (c) is the process of aggregating Altcoin information to generate asynchronous relational impact factors.

In summary, we weight and aggregate the input price sequence with element-wise multiplication on the synchronous method and matrix multiplication on the asynchronous method respectively. The generated relational impact factor sequences will be fed into downstream models for price prediction.

3.3 Deep Learning Models

As mentioned in Sect. 1, deep learning models are widely used in time-dependent data analysis. The most popular models are RNN and its variants of LSTM and GRU. Compared with the typical RNN, LSTM overcomes the vanishing gradient problem [23]. GRU [24] is similar to LSTM, but it combines the forget gate and input gate into one update gate. GRU has a less complex architecture than LSTM so it can be trained faster than standard RNN or LSTM. It has been used to forecast Bitcoin prices in the past, and is as effective as LSTM [25], even better [26].

Since our task is to predict sequences by sequences, a Seq2Seq model is necessary. Since we directly take the last three 1×1 vectors of the hidden layer output as the result, the losses cannot be backward propagated to each RNNcell during the training process, which drives us to use bidirectional models, namely BiRNN, BiLSTM and BiGRU. In the following, we denote the input at timestep t as $\mathbf{x}_t$, which is actually the relational impact factor. We denote the hidden state transmitted between cells as h_t, and the output after the fully connected layers f as Y_t. In this work, we use BiRNN, BiLSTM and BiGRU as downstream models to demonstrate the effectiveness of our methods.

$$\overrightarrow{h_t} = \text{Cell}\left(x_t, \overrightarrow{h_{t-1}}\right)$$
$$\overleftarrow{h_t} = \text{Cell}\left(x_t, \overleftarrow{h_{t+1}}\right) \qquad (7)$$
$$Y_t = f\left(\text{concat}\left(\overrightarrow{h_t}, \overleftarrow{h_t}\right)\right)$$

4   Experiments

In this section, we first describe the datasets, and then present the experimental parameter settings, finally present the results and analysis.

4.1   Dataset

We collect the information of eight cryptocurrencies (Bitcoin and seven other Altcoins), namely Bitcoin, Ethereum, Litecoin (LTC), EOS, IOTA, Ripple (XRP), Stellar (XLM) and Cardano (ADA) on the blockchain from *Binance*[1]. For each cryptocurrency, we intercept the price from June 1, 2018 to May 1, 2020, and use 4 hours as a timestep. Since the results of time-dependent data analysis are strongly influenced by the size of the dataset, we divided the dataset into three proportions, i.e. the ratio of the training set to the test set are 7 : 3, 8 : 2 and 9 : 1, respectively (Table 1).

Table 1. Data description of cryptocurrencies used in this paper.

Cryptocurrency	Min-price ($)	Max-price ($)	Time interval
Bitcoin	3156.26	13960.76	
Ethereum	81.79	628.81	
Litecoin	22.32	145.90	
EOS	1.36	15.68	June 1, 2018
IOTA	0.05	2.01	~
Ripple	0.10	0.80	May 1, 2020
Stellar	0.03	0.35	
Cardano	0.02	0.24	

4.2   Baselines

To illustrate the effectiveness of our C^2RM module, we combine it with three RNN-based models, and compare with machine learning model and MLPs. The parameter settings are summarized in Table 2.

---

[1] https://data.binance.vision/

GBRT. The basic settings and hyperparameters of the baselines remain the same as in our proposed approach, except for the machine learning method. GBRT is a non-parametric statistical learning technique for regression prediction. Since [27] argued that GBRT is no worse than DNN for time series prediction problems, we apply it to our task as well.

RNNs. We employ three of the most common time series prediction models, namely standard **RNN**, **LSTM** and **GRU**, all involving a bi-directional structure. *ReLU* is employed as the activation function in the cells of standard RNN. To control the variables, we use a uniform hyperparameter settings for a fair comparison.

MLPs. We first present a **SmartMLP** method, in which we directly input "**Input window × Number of Coin Types**" into fully connected layers and output a vector with length equal to output window. We also take the same input and output a scalar, and broadcast it to a vector with length equal to output window, which is the **NaiveMLP** method.

Table 2. Hyperparameter settings.

BiRNNs		GBRT	
Shape of LVK	4×4	Number of estimators	200
Hidden dimension	32	Max depth	6
Layers (both directions)	2	Min child weight	1
Input window size	24	L1 regularization factor	0.9
Output window size	3	L2 regularization factor	1
Input dimension	7	Learning rate	0.01
Epochs	2000		
Learning rate	0.01		

4.3   Evaluation Metric

Assume that the predictive value is

$$\hat{\mathbf{y}} = \{\hat{y}_1, \hat{y}_2, \cdots, \hat{y}_n\}, \tag{8}$$

the ground truth is

$$\mathbf{y} = \{y_1, y_2, \cdots, y_n\}. \tag{9}$$

Table 3. Summary of performance on Bitcoin price prediction under different data split schemes in terms of MSE. The highest performance is marked with boldface; the highest performance of baselines is underline.

Methods	Data Split ($MSE \times 10^{-3}$)			Mean($MSE \times 10^{-3}$)
	7:3	8:2	9:1	
GBRT	8.682	3.668	2.513	4.954
Naive-MLP	4.137	4.975	1.017	3.376
Smart-MLP	4.832	5.597	<u>0.885</u>	3.771
BiRNN	<u>2.002</u>	<u>2.498</u>	0.959	<u>1.820</u>
BiLSTM	3.588	3.346	0.916	2.617
BiGRU	2.613	2.541	1.439	2.198
BiRNN-synC^2RM	1.323	0.580	1.036	0.980
BiLSTM-synC^2RM	1.657	0.637	1.014	1.103
BiGRU-synC^2RM	1.127	0.823	1.143	1.031
BiRNN-asynC^2RM	**0.837**	0.445	0.824	**0.702**
BiLSTM-asynC^2RM	0.924	0.494	**0.757**	0.725
BiGRU-asynC^2RM	1.080	**0.420**	0.779	0.760

MSE (Mean Square Error) is a common metric used in regression problems to assess the prediction results. It is defined as the average squared difference between the predictive values and the actual values:

$$MSE = \frac{1}{n} \sum_{i=1}^{n} (\hat{y}_i - y_i)^2 . \tag{10}$$

4.4 Results and Analysis

This section analyses the results of our experiments, including a comparison with baselines, a comparison of synchronous and asynchronous methods, and additional experiments to illustrate the generalization of the asynchronous method.

Enhancement for Bitcoin Price Prediction. Table 3 reports the results of performance comparison between raw methods and their enhanced version (with C^2RM) with different data split schemes, from which we observe that there is a significant boost in prediction performance across all RNN-based methods, suggesting the effectiveness of our C^2RM module on helping existing price prediction methods achieve performance improvement.

Specifically, the machine learning method (GBRT) obtains relative lower performance rankings, indicating the limited expressiveness of the shallow features learnt by GBRT model. The MLP-based methods significantly outperform GBRT in most cases, and gain 23.88% and 31.85% average relative improvements, suggesting that the simple deep models and naive prediction strategies

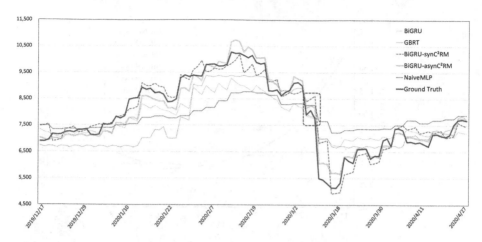

Fig. 3. The results of the 5 price predicting methods as well as the ground truth. The units on the vertical axis are the actual price against the US dollar. The horizontal axis is the actual date corresponding to every 3 consecutive time points at an interval of 24 points.

can provide certain price prediction guidance. The RNN-based methods achieve the best prediction performance across all baselines, indicating that such time series prediction models can effectively capture the time dependence of price fluctuation. Finally, these RNN-based methods (BiRNN, BiLSTM and BiGRU) combined with the proposed C^2RM module obtain higher prediction performance, yielding 45.15%, 57.85% and 46.91% average relative improvements respectively in terms of synchronous method, and 61.43%, 72.30% and 65.42% average relative improvements respectively in terms of asynchronous method, when compared with these RNN-based methods that accept raw price sequence input. Such phenomenon demonstrates that our C^2RM module can effectively extract the impact factors of related Altcoins on Bitcoin, further helping to predict the price of Bitcoin more accurately. Furthermore, we also observe that asynC^2RM totally beat synC^2RM, indicating that the lead-lag relationship between Altcoins and Bitcoin benefits more than the synchronous relationship.

Overall Trend Prediction. We further analyze the performance of different methods in overall trend prediction, as illustrated in Fig. 3, from which we observe that all methods are able to predict the overall trend of Bitcoin price while BiGRU-asynC^2RM represented by the hollow solid line performs best. Specifically, the price curve predicted by BiGRU-asynC^2RM is closest to the ground truth, and BiGRU-synC^2RM is the second closest. Such phenomenon suggests that our C^2RM module can effectively capture the price fluctuation and the asynchronous lead-lag relationship benefits more.

Furthermore, as mentioned in Sect. 1, even for the task of predicting one point in the future, RNNs simply repeat the last day of the input window in a

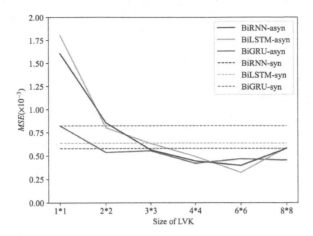

Fig. 4. Effect of LVK size on the performance of BiRNNs.

highly weighted way so that they cannot beat NAIVE methods that repeat the last point exactly. Therefore, it makes more sense to focus on the last two points in a three-point prediction, or the trend in a single point prediction, because the values of the last two points are not inferred from the first point. In the three-point prediction framed by the dashed rectangle, our C^2RM also demonstrates its ability to predict three-point trends while other methods fail. In this output window, the actual price shows a trend of first rising and then falling, which is difficult to predict. Our asyn C^2RM captures such pattern while other methods unsurprisingly employ the naive strategy of repeating the previous trend, i.e. maintaining two consecutive up or down trends.

Impact of LVK Size. We further investigate the impact of the most important hyperparameter—the size of LVK ($n \times n$) in the asyn C^2RM method. Specifically, we vary the number of subwindows n in $1, 2, 3, 4, 6, 8$ and fix other hyperparameters. We present the evaluation results in Fig. 4, from which we observe that larger LVK (with more subsections in input sequence) benefits price prediction more. But when the size arrives at a certain level, improvements become slighter. We speculate that larger LVK can extract more complex and detailed leading-lag relationship between Bitcoin and related Altcoins, yielding more powerful generalization.

5   Conclusion

In this paper, we propose two generic modules for Bitcoin price prediction, including syn C^2RM for extracting synchronous relationship and asyn C^2RM for extracting asynchronous lead-lag relationship. Experiments demonstrate the effectiveness of our methods in enhancing the existing Bitcoin price prediction methods. We believe that the Lead-lag Variance Kernel in asynC^2RM successfully extracts the difference in short-term fluctuation between the historical prices of Altcoins and Bitcoin and the impact on future price fluctuation. Moreover, we also investigate the generalization and effectiveness of LVK in terms of size variation.

Acknowledgments. This work was partially supported by the National Key R&D Program of China under Grant 2020YFB1006104, by the Key R&D Programs of Zhejiang under Grants 2022C01018 and 2021C01117, by the National Natural Science Foundation of China under Grant 61973273, and by the Zhejiang Provincial Natural Science Foundation of China under Grant LR19F030001.

References

1. Nakamoto, S.: Bitcoin: a peer-to-peer electronic cash system. Decentralized Business Review, p. 21260 (2008)
2. Aalborg, H.A., Molnár, P., de Vries, J.E.: What can explain the price, volatility and trading volume of bitcoin? Finan. Res. Let. **29**, 255–265 (2019)
3. Balcilar, M., Bouri, E., Gupta, R., Roubaud, D.: Can volume predict bitcoin returns and volatility? a quantiles-based approach. Econ. Model. **64**, 74–81 (2017)
4. Abay, N.C., et al.: Chainnet: learning on blockchain graphs with topological features. In: 2019 IEEE International Conference on Data Mining (ICDM), pp. 946–951. IEEE (2019)
5. Liu, L.: Are bitcon returns predictable?: evidence from technical indicators. Phys. A Statist. Mech. Appl. **533**, 121950 (2019)
6. Huang, J.Z., Huang, W., Ni, J.: Predicting bitcoin returns using high-dimensional technical indicators. J. Finan. Data Sci. **5**(3), 140–155 (2019)
7. Azari, A.: Bitcoin price prediction: an arima approach. arXiv preprint arXiv:1904.05315 (2019)
8. McNally, S., Roche, J., Caton, S.: Predicting the price of bitcoin using machine learning. In: 2018 26th Euromicro International Conference on Parallel, Distributed and Network-based Processing (PDP), pp. 339–343. IEEE (2018)
9. Matta, M., Lunesu, I., Marchesi, M.: Bitcoin spread prediction using social and web search media. In: UMAP workshops, pp. 1–10 (2015)
10. Figa-Talamanca, G., Patacca, M.: Does market attention affect bitcoin returns and volatility? Dec. Econ. Finan. **42**(1), 135–155 (2019)
11. Mudassir, M., Bennbaia, S., Unal, D., Hammoudeh, M.: Time-series forecasting of bitcoin prices using high-dimensional features: a machine learning approach. Neural Computing and Applications, pp. 1–15 (2020)
12. Giudici, G., Milne, A., Vinogradov, D.: Cryptocurrencies: market analysis and perspectives. J. Indust. Bus. Econ. **47**(1), 1–18 (2020)
13. Li, H.Y., Tseng, V.S., Philip, S.Y.: Enhancing stock trend prediction models by mining relational graphs of stock prices. In: 2020 International Conference on Pervasive Artificial Intelligence (ICPAI), pp. 110–117. IEEE (2020)
14. Sifat, I.M., Mohamad, A., Shariff, M.S.B.M.: Lead-lag relationship between bitcoin and ethereum: evidence from hourly and daily data. Res. Int. Bus. Finan. **50**, 306–321 (2019)
15. Akcora, C.G., Purusotham, S., Gel, Y.R., Krawiec-Thayer, M., Kantarcioglu, M.: How to not get caught when you launder money on blockchain? arXiv preprint arXiv:2010.15082 (2020)

16. Kristoufek, L.: Bitcoin meets google trends and wikipedia: quantifying the relationship between phenomena of the internet era. Sci. Reports **3**(1), 1–7 (2013)
17. Kim, Y.B., et al.: Predicting fluctuations in cryptocurrency transactions based on user comments and replies. PloS one **11**(8), e0161197 (2016)
18. Karalevicius, V., Degrande, N., De Weerdt, J.: Using sentiment analysis to predict interday bitcoin price movements. J. Risk Finan **19** (2018)
19. Gurrib, I., Kamalov, F.: Predicting bitcoin price movements using sentiment analysis: a machine learning approach. Studies in Economics and Finance (2021)
20. Cavalli, S., Amoretti, M.: CNN-based multivariate data analysis for bitcoin trend prediction. Appl. Soft Comput. **101**, 107065 (2021)
21. Akcora, C.G., Dey, A.K., Gel, Y.R., Kantarcioglu, M.: Forecasting bitcoin price with graph chainlets. In: Phung, D., Tseng, V., Webb, G., Ho, B., Ganji, M., Rashidi, L. (eds) Pacific-Asia Conference On Knowledge Discovery and Data Mining, LNCS, vol. 10939, pp. 765–776. Springer, Cham (2018). https://doi.org/10.1007/978-3-319-93040-4_60
22. Crowcroft, J., Maesa, D.D.F., Magrini, A., Marino, A., Ricci, L.: Leveraging the users graph and trustful transactions for the analysis of bitcoin price. IEEE Trans. Network Sci. Eng. **8**(2), 1338–1352 (2020)
23. Hochreiter, S., Schmidhuber, J.: Long short-term memory. Neural Comput. **9**(8), 1735–1780 (1997)
24. Cho, K., et al.: Learning phrase representations using RNN encoder-decoder for statistical machine translation. arXiv preprint arXiv:1406.1078 (2014)
25. Yang, S.: A novel study on deep learning framework to predict and analyze the financial time series information. Future Gener. Comput. Syst. **125**, 812–819 (2021)
26. Rizwan, M., Narejo, S., Javed, M.: Bitcoin price prediction using deep learning algorithm. In: 2019 13th International Conference on Mathematics, Actuarial Science, Computer Science and Statistics (MACS), pp. 1–7. IEEE (2019)
27. Elsayed, S., Thyssens, D., Rashed, A., Jomaa, H.S., Schmidt-Thieme, L.: Do we really need deep learning models for time series forecasting? arXiv preprint arXiv:2101.02118 (2021)

Blockchain-Based UAV-Assisted Forest Supervision and Data Sharing

Lipan Chen[1], Hai Liang[1], Xinyang Li[1], Yong Ding[1,2], Weiguo Huang[1], Yujue Wang[1], and Xiaochun Zhou[3(✉)]

[1] Guangxi Key Laboratory of Cryptography and Information Security, School of Computer and Information Security, Guilin University of Electronic Technology, Guilin 541004, China
[2] Cyberspace Security Research Center, Pengcheng Laboratory, Shenzhen 518038, China
[3] Shenzhen Olym Information Security Technology Co., Ltd., Shenzhen 518101, China
zhouxc@myibc.net

Abstract. Forest supervision is an effective means for preventing forest fires, forest diseases and insect pests, and deforestation. This paper proposes a blockchain-based forest supervision system (BSR) in a multiparty environment to achieve forest supervision, where the collected image data are stored on blockchain and IPFS, and a hybrid encryption of CP-ABE and AES algorithm is employed to realize secure forest data sharing and access control among ground base stations. Theoretical analysis and comparison show that the BSR scheme is effective, and the experimental analysis demonstrates its practicability.

Keywords: Block-chain · UAV · CP-ABE · AES · Hybrid encryption

1 Introduction

With the increasing awareness of ecological protection, the increasing emphasis on forest benefits has made forest research and protection a popular research direction. In order to provide images and data required for forest research and conservation, forest data collection is crucial [1]. With the development of artificial intelligence image processing technology, image processing algorithms using artificial intelligence can be effectively used in forest fire prevention [2], forest pest control [3], investigation of forest resources [4], and collection of various complex forest geographical topography [5], etc. Due to the dependence of artificial intelligence algorithms on data sets, unmanned aerial vehicles (UAV) can be used for image acquisition [6], which is considered as an effective technology to solve the data acquisition problems faced by smart cities and disaster rescue. However, there exist security problems during image acquisition by UAVs, thus the communication between UAVs and ground base stations requires secure protocols to prevent information theft by adversaries. The ground base stations are semi-trusted units, and there needs a reliable mechanism to prevent ground base station from accessing to private information. For achieving information sharing among different departments, the access control mechanism should be guaranteed.

Blockchain technology is a new decentralized technology [7], which has the advantages of decentralization, immutability and traceability. Blockchain is a distributed system, which can effectively avoid single point of failure. The consensus mechanism increases the cost of disrupting the system and improves the system's stability, while smart contracts can improve the independence and stability of the entire system. Mauludi et al. [8] have designed a forest fire warning system, which can predict the forest fires by employing the Internet of Things system. However, their system also faces some problems, for example, sensors are easily damaged, the difficult of facilities installation, and high costs. Taro et al. [9] proposed a system for forest measurement with the help of UAV lidar, which can effectively measure the volume of trees and delineate forest boundaries. Ting et al. [10] used the method of UAV remote sensing to design solutions for UAV aerial photography, image data acquisition and data processing, but lacks security guarantees.

1.1   Related Works

Although many technologies for forest state supervision have been proposed, they have different limitations. For example, Alonso et al. [11] and Koshelev et al. [12] have suggested to use satellite platforms to collect forest image information. However, the use of satellite has many limits, such as high costs, low accuracy of collected image, and inability to mount sensors. Thus, UAVs can be a better choice for data collection. Dash et al. [13] used UAV to collect time series multispectral images to detect forest health, but the cost of using lidar to collect data is high.

There are remain many problems to be solved in forest data collection. For example, Saadat et al. [14] used the UAV system to detect and collect forest image data, but they did not consider the security of the UAV data transmission, and the integrity and security of the data in the UAV system were difficult to be guaranteed. Sreemana et al. [15,16] designed a blockchain and EdgeDrone-based framework for secure data transmission for forest fire monitoring, which guarantees security and reliability during data acquisition and transmission. Note that with its leader UAV Selection (PRELS) algorithm, the UAV with the largest expected remaining energy is always selected as the leader UAV, and the selection algorithm for aggregated UAVs is regular and vulnerable to attack.

Aloqaily et al. [17] proposed a blockchain-assisted 5G-UAV network design guide, and a data acquisition scheme based on the fusion of blockchain and 5G UAV technology, which allows to outsource most of the UAV's computing tasks. However, the edge cloud in the system is also a semi-trusted entity, which cannot guarantee the system's security. Thus, existing forest image data acquisition schemes remain have many problems, such as low level of data security and attack resistance ability, low accuracy and untraceability of data, and inefficiency of data processing.

1.2   Our Contributions

To address the above mentioned issues, this paper proposes a blockchain-based forest state supervision framework (BSR). A new blockchain-based forest image collection method is introduced by taking advantage of the decentralised, non-tampering, and traceability of blockchain, which is combined with encryption and UAV technologies. BSR uses the authentication mechnism of UAV-GS [18] to ensure data security, symmetric encryption technology to encrypt data before being uploaded to the chain, and attribute-based encryption technology CP-ABE [19] to achieve access control of symmetric key. Each node can decrypt the symmetric key through its private key associated with its attributes, and then further decrypt the ciphertext to obtain the plaintext of image data.

2   Preliminaries

2.1   Blockchain

Blockchain is a decentralized distributed system that has decentralization, immutability, and traceability characteristics. As shown in Fig. 1, each block is linked to the next block's header through hash function, and the blocks are connected to form a chain. The merkle tree guarantees the immutability and traceability of data. Multiple blockchain nodes back up the entire copy of blockchain data, so that the security and stability of the system can be guaranteed even if some data is corrupted.

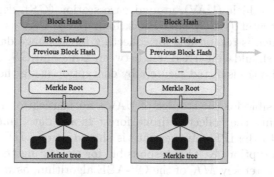

Fig. 1. Blockchain structure

2.2   Smart Contract

Smart contracts are an important tool for blockchain to achieve programmability, which can be run automatically on the blockchain. The contract owner can deploy the smart contract by himself, and users who meet the corresponding conditions can call the interface of contract. A smart contract can be run repeatedly by multiple parties, which can provide a flexible and rich calling mode for blockchain, and make the operation of blockchain more intuitive and transparent.

2.3   Interplanetary File System

Interplanetary file system (IPFS) are point-to-point distributed hypermedia distribution protocols that provide a unified addressing space for the whole world. IPFS provides a high throughput distributed model based on content addressing. IPFS networks are faster, more secure and more open due to their high stability and ability to take advantage of an individual's spare hard disk space and bandwidth.

2.4   Physical Unclonable Functions

A physical unclonable function (PUF) can be used as a hard-based key generator, which provides a non-replicable and unique identity to its device due to the inherent randomness introduced during the manufacturing process. Therefore, PUF is suitable for use as hardware roots of trust and hardware security primitives. Any attempt to tamper with captured PUF will render the PUF unusable. Since each hardware PUF is unique, it is a secure key generation method from PUF.

3   System Model and Security Requirements

3.1   System Model

As shown in Fig. 2, a BSR system consists of five types of entities, namely, unmanned aerial vehicle (UAV), ground base station (GS), department (DP), key generation center (KGC), and Blockchain (BC). UAV is lightweight and small device, which is responsible for collecting forest image data. The authentication process should be carried out between UAV and GS. Then, the forest image data can be transmitted securely by encryption using the negotiated session key.

GS is responsible for the storage of UAV's authentication information, collecting and signing the collected drone forest image data, and uploading the encrypted data to the IPFS. Image data is shared among DP using attribute-based hybrid encryption. KGC is responsible for generating the system parameters PK and master key MK of the CP-ABE algorithm, as well as the private key SK of DP. BC is responsible for storing attribute set U, symmetric key SK encrypted by CP-ABE, forest information, and encrypted forest data, etc.

In the system initialization stage, KGC generates and distributes the system parameters PK and master key MK of the CP-ABE algorithm. With the mutual authentication and signature technologies, DP and KGC can realize secure distribution of private key SK. In the data collection stage, GS first uses the UAV-GS communication protocol to generate the session key. Secure image data is obtained by using session key and encryption and decryption algorithm. In the data processing stage, GS uploads the encrypted data to the IPFS node, links the corresponding hash value, and uses CP-ABE algorithm to construct access structure T to realize the secret sharing among various departments.

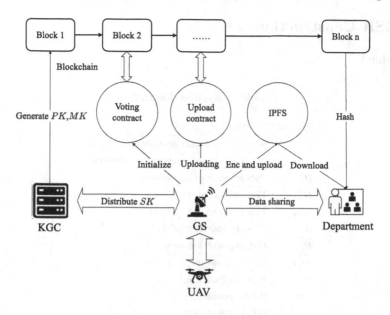

Fig. 2. System model

Finally, the integrity of the uploaded data can be verified by the data uploading smart contract, and the data upload stage can be completed after successful verification.

3.2 Security Requirements

A BSR system should satisfy the following security requirements.

- Data collection security: While collecting data, lightweight small UAVs are vulnerable to spoofing attacks, impersonation attacks, denial of service and message tampering. PUF-based secure UAV-GS authentication protocol is needed to resist these attacks.
- Data storage privacy: The information on the IPFS is stored in ciphertext, so even if the adversary can access the IPFS, the privacy of data can be guaranteed.
- System security: There may be insider attacker trying to upload false data, or even colluding with other GS. The system should deploy smart contracts that can initialize the forest parameters and verify the integrity of forest information. Each uploaded data should be signed so that the source can be traced, which increases the cost of attacks. The system should be resistant to up to 1/2 collusion attacks.
- Data operation security: Non-compliant operations and data cannot pass the verification of smart contracts.

4   BSR Construction

See Table 1.

Table 1. Symbol description

Symbol	Description
F	Secure symmetric encryption scheme
A	Attribute-based encryption schemes
B	Hybrid encryption scheme
DP_i	The i-th department
GS_j	The j-th ground station
U_i	The attribute set of DP_i
R_i	DP_i registration record
S_{DP_i}	DP_i's signature
ψ	KGC's signature
PK	Public parameters
SK_i	DP_i's private key
T	Access structure
N_X	Random nonce
Par	System security parameter
M	Image data
C_k	Data encrypted with symmetric key K
CT	Data encrypted by ABE algorithm
C	The challenge of PUF
R	The response of PUF
K	The session key
$TUID$	Temporary id of UAV
CID	The data's hash

4.1   System Initialization

In the system initialization phase, KGC generates CP-ABE parameters and master key, and issues private keys based on the attribute set from DP.

Step 1: Key generation
KGC selects a secure CP-ABE encryption scheme $A = (Setup, Keygen, Enc, Dec)$ and a secure symmetric encryption scheme $F = (KeyGen, Enc, Dec)$. With the system security parameter Par, the system initialization algorithm generates public parameter PK and system master key MK. Then KGC uploads symmetric encryption scheme F and public parameter PK to the blockchain, while the system master key MK is kept by KGC secretly.

Step 2: Key distribution

DP_i $(i = 1, 2, \cdots, n)$ signs its own attributeset U_i with Cramer-Shoup strong-RSA signature scheme [20] for registering to KGC. If the message passes KGC signature verification, KGC will check if the GS has been registered. If it has been registered, the registration request is rejected. Otherwise, KGC will store the attribute set U_i at local and generate the following registration record:

$$R_i = \{U_i \parallel S_{DP_i}(U_i) \parallel t_i \parallel \psi\}$$

where $S_{DP_i}(U_i)$ is the signature of U_i by DP_i, t_i is the timestamp, and ψ is the signature of KGC on the registration record R_i. Then KGC uploads the register record R_i onto blockchain. KGC runs $A.KeyGen(MK, U_i) \to SK_i$ with the system master key MK and attribute set U_i of DP_i, and sends the private key SK_i to DP_i.

4.2 Forest Information Initialization

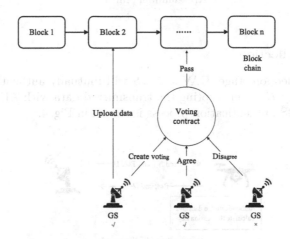

Fig. 3. Forest basic information upload

In this stage, GS can upload the forest information under its jurisdiction to blockchain through smart contract. One GS only manages one forest, and multiple GS can manage the same forest. The upload process of forest basic information is shown in Fig. 3.

- GS_j $(j = 1, 2, \cdots, m)$ uploads its basic information to the blockchain and initiates a voting smart contract.
- Each GS obtains the basic information of GS_j and votes for the GS_j if it thinks the data is true and valid.
- All GS participate in the voting of smart contract. If the number of votes in favor is greater than or equal to 1/2 of the total number of GS, a voting resolution will be adopted. The voting data and results will be uploaded to blockchain by the voting smart contract.

Table 2 shows the basic information of forest initialization, in which Forest-area is the longitude and latitude array data of the forest edge, which can be used to determine the forest boundary by the drawing algorithm. Uavlist is used to store the UAV number owned by the forest base station. GSID is the number of the forest base station, Forest-name and Area-number are the name and area of the forest, respectively.

Table 2. Basic forest information

Name	Types
Forest-area	varchar
Uavlist	varchar
GSID	int
Forest-name	varchar
Area-number	int

4.3   Data Collection

In the data collection stage, UAV and GS will mutually authenticate and generate session key K for encrypting the transmitted data with AES.

The UAV-GS authentication process is shown in Fig. 4.

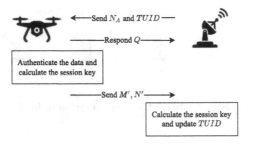

Fig. 4. UAV-GS authentication

- Each UAV stores its challenge response pairs (C, R) in the GS database.
- UAV generates R and $TUID$ through C, then chooses random number N_A, and sends the hash of data to GS.
- GS verifies whether the data is fresh, and generates R after verification. Then R is split into K_1 and K_2. GS chooses a random number N_B, and encrypts the data into Q as follows.

$$X_1 = N_A \oplus K_2$$

$$Y_2 = N_B \oplus X_1 \oplus K_1$$

$$Q = (Y_2 \parallel X_1) \oplus (K_2 \parallel K_1)$$

After received data, UAV decrypts Q with R to obtain N_A and N_B, and chooses random number N_C. The substring of N_C acts as a new challenge C', which is used to generate a new challenge response pairs (C', R') through PUF.

The newly generated data is calculated as M' and N', and the session key K is generated as follows.

$$M' = R' \oplus K_1 \parallel K_2$$

$$N' = N'_C \oplus K_1$$

$$K = (K_1 \oplus N_B) \parallel (K_2 \oplus N_C)$$

UAV sends the hash values of M' and N' to GS. After received the data, GS generates K and updates the challenge response pair (C', R') and $TUID$.

$$TUID'_i = H(K_2 \parallel TUID_i \parallel K_1)$$

– The UAV securely transmits data to the GS using the session key K.

Table 3 summarizes the parameters in UAV data collection. Task-area denotes the area required by the collection task, which is used to check whether the collected image data is missing.

Table 3. Parameters for UAV data collection

Name	Types
Task-area	varchar
UAV number	int
GS ID	int
Forest name	varchar
Time	varchar
Weather	varchar
Image array	varchar

4.4 Data Processing

Step 1: Data upload

– GS_j generates a symmetric key $k \leftarrow F.KeyGen(1^n)$.
– GS_j uploads the encrypted image data to the IPFS network and gets the CID of the data.

Step 2: Encryption key upload

GS_j uses the public parameters PK, MK and attributes selected from the blockchain to construct the access structure T and encrypt the symmetric key K.

$$C_k = F.Enc_k(M)$$
$$CT = A.Enc_{PK_i,T}(k)$$

GS_j uploads CT, CID and a summary of data to the blockchain via the Upload contract. Smart contracts guarantee the security and integrity of data sources.

Step 3: Data sharing

- The department obtains CT and CID from the blockchain and decrypts CT using SK_j and the public parameter PK. If SK_i matches CT, the symmetric key K can be obtained as follows

$$k = A.Dec_{SK_i,PK}(CT)$$

- DP downloads the encrypted data from the IPFS network through CID to obtain the ciphertext C_k and decrypts the encrypted data using the symmetric key K to obtain the image data M uploaded by GS_j.

$$M = F.Dec_k(C_k)$$

5   Security Analysis

Theorem 1. *The proposed BSR system can resist physical attacks, that is, no one can modify the parameters by changing the configuration of UAV.*

Proof. Due to the unclonable property of PUF, if the PUF is tampered with, the authentication between UAV and GS cannot be successfully performed, and the shared key cannot be generated. In other words, if the PUF of UAV cannot correctly generate $R = PUF(C)$, it will not be authenticated by GS, nor generate a key K shared with GS, resulting in the failure of UAV data transmission.

Theorem 2. *The proposed BSR system can resist impersonation attacks. In other words, no entity can impersonate the authorized DP to decrypt the data on blockchain.*

Proof. If some adversary wants to impersonate the authorized department, she must have the private key SK. In the BSR system, after DP registered as chain node, KGC will assign the private key SK to the corresponding DP, which should be kept secretly by DP. Any other unauthorized entity cannot calculate $k = A.Dec_{SK}(CT)$, which means the data on the chain cannot be decrypted.

Theorem 3. *If symmetric encryption scheme F and ABE scheme A are secure, the proposed BSR system can protect the privacy of data. That is, other entities cannot use the encrypted data on the GS chain to obtain decryption keys or infer data in the IPFS network.*

Proof. In the proposed BSR system, only DP with symmetric key k can decrypt the data on the IPFS. Thus, only when DP obtains the symmetric key k, it will be able to calculate the decrypted data through $F.Dec_k(\cdot)$, and only the authorized legal DP could use the private key SK to obtain the symmetric key k from the chain. The adversary does not have the ability to obtain the symmetric key k, thus it will not be able to decrypt the encrypted data. Therefore, the BSR system can protect the privacy of data.

Theorem 4. *If the selected ABE scheme A is secure, the proposed BSR system can support data access control.*

Proof. In the proposed BSR system, ABE technology is used to control the permission, that is, in the encryption process, the sender sets the access structure T and encrypts the data with system parameter PK. Thus, only a department whose property set U in the private key satisfies the access structure T can access and decrypt the data; otherwise, it has no permission to decrypt the data.

Theorem 5. *The proposed BSR system can protect the integrity of data.*

Proof. Only the CID of the uploaded image data set, the encrypted key CT and the data abstract meet the requirements of the Upload Contract and have the signature of the sender GS can be passed the inspection and uploaded.

6   Performance Analysis

We conducted the experiments on the hybrid encryption using Java and a platform with Windows 10 operating system and 16 GB of memory. The security parameter is set as $Par = 128$.

Figure 5 shows the encryption and decryption time overhead of the CP-ABE scheme used. In the experiments, 128-bit AES key is used. It can be seen that the encryption time of CP-ABE increases slowly with the increase of the number of attributes, while the decryption time is almost unchanged, which is determined by the structure of the access tree. For BSR systems, since the AES key length is only 128 bits, the time cost of this part is almost negligible.

Figure 6 shows the time costs of different phases. We selected AES-128-ECB encryption and decryption algorithm to test 100 KB, 1 MB, 10 MB image data. Transcoding and decoding are the conversion time of image data to Bash64 encoding format. Encryption and decryption are the AES encryption and decryption times. Download and Upload are the data uploading and downloading time of IPFS data. The figure shows that the encryption and decryption time and transcoding time of AES account for most of the system overhead. With the increase of image size, the time cost of the system increases slowly.

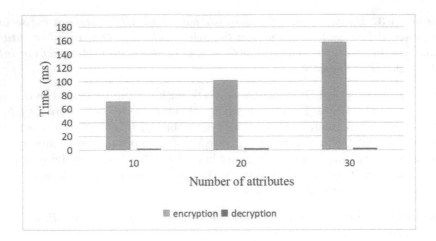

Fig. 5. CP-ABE time cost

Experimental results show that CP-ABE encryption in BSR system enjoys very high time performance, and AES algorithm can still show better performance when the image is larger. For *GS* systems with powerful computing resources, BSR is suitable for dealing with large amounts of high-precision image data.

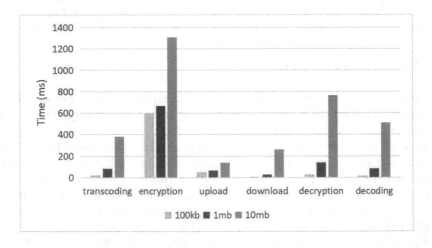

Fig. 6. System time cost

7   Conclusion

This paper studied the data security, privacy and access control issues in data collection, management and sharing for forest supervision, and proposed a blockchain-based forest supervision system (BSR). Our BSR system can support secret data sharing among multiple GS, where GS can apply for the access rights on the interested data. Data integrity and security verification can be achieved through blockchain smart contract. The secret sharing of image data on the blockchain can be realized through the hybrid encryption technology of CP-ABE and AES. Theoretical analysis and experiments showed that the proposed BSR system can realize secure and efficient forest supervision.

Acknowledgments. This article is supported in part by the National Key R&D Program of China under project 2020YFB1006004, the Guangxi Natural Science Foundation under grants AD19245048 and 2019GXNSFGA245004, the National Natural Science Foundation of China under projects 621621017 and 62172119, the Guangdong Key R&D Program under project 2020B0101090002, the Major Key Project of PCL under grants PCL2021A09, PCL2021A02, and PCL2022A03, and the Shenzhen Science and Technology R&D Fund under project JSGG20201102170000002.

References

1. Vastaranta, M., et al.: Laser-based field measurements in tree-level forest data acquisition. Photogramm. J. Finl. **21**, 51–61 (2009)
2. Gnusov, M.A., Popikov, P.I., Malyukov, S.V., Sherstyukov, N.A., Pozdnyakov, A.K.: Improving the efficiency of forest fire prevention and suppression with of forest fire machine. In: IOP Conference Series: Materials Science and Engineering, vol. 919, pp. 032025. IOP Publishing (2020)
3. Karp, D.S., et al.: Forest bolsters bird abundance, pest control and coffee yield. Ecol. Lett. **16**(11), 1339–1347 (2013)
4. Morkovina, S.S., Sibiryatkina, I.V., Konovalova, E.M., Bourtsev, D.S.: Investigation of entrepreneurial structures forest management performance of forestry system in sparsely forest-poor region. Asian Soc. Sci. **10**(23), 20 (2014)
5. Eltner, A., Schneider, D., Maas, H.-G.: Integrated processing of high resolution topographic data for soil erosion assessment considering data acquisition schemes and surface properties. Int. Arch. Photogramm. Remote Sens. Spat. Inf. Sci. **41** (2016)
6. Zhou, H., Kong, H., Wei, L., Creighton, D., Nahavandi, S.: On detecting road regions in a single UAV image. IEEE Trans. Intell. Transp. Syst. **18**(7), 1713–1722 (2016)
7. Yli-Huumo, J., Ko, D., Choi, S., Park, S., Smolander, K.: Where is current research on blockchain technology — a systematic review. PLoS ONE **11**(10), e0163477 (2016)
8. Iqbal Mauludi, M., Aminah, N.S., Budiman, M.: Forest fire alert system. In: IOP Conference Series: Earth and Environmental Science, vol. 830, pp. 012032. IOP Publishing (2021)
9. Suzuki, T., Shiozawa, S., Yamaba, A., Amano, Y.: Forest data collection by UAV Lidar-based 3D mapping: Segmentation of individual tree information from 3D point clouds. Int. J. Autom. Technol. **15**(3), 313–323 (2021)
10. Shi, T.-T., Zhang, X.-B., Guo, L.-P., Huang, L.-Q., Jing, Z.-X.: Application of UAV remote sensing in monitoring of callicarpa nudiflora. China J. Chin. Materia Medica **44**(19), 4078–4081 (2019)

11. Alonso, L., Picos, J., Armesto, J.: Forest cover mapping and pinus species classification using very high-resolution satellite images and random forest. ISPRS Ann. Photogramm. Remote Sens. Spat. Inf. Sci. **3**, 203–210 (2021)
12. Koshelev, A.V., Tkachenko, N.A., Shatrovskaya, M.O.: Decoding of forest belts using satellite images. In: IOP Conference Series: Earth and Environmental Science, vol. 875, p. 012065. IOP Publishing (2021)
13. Dash, J.P., Watt, M.S., Pearse, G.D., Heaphy, M., Dungey, H.S.: Assessing very high resolution UAV imagery for monitoring forest health during a simulated disease outbreak. ISPRS J. Photogramm. Remote Sens. **131**, 1–14 (2017)
14. Saadat, Md.N., Husen, M.N.: An application framework for forest fire and haze detection with data acquisition using unmanned aerial vehicle. In: Proceedings of the 12th International Conference on Ubiquitous Information Management and Communication, pp. 1–7 (2018)
15. Datta, S., Sinha, D.: BESDDFFS: blockchain and EdgEdrone based secured data delivery for forest fire surveillance. Peer Peer Netw. Appl. **14**(6), 3688–3717 (2021)
16. Datta, S., Kumar, S., Sinha, D., Das, A.K.: BSSFFS: blockchain-based sybil-secured smart forest fire surveillance. J. Ambient Intell. Humaniz. Comput., 1–32 (2021)
17. Aloqaily, M., Bouachir, O., Boukerche, A., Al Ridhawi, I.: Design guidelines for blockchain-assisted 5G-UAV networks. IEEE Netw. **35**(1), 64–71 (2021)
18. Alladi, T., Bansal, G., Chamola, V., Guizani, M., et al.: SecAuthUAV: a novel authentication scheme for UAV-ground station and UAV-UAV communication. IEEE Trans. Veh. Technol. **69**(12), 15068–15077 (2020)
19. Bethencourt, J., Sahai, A., Waters, B.: Ciphertext-policy attribute-based encryption. In: 2007 IEEE Symposium on Security and Privacy (SP 2007), pp. 321–334. IEEE (2007)
20. Fischlin, M.: The Cramer-Shoup strong-RSA signature scheme revisited. In: Desmedt, Y.G. (ed.) PKC 2003. LNCS, vol. 2567, pp. 116–129. Springer, Heidelberg (2003). https://doi.org/10.1007/3-540-36288-6_9

Suspicious Customer Detection on the Blockchain Network for Cryptocurrency Exchanges

Haiou Jiang[1], Keming Zhang[2], Xinjian Ma[1], Yanchun Sun[2], and Yun Ma[2(✉)]

[1] Advanced Institute of Big Data, Beijing 100195, China
jiangho@aibd.ac.cn, maxinjian@pku.edu.cn
[2] Peking University, Beijing 100871, China
{zhangsky,sunyc,mayun}@pku.edu.cn

Abstract. Blockchain has rapidly become one of the hottest Internet technologies as a decentralized and distributed data management solution. Cryptocurrency, one of the most successful applications of blockchain, quickly attracted attention from investors because of its high anonymity, flexibility and rapidity. However, cryptocurrencies are also used by some criminals to commit crimes secretly and they integrate illicit funds into real economy through cryptocurrency exchanges, causing serious impact to economies and societies. Traditional methods for exchanges to prevent financial crimes like Know Your Customer (KYC) have limit effect in the peer-to-peer and decentralized blockchain system. In this work, we propose a system aiming to help cryptocurrency exchanges to detect suspicious customers on the blockchain network. Besides the traditional KYC procedures, several machine learning models are used to check the account addresses submitted by the customers and to detect suspicious address in daily transaction. The detection models use the open-source data from websites and forums instead of private data from governments or institutions, and can detect the top five financial crimes in cryptocurrencies simultaneously. Finally, a visualization of transactions is proposed to better demonstrate the fund flows of suspicious customers for further analysis.

Keywords: Blockchain network · Cryptocurrency · Suspicious customer detection · Machine learning · Visualization of transactions

1 Introduction

As a decentralized and distributed data management solution, blockchain has enabled many trustworthy Internet applications among untrusted subjects since it was first proposed by Nakamoto in 2008 [1]. Cryptocurrency is one of the most successful applications of blockchain because of its high anonymity, flexibility and rapidity. There are various kinds of cryptocurrencies, like Bitcoin, Ethereum, etc. They have evolved into huge financial ecosystems with a large number of users and a high degree of activities.

The anonymity means that cryptocurrency addresses are the only information needed in the transactions, that makes cryptocurrencies used by more and more criminals to commit crimes. According to "Chainalysis", a famous company aiming to help government and clients to legitimize the cryptocurrency market, illicit activities in cryptocurrency systems represent roughly $10 billion worth of transfers worldwide in 2020 [2].

Cryptocurrency exchanges are businesses that mainly provide conversion service. They help customers to convert cryptocurrencies into legal currencies or trade them for other assets, like change Bitcoin into dollars or change Bitcoin into Ethereum. According to an industry survey [3, 4], criminals can integrate their illicit funds into real economy through cryptocurrency exchanges, and about 65% of funds from known illicit cryptocurrency entities flow through exchanges. Therefore, detecting suspicious customers in exchanges can be effective to prevent crimes and means a lot to the economies and the society.

However, cryptocurrency exchanges lack effective methods to detect suspicious customers. The traditional KYC procedures used in financial institution only need customers to provide their identity information by themselves, and evaluate their risk by checking the submitted information [5]. It is not enough to detect suspicious customers because criminals can easily forge their identity to bypass these identification procedures [6]. To make matters worse, a global study of 216 exchanges by the reg-tech startup "Coinfirm" found that 69% of these businesses do not even have complete and transparent KYC procedures [7].

In this work, we propose a system aiming to help cryptocurrency exchanges to detect suspicious customers on the blockchain network. Besides the traditional KYC procedures, several popular machine learning models are used to check the account addresses submitted by the customers and to detect suspicious addresses in daily transactions. The detection models use the open-source data from websites and forums instead of private data from governments or institutions and can detect the top five financial crimes in cryptocurrencies simultaneously. Finally, a visualization of transactions is proposed to better demonstrate the fund flows of suspicious customers for further analysis.

Main contributions of this work are listed as follows:

(1) We propose a suspicious customer detection system for cryptocurrency exchanges, consisting of three rounds of KYC procedures and the daily operation detection.
(2) Several popular machine learning models are used in the detection. The model trainings are based open-source data collect from websites and forums and can be updated offline. The main five crimes can be detected simultaneously.
(3) A visualization module is proposed to clearly present transaction flows between addresses, with licit and suspicious ones marked separately. It can help exchanges to do further and detailed analysis.

2   Related Work

Researches on detecting crimes in financial institutions have lasted for decades. In tradition financial institutions, it mainly focuses on customers and data within a single institution. In the cryptocurrency activities, the crime detection can focus overall blockchain network.

2.1 Crime Detection in Traditional Financial Activities

Know Your Customer (KYC) is a procedure widely used in financial institutions. A new customer is required to submit the necessary identity information like full name, date of birth, address, etc. when applying for a new account in the institution.

Based on the KYC information, customer profiling is used to detect suspicious customer. Wang et al. proposed to use decision tree to generate AML rules from customers' profiles to evaluate their money laundering risks [8]. Dreewski proposed the application of social network analysis algorithms to predict the possibility of money laundering [9]. Wang et al. proposed a semi-supervised attentive graph neural network to predict fraud based on users' information and their social networks [10].

Based on the transaction information within the institutions, most of the institutions use the well-designed embedded rules to detect suspicious transactions. With the growing volume of unstructured data, some institutions employ some statistical analysis methods or machine learning model based on their private data. Raza et al. employed a combination of clustering and dynamic Bayesian network to detect anomalies by capturing patterns of a customers' transactional sequences from a real bank [11]. Li et al. used data from CBank and Czech bank to test their proposed multipartite graph model, aiming to detect anomalous fund flows [12]. Liu et al. applied SVM to transaction records from Wuhan Branch of Agriculture Bank in China to detect suspicious accounts based on their business features such as the frequency and the total number of transactions [13].

2.2 Crime Detection in Cryptocurrency Activities

Unlike traditional financial activities where transaction data is only available in the specific institutions involved in the transactions, the full transaction data is available to everyone in the blockchain network. It makes it possible to detect suspicious financial activities based on the complete transaction information. Existing researches focus on the performance of machine learning or deep learning models.

Many suspicious detection models are based on binary classification by identifying one specific type of criminal transactions or addresses. Weber et al. and Tam et al. proposed GCN on Bitcoin transaction networks to identify whether one transaction is illicit or not [14, 15]. Kanemura et al. proposed a vote-based method to label multiple Bitcoin addresses controlled by the same user as a DNM or not [16]. Ackora et al. used the topological data analysis to detect ransomware related Bitcoin addresses [17]. Bartoletti et al. used data mining technique to find Bitcoin addresses related to Ponzi Schemes and used machine learning algorithms to identify Ponzi Schemes addresses [18]. Li et al. collected a large dataset of illicit addresses, proposed three types of features, and used five machine learning algorithms to identify the illicit addresses, and further discussed the class imbalance problem [19]. Although these studies all get good results on identifying their focused type of crimes, it is unsure whether it is effective and practical to generalize these methods to detect other kinds of crimes.

Other researches use multinomial classification to identify addresses of different types, like exchanges, gambling, mixing, mining pool and several crimes. The purpose of these researches is to identify more detailed information of cryptocurrencies addresses, not just whether licit or not. Michalski et al. and Nerurkar et al. proposed machine learning approaches to classify addresses [20, 21]. Chaehyeon et al. further analyzed which address features have the most affect on the classification performance besides categorizing Bitcoin addresses [22]. Ermilov et al. proposed a two-fold Bitcoin address clustering algorithm to cluster addresses for further de-anonymizing analysis [23].

Most of the time, crime information in cryptocurrency is confidential and maintained in governments and certain institutions. Existing open dataset are desensitized and encrypted. And other researches use private datasets [20, 21, 23].

In this work, we aim to help those cryptocurrency exchanges and other businesses which may find it hard to get enough data to solve the problem of detecting suspicious customers in blockchain network by themselves. We propose a system that can not only detect various kinds of mainstream cryptocurrency crimes, but also crawl data from open websites and forums regularly to continuously enrich the training dataset and to improve detection models' performances.

3 Suspicious Customer Detection

In this work, we propose a system aiming to help cryptocurrency exchanges to detect suspicious customers on the blockchain network. Several popular machine learning models are used to detect the suspicious addresses and a visualization module is proposed to clearly present suspicious addresses and transactions.

3.1 Design Goal

The goal of the system is to help exchanges to detect the possibility that a customer may commit financial crimes using cryptocurrency. We collect normal cryptocurrency addresses and marked as licit, and criminal cryptocurrency addresses revealed on open websites and forums and marked as the crime types. The marked dataset can be used to train the multinomial classification models often used in the financial crime detection research area. Then the models are used to classify addresses. The address identified to be a certain type of criminal address is called suspicious address and the related customer is called suspicious customer.

According to the recent industry survey [2], the top five crimes are listed as follows. Most traditional financial crimes like money laundering and ransomware are also committed in cryptocurrency systems widely, and Ponzi, hack, and darknet market rise with the popularity of cryptocurrency.

Money laundering is the process by which the illegal sources of profits are disguised to obscure the link between the funds and the original criminal activity. Characters of cryptocurrencies like flexibility, rapidity, transactional irrevocability and portability increase the effectiveness and efficiency of the money laundering process compared to traditional financial institutions [5].

Ransomware is a type of malicious software which disables the functionality of a computer in some way unless a ransom is paid. Because of the anonymity of cryptocurrencies, criminals can get ransom more secretly, which facilitates the development of ransomwares. In 2020, total amount paid by ransomware victims increased by 311% to reach nearly $350 million worth of cryptocurrencies around the world [2].

Ponzi Schemes is fraudulent investments which repay users with the funds invested by new users that join the scheme, and implode when it is no longer possible to find new investments. Ponzi scheme organizers often use the latest innovation, technology, product or growth industry to scam investors. With the rising use of cryptocurrencies, they become a new tool for fraudster [24].

Hack wallets are often belonged to exchanges or platforms hacked by outsiders. Because of the rising value of cryptocurrencies, especially Bitcoin, cryptocurrency wallets now become the target of hackers. In 2020, over $520 million worth of cryptocurrency was stolen from worldwide services and individuals [2].

Darknet Market is a commercial website on the web that operates via darknets. The emergence of cryptocurrencies enhances its concealment. In 2020, darknet market set a new revenue record about $1.7 billion worth of cryptocurrencies throughout the world.

3.2 System Architecture

As shown in Fig. 1, the system mainly consists of three rounds of KYC procedures and a daily operation procedure. It also has two offline modules run regularly or irregularly, namely dataset update and detection model training.

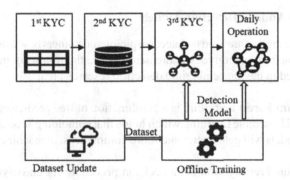

Fig. 1. The architecture of the system.

(1) **1st KYC.** 1st KYC is the traditional KYC procedure. It is still an effective way to evaluate the risk of every customer before they are allowed to create accounts in cryptocurrency exchanges. The new customer is required to fill in the necessary identity information like full name, date of birth, address, etc. for the preliminary review. The new customer is so required to submit photo government-issued identification, such as identification cards and passports to verify the information. Nowadays, with development of image recognition technology, a biometric facial recognition procedure is also compulsory in order to match the customers to their official documents. By asking customers to do a previously undetermined action like blinking or turning their heads, it is more likely to prevent people from forging their identities.

(2) **2nd KYC.** In 2nd KYC, exchanges have a more detailed check on the identity of customers based on the third-party databases, like Refinitiv World-Check and LexisNexis [25], both of which are famous risk information databases that offer financial crime risk data of over millions of entities. The third-party database is widely used in credit industry.

(3) **3rd KYC.** Different from opening a new account in traditional financial institution, the costumer will submit his cryptocurrency account addresses to associate to the new account in the exchanges. Several machine learning models are used to check the addresses submitted by the customers. The customers with suspicious addresses will be declined and reported to the judicial authorities or the regulators.

(4) **Daily Operation.** Exchange regularly or irregularly use the machine learning models in daily operation. All the suspicious address will be associated to the suspicious customer and reported to the judicial authorities or the regulators. A visualization module is proposed to clearly present suspicious addresses and transactions.

(5) **Offline Dataset Update and Models Training.** The open websites and forums are regularly visited and dataset are updated. And the machine learning models are trained if the dataset is update so as to keep or improve the suspicious costumer detection performance.

3.3 Suspicious Address Detection Models

Machine learning models are used to detect suspicious customers based on the transaction information of their cryptocurrency addresses. We use the following machine learning models often used in the financial crime detection research area.

(1) **The Random Forest** algorithm is a combination of tree predictors. It uses a technique called Ensemble Learning which holds that combining several weak machine learning models will get a better and more comprehensive machine learning model [26].

(2) **The Decision Tree** algorithm is a decision procedure for classifying an instance. It starts from a root, and then specifies instances through attribute tests on non-leaf nodes. Every instance will be classified at the bottom of this structure named leaves [27].

(3) **Logistic Regression** is a classic classification algorithm, working in a similar way to linear regression and different in using a special function called Sigmoid function. Logistic Regression can be used in both binary and multiple-class classification problems [28]. One effective way to realize the multiple-class classification is to train models separately for each class and set decision boundaries to separate the targeted class from the others.

(4) **Support Vector Machine (SVM)** is a classification algorithm which can be extended for multiclass problems [29]. It is based on a process called maximum-margin hyperplane and has been applied in many fields since its appearance.

(5) **K-Nearest Neighbor (KNN)** algorithm is a simple classification algorithm. Its core thought is that a new object belongs to the class to which its K-Nearest neighbor belong [30].

We extract 48 features of every address based on the transaction information and addresses' statistics. They can be grouped into the following four groups and the details are listed in Table 1:

(1) number of addresses in transaction inputs and outputs
(2) amount of cryptocurrencies in transaction inputs and outputs
(3) number of transactions involving the target address
(4) address type of the target address, like Pay to Script Hash (P2SH), Pay to Public Key Hash (P2PKH), etc.

3.4 Transaction and Address Visualization

The visualization module is proposed clearly point out transaction flows of addresses and help exchanges to do further analysis on suspicious addresses and customers. It can be used in the 3rd KYC and daily operation procedure.

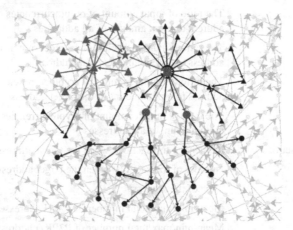

Fig. 2. An example of the transaction and address visualization (Color figure online).

Figure 2 shows an example when the user enters an address and the expected number of transaction hops. The involved addresses and transactions are presented in the form of a directed graph.

The nodes are marked three shapes. Square node represents the submitted address. Triangle node means that this address is on the tracing route that transfers cryptocurrency to other addresses. Circle node means that this address is on the tracking route that receives cryptocurrency from other addresses. The edge between nods is the transaction between the two addresses.

Table 1. Description of features of the addresses.

Group	Description
Number of addresses	Mean/min/max/total number of transaction inputs when the target address is an input/output of the transaction
	Mean/min/max/total number of transaction outputs when the target address is an input/output of the transaction
	The ratio of number of transaction outputs to number of transaction inputs
Amount of cryptocurrencies	Mean/min/max/total input amount of cryptocurrencies when the target address is an input/output of the transaction
	Mean/min/max/total output amount of cryptocurrencies when the target address is an input/output of the transaction
	Mean/min/max/total input amount of cryptocurrencies
	Mean/min/max/total output amount of cryptocurrencies
	The ratio of input amount of cryptocurrencies of the target address to input amount of all addresses
	The ratio of output amount of cryptocurrencies of the target address to output amount of all addresses
	The ratio of output amount of cryptocurrencies of the target address to input amount of the target address
	The ratio of output amount of cryptocurrencies of all address to input amount of all addresses
Number of transactions	Number of transactions when the target address is an input
	Number of transactions when the target address is an output
Address type	Type of the address
	Mean/min/max/total number of P2SH addresses in inputs
	Mean/min/max/total number of P2PKH addresses in inputs
	Mean/min/max/total number of P2SH addresses in outputs
	Mean/min/max/total number of P2PKH addresses in outputs

If the addresses are detected to be suspicious, the nodes will be marked the star shape, and the neighbors, their neighbors' neighbors and the transactions among them are highlighted in red.

4   Evaluation

This section presents the experiments and the performance of the machine learning models.

4.1 Dataset

We use the existing most popular cryptocurrency Bitcoin as an example. Licit addresses are collected from WalletExplorer.com, a website that clusters Bitcoin addresses as wallets. We choose four famous exchanges including Huobi, Bittrex, Luno and Kraken, and suppose that the addresses we select randomly from these exchanges are licit [31]. We collect all the five types of illicit addresses mentioned before from US department of Justice documents, dataset public in [19], and the websites, like Bitcoinabuse.com and WalletExplorer.com.

We collect 12172 addresses in the dataset, including 9532 licit addresses, 482 money laundering addresses, 789 ransomware addresses, 142 Ponzi schemes addresses, 310 hack wallets, and 917 darknet market wallets.

4.2 Evaluation Metrics

In this paper, we use three metrics, including Precision, Recall and F1-score, to evaluate the performance of a model to identify each type of address.

For every address type i, True Positives (TP_i) is the number of addresses of type i that are correctly predicted. False Positives (FP_i) means the number of other types of addresses that are predicted as type i. False Negatives (FN_i) is the number of addresses of type i that are predicted as other types.

Precision is the ability of the models to label a type of addresses correctly.

$$Precision_i = TP_i/(TP_i + FP_i) \tag{1}$$

Recall reflects the ability of the models to find out all illicit addresses.

$$Recall_i = TP_i/(TP_i + FN_i) \tag{2}$$

F1-score is the weighted average of the precision and recall.

$$F1_i = 2 \times Precision_i \times Recall_i/(Precision_i + Recall_i) \tag{3}$$

We use Macro Metrics, including Macro Precision, Macro Recall and Macro F1-score, to evaluate the overall performance of a model to identify all the types of addresses. They are the unweighted mean of their corresponding evaluation metrics of every type of addresses.

$$Macro - Precision = \frac{1}{n}\sum\nolimits_{i=1}^{n} Precision_i \tag{4}$$

$$Macro - Recall = \frac{1}{n}\sum\nolimits_{i=1}^{n} Recall_i \tag{5}$$

$$Macro - F1 = \frac{1}{n}\sum\nolimits_{i=1}^{n} F1_i \tag{6}$$

4.3 Results and Discussions

The overall performances of the machine learning models are shown in Fig. 3. Figure 3(a) shows the macro metrics of all the models. Random Forest performs the best in the experiment, with precision as 0.9306, recall as 0.8412, and F1-score as 0.8754. Decision Tree has the second performance, with precision as 0.8005, recall as 0.816, and F1-score as 0.8005. Logistic Regression has the second performances, with precision as 0.7546, recall as 0.8232, and f1 score as 0.7776.

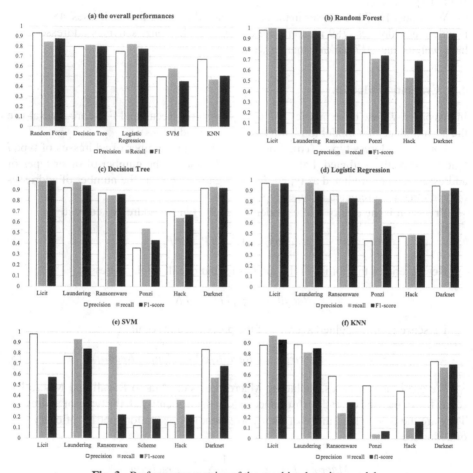

Fig. 3. Performance metrics of the machine learning models.

Figure 3(b) to Fig. 3(f) shows the performance metrics of each model on each type of addresses. Random Forest has the best and balanced performances on each type of addresses. From the view of identifying each type of addresses, all the models perform well in Money laundering, ransomware and darknet market. The performance metrics of Random Forest are all over 90% on the three types. In Decision Tree and Logistic Regression, the performance metrics on the three types are all over 80%.

Most of the models perform bad in Ponzi scheme and hack. We believe that this is caused by their low proportion compared to the other types of addresses, especially licit addresses, which is 1.17% and 2.25% respectively.

It is widely accepted that the performance of machine learning relies on the dataset used to train the models. For example, the imbalance of the dataset in our experiment, especially the extremely low proportion of Ponzi schemes and hack makes their performance much lower than the others. In the suspicious customer detection system, we propose an offline module run regularly to collect data from open websites and forums and update dataset. With the improvement of the quality of the dataset, the performance of the models will definitely improve.

5 Conclusion

Cryptocurrencies have quickly attracted attention from investors because of its high anonymity, flexibility and rapidity since the blockchain was first proposed by Nakamoto in 2008. They are also used commit crimes secretly. And the illicit funds can be integrated into real economy through cryptocurrency exchanges, causing serious impact to economies and societies.

We propose a suspicious customer detection system for cryptocurrency exchanges. It consists two traditional KYC procedures and uses several popular machine learning models to check the account addresses submitted by the customers before opening a new account in the 3rd round KYC procedure, and to detect suspicious address in daily operation procedure. The detection models use the open-source data from websites and forums instead of private data from governments or institutions, and can detect the top five financial crimes in cryptocurrencies simultaneously. The system regularly update dataset and retrain model to improve the detection performance. The system also has a vitalization module to clearly present the addresses and the transactions. Finally, we take some experiments to compare the performance like Precision, Recall, F1-score of the machine learning models.

There are various possibilities for future work. In this paper, we use data from Bitcoin, one future work is to apply our proposed system to identifying suspicious addresses in other cryptocurrencies, like Ethereum. We propose 48 static features in the machine learning model, another future work is to explore some dynamic features to improve classification performance in the machine learning model. For example, the dynamic change in the account balance of a cryptocurrency address may provide more information on the difference among different types of illicit addresses.

Acknowledgements. This work was supported by the National Key R&D Program of China (No. 2020YFB1006000).

References

1. Nakamoto, S.: Bitcoin: a peer-to-peer electronic cash system. https://bitcoin.org/bitcoin.pdf. Accessed 30 Apr 2022

2. The 2021 Crypto Crime Report. https://go.chainalysis.com/2021-Crypto-Crime-Report.html. Accessed 30 Apr 2022
3. 2019 Crypto Crime Report: Decoding Hacks, Darknet Markets, and Scams. https://go.chaina lysis.com/2019-Crypto-Crime-Report.htm. Accessed 30 Apr 2022
4. Foley, S., Karlsen, J.R., Putniņš, T.J.: Sex, drugs, and bitcoin: how much illegal activity is financed through cryptocurrencies? Rev. Financ. Stud. **32**(5), 1798–1853 (2019)
5. Brenig, C., Accorsi, R., Müller, G.: Economic analysis of cryptocurrency backed money laundering. In: ECIS 2015 Completed Research Papers (2015)
6. New OFAC Sanctions and DOJ Complaint for North Korea-Linked Cryptocurrency Laundering Scheme: What You Need to Know (2020). https://blog.chainalysis.com/reports/north-korea-cryptocurrency-addresses-ofac-doj-march-2020/. Accessed 30 Apr 2022
7. Most Crypto Exchanges Still Don't Have Clear KYC Policies: Report. https://alekbo.com/cry ptocoins/most-crypto-exchanges-still-dont-have-clear-kyc-policies-report.html. Accessed 30 Apr 2022
8. Wang, S.-N., Yang, J.-G.: A money laundering risk evaluation method based on decision tree. In: International Conference on Machine Learning & Cybernetics (2007)
9. Rafał, D., Jan, S., Wojciech, F.: The application of social network analysis algorithms in a system supporting money laundering detection. Inf. Sci. **295**, 18–32 (2015)
10. Wang, D., Lin, J., Cui, P., et al.: A semi-supervised graph attentive network for financial fraud detection. In: 2019 IEEE International Conference on Data Mining (ICDM) (2019)
11. Raza, S., Haider, S.: Suspicious activity reporting using dynamic Bayesian networks. Procedia Comput. Sci. **3**, 987–991 (2011)
12. Li, X., Liu, S., Li, Z., et al.: FlowScope: spotting money laundering based on graphs. In: Proceedings of the AAAI Conference on Artificial Intelligence, pp. 4731–4738 (2020)
13. Liu, K., Yu, T.: An improved support-vector network model for anti-money laundering. In: Fifth International Conference on Management of e-Commerce and e-Government, pp. 193–196 (2011)
14. Mark, W., Giacomo, D., Jie, C., et al.: Anti-money laundering in bitcoin: experimenting with graph convolutional networks for financial forensics. arXiv:1908.02591 (2019)
15. Tam, D.S.H., Lau, W.C., Hu, B., et al.: Identifying illicit accounts in large scale e-payment networks-a graph representation learning approach. arXiv:1906.05546 (2019)
16. Kanemura, K., Toyoda, K., Ohtsuki, T.: Identification of darknet markets' bitcoin addresses by voting per-address classification results. In: 2019 IEEE International Conference on Blockchain and Cryptocurrency (ICBC), pp. 154–158 (2019)
17. Akcora, C.G., Li, Y., Gel, Y.R., et al.: Topological data analysis for ransomware detection on the bitcoin blockchain. arXiv:1906.07852 (2019)
18. Bartoletti, M., Pes, B., Serusi, S.: Data mining for detecting bitcoin Ponzi schemes. In: 2018 Crypto Valley Conference on Blockchain Technology (CVCBT), pp. 75–84 (2018)
19. Li, Y., Cai, Y., Tian, H., Xue, G., Zheng, Z.: Identifying illicit addresses in bitcoin network. In: Zheng, Z., Dai, H.-N., Fu, X., Chen, B. (eds.) BlockSys 2020. CCIS, vol. 1267, pp. 99–111. Springer, Singapore (2020). https://doi.org/10.1007/978-981-15-9213-3_8
20. Michalski, R., Dziubałtowska, D., Macek, P.: Revealing the character of nodes in a blockchain with supervised learning. IEEE Access **8**, 109639–109647 (2020)
21. Nerurkar, P., Bhirud, S., Patel, D., Ludinard, R., Busnel, Y., Kumari, S.: Supervised learning model for identifying illegal activities in Bitcoin. Appl. Intell. **51**(6), 3824–3843 (2020). https://doi.org/10.1007/s10489-020-02048-w
22. Lee, C., Maharjan, S., Ko, K., Woo, J., Hong, J.-K.: Machine learning based bitcoin address classification. In: Zheng, Z., Dai, H.-N., Fu, X., Chen, B. (eds.) BlockSys 2020. CCIS, vol. 1267, pp. 517–531. Springer, Singapore (2020). https://doi.org/10.1007/978-981-15-9213-3_40

23. Ermilov, D., Panov, M., Yanovich, Y.: Automatic bitcoin address clustering. In: 16th IEEE International Conference on Machine Learning and Applications (ICMLA), pp. 461–466 (2017)
24. Investor.gov: Investor Alert: Ponzi Schemes Using Virtual Currencies (2013)
25. Norvill, R., Steichen, M., Shbair, W.M., et al.: Demo: blockchain for the simplification and automation of KYC result sharing. In: 2019 IEEE International Conference on Blockchain and Cryptocurrency (ICBC), pp. 9–10 (2019)
26. Leo, B.: Random forests. Mach. Learn. **45**, 5–32 (2001)
27. Utgoff, P.E.: Incremental induction of decision trees. Mach. Learn. **4**, 161–186 (1989)
28. Hosmer, D.W., Lemeshow, S.: Applied logistic regression, vol. 398 (2013)
29. Cortes, C., Vapnik, V.: Support-vector networks. Mach. Learn. **20**, 273–297 (1995)
30. Altman, N.S.: An introduction to kernel and nearest-neighbor nonparametric regression. Am. Stat. **46**, 175–185 (1992)
31. Rajput, V.U.: Research on know your customer (KYC). Int. J. Sci. Res. Publ. **3**(7), 1–6 (2013)

Real-Time Detection of Cryptocurrency Mining Behavior

Ke Ye[1], Meng Shen[2(✉)], Zhenbo Gao[1], and Liehuang Zhu[2]

[1] School of Computer Science, Beijing Institute of Technology, Beijing 100081, China
{yeke,gaozhenbo07}@bit.edu.cn
[2] School of Cyberspace Science and Technology, Beijing Institute of Technology,
Beijing 100081, China
{shenmeng,liehuangz}@bit.edu.cn

Abstract. With the rapid development of blockchain, cryptocurrency gains more attention due to its anonymity and decentralization. However, illegal cryptocurrency mining problems, e.g., unauthorized control of victims' devices or appropriate public resources, become more and more serious. Existing mining detection methods need to be deployed locally and require authorization from administrators, which hardly supervise an entire network segment, as it brings high installation and maintenance costs. To solve this problem, in this paper, we propose a lightweight mining behavior detection method based on traffic analysis, which leverages communication packets in the first n seconds of a flow to achieve a real-time response. The experiment results with real-world datasets prove that the proposed method can achieve 94.04% F1 score using only the first 40 s packets, 98.22% F1 score using the first 120 s packets. Moreover, it can realize unknown cryptomining service discovery for about 96.37% F1 score. Instead of installing antivirus software on the host, the proposed method based on traffic analysis can be deployed at the gateways, which brings convenience for network management.

Keywords: Blockchain · Monero · Mining detection · Traffic analysis · Random forest

1 Introduction

Cryptocurrencies are virtual assets created as a medium of exchange secured by cryptography and a blockchain [16,18], which are used to maintain an anonymous and decentralized record of transactions [6]. To gain cryptocurrencies as rewards, people exert their efforts to solve puzzles using machines with extensive computing power to process hash-like computations, which is known as cryptocurrency mining.

Due to the incentive of financial rewards, multi resources are maliciously exploited for mining, e.g., personal PCs, and company servers. On the one hand, the popularity of cryptomining services, such as CryptoLoot [2], provide conveniences for attackers embedding malicious mining codes in a website to conduct

D. Svetinovic et al. (Eds.): BlockSys 2022, CCIS 1679, pp. 278–291, 2022.
https://doi.org/10.1007/978-981-19-8043-5_20

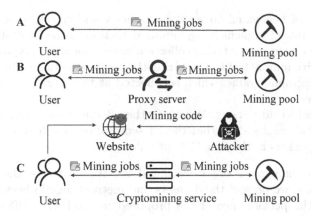

Fig. 1. Three types of cryptocurrency mining scenario

cryptocurrency mining without explicit user content, which is named cryptojacking [14]. The communication process of cryptojacking is shown in Fig. 1-C. On the other hand, several employees occupy the common resources of organizations for mining to fly their own kites, causing resource consumption and economic losses to companies. As shown in Fig. 1-A and B, the client can connect to the pool directly or jump by a proxy server to circumvent security reviews.

To detect cryptocurrency mining, most of the current works focus primarily on the behavior of hosts, e.g., by analyzing the usage of CPU [8] or matching explicit keywords as mining script signatures [7]. However, the technologies of CPU usage limitation and code obfuscation raise the bar for such covert behavior detection. Faced with these challenges, many studies focus on extracting more distinguishing features on target devices, e.g., the regular hash-based computation [9] and JavaScript (JS) runtime execution features [11]. However, these methods require granting the administrator privilege to the antivirus software, thus may not be secure for a normal user. Moreover, these methods need to be deployed on each host of an organization, e.g., an enterprise network, which increases the workload of network administrators.

In this paper, we propose a cryptocurrency mining detecting method by analyzing the communication traffic between clients and mining pools. We make an observation that the features of traffic packets [17,20] reflect the mechanism of cryptocurrency mining process. To abstract the mining process, we extract the packet length, number, interarrival time and flow duration time as features, combining them with machine learning algorithms to construct cryptocurrency mining detectors. Since the traffic analysis approach can be deployed on the gateway [19,21], it is suitable for detecting the mining behavior of the entire network segment, which reduces the maintenance costs of the detection system. The main contributions are summarized as follows:

- We propose a real-time cryptocurrency mining detecting method based on encrypted traffic analysis, which is suitable for both passive cryptojacking and active mining behaviors. Given the simplicity and efficiency of our method, we are capable of implementing mining detection in the early stage.

– We deploy an automatic traffic collection environment for cryptojacking traffic and active mining traffic. Capturing the communication traffic of real users as the background traffic, which is collected at the gateway and mirrored to a data server.

– Using a real-world dataset, We verify the effectiveness of our method. The experimental results show that the F1 score of our method is up to 98.22% using the packets in the first 120 s of a flow.

The rest of the paper is organized as follows. We summarise the related work in Sect. 2. Then, we present the datasets and methodology in Sect. 3. In Sect. 4, we evaluate the performance of the proposed method with different machine learning algorithms and compare it with another previous approach. Finally, this paper is concluded in Sect. 5.

2   Related Work

2.1   Network Communication of Cryptocurrency Mining

In order to strengthen the probability of getting rewards, individuals contribute their processing power to a mining pool, which is a joint group of miners. If the pool is successful in mining for cryptocurrency, rewards are usually divided between the participants according to the contributions. The common protocol used for communication between clients and mining pools is stratum, which is a line-based protocol based on TCP socket, with payload encoded as JSON-RPC format [4]. The communication process is shown in Fig. 2. At the beginning of the session, a miner *subscribes* the connection for receiving mining jobs, describing her computational capability. The mining pool then sends a *subscription response*, containing the subscription ID. Then the client authorizes some workers by sending a *login* message with usernames and passwords. After successful authentication, the mining pool then sends a *difficulty notification* and enters the *job distribution and submission* phase. It starts sending mining jobs, including job ID and several pieces of information the minner needed for calculating. Once the miner finds a *share* according to the difficulty, she submits it to the mining pool. If the share is checked by the pool server, it will respond a *confirmation* message. Finally, the rewards are distributed on the basis of valid submitted shares.

2.2   Summary of Mining Detection Study

Host-Based Methods. Several studies proposed host-based mining behavior detection methods based ont the CPU utilization and the suspicious scripts. [7,8,13]. For example, Hong *et al.* [9] observed that the websites embedded with mining codes spent much time on repeated hash calculations. Due

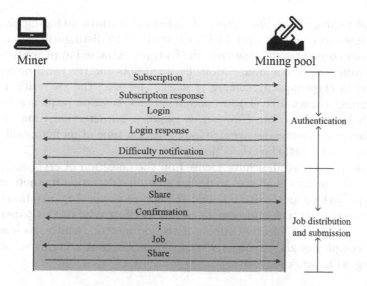

Fig. 2. Stratum protocol communication process

to this, they proposed a mining detector, named CMTracker, to discover cryptojacking based on the hash activity script and stack structure call. Krishnan Konoth *et al.* [12] performed an analysis on Alexa's top 1 million websites about the scale of cryptojacking. Based on the observations, they proposed a detection method, named MineSweeper, which uses intrinsic features of cryptomining codes, e.g., the webassembly module used and the CPU cache events. Kharraz *et al.* [11] combined features leveraged in the above two studies and proposed four more distinctive features, including web worker numbers, identical task numbers, postmessage event numbers and messageloop event numbers, to build an automated cryptojacking detection system.

However, since the above methods mainly focus on cryptojacking detection, several features extracted, e.g., postmessage event numbers, are not suitable for active mining detection, as these features are related to webassembly module, which is a web technology used to improve the performance of native code in the browser [12]. Moreover, these methods need to be deployed locally and require authorization from administrators, which hardly supervise an entire network segment, as it brings high installation and maintenance costs.

Traffic-Based Methods. Very few studies are focused on detecting cryptocurrency mining through network traffic analysis. Antonio *et al.* [15] pay attention to active mining detection (the miner connects to a mining pool directly). They combine 51 features extracted using Tstat tool, a passive sniffer which provides per flow statistics, with machine learning algorithms to detect cryptocurrency mining behaviors. However, cryptojacking traffic, where there is an intermediate service provider, is not considered in this study. Hu *et al.* [10] propose a mining botnet detecting method by analyzing traffic collected from both the botnet stage and mining stage. Four types of statistical features including packet size, packet time, port number and TCP flag are used to distinguish mining botnet traffic from normal traffic. However, the features extracted apply only to botnet mining traffic, as the communications between bots and the C&C server are not contained in cryptojacking. Zhang *et al.* [23] leverage the association between cryptomining packet arrival time and the block creation sequence to achieve mining behavior detection. However, it requires 2 h detection time for monero mining behaviors, since the average long creation time of monero, which makes it not suitable for real-time detection.

Although many studies have focused on the detection of cryptomining traffic, it is still a serious challenge to design an online detection method, suited for both cryptojacking and active mining behavior, to protect organization networks (e.g., enterprise network and campus network) effectively. In this paper, we put forward a simple but effective mining detection method, which has low computational complexity and enables real-time detection, thus bringing advantages in deploying on network gateways.

3 Methodology

In this section, we first introduce the experiment environment and dataset in Sect. 3.1. Next, in Sect. 3.2, we describe our analysis process of extracting mining traffic features through the inherent mechanism of cryptomining. Finally, we introduce four machine learning algorithms used for mining detection in Sect. 3.3.

3.1 Data Collection

As there is no public dataset of mining traffic, we simulate miners connecting to mining pools and collecting traffic to conduct experiments. Figure 3 shows the traffic collection environment. Three devices simulate miners visiting websites that have been injected with malicious code (cryptojacking) or connecting to mining pools actively (active mining behavior). Note that, active miners can connect to mining pools directly or jump by a proxy server to circumvent security reviews based on blacklists of mining pool IP addresses. In addition, there are normal users connected to the switch, which is a gateway to the Internet. Normal users visit legal network services, e.g., sending emails, using instant messaging software and browsing normal webpages. Traffic passing through the gateway is mirrored to the traffic storage server, which is leveraged to build dataset.

Since previous studies indicated that Monero is the most popular cryptocurrency used for cryptojacking [12], in this paper, the main mining traffic is collected from Monero. Mining traffic collected is divided into two parts, cryptojacking and active mining traffic, separately. We define the cryptojacking traffic as D_1, active mining traffic as D_2, background traffic, both web browsing and normal user traffic, as D_3. More details of the three types of traffic are listed in Table 1. For crytojacking traffic, we collect keywords (see Table 1) of core mining code embedded into websites mentioned in previous studies [11,12,22]. Then,

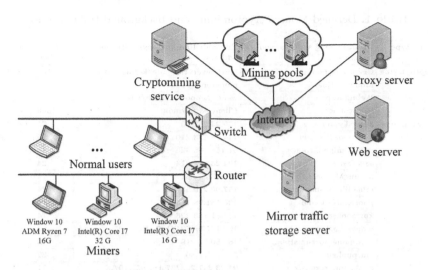

Fig. 3. Traffic collection environment

FOFA [1], a network search engine, is used to collect websites containing these keywords. Finally, removing services that have failed, 4 services are considered. The numbers of flows captured are shown in Table 1. For active mining traffic, we collected 13 commonly used mining pools [3] (see Table 1). Then, XMRig [5], a Menoro mining client, is used to connect to these pools. Finally, as shown in Table 1, 684 active mining flows are collected.

The browsing traffic of non-mining websites and the real traffic of normal users (i.e., traffic generated by normal users' real network activities) are labeled as background. Totally, 3989459 background traffic is collected, 1546 times as much as mining traffic, which makes the dataset imbalanced.

3.2 Feature Extraction

Since the encryption algorithm is applied, features related to key strings in the packet payload are invalid. Due to this reason, through analyzing the inherent communication mechanism of mining, we propose four types of statistical features to distinguish it from normal traffic. The feature extraction process is shown as Algorithm 1.

Packet Inter-arrival Time. When a miner receives a job, she will exert efforts to solve hashes, which takes a period of time depending on the complexity of the problem and the performance of the CPU. Once the answer is figured out, it will be sent back to the pool immediately. If the current puzzle has been solved, the mining pool will distribute the next job. From the process, we can observe that the packet inter-arrival time largely depends on the calculation speed of miners, which reflects the inherent feature of mining. Based on this observation, we select the standard deviation of *up_packet_interarrival_time* as a feature (up

Table 1. Detailed Monero cryptomining and background traffic Dataset.

Traffic type	Cryptomining services/pool domains	Embedded mining keyword/pool address	Flow number	Total number
Cryptojacking	Crypto Webminer	trustiseverything.de/karma/karma.js?	161	1896
	Monero Miner	monerominer.rocks	106	
	Webminerpool	webminepool.com/lib/base.js	273	
	CryptoLoot	Client.Anonymous	1356	
Active mining	auto.skypool.xyz	175.24.252.40	75	684
	xmr.pool-pay.com	144.76.173.210	25	
	pool.semipool.com	51.158.186.32	75	
	asia.fastpool.xyz	194.233.68.213	24	
	MiningMadness.com	147.135.70.51	74	
	mine.liberty-pool.com	157.90.210.50	74	
	pool.xmrfast.com	135.181.78.174	74	
	xmrpool.sargatxet.cloud	172.81.183.226	74	
	monerohash.com	107.191.99.221/107.191.99.95	53	
	gulf.moneroocean.stream	18.180.72.219	73	
	xmrpool.eu	51.89.217.80	22	
	pool.supportxmr.com	94.23.247.226/37.187.95.110/...	21	
	auto.c3pool.org	5.161.50.27/5.161.70.189/...	20	
Background	–	–	3989459	

packets refer to packets sent from clients to pools, down packets represent packets in the reverse direction). The reason that we do not consider down packets is that the pool may send consecutive packets if a block is created before the miner solves hashes [23].

Packet Length. In the job distribution and submission phase (see Fig. 2), the transferred data is relatively fixed (i.e., job, share, and confirmation packet). Specifically, uplink packets transmit only share, which contains the message id, message type, job id, nonce, etc. The change of several fields may cause the packet length to become longer. For example, when the job id changes from 9 to 10, the job length increases by 1. However, the increase in length is not significant compared with normal traffic. Based on this observation, we calculate the mean value of *up_packet_length* to reflect the inherent characteristic of the mining process.

The Duration of Flow. The duration of flow reflects mining time directly. On the one hand, the miner needs to calculate hashes, which increase the duration of flow. On the other hand, the longer the mining goes on, the more rewards get. For cryptojacking, as the attacker expects to gain more rewards, the mining process usually continues until the user closes the website voluntarily. For active mining behavior, the miner runs the mining program for a quite long time to generate uninterrupted revenue. Considering the motivation for mining, we select the *flow_duration* as a feature.

Packet Number. The normal traffic, for example, the web browsing traffic, contains vast fully loaded downlink packets, as the server needs to transmit a lot of resources to the client. Compared with web browsing traffic, the mining traffic has fewer packets, since the mining process does not contain a lot of information exchange. In the job distribution and submission phase, only three types of packets are involved, i.e., the job distribution packet, the share submission packet and the confirmation packet. Considering the stable communication pattern, the *up_packet_number* and *down_packet_number* are extracted as two features.

Algorithm 1: Traffic feature extraction process

Input: a traffic C, time threshold T
Output: the extracted feature set F

1 Initialize three arraies up_packet_length, up_packet_arrival_time, down_packet_arrival_time;
2 **foreach** *packet P in C* **do**
3   **if** *the timestamp of P $\geq T$* **then**
4   break;
5   **end**
6   **if** *P is an up packet* **then**
7   add the length of P into up_packet_len;
8   add the arrival time of P into up_packet_arrival_time;
9   **else**
10   add the arrival time of P into down_packet_arrival_time;
11   **end**
12 **end**
13 Calculate up_packet_interarrival_time from up_packet_arrival_time;
14 Calculate the standard deviation of up_packet_interarrival_time, the mean value of up_packet_length, the duration of flow and the packet number as the feature F.

3.3 Machine Learning Classifier

We compare the following machine learning algorithms in mining traffic detection.

Logistic Regression (LR). LR is a statistical model using a logistic function to solve binary classification problems, which does not require a linear relationship between inputs and output variables. The small number of parameters makes it easy to implement, interpret, and efficient train.

k-Nearest Neighbor (k-NN). For a classification problem, a sample is classified by a plurality vote of its k nearest neighbors, which contains objects have close distances to it. The distant calculation methods include Euclidean distance, Manhattan distance, etc. Then the sample is assigned to the class closest to it among its neighbors.

Random Forest (RF). RF is an ensemble learning method based on bagging algorithm, which can be used to solve classification problems. The classification results depend on a vote of all decision trees in the forest. The training algorithm of bootstrap aggregating makes RF less sensitive to noise samples since the trees are not correlated.

Gradient Boosting Decision Tree (GBDT). GBDT is an ensemble learning method based on boosting algorithm, which generates a stronger classifier in the form of an ensemble of decision trees (for classification tasks). The tree of each stage attempts to correct the errors of its predecessor. Through constantly fit trees to pseudo-residuals, the ensemble classifier performs better than a single weak classifier.

4   Performance Evaluation

In this section, we evaluate the proposed mining traffic detection methods, including the effectiveness, robustness and time-consuming evaluation.

4.1   Preliminary

The core goal of mining traffic detection is to be accurate, i.e., reducing missed and false positives. We consider four metrics to measure the detector, namely recall, false positive rate (FPR), precision (Prec) and F1 score. Note, we do not involve accuracy and error rate in evaluation metrics, as the dataset is largely imbalanced, which makes the two metrics can not reflect the effectiveness of the classifier. Specifically, recall is the ratio of positive instances that are retrieved, FPR gives the ratio of false predictions in positive class, precision is the ratio of positive predictive samples in positive class and F1 is the harmonic mean of precision and recall.

4.2   Effectiveness Evaluation

We use the D_1, D_2 and D_3 described in Sect. 3.1 to conduct the experiment. In this experiment, features, the input of the machine learning model, are extracted from the first 120s of a flow. To reflect the effectiveness, k-flod cross validation is leveraged as the evaluation method. Table 2 shows the recall, FPR, Prec and F1 of classification results using four machine learning algorithms.

Both RF and GBDT achieve a recall rate higher than 97%, followed by the k-NN algorithm with 93.43%. The LR classifier does not perform well, as its linear structure is not suitable for complex classification. The F1 scores of k-NN, RF and GBDT are high than 98%, showing great effectiveness in mining traffic detection.

In order to present comprehensive instructions on the contribution of this work. We compare our methods with the features proposed in [10]. The experiments are carried out on D_1, D_2 alone, i.e., traffic collected from cryptojacking and active mining respectively, as well as both cryptojacking and active mining traffic, denoted as $D_1 + D_2$. As RF has the best performance in their study, we select RF as the classifier.

Table 2. The recall, FPR, Prec, and F1 of effectiveness evaluation under four machine learning classifiers.

	Recall	FPR	Prec	F1
LR	56.94%	0.67%	87.97%	69.08%
k-NN	93.43%	0.14%	98.11%	95.71%
RF	97.12%	0.05%	99.35%	98.22%
GBDT	97.13%	0.03%	99.68%	98.39%

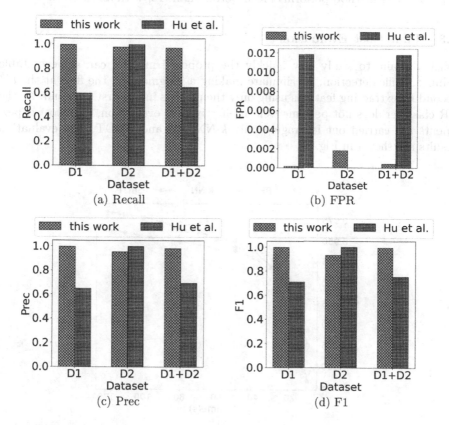

Fig. 4. The recall, FPR, Prec, and F1 of effectiveness evaluation under four machine learning classifiers.

Figure 4 shows the recall, FPR, Prec, and F1 of two methods on three dataset. From the results, we can see that both feature sets proposed in [10] and our work performs well on active mining traffic detection (D_2). However, the features extracted in [10] are less effective in cryptojacking traffic detection(D_1). For example, the packet length and interarrival time of the first n packets are leveraged as features in [10]. Nevertheless, the cryptojacking traffic is transmitted under TLS protocol, where the first few packets contain handshake messages, which have little difference from normal TLS communication traffic. On the contrary, our method shows great performances on both D_1 and D_2 datasets, as the features extraction is based on internal mechanism analysis, which is universal in both passive and active mining behavior. Our method performs slightly better on D_1 than on D_2, as the unstable connections of some mining pools, the duration times of some mining traffic in D_2 are less than 120s, which makes the features less significant. In order to simulate various real-world situations, we didn't remove these connections. In a comprehensive perspective, on dataset $D_1 + D_2$, our method performs much better than [10] with all metrics.

4.3   Time Cost Evaluation

With the aim to study how quickly the proposed method can achieve stable mining traffic detection, we simulate making a judgment on the flow at the kth second by extracting features using only the packets in the first k second. As the LR classifier does not perfome well in effectiveness evaluation, time cost experiments are carried out leveraging only k-NN, RF and GBDT. The evaluation results are shown in Fig. 5.

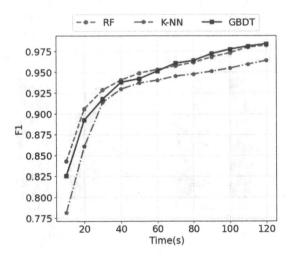

Fig. 5. The F1 score of detection using only packets in the fisrt n seconds.

The figure shows that the detection results using only the first 10 seconds is not ideal. The reason is that there are few packets transmitted during the first 10 s, as the miners need time to solve hash problems, which blocks the job delivery of the mining pools. With job distribution and submission, the F1 score grows rapidly from 10 to 40 s and achieves more than 93% using only the first 40 s packets for RF and GBDT. From 40 to 120 s, as the number of packets increases, the F1 score grows gently.

4.4   Roubustness Evaluation

To present the robustness of the proposed feature set, we devide D_1 to D_{11}, D_{12}, D_{13} and D_{14}, representing cryptojacking traffic collected from four different cryptomining services shown in Table 1. Three of the sub datasets and 70% of the D_3 are used as the training set, the remaining one and 30% of the D_3 are used as the test set. This scenario is designed to prove whether the features are suitable for unknown cryptomining service discovery.

Table 3. The recall, FPR, Prec, and F1 of robustness evaluation with four subsets.

Train	Test	Recall	FPR	Prec	F1
$D_{11}D_{12}D_{13}$	D_{14}	95.06%	0.28%	96.05%	95.55%
$D_{11}D_{12}D_{14}$	D_{13}	90.84%	0.00%	99.99%	95.20%
$D_{11}D_{13}D_{14}$	D_{12}	96.23%	0.07%	94.44%	95.33%
$D_{12}D_{13}D_{14}$	D_{11}	98.76%	0.00%	99.99%	99.38%

To compared with results of D_1 in Fig. 4, RF is leveraged as the classifier. The experiment results are shown in Table 3. We can find that in this scenario, the F1 score of D_{11}, D_{12}, D_{13} and D_{14} are 95.55%, 95.20%, 95.33% and 99.38%, decreasing only 4.1%, 4.45%, 4.32% and 0.27% compared with results of D_1 in Fig. 4. The recall of all experiment results is higher than 90%, the precision is higher than 94%, which proves that the features are suitable for unknown cyptomining service discovery.

5   Conclusion

In this paper, we proposed a real-time mining traffic detection method, which is suitable for both cryptojacking and active mining traffic. We build a dataset of Monero mining traffic as well as normal user traffic. Inherent features are extracted through mining mechanism analysis, using only the statistics of packet number, time and length, which are suitable for encrypted traffic detection. Four machine learning algorithms are used as a classifier. Experiment results suggest that GBDT and RF perform best in mining traffic detection, which can achieve over 93% of F1 score using only packets in the first 40 s, over 98% of F1 score using packets in the first 120 s. In the future work, we plan to further expand the dataset and consider unknown mining pool node discovery through traffic behavior analysis.

Acknowledgments. This work is supported by National Key R&D Program of China with No. 2020YFB1006101.

References

1. FOFA. https://fofa.info/
2. CryptoLoot (2022). https://www.crypto-webminer.com/integrate.html?. Accessed 17 May 2022
3. Mining pool (2022). https://miningpoolstats.stream/monero. Accessed 20 May 2022
4. Stratum (2022). https://zh.braiins.com/stratum-v1/docs. Accessed 17 May 2022
5. XMRig (2022). https://xmrig.com/. Accessed 20 May 2022
6. Bijmans, H.L., Booij, T.M., Doerr, C.: Inadvertently making cyber criminals rich: a comprehensive study of cryptojacking campaigns at internet scale. In: 28th USENIX Security Symposium (USENIX Security 2019), Santa Clara, CA, pp. 1627–1644. USENIX Association, August 2019. https://www.usenix.org/conference/usenixsecurity19/presentation/bijmans
7. Eskandari, S., Leoutsarakos, A., Mursch, T., Clark, J.: A first look at browser-based cryptojacking. In: 2018 IEEE European Symposium on Security and Privacy Workshops (EuroS&PW), pp. 58–66. IEEE (2018)
8. Gomes, F., Correia, M.: Cryptojacking detection with CPU usage metrics. In: 2020 IEEE 19th International Symposium on Network Computing and Applications (NCA), pp. 1–10. IEEE (2020)
9. Hong, G., et al.: How you get shot in the back: a systematical study about cryptojacking in the real world. In: Proceedings of the 2018 ACM SIGSAC Conference on Computer and Communications Security, pp. 1701–1713 (2018)
10. Hu, X., Shu, Z., Song, X., Cheng, G., Gong, J.: Detecting cryptojacking traffic based on network behavior features. In: 2021 IEEE Global Communications Conference (GLOBECOM), pp. 01–06. IEEE (2021)
11. Kharraz, A., et al.: OUTGUARD: detecting in-browser covert cryptocurrency mining in the wild. In: The World Wide Web Conference, pp. 840–852 (2019)
12. Konoth, R.K., et al.: MineSweeper: an in-depth look into drive-by cryptocurrency mining and its defense. In: Proceedings of the 2018 ACM SIGSAC Conference on Computer and Communications Security, pp. 1714–1730 (2018)
13. Musch, M., Wressnegger, C., Johns, M., Rieck, K.: Web-based cryptojacking in the wild. arXiv preprint arXiv:1808.09474 (2018)
14. Naseem, F., Aris, A., Babun, L., Tekiner, E., Uluagac, S.: MINOS: a lightweight real-time cryptojacking detection system. In: 28th Annual Network and Distributed System Security Symposium, NDSS (2021)
15. Pastor, A., et al.: Detection of encrypted cryptomining malware connections with machine and deep learning. IEEE Access 8, 158036–158055 (2020)
16. Shen, M., Duan, J., Zhu, L., Zhang, J., Du, X., Guizani, M.: Blockchain-based incentives for secure and collaborative data sharing in multiple clouds. IEEE J. Sel. Areas Commun. 38(6), 1229–1241 (2020)
17. Shen, M., Gao, Z., Zhu, L., Xu, K.: Efficient fine-grained website fingerprinting via encrypted traffic analysis with deep learning. In: 2021 IEEE/ACM 29th International Symposium on Quality of Service (IWQOS), pp. 1–10. IEEE (2021)
18. Shen, M., et al.: Blockchain-assisted secure device authentication for cross-domain industrial iot. IEEE J. Sel. Areas Commun. 38(5), 942–954 (2020)
19. Shen, M., Liu, Y., Zhu, L., Du, X., Hu, J.: Fine-grained webpage fingerprinting using only packet length information of encrypted traffic. IEEE Trans. Inf. Forensics Secur. 16, 2046–2059 (2020)

20. Shen, M., Ma, B., Zhu, L., Mijumbi, R., Du, X., Hu, J.: Cloud-based approximate constrained shortest distance queries over encrypted graphs with privacy protection. IEEE Trans. Inf. Forensics Secur. **13**(4), 940–953 (2017)
21. Shen, M., Zhang, J., Zhu, L., Xu, K., Du, X.: Accurate decentralized application identification via encrypted traffic analysis using graph neural networks. IEEE Trans. Inf. Forensics Secur. **16**, 2367–2380 (2021)
22. Varlioglu, S., Gonen, B., Ozer, M., Bastug, M.: Is cryptojacking dead after coinhive shutdown? In: 2020 3rd International Conference on Information and Computer Technologies (ICICT), pp. 385–389. IEEE (2020)
23. Zhang, S., et al.: MineHunter: a practical cryptomining traffic detection algorithm based on time series tracking. In: Annual Computer Security Applications Conference, pp. 1051–1063 (2021)

Traffic Correlation for Deanonymizing Cryptocurrency Wallet Through Tor

Xiangdong Kong[1], Meng Shen[1(✉)], Zheng Che[2], Congcong Yu[2],
and Liehuang Zhu[1]

[1] School of Cyberspace Science and Technology, Beijing Institute of Technology,
Beijing 100081, China
{xiangdongkong,shenmeng,liehuangz}@bit.edu.cn
[2] School of Computer Science, Beijing Institute of Technology, Beijing 100081, China
{chezheng,yucongcong}@bit.edu.cn

Abstract. Cryptocurrencies have increasingly become the preferred choice for private transactions due to their anonymity and decentralized features. When a user creates transactions using wallet software with built-in Tor module, their identity information is further protected. At the same time, however, this combination of Tor and cryptocurrency is misused to carry out illegal acts, while the perpetrators are difficult to detect. Therefore, it is important to study traffic correlation methods for cryptocurrencies over Tor to maintain a healthy blockchain ecosystem. In this paper, based on existing work, we propose CryptoCorr, a traffic analysis model for cryptocurrency wallets, which can screening the collected Tor traffic data based on time window and flow features, and implement traffic correlation for cryptocurrency wallets based on deep learning architecture. We validate the proposed model by constructing a dataset with 82077 collected packets of wallet, and the experiment results demonstrate the effectiveness of the CryptoCorr model.

Keywords: CryptoCurrency · Tor · Wallet RPC · Deanonymizing · Traffic analysis

1 Introduction

The development of information technology has spawned many anonymity technologies, which often have double sides. On the one hand, they are applied as privacy protection technologies to escort personal information in our daily lives. On the other hand, they are also abused for illegal purposes, and the identities of criminals are often difficult to trace.

Today, we are faced with two state-of-the-art technologies that can hide the identity of users: cryptocurrencies and the Tor network. Cryptocurrency is a peer-to-peer electronic cash transaction system based on blockchain technology [1,2]. It has attracted the attention of many parties due to its decentralization and anonymity, which allow users to conduct financial transactions anonymously without revealing their real identities and enable users to transfer assets across borders instantly and cheaply. Due to the popularity of the digital currency, its market value is rising drastically. According to data from the famous digital currency website CoinMarketCap, as of April 2022, the total market capitalization of cryptocurrencies has reached $1967billion. At the same time, however, there is overwhelming evidence that cryptocurrencies are being used for financial crimes, such as money laundering [3], Ponzi scheme [4], ransome software [5], etc. These criminal activities have caused significant damage to people's financial safety and social stability.

Similar to cryptocurrencies, Tor also has double sides. Tor is an anonymous communication technology that comprehensively utilizes data forwarding, information encryption, traffic obfuscation, and other technologies to hide communication entities. Tor is proposed to protect the user's IP address and prevent network layer privacy from being destroyed by traffic analysis technologies such as traffic filtering and sniffing analysis. However, this anonymity feature also breeds many illegal and criminal activities, such as the illegal trafficking of drugs, guns, and arms.

While there has been some work analyzing the abuse of Tor [6] or cryptocurrencies [7], most of these studies have only looked at one technology in cryptocurrencies or Tor alone, and only a few [8,9] have looked at a combination of digital currency and Tor technologies. Foley et al. measured the amount of bitcoins used for illegal commodity transactions based on historical transaction data of bitcoins and derived the characteristics of illegal transactions based on this analysis [9]. Seunghyeon et al. went a step further to track and verify the transaction characteristics and the flow of funds based on the collection of illegal transaction data in the dark web. However, they still have serious limitations. They all need to spend a lot of computational resources to collect transaction data in the dark web, and these data are relatively old. Most importantly, these studies focus on the characteristics of these digital currency transactions in real-world applications, without examining the source of illegal transaction initiation. When a user initiates a transaction using digital currency wallet with a built-in Tor, the current studies can not effectively identify the user entity for such transactions. Therefore, studying the traffic correlation for digital currency wallets with built-in Tor is essential.

As mentioned above, the main goal of this paper is to perform an in-depth analysis of the traffic of digital currency wallets using Tor proxies (referred to as *anonymous wallets*), focusing on the correlation between exit traffic and entrance traffic of the corresponding Tor network circuits. However, conducting this research is not an easy process, as it suffers from two key challenges. First, due to the limitations of Tor usage scenarios, it is difficult to collect and analyze traffic data on a large scale, especially for anonymous wallets. Second, generic network packet capture software (e.g., TcpDump) works at Ethernet layer, and the captured traffic data contains a large amount of background traffic, which creates difficulties in screening anonymous wallet traffic.

To address these challenges, we design **CryptoCorr**, a data collection and analysis model for anonymous wallet traffic, which collects inbound and outbound traffic of Tor circuit by deploying proxies. Then it extracts wallet traffic from large background traffic based on time window, flow packet rate, information of Tor relays, and packet size distribution. Finally, a deep learning model is used to implement a correlation analysis of anonymous wallet traffic.

Our contributions are summarized as follows.

- We design a traceability model CryptoCorr for sensitive transactions using anonymous wallets, which dynamically chains and listens to addresses or behaviors of interest, and analyzes the anonymous wallet traffic carrying out this behavior. First, we use a proxy to collect the ingress and egress traffic of the Tor circuit, and purify the traffic sent from the anonymous wallets to remote RPC nodes through them, so as to realize the screening and correlation analysis of the anonymous wallet traffic and finally achieve the purpose of traceability.
- We take Bitcoin as an example and introduce probe nodes to continuously listen to the transactions sent by the target RPC server according to its transaction propagation pattern, set up a rule matching mechanism to be able to dynamically update the transaction layer rules for sensitive transactions, and give a method to delineate the traffic time window for the process of this transaction occurrence.
- We design an anonymous wallet traffic identification method for the characteristics of digital currency and Tor traffic. The method can first remove non-Tor background traffic, and then mine the characteristics of anonymous wallet traffic to make it distinguishable from regular Tor Browser traffic. This method can effectively reduce the interference of background traffic with anonymous wallet traffic.
- We take a bitcoin wallet *Electrum* with a built-in Tor proxy as an example, and collect the traffic generated by the wallet during the transaction process to build a test set to validate the proposed model, and the experimental results demonstrate the effectiveness of the proposed model.

The article is organized as follows:

Section 2 briefly introduces the related work. Section 3 describes the overall architecture of CryptoCorr and how each component works. Section 4 evaluates and assesses the performance of CryptoCorr in digital currency trading scenarios. The final section concludes the entire paper.

2   Related Works

Most of the existing work focuses only on Tor's traffic correlation or digital currency anti-anonymity alone, with less research on both of them combined. This section briefly summarizes the existing related research work.

Tor Traffic Correlation Analysis. Edman et al. [10] found an attack that uses AS (Autonomous Systems) traffic monitoring to correlate Tor traffic, while Akhoondi et al. [11] designed an efficient algorithm to determine whether a Tor link can be correlated by an AS and designed a new Tor client LASTor based on this algorithm. Sum et al. [12] proposed an efficient Tor traffic association model, RAPTOR, which can exploit dynamic properties of Internet routing (e.g., routing asymmetry, routing fluctuations, and routing attacks), enabling an AS-level adversary to effectively compromise user anonymity. Nasr et al. designed a traffic association model, DeepCorr [13], using deep learning approach to learn traffic correlation functions applicable to Tor's complex network, which can correlate Tor's ingress traffic with egress traffic with a high degree of accuracy.

Deanonymization of Cryptocurrency. Research on anti-anonymity for cryptocurrencies can be divided into two main categories. One is network layer traceability. This type is represented by the work of Biryukov et al. [14] The core idea is to deploy a "super node" in the Bitcoin network that can establish connections with most customer nodes in the Bitcoin network. The controllable node sends the transaction to the network, and then infers the propagation path of the message according to the time when the "super node" receives the transaction from the adjacent nodes, and then analyzes the originating node of the transaction. The other type is transaction layer traceability. This type is represented by the work of Reid et al. [15] The core idea is to use address clustering method to associate multiple transaction addresses controlled by the same user according to the user's transaction habits.

There are also recent studies that analyze the technical mix of Tor and cryptocurrencies. For example, Seunghyeon et al [8] proposed the MFScope framework, which can collect data on illegal transactions in the dark web and track and verify the transaction characteristics and money flow in the dark web. However, this study requires a large amount of computational resources to collect transaction data in the dark web and does not trace the source of illegal transaction initiation. This thesis analyzes the transactions issued by anonymous wallets from the network level, aiming to correlate the exit traffic of anonymous wallets with the entrance traffic and find the originators of anonymous transactions.

3   Methodology

Based on the research of existing works [16–19], we design a traffic correlation analysis architecture for anonymous wallets, which can match the rules of transactions in the P2P network by probe nodes, select the transactions of interest and dynamically update the rules, then capture the incoming and outgoing traffic of anonymous wallets by means of proxies. According to the destination IP and port of the captured traffic, flow packet rate, MTU(Max Transmission Unit) occupancy and packet size distribution obtained from the traffic that we can screen the anonymous wallet traffic. Finally, the correlation analysis of this traffic is completed by deep learning model to achieve the effect of traceability.

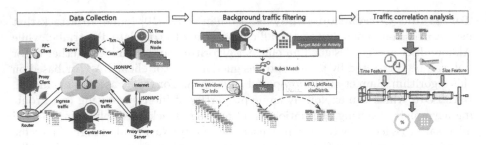

Fig. 1. The architecture of CryptoCorr

3.1   System Overview

According to the digital currency wallet, the message dissemination mechanism of digital currency and the working principle of Tor, we try to build a probe node to monitor the transactions in the blockchain P2P network and focus on sending outgoing connections to the target RPC server to monitor it, while using the traffic features to filter, extract, and correlate the traffic of anonymous wallets. Figure 1 shows the overall architecture and workflow of CryptoCorr, which is mainly composed of three components.

The first component is data collection, which implements the function of collecting the ingress and egress traffic of the Tor network by deploying a pre-proxy at the entrance of the Tor client of anonymous wallet, so that the traffic can directly reach the transit proxy server after passing through the Tor circuit. By deploying the probe node at a place close to the RPC node network and the connection is stable, it only sends a *CONN* request to the target RPC server to establish an outgoing connection to receive transaction information in the blockchain network. It does not matter whether the transaction received by the probe is originated by the RPC node, because from the macro scenario, if the attacker or supervisor can listen to a vast majority of the RPC servers, which is not that many, or the RPC server can jointly launching a supervision request for a hacker's address without a hard fork to the blockchain, this model can deter hackers greatly. The proxy server in the first component will collect and store the network traffic, and the probe node interacts with the second component to determine whether the association mechanism needs to be triggered. If triggering is not required, continue monitoring, if triggering is required, the proxy server will send the set of traffic within the time window to the central computing server for screening and correlating. Then, the rules that need to be matched in the database are updated according to the blockchain state changes generated by the transaction, so as to achieve continuous chain tracking.

The second component is Rules Match & Background traffic filter. During the interaction with the first component, this component performs rule matching on the transaction received by the probe node. If the transaction matches the address or procedure in the rule, then returns the trigger signal. Besides, the second component can extract the traffic belonging to the Tor network according to the IP address and port number of the record about the Guard Node and Exit node in the Tor Directory Server within a day, and then according to the port number, flow packet rate, in-flow packet size distribution and MTU full-occupancy rate features filter anonymous wallet traffic from background traffic to form a data set.

The third component is Traffic correlation analysis, which can use the trained deep learning model to complete the correlation analysis of the wallet traffic data set generated above.

3.2   Data Collection

We accomplish the capturing of anonymous wallet traffic by deploying a pre-proxy and staging proxy server. Since digital currency wallets are often resource-constrained personal devices (smartphones, laptops, etc.), they do not store complete copies of blocks. When a user initiates a transaction request using a light digital wallet, the transaction needs to be verified by requesting the block that may contain the transaction from a full node of the blockchain. After the verification is passed, it is broadcast by the remote full node to other nodes in the network. Using this mechanism, we set up a front proxy client at the traffic exit of the anonymous wallet that wraps the request packet as a proxy packet in a nested SSR proxy, with the destination IP of the proxy packet pointing to the remote transit SSR proxy server. At the same time, we capture the ingress traffic using *tcpdump* software deployed in the front proxy client. After the proxy data packets pass through Tor's entry node, intermediate node and exit node in sequence, they will flow to the transit SSR proxy server. This server verifies the received proxy data packets and parses its destination, and then establishes a connection with the RPC server to complete the data exchange. Meanwhile, we capture egress traffic using *tcpdump* software deployed in the transit proxy client. The captured ingress and egress traffic is then dumped to the central server. So far, we have successfully captured the ingress and egress traffic of the anonymous wallet.

3.3   Background Traffic Filtering

After collecting of Tor ingress and egress traffic, the filtering of the background traffic is followed. This process can be divided into two steps: time window filtering and packet characteristic screening. Table 1 describes the relevant parameters and their meanings that appear in this section and subsequent subsections.

Step 1: Time Window Filter. The core idea of time window filtering of anonymous wallet traffic is that, in order to meet the basic number of valid packets for correlation in the third component, a time window can be determined in which the number of packets generated by the anonymous wallet interacting with the remote node contained in this window meets the minimum number $SIZE_{flow}$ of packets required by the correlation stage, taking into account the frequency of packets sent by the specific wallet software and the activity of the addresses in the rule. However, it is important to note that timestamp is not included in the transaction structure of major cryptocurrencies such as Bitcoin and Ethereum. Also, the transaction time displayed in many blockchain browsers (e.g., btc.com, etherscan.io, etc.) is not the time when the transaction was created, but the time when the transaction is added to the site's memory pool. Therefore, we make the calculated transaction creation time more accurate by deploying the full node and counting the time when the target transaction arrived at that node. We use this time as the transaction time t_{tx}.

Table 1. Symbols and notations.

Notations	Descriptions
r	Flow rate of wallet heartbeat
t_{tx}	Earliest time when the transaction packet arrives at the server
$t_{tx_{recvd}}$	Timestamp of the transaction broadcast received by the probe node
$delay_{net}$	Ping latency between probe and target RPC server
$delay_{node}$	Intermediate delay for full node broadcasting to each neighbor
$SIZE_{flow}$	Minimum packets demand to achieve a correlation task
$FLOW_{rate}$	Flow rate under a certain situation(e.g. wallet and network config)
W	Window of opportunity for targeted traffic to emerge
w_{start}	Start timestamp of the window
w_{end}	End timestamp of the window
w_{size}	Size of opportunity window
$\hat{p}_{i,j}$	Predicted traffic correlation probability
N_i	Coefficients of a certain value
MTU_{ratio}	Ratio of packets in a flow take up a full MTU

After the probe node receives the transaction, it records the current time $t_{tx_{recvd}}$, the time window $W = \{w_{start}, w_{end}\}$ needs to be calculated.

$$t_{tx} = t_{tx_{recvd}} - MIN\{delay_{node}\} - AVERAGE\{delay_{net}\} \tag{1}$$

$$w_{end} = t_{tx} \tag{2}$$

$$w_{size} = \frac{size_{flow}}{FLOW_{rate}} \tag{3}$$

$$w_{start} = w_{end} - w_{size} \tag{4}$$

After the time window is calculated, only the traffic data in the traffic window can be analyzed, which reduces the workload of subsequent analysis.

After that, we obtain the active nodes published daily at UTC 0:00 from the Tor directory server (e.g. torproject.org), which contains comprehensive information about the node including IP address and port number. We can use IP: PORT as a feature to screen only the Tor traffic we are interested in.

Step 2: Flow Characteristic Filter. After Step1 filtering, we proceed to count the flow packet rate of traffic included in this time window, the packet volume distribution and the proportion of packets that fully occupied the RFC864 [20] standard MTU to determine whether a traffic belongs to anonymous wallet. Since the frequency of interaction between anonymous wallets and full nodes is much lower compared to the frequency of interaction between clients and servers for web activities such as browsing the web and watching videos, it makes the transaction traffic of crypto wallets have a much smaller flow rate and the volume of data for one interaction is much tinier. Based on this observation, we combine the experimental data analysis and mark packets with low flow packet rate, high percentage of small packets, and very few packets that occupy full MTU as crypto wallet traffic. In addition, to mitigate the high noise and high uncertainty of user interactions caused by Tor network congestion, we add the parameter N_1 to better cope with such cases.

Algorithm 1 describes the screening of wallet traffic from a noisy background traffic.

Algorithm 1. Massive Traffic Data Filter of **CryptoCorr**

Input: Massive traffic flow from double ends F_{in}, F_{out}; $MTU_{ratio}, FLOW_{rate}$ according to different wallet softwares and network config; N_i

Output: Potential wallet traffic $F_{in_{wallet}}, F_{out_{wallet}}$ to be correlated

1: $t_{tx_{recv}} \leftarrow getNowTimeStamp()$
2: $W \leftarrow calculateTimeWindowSize(t_{tx_{recvd}})$
3: $F_{in}, F_{out} = cutFlowInWindowOfTor(W, TorRelayList, F_{in}, F_{out})$
4: $F_{out_{wallet}} = filterRpcDestination(F_{out}, RpcServerInfo)$
5: **for** each $flow \in F_{in}$ **do**
6:     **if** $flow.dst \in Tor_{guard}$ **then**
7:         **if** $flow.rate < N_1 * FLOW_{rate}$ && $flow.fullMTU < MTU_{ratio}$ && $flow.smallRatio < SMALL_{ratio}$ **then**
8:             $F_{in_{wallet}}$.append($flow$)
9:         **end if**
10:     **end if**
11: **end for**
12: **return** $F_{in_{wallet}}, F_{out_{wallet}}$

During the wallet-RPC interaction process, the IP address and port number of the RPC server to be monitored are known, so the required egress traffic data set can be directly obtained. However, the Tor traffic at the ingress part is still complex, especially the scene collected on the switch in the backbone network center in reality. Therefore, the anonymous wallet traffic at the ingress is mainly screened here.

Combining the time window with Tor Relay IP port filtering and packet feature filtering together, we successfully screen out anonymous wallet traffic from background traffic. After that, the filtered anonymous wallet dataset will be sent to the Traffic correlation analysis section as the traffic to be analyzed.

3.4   Traffic Correlation Analysis

This section focuses on correlation analysis of anonymous wallet traffic by drawing on the Deepcorr deep learning model proposed by Nasr et al. [13]. Since the encrypted traffic of anonymous wallets hides most of the information in the traffic, we follow the traffic characteristics common to the analysis work on encrypted traffic: packet time and packet size. Packet time is the relative time of a flow packet, i.e., the time interval between flow packets (inter packet delay, IPD). Packet size is the number of bytes contained in each flow packet. We define a flow pair by this formula:

$$F_i = [T_i^u, S_i^u, T_i^d, S_i^d] \tag{5}$$

In the above equation, T stands for IPD and S stands for the number of bytes of packets. u indicates that the collected traffic is upload traffic and d indicates that the collected traffic is download traffic.

By observation, we find that in the actual traffic distribution, the flow size is not consistent for each flow or each time period. Here, we also draw on the experience of Nasr et al. and only take the first $size_{flow}$ packets for the study. If the number of packets in a flow cannot reach the requirement of $size_{flow}$, the IPD and size are padded 0 to make up. Here, $size_{flow}$ is chosen as 300. We select two flows F_i and F_j from the input traffic $F_{in_{wallet}}$ and output traffic $F_{out_{wallet}}$ of the anonymous wallet to form a flow pair.

$$\hat{F}_{i,j} = (F_i, F_j) = [T_i^u, S_i^u, T_i^d, S_i^d, T_j^u, S_j^u, T_j^d, S_j^d] \tag{6}$$

The neural network architecture is identical as the Deepcorr that it extracts time and size features to learn a correlation function and finally outputs the correlation confidence of the two selected streams.

$$\hat{p}_{i,j} = \Psi(\hat{F}_{i,j}) \tag{7}$$

Since a correlation function is to be trained in this process, its input is the flow pair, and the output is the correlation probability. Therefore, in the training process, if we want to achieve a better correlation effect, the data set used for training needs to meet the data set used in the target correlation scene. The loss function for training adopts the cross entropy function:

$$\mathcal{L} = -\frac{1}{|\mathcal{F}|} \sum_{F_{i,j} \in \mathcal{F}} y_{i,j} log\Psi(F_{i,j}) + (1 - y_{i,j})log(1 - \Psi(F_{i,j})) \tag{8}$$

With Deepcorr's model, traffic correlation analysis of anonymous wallets can finally be accomplished.

4   Evaluation

In this section, we will first present the preparation of the experiment, including information about the device configuration of the different components in the system and the geographical location where they are located. We will then evaluate the differentiation between the streams generated when a wallet send a transaction and the common web-page browsing streams in the Tor network to demonstrate the effectiveness of the stream filtering approach. After determining the difference, we will verify the effectiveness of the correlation method based on the incoming and outgoing flows of Tor captured above.

4.1   Prerequisite Knowledge

For this experiment, we ran the most classic bitcoin wallet software, *Electrum*, deployed on a Windows OS with an Intel Core i5-10210U CPU @1.60 GHz and 16 GB of RAM, which would be perfectly suited to the wallet software's running configuration. We connected the wallet software to a proxy client running the SSR protocol and then interacted with the Tor network through a router running OpenWRT. Our probe node is deployed in Qingdao, Shandong Province, with an i7-4770 processor and 16G of RAM.

To verify the correlation between Tor ingress and egress traffic when using a wallet to interact with a P2P network via Tor, we initiate transactions in the Bitcoin test network and collect traffic-related information and then validate the scenario using Deepcorr. Deepcorr is designed to correlate ingress and egress traffic when accessing web pages via Tor, which is similar to our scenario. We use confidence value to evaluate the correlation of the two flows, which reflects the probability that these two flows are correlated.

4.2   The Difference Between Wallet Stream and Normal Stream

When we capture transaction-related streams on the router, we also capture data streams from other applications accessing the web. Therefore, differentiating the transaction streams from the background traffic just from the information of the streams themselves is a very critical step, and in this subsection, we evaluate the difference in number of packets and packet size distribution between the two. We counted the number of upstream and downstream packets over time when accessing the web page and accessing the RPC Server through Tor, respectively, as shown in the figure. It is clear that the packet growth rate is much lower when the wallet accesses the RPC Server than when it accesses the web page. This is understandable. When accessing a web page, the client and server need to interact frequently to deliver the required text, images, audio and other resources. But when the wallet accesses the RPC Server, only a small amount of textual information related to the transaction needs to be transferred.

The wallet software shows a clear stepwise distribution in the number of packets when interacting with the RPC Server via Tor. This is because the wallet regularly accesses the RPC Server to query information such as the current

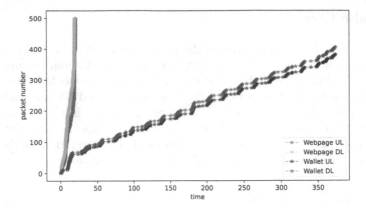

Fig. 2. Drastic differences between webpage and wallet traffic in flow rate

block height and also to verify that the RPC Server is accessible. During the query period (10–15 s in Fig. 2), the number of interaction packets increases significantly, while the rest of the time there are only a few communication packets.

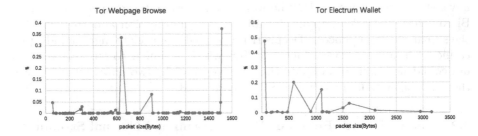

Fig. 3. Packet size distribution in bytes

We further counted the distribution of downstream packet sizes for wallet access to the RPC server and Tor Browser accesses to normal web pages. As clearly shown in Fig. 3, The streams generated when the wallet accesses the RPC server show a clear distribution of small packets. While the Tor Browser will show a distribution of medium and large packets when accessing web pages.

When an application accesses a web page, the packets usually reach the Maximum Transmission Unit (MTU), and the MTU value is generally set in relation to the router, 1500 is the most common value, so when accessing a web page, more than 35% of the packet size is around 1500. When the wallet accesses the RPC server via Tor, the most frequent interaction messages are, wallet queries the current block height and the RPC server returns current status information. Thus less information is transmitted, with more than 40% of the packets having a length of less than 100 bytes.

The experimental results show that there is a significant difference in packet growth rate and packet size distribution between the data stream when accessing the RPC server via Tor and when accessing a regular web page. Combined with the filtering algorithm proposed in the previous section, we filtered 82077 anonymous wallet-related traffic packets from the background traffic. Afterwards, we correlate these flows for correlation analysis.

4.3   Correlation Analysis of Inbound Flow and Outbound Flow

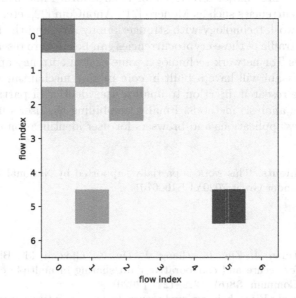

Fig. 4. Flow correlation analysis. (Color figure online)

In this subsection, we will use Deepcorr to perform a correlation analysis on the collected ingress and egress flows. Note that this correlation analysis is performed for both flows, and then a similar probability, called confidence, is calculated. The figure shows a hotspot plot based on the confidence level, with the flow indexes on each axis, and the same index number indicating the correlated flow. The result shows that the correlation confidence value between the inlet flow and the outlet flow of the same flow is significantly higher than that of other flow pairs, as the orange and brown mark shows, darker squares indicate that the two flows are more related. For the colored squares on the off-diagonal, since when inputting data to the neural network, for one of the two streams in a pair of flows, it is fed into the neural network as the input and output streams, respectively. So as long as there are no two dark blocks symmetrical along the main diagonal in this matrix, it means that the correlation is not as high as the diagonal elements. Therefore, among the 7 related flow pairs in the figure, 4 highly correlated incoming and outgoing flows are determined (Fig. 4).

5 Summary

Based on the existing work, this paper proposes a traffic analysis model Crypto-Corr for anonymous wallets. The model is mainly composed of three components: Data Collection, Background traffic filtering and Traffic correlation analysis. It realizes the collection, screening and correlation analysis of anonymous wallet traffic. We verify the proposed model by constructing a dataset of 82,077 wallet data packets collected, and the final experimental results demonstrate the effectiveness of the CryptoCorr model.

We perceive three major directions for future work. First, some mainstream privacy cryptocurrencies such as Monero [21], AnonCoin [22], etc. adopt the I2P anonymity network technology with stronger anonymity, and the analysis of the cryptographic traffic of these cryptocurrencies can be a future research direction. Second, besides Tor network technology, some digital currency application wallets such as Wasabi will have a built-in coin mixing mechanism *CoinJoin*, and it is a valuable research direction to analyze the identity of participating users by using traffic analysis methods. Finally, combining the user's usage traces in digital currency applications and browsers for user identification can be studied in more depth.

Acknowledgements. This work is partially supported by National Key R&D Program of China under Grant 2020YFB1006101.

References

1. Shen, M., Duan, J., Zhu, L., Zhang, J., Du, X., Guizani, M.: Blockchain-based incentives for secure and collaborative data sharing in multiple clouds. IEEE J. Sel. Areas Commun. **38**(6), 1229–1241 (2020)
2. Shen, M., et al.: Blockchain-assisted secure device authentication for cross-domain industrial IoT. IEEE J. Sel. Areas Commun. **38**(5), 942–954 (2020)
3. de Balthasar, T., Hernandez-Castro, J.: An analysis of bitcoin laundry services. In: Lipmaa, H., Mitrokotsa, A., Matulevičius, R. (eds.) NordSec 2017. LNCS, vol. 10674, pp. 297–312. Springer, Cham (2017). https://doi.org/10.1007/978-3-319-70290-2_18
4. Chen, W., Zheng, Z., Cui, J., Ngai, E., Zheng, P., Zhou, Y.: Detecting Ponzi schemes on Ethereum: towards healthier blockchain technology. In: WWW 2018 (2018)
5. Raheem, A., Raheem, R., Chen, T.M., Alkhayyat, A.: Estimation of ransomware payments in bitcoin ecosystem, pp. 1667–1674 (2021)
6. Biryukov, A., Pustogarov, I., Thill, F., Weinmann, R.-P.: Content and popularity analysis of tor hidden services. In: 2014 IEEE 34th International Conference on Distributed Computing Systems Workshops (ICDCSW), pp. 188–193 (2014)
7. Christin, N.: Traveling the silk road: a measurement analysis of a large anonymous online marketplace. In: Proceedings of the 22nd International Conference on World Wide Web, WWW 2013, pp. 213–224. Association for Computing Machinery, New York (2013)
8. Lee, S., et al.: Cybercriminal minds: an investigative study of cryptocurrency abuses in the dark web, January 2019

9. Foley, S., Karlsen, J., Putnins, T.: Sex, drugs, and bitcoin: how much illegal activity is financed through cryptocurrencies? Rev. Finan. Stud. **32**, 1798–1853 (2019)
10. Edman, M., Syverson, P.: As-awareness in tor path selection, pp. 380–389, January 2009
11. Akhoondi, M., Curtis, Yu., Madhyastha, H.: LASTor: a low-latency as-aware tor client. IEEE/ACM Trans. Netw. **22**, 476–490 (2012)
12. Sun, Y., et al.: RAPTOR: routing attacks on privacy in Tor. In: Proceedings of the 24th USENIX Security Symposium, March 2015
13. Nasr, M., Bahramali, A., Houmansadr, A.: DeepCorr: strong flow correlation attacks on tor using deep learning, August 2018
14. Biryukov, A., Khovratovich, D., Pustogarov, I.: Deanonymisation of clients in bitcoin P2P network, May 2014
15. Reid, F., Harrigan, M.: An analysis of anonymity in the bitcoin system. Secur. Priv. Soc. Netw. **3**, 07 (2011)
16. Shen, M., Liu, Y., Zhu, L., Du, X., Hu, J.: Fine-grained webpage fingerprinting using only packet length information of encrypted traffic. IEEE Trans. Inf. Forensics Secur. **16**, 2046–2059 (2021)
17. Shen, M., Gao, Z., Zhu, L., Xu, K.: Efficient fine-grained website fingerprinting via encrypted traffic analysis with deep learning. In: 29th IEEE/ACM International Symposium on Quality of Service, IWQOS 2021, Tokyo, Japan, 25–28 June 2021, pp. 1–10. IEEE (2021)
18. Shen, M., Wei, M., Zhu, L., Wang, M.: Classification of encrypted traffic with second-order Markov chains and application attribute bigrams. IEEE Trans. Inf. Forensics Secur. **12**(8), 1830–1843 (2017)
19. Shen, M., Zhang, J., Zhu, L., Xu, K., Du, X.: Accurate decentralized application identification via encrypted traffic analysis using graph neural networks. IEEE Trans. Inf. Forensics Secur. **16**, 2367–2380 (2021)
20. Postel, J.: RFC864, May 1983
21. van Saberhagen, N.: CryptoNote v 2.0, October 2013
22. van Saberhagen, N.: Anoncoin (2013)

FL-MFGM: A Privacy-Preserving and High-Accuracy Blockchain Reliability Prediction Model

Jianlong Xu$^{(\boxtimes)}$, Weiwei She, Jian Lin, Zhuo Xu, Hao Cai, Zhi Xiong, and Changsheng Zhu

Colleage of Engineering, Shantou University, Shantou 515061, China
{xujianlong,17wwshe,20jlin3,20zxu3,haocai,zxiong,cszhu}@stu.edu.cn

Abstract. Reliability prediction mechanism plays an important role in selecting reliable peers for blockchain users. Traditionally, reliability prediction approaches are performed by collecting a large amount of user data and conducting centralized training. Although these methods can achieve high accuracy, they may lead to malicious attacks by third-party services on users' private data. As a privacy-preserving approach to addressing privacy leakage caused by centralized training, federated learning can enable users to learn a shared prediction model by providing gradients to a central server instead of raw data. However, uploading complete gradients directly may be exposed to a gradient attack and cause privacy leakage. To address the privacy data leakage from centralized training and prevent the attack threat from uploading gradients, we propose a privacy-preserving and high-accuracy blockchain reliability prediction model, namely FL-MFGM. Based on federated learning architecture, the model protects user privacy by uploading the gradients of matrix factorization. Specifically, in order to enhance the privacy-preserving capability of our model, we employ gradient compression with momentum correction for federated matrix factorization. To validate the effectiveness of our approach, sufficient experiments are conducted, which indicate that our approach can achieve higher prediction accuracy than other approaches with privacy-preserving based on federated learning architecture.

Keywords: Blockchain · Reliability prediction · Privacy protection · Federated learning · Matrix factorization

1 Introduction

Blockchain technology has received wide attention from industry and academia because of its decentralized, persistent, and auditable features. These features are derived from the working mechanism of blockchain system. Blockchain is a shared digital ledger and each transaction is public [1]. The communication technology of the system is Peer-to-Peer (P2P), where communication between peers does not need to rely on a third party. Each participant peer in such a

D. Svetinovic et al. (Eds.): BlockSys 2022, CCIS 1679, pp. 306–321, 2022.
https://doi.org/10.1007/978-981-19-8043-5_22

system maintains a blockchain and acts in the roles of both client and server, i.e., each peer can request content or services from other peers and act as a server to provide content or services to other peers [2]. The way to maintain the blockchain is through a consensus mechanism. Once a peer finds a proof-of-work, it broadcasts the block to all peers and receives a reward [1].

In order to get rewards [3] or verify transactions [4], users in the blockchain network need to request the latest block information from neighboring peers. However, not all the peers would return the latest block information because of the network latency, malicious attacks, etc. If a peer returns incorrect or outdated block information, it would waste the users' time and resources. The users may even be vulnerable to being attacked as a result [3].

In order for users to select more secure and reliable blockchain peers, one simple solution is to use known reliability information (e.g., successful request rates from users to peers) to predict the unknowns. Many existing approaches are designed for centralized training, which collects users' raw data in the central servers. However, large-scale collection of sensitive data entails risks [5]. For example, malicious third parties can steal sensitive data by attacking the server and untrustworthy data collectors may disclose users' private data [6]. Therefore, it is necessary to enhance the privacy protection of reliability prediction.

Federated learning is an effective method to protect user privacy. Current researches based on federated learning include edge computing, Internet of Things, and smart healthcare [7–9]. The main idea of federated learning is to enable users to leave the training data distributed on the mobile devices and learn a shared model by aggregating locally-computed updates (e.g., gradient information) [10]. However, the canonical federated learning involves two big challenges: First, shared gradients publicly may lead to leakage of private training data [11]; Second, communication in federated networks can be much more expensive than that in classical data center environments because of comprised of a massive number of devices (e.g., millions of smartphones) [12].

In this paper, we propose a privacy-preserving and high-accuracy blockchain reliability prediction model based on federated matrix factorization with gradient compression and momentum correction (FL-MFGM). FL-MFGM achieves privacy preservation in blockchain reliability prediction by federated matrix factorization and gradient compression. The main contributions of this paper are summarized as follows:

(1) We propose a blockchain reliability prediction model based on federated matrix factorization to protect user privacy.
(2) We design a gradient compression method to reduce the uploaded gradients, which enables our model to defend against gradient attacks.
(3) We adopt momentum correction to ensure the prediction accuracy.
(4) We verify the effectiveness of our model through sufficient experiments.

The rest of the paper is structured as follows: Sect. 2 introduces the related work. Section 3 includes details of the approach in this paper. Section 4 elaborates on the experiments and discusses the results of the experiments. Section 5 concludes the work of this paper and gives the vision for the future work.

2   Related Work

This section focuses on reviewing current approaches to blockchain reliability prediction and privacy protection based on federated learning, which are relevant to this paper.

Blockchain Reliability Prediction. Current approaches to blockchain reliability prediction are based on studies of software reliability prediction. Zheng et al. [4] proposed a hybrid blockchain reliability prediction (H-BRP), which takes blockchain-related factors (e.g., block hash, block height) into consideration and finds the similarity among users and among peers to do the prediction. However, H-BRP is a centralized training model that must collect the data of all users to calculate the similarity between peers, which may cause sensitive data leakage. Xu et al. [13] proposed a high-accuracy reliability prediction approach for block-chain services under BaaS (BSRPF), using matrix factorization. BSRPF is also a centralized training model, but it inspired our work in this paper that we can use matrix factorization based on federated learning to predict reliability effectively and protect user privacy by not sharing raw data.

Privacy Protection Based on Federated Learning. Federated learning can significantly reduce privacy and security risks by sharing model updates instead of uploading a local dataset [10]. However, it may still reveal sensitive information to third parties or central servers [12]. Zhu et al. [11] demonstrated that attackers can extrapolate the local data from the high-density gradient communication. They also summarize the practical methods to defend against this kind of attack effectively without a dropped performance, including gradient compression and homomorphic encryption.

Homomorphic encryption is a kind of cryptology that is the most secured defense. But it has limitations: the gradients required should be an integer [5], homomorphic encryption is only for parameter servers [14]. Gradient compression can be used universally because it has no limitations on gradients or servers and is easy to be implemented. Many studies have focused on two aspects to optimize gradient compression: the choice of sparsification threshold and the problem of accuracy loss and low convergence rate.

Strom Nikko [15] developed a gradient compression method with a fixed threshold. But it is difficult to choose an available threshold due to the variation of gradients. Tao et al. [16] proposed an approach to solving this problem. They set a threshold according to gradient average value and designed a momentum residual accumulation for tracking the residual gradients. It can also recover the low convergence caused by gradient sparsification. However, the convergence comes with nearly a thousand iterations, which was exceeding our expectations. Lin et al. [17] proposed a deep gradient compression (DGC), using warm-up training and gradient sparsification with momentum correction and gradient clipping to solve the problem of low accuracy and low convergence rate. DGC achieves a gradient compression ratio of about 600× without losing accuracy.

Although the existing reliability prediction methods of blockchain have achieved relatively high accuracy, these methods are based on centralized training and lack consideration for user privacy protection, which may be attacked by third-party services. To address the privacy data leakage from centralized training and prevent the attack threat, inspired by federal learning, we focus on the privacy protection of blockchain reliability prediction in this paper, hoping to ensure the accuracy of prediction while protecting users' privacy.

3 Privacy-Preserving Blockchain Reliability Prediction Model

In this section, we first present a framework of our FL-MFGM model in Sect. 3.1. Then, We illustrate the federated matrix factorization approach for our model in Sect. 3.2 and introduce how to achieve gradient compression with momentum correction for our model in Sect. 3.3. Finally, we show the implementation in Sect. 3.4.

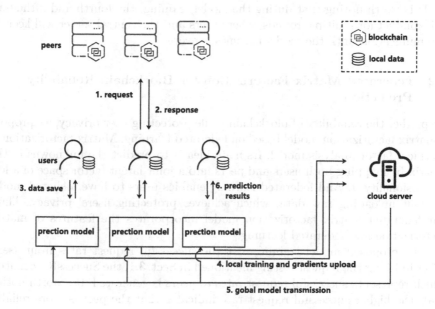

Fig. 1. The framework of FL-MFGM model

3.1 Model Framework

The main idea of FL-MFGM is that users train the model respectively using the data stored locally, and upload the gradients generated by the local model update to the central server, which updates the global model and transmit it to users. As the iterations proceed, the model gradually converges, and users can use the model to predict the reliability of candidate peers for selecting a more reliable peer. As shown in Fig. 1, the model framework mainly consists of six steps:

(1) Users randomly request blockchain data from candidate peers over a period of time.
(2) The requested peers respond and return data (e.g., block hash, block height).
(3) Users compile the information responded from peers and save the data locally.
(4) Users take a certain number of iterations to update the local model based on their local data. After local training, they compute gradients and send them to the central server.
(5) The central server aggregates the gradients from users and updates the global model. The improved global model will be transmitted to users for the next training.
(6) After the model becomes converged, users can predict the reliability of candidate peers and select the ones that meet their reliability requirements.

It is worth noting that during the model training, the fourth and fifth steps will conduct for multiple rounds, where users and the central server will keep in communication until the model becomes converged.

3.2   Federated Matrix Factorization for Blockchain Reliability Prediction

To predict the reliability of blockchain while protecting user privacy, we propose a matrix factorization model based on federated learning. Matrix factorization is a typical factor analysis model. Its main idea is to predict the unknowns in the matrix by mapping both users and peers into a joint latent factor space of a low dimensionality d. And federated learning enables users to have a shared model without uploading raw data, which achieves protecting users' privacy. Thus, our federated matrix factorization model incorporates the features of matrix factorization and federated learning.

The proposed model training uses the successful request rates from users. After finishing the request testing mentioned in Sect. 3.1, the SuccessRate matrix which represents successful request rates to peers is generated. It's worth noting that, the higher successful request rate indicates that the peer is more reliable to the user [4].

We update the matrix factorization model, including user profile matrix and peer profile matrix by the SuccessRate matrix. To prevent the server from directly knowing users' raw data or learned profiles, users will update the user profile matrix and peer profile matrix only locally using their SuccessRate matrix, and share gradients of peer profile matrix to the server for updating the global model [18].

We assume there are N users and M peers. The SuccessRate matrix for user i is denoted as $R^i \in \mathbb{R}^{1 \times M}$, and the element of column j of R^i denotes the successful request rate from user i to peer j. For user i, the local matrix factorization model consists latent user factors $U^i \in \mathbb{R}^{1 \times d}$ and latent peer factors $P^i \in \mathbb{R}^{M \times d}$. Thus, we aim to minimize the objective function with regularization terms [19]:

$$\mathcal{L}^i = \frac{1}{2} \sum_{j=1}^{M} I_j^i \left(R_j^i - U^i \left(P_j^i \right)^T \right)^2 + \frac{\lambda_U}{2} \|U^i\|_F^2 + \frac{\lambda_P}{2} \|P^i\|_F^2, \tag{1}$$

where I_j^i acts as an indicator that equals to 1 if R_j^i is observed, and 0 otherwise. λ_u and λ_p are the regularization coefficients to control the degree of regularization, and $\| \cdot \|_F^2$ denotes the Frobenius norm [19]. We employ the stochastic gradient descent method (SGD) [20] to train our model. For each successful rate from user i to requested peer j, we have the following pairwise loss function:

$$\ell \left(U^i, P_j^i \right) = \frac{1}{2} \left(R_j^i - U^i \left(P_j^i \right)^T \right)^2 + \frac{\lambda_u}{2} \|U^i\|_2^2 + \frac{\lambda_p}{2} \|P_j^i\|_2^2, \tag{2}$$

where $\| \cdot \|_2^2$ denotes the Eulerian norm. Instead of directly minimizing $\mathcal{L}$, SGD relaxes to minimize the pairwise loss function ℓ [21]. We compute gradients of U^i and P_j^i respectively:

$$\frac{\partial \ell}{\partial U^i} = \left(U^i \left(P_j^i \right)^T - R_j^i \right) P_j^i + \lambda_u U^i \tag{3}$$

$$\frac{\partial \ell}{\partial P_j^i} = \left(U^i \left(P_j^i \right)^T - R_j^i \right) U^i + \lambda_p P_j^i \tag{4}$$

Then the local matrix U^i and P^i would update using Eq. (5) and Eq. (6) respectively:

$$U^i = U^i - \alpha \cdot \frac{\partial \ell}{\partial U^i} \tag{5}$$

$$P_j^i = P_j^i - \alpha \cdot \frac{\partial \ell}{\partial P_j^i}, \tag{6}$$

where α is the learning rate of our model.

The local training will perform for a certain number of iterations to reduce the rounds of communication needed between the server and users. After local updates, the user computes gradients for P^i and sends them to the server. To distinguish the global model from the local model, we use $\hat{P}$ to denote the global model and P^i to denote the local model of user i. The gradients generated by the local training of user i are denoted as:

$$g^i = \hat{P} - P^i \tag{7}$$

The central server aggregates the gradients uploaded by users and updates the global model $\hat{P}$:

$$\hat{P} = \hat{P} - \frac{1}{N} \sum_{i=1}^{N} g^i \tag{8}$$

After the global model has been updated, the central server broadcasts it to users for the next training round. During the training process, the server keeps providing the global model for all the users to download. The training rounds and model updates will keep going until the model becomes converged. As a result, all the users can gain an effective blockchain reliability prediction model without sharing their raw data, which will achieve the preservation of private data.

3.3   Gradient Compression

To protect users' privacy, we transmit the gradients for model updating instead of users' raw data during the training process. However, sharing gradients is considered insecure in federated learning. For example, malicious third parties can deduce the user's raw data from the shared gradients [11]. To enhance the privacy preservation of our model and defend against gradient attacks, we proposed gradient compression with momentum correction.

Gradient Sparsification. Gradient compression only uploads the important gradients which are larger than a threshold [17]. Due to the uncertainty of data, it is difficult to set a fixed threshold. Thus, we set a sparsity to choose the larger gradients instead of a threshold. We assume that the gradient matrix generated by user i is g^i, and set a sparsity $ratio \in (0,1]$. The proportion of uploaded gradients to the overall number is the $ratio$, whose values are all larger than the gradients that do not need to be uploaded. Especially, when $ratio$ fetches 1, all the gradients will be uploaded.

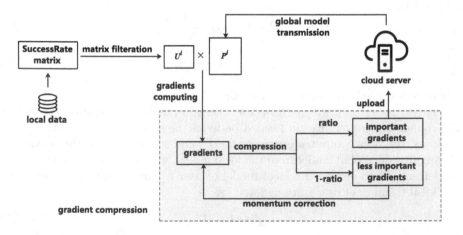

Fig. 2. FL-MFGM model training for user i.

Momentum Correction. With the increasing of sparsity, the model becomes tougher and tougher to converge [17], because gradient sparsification only retains the important gradients. To solve this problem, we design a momentum correction method. The gradients which are not available to be uploaded in the previous iteration will be saved on the local device and accumulated with the newly gradients using momentum correction method. We perform momentum correction locally before gradient sparsification. The momentum correction method in iteration t is shown in Eq. (9) and Eq. (10).

$$u^{(i,t)} = m \cdot u^{(i,t-1)} + g^{(i,t)}, \quad v^{(i,t)} = v^{(i,t)} + u^{(i,t)}, \quad g^{(i,t)} = \text{Sparsification}\left(v^{(i,t)}\right), \tag{9}$$

where m is the momentum coefficient, $u^{(i,t)}$ denotes the result of momentum correction, $g^{(i,t)}$ is the gradients of this iteration, $v^{(i,t)}$ is used for subsequent sparsification and accumulation, and $Sparsification(v^{(i,t)})$ is for gradient compression. The details of gradient compression is shown in Fig. 2. After determining the gradients to be uploaded, $v^{(i,t)}$ will store the gradients that have not been uploaded:

$$v^{(i,t)} = v^{(i,t)} - g^{(i,t)} \tag{10}$$

Figure 2 is mainly a more detailed explanation of the model training. The "gradient compression" part shows the workflow of the proposed gradient compression method in one iteration. Based on the existing SuccessRate matrix and the global model, we use matrix factorization to update model and compute gradients. We perform gradient compression: According to the sparsity, the larger gradients will be uploaded, and the remaining will be saved locally and accumulated with the newly computed gradients by the momentum correction method. As to reduce the times of communication, the local model training and update will perform a certain of rounds and then compute gradients to upload. After the central server updates the model and transmits it to user i, user i can update the training model and move on to the next iteration. Model training and communication between the user and the central server will keep on until the model converges.

3.4   FL-MFGM Algorithm

The pseudo code of our FL-MFGM is shown in Algorithm 1.

Algorithm 1. FL-MFGM Algorithm

Input:

    The dataset and parameters of training: $\{R, N, iteration, m, ratio\}$

Output: A convergence model P

1: Divide R into a training set and a test set $\{trainMatrix, testMatrix\}$
2: Initialize the user matrix U^i and peer matrix P^i for user i
3: $u \leftarrow 0, v \leftarrow 0$
4: **for** $t = 1$ to $iteration$ **do**
5:     **for** $i = 1$ to N **do**
6:        $g^{(i,t)} \leftarrow 0$
7:        $U^i, \quad P^i \leftarrow \text{UserUpdate}\left(U^i, P^i, \mathrm{R}^i\right)$
8:        $g^{(i,t)} \leftarrow P - P^i$
9:        $u^{(i,t)} \leftarrow m \cdot u^{(i,t-1)} + g^{(i,t)}$
10:       $v^{(i,t)} \leftarrow v^{(i,t-1)} + u^{(i,t)}$
11:       $g^{(i,t)} \leftarrow \text{Sparsification}\left(v^{(i,t)}, ratio\right)$
12:       $v^{(i,t)} \leftarrow v^{(i,t)} - g^{(i,t)}$
13:     **end for**
14:    $P \leftarrow \frac{1}{N} \sum_{i=1}^{N} g^{(i,t)}$
15: **end for**
16: **return** P

Specially, the iterative updating process of the global model decomposes into two parts that are performed on the user side (Line 5–13) and the server side (Line 14), respectively. The global model updating will keep on until convergence. Especially, the model updating operations on the user side are defined as a function $UserUpdate\left(U^i, P^i, \mathrm{R}^i\right)$. After the local model updating, users will compute the gradients which are required for the model updating. Note that for newly computed gradients, we first accumulate them with the remaining gradients of the previous iteration by momentum correction (Line 9–10) and then conduct gradient sparsification (Line 11). The operations of gradient sparsification are defined as a function $Sparsification\left(v^{(i,t)}, ratio\right)$, according to the details described in the gradient sparsification part in Sect. 3.3. Another important point is that the user would save the remaining gradients locally after gradient sparsification (Line 12). The uploaded gradients from users will be aggregated on the server side and used for the global model updating (Line 14). As such, our model can protect users' privacy as it enables users to keep their raw data on device and compress the uploaded gradients.

4 Experiments and Analysis

In this section, sufficient experiments are conducted in real-world datasets to answer the following questions:

    Q1: Is our proposed approach effective for blockchain reliability prediction?

    Q2: What is the effect of gradient compression and momentum correction on prediction accuracy?

    Q3: What is the impact of different sparsity on prediction accuracy?

Our experiments were conducted on an AMD Ryzen 5 3600 6-core processor and 8GB of RAM, running on Python 3.7 and windows 10 (64-bit). In the following subsections, we will introduce the experimental settings, and then conduct experiments and analysis according to the above three questions.

4.1 Experiment Settings

Dataset and Parameter Setting. In this paper, we use the real dataset proposed by Zheng et al. [4]. It is a 100×200 SuccessMate matrix between 100 blockchain users and 200 blockchain peers. It is worth noting that, the successful request rate range from 0 to 1 and the higher successful request rate indicates that peer j is more reliability to user i. We use *MaxRTT* to indicate the maximum tolerable request round-trip time and use *MaxBlockBack* to indicate the maximum tolerable return block backward to the latest block [4]. We set four different combinations of *MaxBlockBack* and *MaxRTT* for our experiments: $<MaxBlockBack = 0, \quad MaxRTT = 1000>$, $<MaxBlockBack = 12, \quad MaxRTT = 1000>$, $<MaxBlockBack = 12, \quad MaxRTT = 2000>$, $<MaxBlockBack = 100, MaxRTT = 5000>$, and the density of the training matrix is set as *Density = 30%, 50%, 65%, 95%*.

Evaluation Metric. We use the root mean square error (RMSE) to measure the difference between the predicted and real values. A smaller RMSE value represents higher prediction accuracy. The formula for calculating the root mean square error is:

$$RMSE = \frac{\sum_{(i,j,R_{i,j}) \in T} \left| \hat{R}_{i,j} - R_{i,j} \right|}{|T|}, \tag{11}$$

where $R_{i,j}$ is the known real record value, which indicates the success rate of user i to the peer j, $\hat{R}_{i,j}$ denotes the success rate predicted by FL-MFGM, T indicates the records in training set.

4.2 Prediction Accuracy Comparison (RQ1)

To verify the prediction accuracy of FL-MFGM, we compare it with some baseline methods for reliability prediction: the user similarity-based prediction method UPCC [22], the item similarity-based prediction method IPCC [23], the mixed user and item similarity-based prediction method UIPCC [24], and the mixed block information-based prediction method H- BRP [4]. We set the sparsity of FL-MFGM is 99% which means users can only upload the top 1% of the large gradients. The results are shown in Table 1.

From Table 1, we can observe that RMSE of H-BRP is the lowest among the baseline method and the performance of our FL-MFGM model is even better than H-BRP. Concretely, for $<MaxBlockBack = 12, MaxRTT = 1000>$, the RMSE of FL-MFGM is 27.9%–51.4% lower than that of H-BRP at different matrix densities, which means that FL-MFGM achieves 27.9%–51.4% improvement on prediction accuracy. And for $<MaxBlockBack = 100, MaxRTT = 5000>$,

Table 1. Comparison of RMSE among FL-MFGM and baseline approaches.

Parameter	Method	Density = 30%	Density = 50%	Density = 65%	Density = 95%
MaxBlockBack = 0 MaxRTT = 1000	UPCC	0.2823	0.2791	0.2769	0.2758
	IPCC	0.0821	0.0777	0.0764	0.0748
	UIPCC	0.0851	0.0806	0.0791	0.0773
	H-BRP	0.0791	0.0716	0.0711	0.0670
	FL-MFGM	**0.0637**	**0.0565**	**0.0399**	**0.0397**
	Improve.(%)	19.5%	21.1%	43.9%	40.7%
MaxBlockBack = 12 MaxRTT = 1000	UPCC	0.3627	0.3591	0.3566	0.3559
	IPCC	0.1009	0.0949	0.0919	0.0920
	UIPCC	0.1053	0.0994	0.0963	0.0961
	H-BRP	0.1017	0.0908	0.0901	0.0834
	FL-MFGM	**0.0718**	**0.0655**	**0.0438**	**0.0466**
	Improve.(%)	29.4%	27.9%	51.4%	44.1%
MaxBlockBack = 12 MaxRTT = 2000	UPCC	0.3793	0.3775	0.3758	0.3760
	IPCC	0.0810	0.0785	0.0765	0.0751
	UIPCC	0.0887	0.0864	0.0845	0.0831
	H-BRP	0.0641	0.0546	0.0528	0.0451
	FL-MFGM	**0.0461**	**0.0439**	**0.0330**	**0.0328**
	Improve.(%)	28.1%	19.6%	37.5%	27.3%
MaxBlockBack = 100 MaxRTT = 5000	UPCC	0.4595	0.4585	0.4569	0.4574
	IPCC	0.0921	0.0887	0.0842	0.0774
	UIPCC	0.1022	0.0993	0.0954	0.0895
	H-BRP	0.0635	0.0547	0.0524	0.043
	FL-MFGM	**0.051**	**0.0478**	**0.0328**	**0.0327**
	Improve. (%)	19.7%	12.6%	37.4%	24.0%

FL-MFGM achieves 12.6%–37.4% improvement on prediction accuracy. According to the results, our FL-MFGM approach significantly outperforms the other approaches over RMSE. And as the density of the training set increases, the RMSE of FL-MFGM decreases correspondingly indicating that its prediction accuracy also increases. We verify that our FL-MFGM model can achieve higher accuracy than existing approaches for blockchain reliability prediction.

4.3 Effect of Gradient Compression and Momentum Correction (RQ2)

Gradient compression is an important method to defend against gradient attacks. However, it would reduce the accuracy of the prediction due to the reduction of the uploaded gradients. As discussed in Sect. 3.3, we recover the accuracy by momentum correction. To study the performance of our gradient compression method which contains gradient sparsification and momentum correction, we compare the prediction accuracy of FL-MFGM with two methods, named FL-MF and FL-MFG respectively. FL-MF and FL-MFG are both blockchain reliability prediction approaches based on federated matrix factorization. Compared with FL-MFGM,

FL-MF performs without gradient compression or momentum correction, and FL-MFG performs gradient compression without momentum correction. And we set sparsity, $ratio = 99\%$. The experimental results are shown in Table 2.

Table 2. Effect of gradient compression and momentum correction on prediction accuracy.

Parameter	Method	Density = 30%	Density = 50%	Density = 65%	Density = 95%
MaxBlockBack = 0 MaxRTT = 1000	FL-MF	0.0626	0.0569	0.0382	0.0382
	FL-MFG	0.0687	0.0665	0.0794	0.0800
	FL-MFGM	**0.0637**	**0.0565**	**0.0399**	**0.0397**
MaxBlockBack = 12 MaxRTT = 1000	FL-MF	0.0717	0.0679	0.0398	0.0395
	FL-MFG	0.0825	0.0929	0.0989	0.1029
	FL-MFGM	**0.0718**	**0.0655**	**0.0438**	**0.0466**
MaxBlockBack = 12 MaxRTT = 2000	FL-MF	0.0462	0.0441	0.0313	0.0304
	FL-MFG	0.0489	0.0452	0.0404	0.0426
	FL-MFGM	**0.0461**	**0.0439**	**0.0330**	**0.0328**
MaxBlockBack = 100 MaxRTT = 5000	FL-MF	0.0503	0.0470	0.0308	0.0308
	FL-MFG	0.0518	0.0490	0.0508	0.0431
	FL-MFGM	**0.0510**	**0.0478**	**0.0328**	**0.0327**

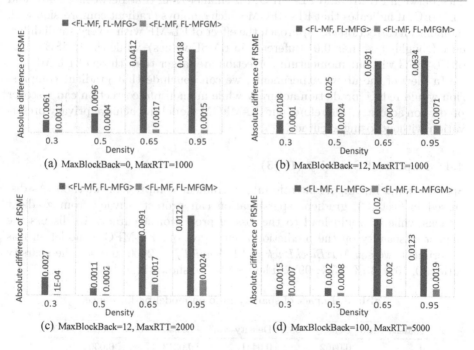

(a) MaxBlockBack=0, MaxRTT=1000

(b) MaxBlockBack=12, MaxRTT=1000

(c) MaxBlockBack=12, MaxRTT=2000

(d) MaxBlockBack=100, MaxRTT=5000

Fig. 3. Performance comparison of gradient compression and momentum correction on prediction. Note: <*FL-MF, FL-MFG*> means the absolute value of the difference between the RMSE of FL-MF and FL-MFG. <*FL-MF, FL-MFGM*> means the absolute value of the difference between the RMSE of FL-MF and FL-MFGM.

From Table 2, we find that FL-MF without gradient compression achieves highest accuracy in most cases. The prediction accuracy of FL-MFGM is very close to that of FL-MF. It is worth noting that, the RMSE values of FL-MFGM are lower than those of FL-MF when $Density = 50\%$ and $MaxBlockBack = 12$, which means that the prediction accuracy of FL-MFGM can be higher than that of FL-MF. With the increase of $Density$, the RMSE values of FL-MF and FL-MFGM show a tendency of decreasing which means the accuracy is improving, while the accuracy of the FL-MFG method without a decreasing trend is the lowest among these three methods. It reflects that FL-MFGM and FL-MF are much more effective than FL-MFG.

To observe the effect of compression and momentum correction on the prediction accuracy more clearly, we compute the absolute value of the RMSE difference between FL-MF and FL-MFG and also compute it for FL-MF and FL-MFGM. The results are shown in Fig. 3.

From Fig. 3, we can find that the difference between FL-MF and FL-MFG becomes larger with the increasing $Density$, as well as between FL-MF and FL-MFGM. While the maximum RMSE difference between FL-MF and FL-MFGM is 0.0071 and the maximum difference between FL-MF and FL-MFG is 0.0634. Notably, with a fixed $Density$, $MaxRTT$, and $MaxBlockBack$, the difference between FL-MF and FL-MFGM is smaller than that between FL-MF and FL-MFG. It indicates that FL-MFGM which employs gradient compression with momentum correction can approach the effect of FL-MF with a very small difference (roughly less than 0.01 difference in RMSE values), while the RMSE values of FL-MFG without momentum correction are larger than those of FL-MF.

In view of the above experiments, we can conclude that gradient compression would reduce prediction accuracy while momentum correction can rescover prediction accuracy. Therefore, our FL-MFGM model can achieve privacy preservation without losing accuracy.

4.4   Impact of Sparsity (RQ3)

Sparsity plays an important role in our gradient compression method. As discussed in Sect. 3.3, gradient sparsification can protect privacy from gradient attacks while it would lead to the loss of prediction accuracy. To discuss the impact of sparsity on the prediction accuracy of our FL-MFGM model, in this experiment, we set $MaxBlockBack = 12$, $MaxRTT = 2000$ and set the sparsity ratio $= 0$, 10%, 30%, 65%, 99%. The results are shown in Table 3.

Table 3. Impact of sparsity ratio on model performance.

Sparsity ratio	Density = 30%	Density = 50%	Density = 65%	Density = 95%
0	0.0462	0.0441	0.0313	0.0304
10%	0.0460	0.0442	0.0337	0.0320
35%	0.0462	0.0440	0.0342	0.0331
65%	0.0465	0.0440	0.0336	0.0326
99%	0.0464	0.0442	0.0340	0.0330

From Table 3, we can observe that when the sparsity ratio is fixed, the RMSE of FL-MFGM shows a gradually decreasing trend with *Density* increasing. When we keep *Density* constant, the prediction error is not significantly different when sparsity ratio is changed. Specifically, when *Density* = 65%, the maximum RMSE difference between different ratios obtains the largest value (about 0.0029), while *Density* = 10%, the maximum RMSE difference between different ratios obtains the smallest value (about 0.0002). The results show that the variation of sparsity has little effect on the prediction accuracy of our model. It turns out that FL-MFGM can achieve high accuracy at different sparsity even when the degree of sparsity ratio reaches 99%.

5   Conclusion and Future Work

In this paper, we propose a privacy-preserving and high-accuracy blockchain reliability prediction approach based on federated matrix factorization with gradient compression and momentum correction. Firstly, we propose a matrix factorization model based on federated learning, which enables users to learn an effect global prediction without sharing private data. Secondly, we use gradient compression method to defend against gradient attacks by sparsifying the gradient matrix. Thirdly, we design the gradient compression with momentum correction which fixes the accuracy degradation caused by compression. Finally, the experimental results verify that our approach can improve prediction accuracy while achieving privacy preservation. And the proposed approach achieves a high gradient compression rate and reduces the communication bandwidth without compromising the prediction accuracy.

In our future research, we plan to improve our model performance by considering the impact of other block information, such as block height and block hash. We will also explore ways to improve the model's ability to resist attacks. In addition, our proposed approach is based on the condition of trusted users and trusted servers, and further work will consider the credibility of users and servers.

Acknowledgments. This research was financially supported by 2021 Guangdong Province Special Fund for Science and Technology ("major special projects + task list") Project (No. STKJ2021201), Guangdong Province Basic and Applied Basic Research Fund (No.2021A1515012527) and in part by 2020 Li Ka Shing Foundation Cross-Disciplinary Research Grant (No. 2020LKSFG08D).

References

1. Nakamoto, S.: Bitcoin: A peer-to-peer electronic cash system (2008). http://Bitcoin.org/Bitcoin.pdf
2. Bhutta, M.N.M., et al.: A survey on blockchain technology: evolution, architecture and security. IEEE Access **9**, 61048–61073 (2021)

3. Gervais, A., Karame, G.O., Wüst, K., Glykantzis, V., Ritzdorf, H., Capkun, S.: On the security and performance of proof of work blockchains. In: Proceedings of the 2016 ACM SIGSAC Conference on Computer and Communications Security, pp. 3–16 (2016)
4. Zheng, P., Zheng, Z., Chen, L.: Selecting reliable blockchain peers via hybrid blockchain reliability prediction. arXiv preprint arXiv:1910.14614 (2019)
5. Bonawitz, K., et al.: Practical secure aggregation for federated learning on user-held data. arXiv preprint arXiv:1611.04482 (2016)
6. Liu, J., Meng, X.: Survey on privacy-preserving machine learning. J. Comput. Res. Dev. **57**(2), 346 (2020)
7. Lu, Y., Huang, X., Dai, Y., Maharjan, S., Zhang, Y.: Differentially private asynchronous federated learning for mobile edge computing in urban informatics. IEEE Trans. Ind. Inform. **16**(3), 2134–2143 (2019)
8. Ren, J., Wang, H., Hou, T., Zheng, S., Tang, C.: Federated learning-based computation offloading optimization in edge computing-supported internet of things. IEEE Access **7**, 69194–69201 (2019)
9. Wang, X., Han, Y., Wang, C., Zhao, Q., Chen, X., Chen, M.: In-edge AI: intelligentizing mobile edge computing, caching and communication by federated learning. IEEE Netw. **33**(5), 156–165 (2019)
10. McMahan, B., Moore, E., Ramage, D., Hampson, S., Arcas, B.A.: Communication-efficient learning of deep networks from decentralized data. In: Artificial Intelligence and Statistics, pp. 1273–1282. PMLR (2017)
11. Zhu, L., Liu, Z., Han, S.: Deep leakage from gradients. In: Advances in Neural Information Processing Systems 32 (2019)
12. Li, T., Sahu, A.K., Talwalkar, A., Smith, V.: Federated learning: challenges, methods, and future directions. IEEE Signal Process. Mag. **37**(3), 50–60 (2020)
13. Xu, J., Zhuang, Z., Wang, K., Liang, W.: High-accuracy reliability prediction approach for blockchain services under BaaS. In: Zheng, Z., Dai, H.-N., Fu, X., Chen, B. (eds.) BlockSys 2020. CCIS, vol. 1267, pp. 648–660. Springer, Singapore (2020). https://doi.org/10.1007/978-981-15-9213-3_50
14. Aono, Y., Hayashi, T., Wang, L., Moriai, S., et al.: Privacy-preserving deep learning via additively homomorphic encryption. IEEE Trans. Inf. Forensics Secur. **13**(5), 1333–1345 (2017)
15. Strom, N.: Scalable distributed DNN training using commodity GPU cloud computing. In: Sixteenth Annual Conference of the International Speech Communication Association (2015)
16. Tao, Z., Li, Q.: {eSGD}: communication efficient distributed deep learning on the edge. In: USENIX Workshop on Hot Topics in Edge Computing (HotEdge 2018) (2018)
17. Lin, Y., Han, S., Mao, H., Wang, Y., Dally, W.J.: Deep gradient compression: Reducing the communication bandwidth for distributed training. arXiv preprint arXiv:1712.01887 (2017)
18. Chai, D., Wang, L., Chen, K., Yang, Q.: Secure federated matrix factorization. IEEE Intell. Syst. **36**(5), 11–20 (2020)
19. Salakhutdinov, R., Mnih, A.: Probabilistic matrix factorization. In: Proceedings of the 20th International Conference on Neural Information Processing Systems, pp. 1257–1264 (2007)
20. Shapiro, A., Wardi, Y.: Convergence analysis of gradient descent stochastic algorithms. J. Optim. Theory Appl. **91**(2), 439–454 (1996)

21. Zhu, J., He, P., Zheng, Z., Lyu, M.R.: Towards online, accurate, and scalable QoS prediction for runtime service adaptation. In: 2014 IEEE 34th International Conference on Distributed Computing Systems, pp. 318–327. IEEE (2014)

22. Breese, J.S., Heckerman, D., Kadie, C.: Empirical analysis of predictive algorithms for collaborative filtering. arXiv preprint arXiv:1301.7363 (2013)

23. Sarwar, B., Karypis, G., Konstan, J., Riedl, J.: Item-based collaborative filtering recommendation algorithms. In: Proceedings of the 10th International Conference on World Wide Web, pp. 285–295 (2001)

24. Zheng, Z., Lyu, M.R.: Collaborative reliability prediction of service-oriented systems. In: 2010 ACM/IEEE 32nd International Conference on Software Engineering, vol. 1, pp. 35–44. IEEE (2010)

WaLi: Control-Flow-Based Analysis of Wasm Smart Contracts

Shuo Yang[1], Huizhong Li[2(✉)], and Zibin Zheng[1]

[1] School of Software Engineering, Sun Yat-sen University, Zhuhai 519000, China
zhzibin@mail.sysu.edu.cn
[2] WeBank, Shenzhen 518055, China
wheatli@webank.com

Abstract. With the proliferation of various types of blockchain applications, smart contracts are getting more and more essential in developing decentralized applications due to their powerful expressing capabilities. However, security vulnerabilities of smart contracts keep arising in recent years, which has attracted a lot of attention. Most of the related research mainly focuses on smart contracts deployed on Ethereum. But in the meantime, more and more types of smart contracts adopt Wasm as their bytecode format due to its smaller size and higher operating efficiency in blockchain. To avoid the recurrence of exploited vulnerabilities in Wasm smart contracts, we develop WaLi, a control-flow-based analyzer for security vulnerabilities. In particular, we first construct a control flow graph based on the Wasm bytecode and define a critical path identification method to locate possible paths that may contain vulnerabilities. Then we adopt a Wasm virtual machine to simulate a runtime environment when tracing the critical paths and report the result based on our vulnerability detection patterns. We choose Liquid smart contracts on FISCO-BCOS to illustrate our approach and the experimental results show that WaLi performs well in detecting the access control vulnerabilities.

Keywords: Blockchain · Smart contract · Control flow · Static analysis · WebAssembly

1 Introduction

Blockchain is a pioneering distributed ledger database based on a peer-to-peer (P2P) network [24]. And smart contracts [16] enable diverse decentralized applications (DApps) to deploy on blockchains owing to the powerful expressing capabilities brought by Turing-complete programs [7]. Specifically, smart contracts written in Solidity can be deployed on Ethereum [19] and run inside the Ethereum Virtual Machine (EVM) in the form of EVM bytecodes. The advent of smart contracts has boosted the growing prosperity of DApps to promote the development of blockchain [23].

However, like other software systems, the birth of the blockchain is accompanied by a series of security vulnerabilities [8]. Due to the immutability of smart contracts and the freedom of participants deploying smart contracts, it is almost inevitable for developers to avoid every potential vulnerability when designing smart contracts [22]. Take the Parity Multi-Sig Wallet Attack [11] as an example, an estimated USD 30,000,000 was lost to hostile attackers due to the access control vulnerability [12]. The problems of the public blockchains are gradually exposed and getting worse [1]. To deal with this issue, there are a lot of studies such as [2,4,9,15,17] etc. focusing on the security of Solidity smart contracts on Ethereum. They perform well in detecting vulnerabilities of Solidity smart contracts based on EVM bytecode or contract source code.

But in the meantime, WebAssembly (Wasm) becomes a favorable bytecode format of smart contracts on more and more blockchains [10]. Different from EVM bytecode, Wasm bytecode has a smaller size and higher operating efficiency, making the blockchain run smart contracts faster and more stable [21]. So a lot of blockchains adopt Wasm to improve the performance and Transaction Per Second (TPS). With the development of the blockchain and widespread use of the Wasm bytecode format, the security of Wasm smart contracts has attracted a lot of attention [6,13,18,20] and the significance of Wasm is growing.

For all these reasons, we chose to focus on avoiding potential vulnerabilities in Wasm smart contracts via static analysis. Specifically, Our work reasonably prevents the recurrence of access control vulnerabilities in new scenarios. To illustrate the method and the performance of our work, we chose Liquid[1] smart contracts on FISCO-BCOS[2] from several Wasm smart contracts as our subject.

In this paper, we develop WaLi, a control-flow-based analyzer for Liquid smart contracts. The main idea of WaLi works as follows. Firstly, we define the features of access control vulnerabilities in Liquid smart contracts based on FISCO-BCOS Environment Interfaces[3] (FBEIs) and label the target functions. Secondly, we build a control flow graph based on the Wasm bytecode of the compiled smart contract and locate the critical paths related to the vulnerabilities. Thirdly, we adopt a Wasm virtual machine to simulate the running environment. During its tracing of the critical paths, it updates the parameters manually set in the virtual machine which demonstrate some key properties related to vulnerability detection. After tracing all the paths, WaLi reports the access control vulnerabilities based on those preset parameters. Furthermore, We convert the Solidity smart contracts in the dataset of SmartBugs [5] into Liquid smart contracts and compile them to Wasm bytecode to conduct the experiment. The results of the experiment demonstrate the effectiveness of WaLi to detect access control vulnerabilities.

We summarize our contributions of this paper as follows:

1. We propose a method to identify the critical paths strongly related to vulnerabilities, which improves detection efficiency.

---

[1] https://liquid-doc.readthedocs.io/zh_CN/latest/.
[2] https://fisco-bcos-doc.readthedocs.io/zh_CN/latest/.
[3] https://liquid-doc.readthedocs.io/zh_CN/latest/docs/advance/fbei.html.

2. We design a set of patterns that checks the properties related to vulnerability detection.
3. We perform an evaluation on a converted dataset and the result shows the capability of our work.

The rest of this paper is organized as follows: Sect. 2 presents some related works of this research. Section 3 illustrates the overview and details of our approach. Section 4 presents experimental results and case studies to evaluate the efficiency of the approach. Finally, we briefly make a conclusion of this paper in Sect. 5.

2   Related Work

Since the attacks on smart contracts account for the vast majority of blockchain security attacks [14], the security vulnerabilities of smart contracts have attracted the great attention of our research community. But most of these researches [2,4,9,15,17] focus on Solidity smart contracts on Ethereum. In addtion, it is worth noting that the current detection tools for Wasm smart contracts are concentrated in EOS, and the exploitable vulnerabilities are almost all unique to EOS smart contracts. So they cannot be applied to the vulnerability detection of other scenarios.

Specifically, Quan et al. brought forward EVulHunter [13], a static analysis tool for EOS smart contracts, realizing the detection of *fake transfer* vulnerability based on the Wasm bytecode. He et al. proposed EOSafe [6], the first static analysis tool at the Wasm bytecode level of EOS smart contracts, which adopted a symbolic execution engine to detect four popular vulnerabilities in EOS smart contracts. And WANA [18] was proposed by Wang et al. to detect vulnerabilities in smart contracts on both EOS and Ethereum based on symbolic execution of Wasm bytecode. Yang et al. developed Seraph [20] which can detect vulnerabilities for EVM and Wasm smart contracts. Seraph introduced a set of general connector APIs to abstract interactions between the virtual machine and blockchain.

Our work is the first attempt to develop a static analysis tool for detecting access control vulnerabilities in Wasm smart contracts. And we illustrate and implement the method based on Liquid smart contracts on the prevailing FISCO-BCOS blockchain specifically.

3   Methodology

3.1   Overview

Figure 1 shows the overall process of WaLi detecting access control vulnerabilities of Liquid smart contracts. Taking the Wasm bytecode generated by the compilation of the Liquid smart contract as input. First, in the process of path

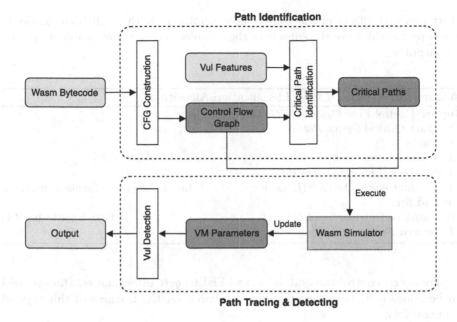

Fig. 1. The architecture of WaLi.

identification, the control flow graph is constructed based on Octopus[4]. Then, incorporating vulnerability features and labeled target functions, the critical paths are identified. Next, in the process of path tracing and detection, the control flow graph and critical paths information are fed into a designed Wasm virtual machine which contains some manually set parameters flagging the properties of the access control setting. During the path tracing process, the preset parameters are updated accordingly. Finally after all paths are traced over, WaLi reports the detection outputs based on those parameters.

3.2   Critical Path Identification

After the control flow graph is constructed, Algorithm 1 is used to find the offsets of the key function call points in the control flow graph. The critical paths are identified accompanied by predefined vulnerability features which specify the target FBEIs. Specifically, the control flow graph and those target FBEIs are inputs of the algorithm. Then, for every basic block in the main function of Wasm bytecode, we use a LOCATE function to scan the occurrence of those FBEIs and record the offsets. Subsequently, we use a general graph data structure and perform a depth-first search algorithm to calculate the possible paths between

---

[4] https://github.com/pventuzelo/octopus.

start and end offsets in the control flow graph. After that, all basic blocks in those paths which are the subsets of the complete control flow graph are gotten as output.

Algorithm 1. Critical Path Identification Algorithm

Input: Control Flow Graph: CFG; Target FBEIs: F_s;
Output: Critical Paths: $Paths$;
 1: $Paths \leftarrow [\,]$;
 2: $start \leftarrow 0$, $end \leftarrow 0$;
 3: **for** $block \in$ main function **do**
 4:    $start, end \leftarrow$ LOCATE($block, F_s$);   ▷ Locate blocks by function matching
 5: **end for**
 6: $Paths \leftarrow$ DFS($start, end, CFG$);   ▷ Search paths in CFG
 7: **return** $Paths$;

For access control vulnerabilities, two FBEIs, *getCaller*, and *setStorage* need to be concerned. We define logical rules based on the features of this type of vulnerability.

Firstly, the visibility of the function is public, which can be called and executed by external users. In Wasm, this kind of method is defined in the main function of the bytecode. Secondly, from the internal logic of the Liquid smart contracts: (1) the parameter of *setStorage* operation is exposed by the public function, (2) the value of the function address type parameter or the address obtained by *getCaller* is not constrained (e.g., no if statement to verify the address). To sum up, the logical expression of the complete access control vulnerability can be expressed as expression 1. In this expression, the existence of *getCaller* and *setStorage* operations are represented by propositions C and S respectively. And propositions P and I denote the visibility of the function and the existence of constraint operations separately.

$$P \wedge (\neg C \vee (C \wedge S \wedge \neg I)) \Rightarrow Vul \qquad (1)$$

Through the control flow information obtained before, a depth-first search algorithm is utilized to find the offsets of call points of these methods in the main function, that is, the key start point and end point of the identification of possible vulnerability occurrences.

And we intend to use Fig. 2 to illustrate the identification method further. First, we find the block in the main function that contains a *bcos.getCaller* instruction and record the offset as the start point (e.g., 32 in Fig. 2). And in some other basic block, we find an instruction that calls a function containing a *bcos.setStorage* instruction at offset 129 indirectly. We take the calling point of this indirect call (e.g., 101 in Fig. 2) rather than the target function call site. Then we recognize this indirect call through the depth-first search algorithm which calculates call paths from the main function to our target function. It is worth noting that we only focus on the offsets calculated in the main function as the subsequent search algorithm should locate the blocks in the main function which cover those offsets. Next, the DFS function searches all the possible paths from the start block to the end block based on directed edges in the control flow graph of the main function. Eventually, the critical paths are identified.

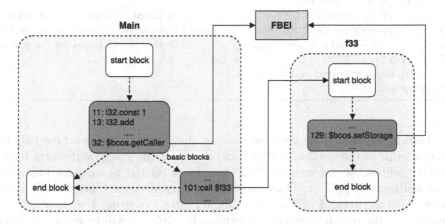

Fig. 2. An example to illustrate the critical path identification algorithm.

3.3 Path Tracing and Detection

Path Tracing. In the procedure of path tracing, in order to deduce whether the value obtained by *getCaller* has been verified by the if statement, a Wasm virtual machine is constructed to simulate a runtime environment, monitor and record the stack changes, memory, variables, etc. During the execution of these paths, when the key operations are executed, the preset parameters in the virtual machine will be updated.

In the Wasm virtual machine, a variety of instructions are symbolically modeled, such as constant instructions, arithmetic operation instructions, variable loading and storing instructions, memory instructions, etc. Additionally, we use symbolic values to replace actual values of elements in the stack. Real values that should be obtained in real runtime are represented by 0. And we model stack and memory-related opcodes according to Quan et al.'s work [13].

We use Algorithm 2 to illustrate the high-level idea of our path-tracing method. We take the control flow graph and critical paths identified in Sect. 4.1 as input. First, we assume that all smart contracts have access control vulnerabilities. Then, for every path in the identified critical paths, we define a Wasm virtual machine to initialize a simulation environment and use a TRACE function to execute every instruction of the basic blocks in the path. During this time, the self-updating mechanism works to change values of those preset parameters. The parameters are designed to check the compliance and violation of some patterns related to the existence of the access control settings. At last, the DETECT function reports the results based on the parameters after all paths are traced.

Algorithm 2. Path Tracing Algorithm
___
Input: Control Flow Graph: CFG; Critical Paths: $Paths$;
Output: Vulnerability: Vul;
1: $Vul \leftarrow$ True;
2: **repeat**
3:    **for** $path \in Paths$ **do**
4:       $vm \leftarrow$ WASMVM(CFG); $\triangleright$ Create a Wasm virtual machine
5:       $params \leftarrow$ TRACE$(path)$; $\triangleright$ Trace blocks in the Wasm virtual machine
6:       $Vul \leftarrow$ DETECT$(params)$; $\triangleright$ Detect vul based on vm params
7:    **end for**
8: **until** all paths traced or Vul is False
9: **return** Vul;

During the simulated execution process, the Wasm virtual machine puts the return value of the *getCaller* FBEI on the top of the stack, and stores it in a specific address of the memory list. Operations related to memory loading of that address are paid attention to when tracing all basic blocks of the entire critical path. Taking Fig. 3 as an example, after executing the instruction of sequence a, the return value obtained through *getCaller* will be placed on top of the stack, and its value is set to X. Then, the instruction of sequence b assigns the value X on top of the stack to the local variable L_0, so the value of L_0 in the variable table is updated to X. Next, when executing the instruction of sequence d, the value of local variable L_0 will be loaded on top of the stack. Along with the instruction of sequence c and e, the Wasm virtual machine stores the value of variable L_0 into the memory list at address Y. Therefore, this sequence of instructions implements the operation of placing the return value X of the *getCaller* FBEI into the memory address Y in the end.

Vulnerability Detection. In the Wasm virtual machine, instructions of basic blocks in the paths are executed in simulation. It is worth noticing that load-related operations of the value in the memory address Y is concerned. If the reloaded value is placed on top of the stack and relevant instructions for comparison are performed, it means that the smart contract logic includes an access control setting, so there is no access control vulnerability.

During the execution of the virtual machine, elements in the stack and the variable table will be continuously updated, and more and more values will be stored in the memory. Based on the above consideration, we focus on those instructions that reload the value from the specific address which stores the return value of *getCaller*. For instance, in the process of verifying the address of the contract caller, the value of the memory address Y will be reloaded to top of the stack, and its value will be related to the comparison operation. If there is such an operation, it is considered that the access control mechanism is set in the smart contract design logic.

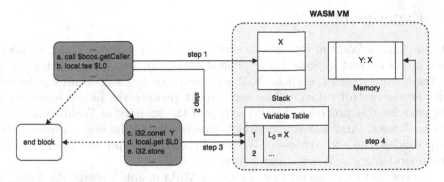

Fig. 3. An example of data transmission from stack to specific address in memory list during Wasm execution.

Patterns Setting. To monitor the execution process of the Wasm virtual machine, we define three patterns that are logically progressive as logic gates to help detect vulnerabilities. It means that only after pattern 1 is complied, the verification of pattern 2 can be available, and so forth. We consider the compliance of pattern 3 as a symbol of the set of access control mechanism which means smart contracts do not have that kind of vulnerability. Table 1 shows the meaning and logical expression of each pattern.

Table 1. Meaning and logical expression of each pattern.

Name	Meaning	Logical Expression
Patt. 1	Load *getCaller* value from memory	Load ∧ stack[top] = key address
Patt. 2	Find the function that contains a load instruction and the return value of *getStorage*	Patt. 1 = true ∧ *getStorage*
Patt. 3	Check the comparison operation	Patt. 2 = true ∧ comparison

It is worth noting that we also consider the *getStorage* FBEI into our settings to check whether there is a function that contains the load operation of the value of *getCaller* from memory and the return value of *getStorage* simultaneously. The access control settings are always reflected in these scenarios.

To sum up, we set corresponding parameters in the virtual machine to flag the compliance and violation status of these patterns. And these manually set parameters will be updated during the path tracing process. Eventually, an access control setting is recognized according to the parameters related to pattern 3. And the nonexistence of vulnerability is reported.

4   Experiment

We implement WaLi in Python. To verify the efficiency of our WaLi, we adopt part of the dataset in SmartBugs[5]. This dataset was used by T. Durieux et al. in their large scale experiment [3]. Specifically, we focus on contracts labeled with access control vulnerabilities and convert them to the Liquid source code. We exercise this procedure to fill the gap of the scarcity of Wasm smart contracts dataset. And as we understand, this converted dataset can reasonably help validate the effectiveness of WaLi and thus help to prevent the recurrence of vulnerabilities in Wasm smart contracts.

We conduct experiments to evaluate our WaLi mainly towards the following research questions.

- RQ1: How does WaLi perform on converted dataset?
- RQ2: Is the critical path identification method effective in locating the scope of possible vulnerabilities?
- RQ3: Do the set patterns have strong generalization capability in various situations?

4.1   Performance on Converted Dataset

As we mentioned in Sect. 1, it appears that there are no available benchmarks on vulnerable Liquid smart contracts. So we converted a labeled dataset from vulnerable Solidity smart contracts to Liquid. At last, we have successfully converted 13 smart contracts out of 18 labeled samples. We failed to convert 5 of the benchmark because there are no corresponding environment interfaces in FISCO-BCOS like suicide and delegatecall to make the program semantics the same.

Table 2. The overall experiment result.

	True positive	False negative	Precision	Accuracy	F1
Access control	11	2	100%	84.6%	0.917

Table 2 shows the detection result of our experiment. For access control vulnerability, our tool could achieve an accuracy of 84.6% on the dataset. It is worth mentioning that the precision and recall of our tool could achieve 100%, and the reported false negatives were all due to the timeout.

4.2   Search Scope Narrowing Strategy Analysis

This research brings forward the idea of narrowing the search scope of finding the vulnerability based on extracted features. For the access control vulnerability, we propose a critical path identification method to locate paths between two

[5] https://github.com/smartbugs/smartbugs.

essential FBEIs. This section aims to verify the correctness and effectiveness of WaLi to locate search paths and its important role in facilitating vulnerability finding. We modify WaLi to perform the ablation experiment on a specific example shown in Listing 1.1. At line 19, there is an access control vulnerability that ignores the permission check.

Listing 1.1. An example of vulnerable contract in our dataset.

```
1   #[liquid::contract]
2   mod missing {
3       use super::*;
4       #[liquid(storage)]
5       struct Missing {
6           owner: storage::Value<Address>,
7       }
8       #[liquid(methods)]
9       impl Missing {
10          pub fn new(&mut self) {}
11          // modifer semantic
12          pub fn onlyowner(&mut self, address: Address) -> bool {
13              ...
14          }
15          // The name of the constructor should be Missing
16          // Anyone can call the IamMissing once the contract is
                deployed
17          // <yes> <report> ACCESS_CONTROL
18          pub fn IamMissing(&mut self) {
19              self.owner.set(self.env().get_caller());
20          ...
```

In the experiment, we took down the time to run with and not with the strategy. Specifically, the modified tool ran timed out during finding the access control vulnerability, while WaLi recognized the vulnerability in 17.47 s and reported it correctly. The result of our experiment demonstrates the effectiveness and correctness of narrowing the vulnerability search scope with the critical path identification method.

Due to the number of edges in the whole control flow graph, and the iteratively tracing paths in Wasm virtual machine on a function level granularity, there will be path explosion problems. So it is reasonable and effective to propose a critical path identification method to narrow the search scope of vulnerabilities.

4.3 Generalization Capability of Patterns

In the iterative path tracing process, the pattern setting strategy helps to show the detection idea in Wasm virtual machine. The generalization capability of these patterns reflects the robustness of our method. Therefore, in this section, we aim to show some case studies to illustrate our approach further.

Comparing with Constant Parameters. The MultiOwnable in Listing 1.2 is a vulnerable smart contract that makes a comparison between an external address type parameter and a constant. The original intention of the contract is to set a new owner of the contract after permission. However, the contract is susceptible to be attacked by anyone because there is no valid access control setting. At line 16, there is an if statement to check the external parameter with the default value of the address type variable, but this comparison can not guarantee the caller of the contract is one of the owners.

Listing 1.2. Multiowned vulnerable contract in the dataset.

```
1   #[liquid::contract]
2   mod multiownable {
3       use super::*;
4       #[liquid(storage)]
5       struct MultiOwnable {
6           owners: storage::Mapping<Address, Address>,
7       }
8       #[liquid(methods)]
9       impl MultiOwnable {
10          /**
11           * @dev Adding new owners
12           * Note that the "onlyOwner" modifier is missing here.
13           */
14          // <yes> <report> ACCESS_CONTROL
15          pub fn newOwner(&mut self, _owner: Address) -> bool {
16              if _owner != Address::default() {
17                  self.owners[&_owner] = self.env().get_caller();
18          ...
```

In this case, the WaLi will focus on the comparison objects in the if statement. Unless the contract caller and the storage variable are put in the comparison, the if statement may not be considered to be an access control setting to perform the permission check. So in this case, an access control vulnerability is reported.

Missing Critical Access Control Setting. As shown in Listing 1.3, the contract Rubuxi is a smart contract that contains all factors that we concern in our method. It contains *getCaller*, *getStorage*, *setStorage* operations and seemly valid access control setting in function `onlyowner` via an if statement. But the access control setting is missing in the critical storage set function `DynamicPyramid`.

Listing 1.3. Rubixi vulnerable contract in the dataset.

```
1   #[liquid::contract]
2   mod rubixi {
3       use super::*;
4       #[liquid(storage)]
5       struct Rubixi {
6           ...
7           creator: storage::Value<Address>,
8       }
9       #[liquid(methods)]
10      impl Rubixi {
11          ...
12          // Sets creator
13          // <yes> <report> ACCESS_CONTROL
14          pub fn DynamicPyramid(&mut self) {
15              self.creator.set(self.env().get_caller());
16          }
17          // modifer
18          pub fn onlyowner(&mut self) -> bool {
19              if self.creator.eq(&self.env().get_caller()) {
20          ...
```

At line 19, the contract caller is compared with the storage variable `creator`. However, this kind of access control setting is missing in `DynamicPyramid` which performs the *setStorage* operation. The WaLi recognizes this negligence of critical access control setting that works to verify the caller address.

The output results of different situations demonstrate that WaLi can correctly recognize diverse cases of access control vulnerabilities.

To sum up, Sect. 4.1 shows the overall effectiveness of WaLi on the converted dataset and Sect. 4.2 elaborates the efficiency of path searching scope narrowing strategies. This section aims to verify the robustness and correctness of our patterns. By identifying the critical path of searching, WaLi concentrates on those basic blocks closely related to vulnerabilities and performs detection based on preset patterns. The results of the experiments show us the effectiveness of WaLi.

5   Conclusion

In this paper, we present a static analyzer WaLi to detect access control vulnerabilities. Firstly, we analyze the features of the vulnerability and label the target FBEIs which are essential to critical path identification. During pathfinding, we use a search algorithm to calculate paths from the main function to the call point of target FBEIs and locate the key offsets. Then we find all possible paths related to the vulnerability in a small subset of the whole control flow graph. Secondly, we adopt a Wasm virtual machine to simulate the runtime of bytecodes. Specifically, we set some patterns according to our detection method. And during the execution of instructions in the path, the parameters that reflect the compliance and violation of these patterns will be updated simultaneously. Lastly, we concatenate these two methods and develop WaLi to detect the access control vulnerabilities in Liquid smart contracts, the output of WaLi is based on those parameters after tracing all paths. The results and case studies in experiments show that our WaLi can effectively and efficiently detect the access control vulnerability.

For future work, we may take into account more vulnerabilities exploited in Solidiy smart contracts to prevent the recurrence of them in Wasm smart contracts. Furthermore, to improve the efficiency of the detection, we intend to propose a more precise path trimming method to reduce the search time, and make the design of the Wasm virtual machine more scalable to make WaLi more efficient and effective.

Acknowledgements. The work described in this paper is supported by the National Natural Science Foundation of China (62032025), the Science and Technology Program of Guangzhou, China (202103050004) and is sponsored by WeBankScholars Program.

References

1. Atzei, N., Bartoletti, M., Cimoli, T.: A survey of attacks on Ethereum smart contracts (SoK). In: Maffei, M., Ryan, M. (eds.) POST 2017. LNCS, vol. 10204, pp. 164–186. Springer, Heidelberg (2017). https://doi.org/10.1007/978-3-662-54455-6_8
2. Brent, L., Grech, N., Lagouvardos, S., Scholz, B., Smaragdakis, Y.: Ethainter: a smart contract security analyzer for composite vulnerabilities. In: Proceedings of the 41st ACM SIGPLAN Conference on Programming Language Design and Implementation, pp. 454–469 (2020)
3. Durieux, T., Ferreira, J.F., Abreu, R., Cruz, P.: Empirical review of automated analysis tools on 47,587 Ethereum smart contracts. In: Proceedings of the ACM/IEEE 42nd International Conference on Software Engineering, pp. 530–541 (2020)
4. Feist, J., Grieco, G., Groce, A.: Slither: a static analysis framework for smart contracts. In: 2019 IEEE/ACM 2nd International Workshop on Emerging Trends in Software Engineering for Blockchain (WETSEB), pp. 8–15. IEEE (2019)
5. Ferreira, J.F., Cruz, P., Durieux, T., Abreu, R.: SmartBugs: a framework to analyze solidity smart contracts. In: Proceedings of the 35th IEEE/ACM International Conference on Automated Software Engineering, pp. 1349–1352 (2020)
6. He, N., et al.: {EOSAFE}: security analysis of {EOSIO} smart contracts. In: 30th USENIX Security Symposium (USENIX Security 2021), pp. 1271–1288 (2021)
7. Jansen, M., Hdhili, F., Gouiaa, R., Qasem, Z.: Do smart contract languages need to be turing complete? In: Prieto, J., Das, A.K., Ferretti, S., Pinto, A., Corchado, J.M. (eds.) BLOCKCHAIN 2019. AISC, vol. 1010, pp. 19–26. Springer, Cham (2020). https://doi.org/10.1007/978-3-030-23813-1_3
8. Li, X., Jiang, P., Chen, T., Luo, X., Wen, Q.: A survey on the security of blockchain systems. Future Gener. Comput. Syst. **107**, 841–853 (2020)
9. Luu, L., Chu, D.H., Olickel, H., Saxena, P., Hobor, A.: Making smart contracts smarter. In: Proceedings of the 2016 ACM SIGSAC Conference on Computer and Communications Security, pp. 254–269 (2016)

10. Mokdad, I., Hewahi, N.M.: Empirical evaluation of blockchain smart contracts. In: Khan, M., Quasim, M., Algarni, F., Alharthi, A. (eds.) Decentralised Internet of Things, pp. 45–71. Springer, Cham (2020). https://doi.org/10.1007/978-3-030-38677-1_3

11. Palladino, S.: The parity wallet hack explained. https://blog.zeppelin.solutions/on-the-parity-walletmultisig-hack-405a8c12e8f7

12. Praitheeshan, P., Pan, L., Yu, J., Liu, J., Doss, R.: Security analysis methods on ethereum smart contract vulnerabilities: a survey. arXiv preprint arXiv:1908.08605 (2019)

13. Quan, L., Wu, L., Wang, H.: EVulHunter: detecting fake transfer vulnerabilities for EOSIO's smart contracts at webassembly-level. arXiv preprint arXiv:1906.10362 (2019)

14. Sayeed, S., Marco-Gisbert, H., Caira, T.: Smart contract: attacks and protections. IEEE Access 8, 24416–24427 (2020)

15. Schneidewind, C., Grishchenko, I., Scherer, M., Maffei, M.: eThor: practical and provably sound static analysis of Ethereum smart contracts. In: Proceedings of the 2020 ACM SIGSAC Conference on Computer and Communications Security, pp. 621–640 (2020)

16. Szabo, N.: Formalizing and securing relationships on public networks. First Monday (1997)

17. Tikhomirov, S., Voskresenskaya, E., Ivanitskiy, I., Takhaviev, R., Marchenko, E., Alexandrov, Y.: SmartCheck: static analysis of Ethereum smart contracts. In: Proceedings of the 1st International Workshop on Emerging Trends in Software Engineering for Blockchain, pp. 9–16 (2018)

18. Wang, D., Jiang, B., Chan, W.: WANA: symbolic execution of Wasm bytecode for cross-platform smart contract vulnerability detection. arXiv preprint arXiv:2007.15510 (2020)

19. Wood, G., et al.: Ethereum: a secure decentralised generalised transaction ledger. Ethereum Project Yellow Paper 151(2014), pp. 1–32 (2014)

20. Yang, Z., Liu, H., Li, Y., Zheng, H., Wang, L., Chen, B.: Seraph: enabling cross-platform security analysis for EVM and WASM smart contracts. In: 2020 IEEE/ACM 42nd International Conference on Software Engineering: Companion Proceedings (ICSE-Companion), pp. 21–24. IEEE (2020)

21. Zheng, S., Wang, H., Wu, L., Huang, G., Liu, X.: VM matters: a comparison of WASM VMS and EVMS in the performance of blockchain smart contracts. arXiv preprint arXiv:2012.01032 (2020)

22. Zheng, Z., et al.: An overview on smart contracts: challenges, advances and platforms. Future Gener. Comput. Syst. 105, 475–491 (2020)

23. Zheng, Z., Xie, S., Dai, H.N., Chen, X., Wang, H.: Blockchain challenges and opportunities: A survey. Int. J. Web Grid Serv. 14(4), 352–375 (2018)

24. Zheng, Z., Xie, S., Dai, H., Chen, X., Wang, H.: An overview of blockchain technology: Architecture, consensus, and future trends. In: 2017 IEEE International Congress on Big Data (BigData Congress), pp. 557–564. IEEE (2017)

Blockchain Policy Tool Selection in CHina's Blockchain Industry Clustering Areas

Jiqiang Tang[1], Zhen Wu[1], Yuxi Zhang[2(✉)], Xiaotuo Qiao[3], and Haifeng Guo[4]

[1] National Internet Emergency Center, CNCERT/CC, Beijing 100044, China
[2] School of Management, Harbin Institute of Technology, Harbin 150001, China
yuximanman@163.com
[3] School of Finance, Zhongnan University of Economics and Law, Wuhan 430073, China
[4] School of Finance, Southwestern University of Finance and Economics, Chengdu 610000, China

Abstract. According to the data from Cyberspace Administration of China, the formation time of China blockchian industry clustering coincided with the release time of related policies that support the development of blockchian industry. To detect the relationship between regional blockchain industry clustering and the policy tools used when different regions release blockchain related policies, we conduct text analysis on regional blockchian industry indicators and blockchain related policies using K-means clustering method. The results show that in provinces which have higher blockchain industry clustering, regions with better economy and technology pay more attention to innovative R&D support in environment-side policy tools, while less developed regions pay more attention to supply-side and demand-side policy tools. Besides, provinces with lower blockchain industry clustering mainly focus on strategic measure or target planning in environment-side policy tools.

Keywords: Blockchian industry · Industry clustering · Policy tools · Text analysis

1 Introduction

Since Chinese government expressed its support for the development of blockchain industry in 2016, China's large IT and internet companies began to layout blockchain one after another. Blockchain-related start-ups entered a blowout mode, the frequency and amount of investment and financing increased dramatically. The structure of Chinese blockchain industry was initially formed in 2018. According to the data of "blockchain home" website, enterprises of Chinese blockchain industry can be divided into five categories: application products, underlying platforms, solutions, infrastructure, and industry services. The scale of blockchain industry remains expanding. As of 2020, the Cyberspace Administration of China has recorded a total of 1015 blockchain information service names and numbers, involving 814 companies. Up to now, the application of blockchain has extended from a single digital currency to various fields of economy and society such as financial industry, copyright protection, traceability and anti-counterfeiting, energy industry, sharing economy, internet of things, etc. The blockchain industry is gradually scaling up.

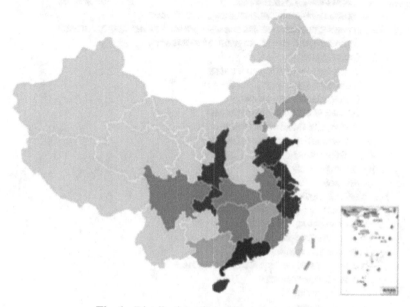

Fig. 1. Distribution of blockchain enterprises

We visualized the enterprises of each region that has been recorded using Arcgis in Fig. 1, as can be seen, Sichuan is the most advanced blockchain project development province among inland regions, besides, regions along Yangtze and Yellow River basins such as Chongqing, Shanxi, Hunan, Hubei and Anhui also have a large number of blockchain projects.

On April 20th, 2020, the National Development and Reform Commission officially announced that blockchain will be included in the scope of "new infrastructure". Thereafter, on July 7th, the China Securities Regulatory Commission (CSRC) issued "Letter on Approving the Construction of Blockchain in Five Regional Equity Markets including Beijing, Shanghai, Jiangsu, Zhejiang and Shenzhen", agreeing the participation of above five markets in the pilot of blockchain construction. Under the guidance of top-level design and national policies, many regions rush out support plans, more than 50 cities such as Hangzhou, Beijing, Shenzhen and Guiyang have issued special support policies for the blockchain industry. Chinese blockchain industry has entered a stage of rapid growth. However, due to different economic and technological foundations, the policies of different regions on blockchain industry are not unified.

Referring to the release conditions of blockchain policies in each region in Fig. 2, we can clearly see that in regions with high blockchain industry clustering, the policy support from government is also in the forefront of the whole country. In addition to policy support, to strengthen leadership and create development atmosphere, the government

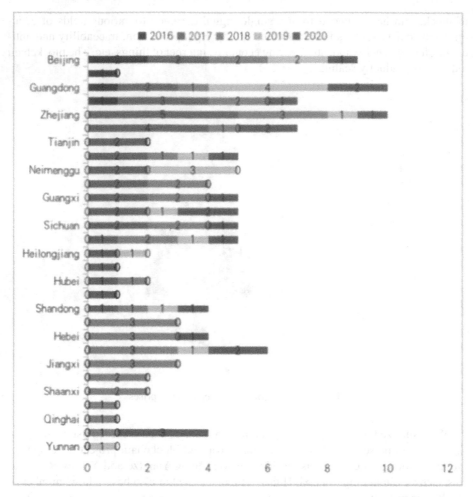

Fig. 2. Quantity of blockchain policies of each region on December, 2016–2020.

will also give specific guidance or financial and material support for technological break-throughs, industrial applications or overall ecological cultivation following the strategic planning.

For instance, cities such as Changsha, Guiyang, Chongqing, Shanghai, Guangzhou, Hangzhou and Qingdao have issued special guidance on blockchain industry at the municipal or district level. The detailed policies cover various aspects, including funding and financial support, enterprise management support, construction of industrial aggregation platform and innovation service platform, talent introduction and cultivation, technology and application support, activities and training subsidies, etc. According to earlier analysis, the development of blockchain industry in these regions have been at the forefront of China.

Research on blockchain policies is relatively few in domestic due to the special attributes of blockchain industry. When blockchain first appeared in public view, it was related to virtual currency such as Bitcoin, almost all blockchain-related progress is tied to virtual currencies. In addition, the anonymity and decentralization attributes of blockchain provide more space for illegal financial activities such as illegal fundraising. Therefore, the public attention to blockchain-related topics mainly focuses on its direct benefits, but not on blockchain technology itself. However, as the underlying technology of internet, if blockchain can be researched and updated, it will bring great convenience and technological development to many industries. Bypassing the direct financial benefits of blockchain and choosing to develop the technology itself requires enterprises' implementation. Moreover, only the government can afford the alternative cost of this process, except for the huge enterprises with foresight. As for the government support on technology development, direct policy promulgation works best. To detect the impact of policy tools on blockchain industry clustering, we firstly conduct cluster analysis on the distribution of blockchain industry and the blockchain policies promulgated by each province, and then match two results to discuss the influence of blockchain policy on the industry distribution.

2 First Section

Due to the large number and volume of policy release regions and the great difference in the content of policy texts in different regions, it is difficult to completely summarize the expression rules of policy texts. In addition, in the field of text analysis, there is still a lack of perfect and standardized policy lexicon, so it is difficult to identify policy tools based on rules and keywords.

To make sure the classification of blockchain policy tools objectively, we use K-means model to perform cluster analysis on blockchain policy texts. Our analysis consists of five steps: data acquisition, data preprocessing, text vectorization, text clustering and model evaluation.

2.1 Data Acquisition

The policy tools used in this paper come from the law database of Peking University and the official website of each province and cities. The data is captured and saved using Python. For the obtained raw data, we classify related texts to different groups according to region and year. Since many policies are not issued independently, but together with other policies, we need to exclude irrelevant policies. We search text location and content by blockchain-related keywords, including: blockchain, distributed, decentralized, data encryption, etc. Further checks are also performed on the screened texts to ensure accuracy.

2.2 Text Segmentation

Word segmentation is the process of cutting text into individual words, words or phrases using word segmentation algorithms. For English text, words are separated by Spaces.

English text can be sliced directly using Spaces without ambiguity. However, there is no space between characters, words and phrases in Chinese text. They are rendered as consecutive strings. In this paper, the N-gram language model based on Jieba word segmentation algorithm in Python is used for word segmentation of policy text. Suppose that the random variable S is a sequence of Chinese characters. W is all possible syncopated paths on S. Word segmentation is actually solving the segmentation path W* that maximizes the conditional probability P(W|S). The formula is as follows:

$$W^* = {}_W{}^{argmax} P(W|S) \tag{1}$$

According to Bayes' formula:

$$W^* = {}_W{}^{argmax} \frac{P(W)P(S|W)}{P(S)} \tag{2}$$

Since P(S) is a normalized factor and P(S|W) is always 1, we need only find the solution P(W). The N-gram language model is used to calculate P(W). The formula is as follow:

$$P(W) = P(w_0, w_1, \ldots, w_n) = P(w_0)P(w_1|w_0)P(w_2|w_1) \ldots P(w_n|w_{n-1})$$
$$= P(w_0) \prod_{t=1}^{n} P(w_n|w_{n-1}) \tag{3}$$

The matching degree of each segmentation path can be judged by conditional probability P(W|S).

2.3 Remove Stop-Words and Illegal Characters

After word segmentation, the original text becomes a set of single words, which can be called word segmentation result set. However, there are many function words, such as adverbs and symbols in this set. These words are called stop-words which have no practical meaning. Deleting stop-words can reduce the dimension of features without decreasing the accuracy of classification. In this paper, Harbin Institute of Technology (HIT) vocabulary table is used for word segmentation.

In addition, the text categorization data set used for the actual operation is retrieved from web pages. Web pages are made up of hypertext Markup language (HTML), which contains many tags. These labels have the potential to slip into the data set. Illegal format characters don't just refer to HTML tags. They can be generalized to all characters that are invalid for text categorization, such as symbols, emoticons, URLS, etc. In order to reduce the interference of these characters to the subsequent analysis, this paper adopts the localization deletion process.

2.4 Text Vectorization

Since the K-means algorithm used for policy text clustering needs to rely on vectors to judge a sample subordinate category, this paper first needs to carry out lexicographical quantization of the text. The K-means model determine the category of a sample based on the vector. There are two main methods for text vectorization: one hot encoding (OHE) and term frequency/inverse document frequency (TF/IDF). OHE vector can only show whether a term appears in the document (1 if appears and 0 otherwise) but cannot describe the frequency of the term appearance. TF/IDF makes up for this deficiency. So, after text segmentation, we use TF/IDF technique to vectorize the blockchain policies.

TF/IDF is one of the common techniques to describe the importance of a term in a document. Term frequency (TF) shows how frequently a term occurs in a document, it is the normalization of term count and can prevent the bias of long documents. Inverse document frequency (IDF) measures how important a term is. The IDF is calculated as the logarithm for the total number of documents divided by the number of documents with the term appeared in. A high TF/IDF score indicates that a term has high frequency of appearance in a certain document, but low frequency of appearance in entire document. Therefore, TF/IDF can be used to filter common terms and keep important terms.

2.5 Policy Text Clustering

As an unsupervised machine learning algorithm, K-means is a classic algorithm in clustering analysis. It can continuously adjust the classification after the first rough classification until a satisfactory condition is reached. K-means algorithm starts with k number of randomly selected centroids, and then calculate the Euclidean distance from other data points to each centroid as follows:

$$d_q(x, y) = \left[\sum\nolimits_{k=1}^{p} |x_k - y_k|^q \right]^{\frac{1}{q}}, q > 0 \qquad (4)$$

When q = 2, the Euclidean distance can be expressed as:

$$d_2(x, y) = \left[\sum\nolimits_{k=1}^{p} |x_k - y_k|^2 \right]^{\frac{1}{2}} \qquad (5)$$

After that, allocating every data point to the nearest centroid. Every centroid and the data points aggregated together refer to a cluster. When the data points are allocated in each cluster, we can get k clusters, the K-means algorithm performs iterative (repetitive) calculations to optimize the position of the centroids. The goal of the K-means algorithm is to make good, meaningful clusters, the chosen of k value is important for the cluster quality. We use inertia to measure whether k value is appropriate. Inertia is also called within-cluster sum of squared errors (SSE), it tells how far away the points within a cluster are. The smaller the inertia value, the better the clustering effect, so a small inertia is aimed for.

To determine the optimal k value, we carry out hyperparameter optimization in this paper, taking the k value between 1 to 13, each value is clustered once. We continuously adjust the value of the initial k, and finally obtain the optimal k value (k = 13).

2.6 Model Evaluation

When the text category is unknow, the silhouette score can be used to measure the cluster quality, it tells how far away the data points in one cluster are. The range of silhouette score is from -1 to 1, and the score should be closer to 1 than -1. The silhouette score for a particular data point i is:

$$SC(d_i) = \frac{b(i) - a(i)}{max\{a(i), b(i)\}} \tag{6}$$

where is the average distance between i and all the other data points in the cluster to which i belongs, is the average distance from i to all clusters to which i does no belong. We will then calculate the average silhouette for every cluster as:

$$SC = \frac{1}{N} \sum_{i=1}^{N} SC(d_i) \tag{7}$$

The final silhouette score in this paper is 0. 18, indicating that the cluster quality is above average.

3   Policy Tool Choice

3.1   Generate Word Cloud

After setting the initial centroids and the highest iteration, we conduct the clustering and show the results in the form of word clouds. This p only shows part of the word clouds due to space limitations (Fig. 3).

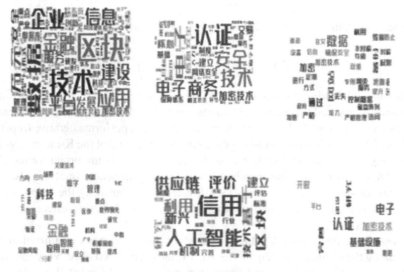

Fig. 3. Policy word clouds

3.2 The Classification of Policy Tools

The classification of policy tools is the basis for the policy tool analysis. There are many classification models for policy tools in academia. Based on above results of clustering analysis, we choose the model of Rothwell and Zegveld to classify the policy tool texts to three categories: supply-side policy, demand-side policy, and environment-side policy, including 13 sub-categories such as talent support. Supply-side policy tools help the development of blockchain industry in terms of economy, talents and supporting facilities. Demand-side policy tools drive the market demand of each industry on blockchain products. Environment-side policy tools have indirect influence and penetration on blockchain industry (Table 1).

Table 1. Category of policy tools

Category	Policy tool name	Implication
Supply	Talent support	Attract blockchain professionals by cultivating, introducing, strengthening training, encouraging enterprises and research institutes to improve treatment, and relaxing policies
	Public service	Government provides corresponding supporting services for the healthy development of blockchain industry by administrative measures
	Financial & tax support	Support the development of blockchain enterprises, scientific research and education by financial investment. Provide subsidies for financing, loan and risk guarantees to blockchain industry. Conduct tax relief, subsidies, rewards and other incentives to enterprises and individuals who engage in blockchain research, production, investment or consumption
	Technical support	Government actions to promote development of scientific research, such as establishing research labs, providing funds for research, etc
	Infrastructure construction	Provide infrastructure such as industrial bases, official platforms, facilities and equipment, application centers or residences for blockchain industry

(continued)

Table 1. (*continued*)

Category	Policy tool name	Implication
Demand	Government application	Government purchases blockchain projects or services using financial funds or entrusts blockchain R&D and innovation projects to scientific research institutes or innovative talents
	Financial & supply chain application	The application and promotion of blockchain technology in financial industry
	Trade support	Promote the development of blockchain industry by guiding and expanding market demand
	Project pilot	Carry out pilot demonstration projects for the application of blockchain industry, summarize and promote experience
Environment	Regulatory control	Manage the behavior of blockchain industry entities by enacting related laws and regulations and industry standard, create favorable policy environment for the development of blockchain industry
	Target planning	Describe and conceive the targets and prospects of blockchain industry
	Strategic measure	Provide support and incentives to key object by formulating short-term policies
	Innovative R&D support	Encourage enterprises and research institutes to carry out blockchain technology and product innovation by formulating related policies

3.3 Provinces Match Policy Tools

The policy text matching policy tools is classified and visualized according to regions. The result is shown in Fig. 4:

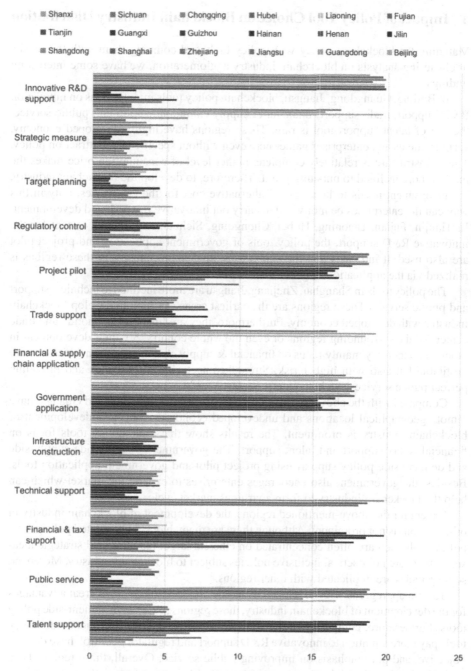

Fig. 4. The result of provinces match policy tools

4   Impact of Policy Tool Choice on Blockchain Industry Distribution

Matching the blockchain policy with policy tools and combing them with the results of clustering analysis on blockchain industry agglomeration, we have some interesting findings.

In Beijing, Guangdong, Jiangsu, blockchain policy tools mainly focus on innovation R&D support, trade support, financial & supply chain application and public service, the use of talent support tool is rare. These regions have highly developed economy, various talents and enterprises gather here even without specific talent attraction policy. The infrastructure is relatively complete, higher level of consumption price makes the market more inclined to pursuing profit. Therefore, to develop the blockchain industry, the government needs to bear part of alternative cost for the enterprises, only in this way can the enterprises be motivated to carry out innovative research and development. In Tianjin, Fujian, Liaoning, Hubei, Chongqing, Sichuan and Shanxi, except for the innovative R&D support, the policy tools of government application and project pilot are also used. It indicates that the support on blockchain industry in these regions is realized via the application of government level.

The policy tools in Shanghai, Zhejiang, Jiangsu are more inclined to technical support and public service. These regions are the earliest areas in China to develop blockchain industry with developed economy. Furthermore, they are financial, economic and trade centers of the surrounding regions or even the whole country. So, their development in blockchain industry mainly focus on financial & supply chain application which is more profitable but also with higher risk. Strengthening technical guidance and providing perfect public services can help enterprises avoid risks.

Compared with the above regions, Jilin, Henan, Hainan, Guizhou and Guangxi have remote geographical locations and undeveloped economies, but their development of blockchain industry is prominent. The results show that their policy tools focus on financial & tax support and talent support. The government also provide supply-side and demand-side policy support using project pilot and government application tools. Besides, the government also encourages enterprises to expand the market which can help the blockchain industry to form a virtuous market cycle.

Except for the above-mentioned regions, the development of blockchain industry in other regions is not prominent. Although there are many blockchain-related policies, the policy tools used are often concentrated on ethereal target planning and strategic measures, there are no practical inclusive policies subject to blockchain industry. Moreover, some policies are duplicated with other regions.

To sum up, regions with developed economy and technology have great advantages for the development of blockchain industry, these regions prefer environment-side policy tools. Furthermore, comparing to the strategic measure, their environment-side policy tools pay more attention to innovative R&D support and regulatory control, have definite objective, and put emphasis on improving public service. Overall, these regions have created a better industrial environment for the development of blockchain enterprises. In regions with undeveloped economy and technology, in comparison with other areas, areas with prominent blockchain industry development pay more attention to government policies and tend to use supply-side and demand-side policy tools, try to make up the gap on economy, technology, talent and market with developed regions from the angle of government governance, and provide all-round support to blockchain enterprises.

5 Conclusion

In government governance, policy tools are direct governing measures for the blockchain industry which are used in different ways by local governments in different regions. In regions with developed economy and dense population, the government policies are more inclined to encourage enterprises to conduct innovative R&D, improve the level of public service, and intervene earlier to regulate the blockchain industry. While in regions with high blockchain industry agglomeration but low economy development, the governments prefer supply-side policy, provide enterprises with financial support, help enterprises with talent attraction, committee to create a broader market for blockchain products and services, form a virtuous circle for local blockchain industry. Besides, in regions with low blockchain industry agglomeration, the policy tools are more inclined to general strategic measure and target planning, do not implement government work to the development of blockchain industry. Many policy documents are just copied from the guidance documents issued by the central government.

As the underlying technology of emerging internet, the blockchain technology has tremendous utilization value in big data and cloud storage, but the development of blockchain industry need more accumulation. The government should take precautions and plan ahead, make corresponding support policies according to the local condition. Moreover, the government should strengthen relevant knowledge training of officials to make sure that they have scientific and technological sensitivity and can flexibly and purposefully assist the development of blockchain enterprises in actual work.

Acknowledgments. This work was supported by The National Key Research and Development Program of China (2020YFB1006104).

References

1. Janjua, F., Masood, A., Abbas, H., Rashid, I., Zaki, M.M., Khan, M.: Textual analysis of traitor-based dataset through semi supervised machine learning. Future Gener. Comput. Syst. **125**, 652–660 (2021)
2. Tang, Z., Li, W., Li, Y., Zhao, W., Li, S.: Several alternative term weighting methods for text representation and classification. Knowl.-Based Syst. **207**, 106399 (2020)
3. Singh, K.N., Devi, S.D., Devi, H.M., Mahanta, A.K.: A novel approach for dimension reduction using word embedding: an enhanced text classification approach. Int. J. Inf. Manag. Data Insights **2**(1), 100061 (2022)
4. Taşcı, Ş., Güngör, T.: Comparison of text feature selection policies and using an adaptive framework. Expert Syst. Appl. **40**(12), 4871–4886 (2013)
5. Noh, H., Jo, Y., Lee, S.: Keyword selection and processing strategy for applying text mining to patent analysis. Expert Syst. Appl. **42**(9), 4348–4360 (2015)
6. Niemann, H., Moehrle, M.G., Frischkorn, J.: Use of a new patent text-mining and visualization method for identifying patenting patterns over time: concept, method and test application. Technol. Forecast. Soc. Chang. **115**, 210–220 (2017)

Lock-Based Proof of Authority: A Faster and Low-Forking PoA Fault Tolerance Protocol for Blockchain Systems

Zhenbang Huang[1] , Peilin Zheng[1](✉) , Zibin Zheng[1] , and Yin Li[2]

[1] Sun Yat-sen University, Guangzhou 510006, Guangdong, China
{huangzhb23,zhengpl3}@mail2.sysu.edu.cn, zhzibin@mail.sysu.edu.cn
[2] Institute of Software Application Technology,
Guangzhou 511458, Guangdong, China
liyin@gz.iscas.ac.cn

Abstract. A key component of a blockchain system is the consensus protocol, which directly affects the reliability and performance of blockchain systems. There are lots of blockchain consensus protocols. Proof of Authority (PoA) is a popular consensus protocol, and it has been embedded in many blockchain systems. However, PoA protocol cannot satisfy high transaction throughput, low transaction latency, and low forking rate at the same time, and can only take parts of them. This contradiction limits the practical application of PoA and needs to be resolved. Facing the challenges, in this paper, we present LPoA (Lock-based Proof of Authority), a new improved PoA consensus protocol. The experimental results show that LPoA delivers around 3x throughput, 1/3 transaction latency, and almost 0 forking rate over PoA under the same transactions.

Keywords: Blockchain · Consensus · Proof of authority · Performance · Throughput

1 Introduction

Since Bitcoin [1] was introduced in 2008, blockchain has been widely used in many fields [2,3]. It enables an individual or a single entity to trust others without a central third-party authority. Blockchain is essentially a distributed system, and the key to it is decentralization [4–6], which relies on a consensus protocol to reach an agreement on transactions among the peer nodes [7–9]. A consensus protocol is an algorithm that the nodes obey to reach a unanimous agreement [10,11]. There are a lot of blockchain consensus protocols, such as Proof of Work (PoW) [12], Proof of Stake (PoS) [13], PoA [14], Practical Byzantine Fault Tolerance (PBFT) [15], Raft [16], etc. A consensus protocol, as a key component in a blockchain system [17,18], determines the performance of the blockchain system. However, as reported by [19,20], most protocols suffer from poor performance, such as low transaction throughput and high latency, which hinders the application of blockchain systems.

D. Svetinovic et al. (Eds.): BlockSys 2022, CCIS 1679, pp. 348–361, 2022.
https://doi.org/10.1007/978-981-19-8043-5_25

PoA is a consensus protocol originally designed for Ethereum as an alternative to PoW and PoS [14]. PoA is a faster and more simple protocol. The participants of PoA are assumed to be trusted, through a strict identity certification. A set of nodes are selected as authorities to join in the consensus process of PoA, responsible for proposing and validating blocks. Each block is generated by an authority node. There is a fixed interval between two blocks, called block time. All the authority nodes are required to propose new blocks in turns. PoA has been embedded in many blockchain systems, such as Go-Ethereum [21], OpenEthereum [22], Quorum [23]. PoA is already used in several Ethereum testnets. And moreover, Binance Smart Chain [24], having a locked on-chain cryptocurrency with a market cap of over 13 billion dollars recently[1], also adopts a hybrid consensus protocol of Delegated PoS and PoA to support its system.

For those consensus protocols that provide probabilistic finality [8], it is difficult to meet the requirements of both high transaction throughput and low transaction latency. This is because lower transaction latency demands shorter block time, which will cause more forking and incur extra computation overhead. And forking lowers the throughput and leads to inconsistency and reduction in reliability [25]. In our evaluation in Sect. 4.1, we prove that PoA does have this issue, especially with great stress. The motivation of achieving high performance prompts us to figure out an improvement for PoA.

In this paper, we propose a novel consensus protocol called Lock-based Proof of Authority (LPoA). The main idea of LPoA is to make an agreement on which node has the right of proposing a new block rather than let the nodes compete to propose a new block, so as to avoid forking. In this way, it only incurs a little overhead rather than the overhead of reverting orphan blocks when forking occurs, which will also be evaluated in Sect. 4.

We implement LPoA on Go-ethereum, which is one of the most popular blockchain clients. Specifically, it is based on Clique, the PoA consensus engine of Go-Ethereum. To evaluate the performance of LPoA and to compare it with PoA, we carry out a set of experiments on Tencent Cloud. A baseline of a total of one million transactions is used to conduct stress tests. The results turn out that LPoA has advantages over PoA in performance with great stress. And LPoA has alike performance with PoA with low stress. Moreover, experiments on Go-Quorum system with a similar experiment setup is carried out to make a comparison across analogous consensus protocols, including Istanbul BFT (IBFT), QBFT(Improved version of IBFT) and Raft. In summary, LPoA delivers around 2-4x throughput, 1/2–1/20 transaction latency and almost 0 forking rate over PoA. And LPoA is able to handle greater transaction stress compared with all the other protocols mentioned above.

Contributions. In summary, the main contributions of our work are listed as follows.

1. We propose a novel improved PoA consensus protocol, LPoA, which enables high transaction throughput together with low transaction latency and low probability of forking in blockchain systems.

---

[1] https://defillama.com/chain/BSC.

2. We introduce a new idea of the lock mechanism and pre-consensus to avoid forking, which is designed for consensus protocols providing probabilistic transaction finality, and it is proved effective.
3. An implementation of LPoA is realized based on Clique, the PoA consensus engine of Go-Ethereum. Experiments are conducted to demonstrate the effectiveness of our implementation of LPoA.

2   Design of LPoA

In LPoA, the consensus is reached block by block. The nodes can reach consensus on a new block in a consensus cycle. As consensus cycles pass, consensus on new blocks is reached. To finish a consensus cycle, a pre-consensus process to determine which node has the right to propose a new block is conducted. The pre-consensus process is implemented through a lock mechanism, in which each node holds a lock variable to record its lock state. Depending on the lock state, the nodes behave differently. In the beginning, they send requests and respond to the requests to exchange messages. And then, one of the nodes gets the right to propose a new block first. After that, the node will generate a new block and broadcast it. In addition, an extra state called turn state is introduced to help with the consensus process. The detailed mechanisms in LPoA are as follows.

2.1   Mechanism

Consensus Cycle. The consensus cycle is defined as the process of the blockchain nodes reaching a consensus on a block. It begins with the trying of the nodes to propose a new block and ends with the consensus on the block. Each consensus cycle can be identified by the block height of the system. In a consensus cycle, the nodes in the blockchain system firstly try to get the right of proposing a new block. When a node gets the right, it will generate a new block and broadcast the block to the other nodes. The other nodes will verify and accept the block. Then the consensus on the block is reached and the consensus cycle ends. Next, a new consensus cycle starts.

Turn State. In a consensus cycle, a specific node is selected to be "inturn", and the other nodes are "not-inturn". Inturn denotes the priority of the proposing right among the nodes in a consensus cycle. And the inturn node will serve as the center node to be asked for approval from the not-inturn nodes when they want to get the proposing right (details in Sect. 2.2). This state of inturn or not-inturn is called "turn". A turn determines which node is the inturn node and the other nodes not-inturn. In a different turn, the change is that another node is the inturn node, but the block height of the new block is unchanged, i.e. the consensus cycle is the same. The inturn node is determined by the block height of the block in the consensus cycle. The nodes are arranged in turn-order and become the inturn node in turns along with the block height increasing by 1 from 0. Taking a 4-node blockchain system as an example, node-1, node-2, node-3, node-4 are in the turn-order, and they will take turns to be the inturn-node.

P-right. To avoid randomly proposed blocks in PoA and reduce forking among the nodes, Proposing right (p-right) is introduced. P-right is the right to propose a new block in a consensus cycle. In a certain consensus cycle, when a node wants to propose a new block, it needs to get the p-right first. The process for a node to get p-right is regarded as a pre-consensus process before the nodes reach consensus on a new block. In a consensus cycle, every node is allowed to get the p-right but only one will win and get the p-right.

P-request. A proposing request (p-request) is a request used in the process to get the p-right. The p-request is sent from a node to the other nodes to ask for approval. The p-requests made by a node will carry some necessary information, such as the block height the node expects to propose. Before a node in the blockchain system is able to propose a new block, the p-right is required. To continue, the process to get the p-right starts. The node needs to put itself in "p-locked" state first (details in Sect. 2.1), and then makes a p-request and sends it to each of the other nodes so as to collect approval messages. To get the p-right, approval messages from more than half of the nodes in the blockchain system (including the node itself) are required. Once the node receives enough approval messages, it is deemed to get the p-right and will proceed to generate a new block and broadcast it. Otherwise, the node will waive its try to get the p-right this time. Note that the node is still allowed to get the p-right in the consensus cycle as long as it continues with the process to get the p-right.

P-lock State. We define proposing-lock (p-lock) state of a node, which determines the behavior of the node. The p-lock state is used to determine which node will get the p-right. There are two p-lock state values, "p-locked" and "p-unlocked". For nodes in the p-locked state, they will reject all p-requests from other nodes and they will not try to start the process to get the p-right as well. This guarantees that a node will not approve p-requests from more than one node at a time in a consensus cycle, promoting the process of a node getting the p-right. As for nodes in the p-unlocked state, each node will verify p-requests from other nodes by verifying the signatures and checking whether the block height of each p-request equals their block height plus one. If the verification passes, the node will approve the p-request. If node B approves the p-request from node A, it will send back an approval message (appr) to inform node B as a response. Similarly, if node B rejects the p-request from node A, it will send back a rejection message (rej) to inform node B as a response.

During the procedure the nodes try to get the p-right, a node may send p-requests to the other nodes. If the node receives some *apprs* from other nodes but fails to get the p-right because of not enough approval messages from other nodes or somehow, it will waive its try to get the p-right this time. Then the node needs to send a returning message (ret) to each of the nodes that approve its p-requests. Such returning messages are required because the nodes that approve the p-requests put themselves in the p-locked state and reject other p-requests. This hampers other nodes' getting the p-right. Thus when they receive the returning messages, the nodes will put themselves in the p-unlocked state. This allows them to continue to get the p-right or approve p-requests from another node, making the consensus process go on.

Timeout. Generally, The LPoA protocol runs stably as long as the nodes work well. However, some nodes may be faulty in practice, which will result in blocking the consensus cycle. A timeout mechanism is introduced to solve the problem. In a specific consensus cycle, A node, marked as $node_i$, will start a timer of duration $time_{out}$. Before the countdown ends, if a new block is proposed, indicating the success of the consensus cycle, the timer will be reset and the countdown will restart. Otherwise, indicating the failure of proposing a new block, the timeout is triggered. $Node_i$ will skip the current turn and get into the next turn. As the turn changes, the inturn node (including the node itself) will be skipped, and the next node in the turn-order will be regarded as the new inturn node. Moreover, for $Node_i$, if it is in the p-locked state when the timeout is triggered, it will put itself in the p-unlocked state. This allows $Node_i$ to continue with the consensus process in the new turn.

As a special situation, in a consensus cycle, a not-inturn node $Node_{not}$ sends a preempting p-request to the inturn node and gets the appr but does not propose a new block within $time_{out}$. The timeout mechanism will be triggered. In case $Node_{not}$ is faulty and blocks the consensus process, the inturn node will mark $Node_{not}$ "limit" and reject any other p-request of $Node_{not}$ until the consensus on a new block is reached. And if the inturn node accepts or itself generates a new block, it will clear all the limit marks, allowing the limit-marked nodes to send p-request to itself again. This makes the system continues to work even if there are faulty nodes. We name this mechanism "preempting limit".

2.2   Consensus Process

Taking a 4-node blockchain system as an example, we describe here how the LPoA system works. In a consensus cycle, there are two cases of consensus processes distinguished by the inturn or not-inturn state of the node that proposes a new block. Case one is that the inturn node will propose a new block, and case two is the not-inturn node. Figure 1 and Fig. 2 show the two cases respectively. The four nodes are identified by 1 to 4 respectively. The inturn node is marked "in" and the not-inturn nodes are marked "out". The p-locked nodes are colored red and the p-unlocked nodes are colored green.

Block Proposed by the Inturn Node

Figure 1 shows how a consensus cycle processes when a new block is proposed by the inturn node identified by 1.

Phase 1. Initial is the initial state of the consensus process, as shown in Fig. 1(a). At the first of the consensus cycle, the four nodes are all in the p-unlocked state. And they are ready to start the consensus process.

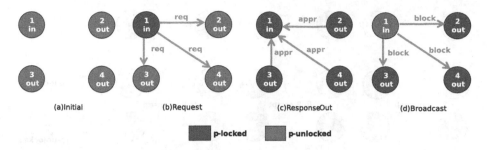

Fig. 1. The consensus process of a new block proposed by an inturn node in a 4-node system.

Phase 2. Request is the phase when the inturn node makes p-requests to get the p-right, as shown in Fig. 1(b). Node 1 wants to get the p-right, and it puts itself in the p-locked state first. And then, it makes a p-request (req) and sends it to each of the other 3 not-inturn nodes, namely nodes 2, 3, and 4.

Phase 3. Response-Out is the phase when the inturn node receives responses from the not-inturn nodes, as shown in Fig. 1(c). Nodes 2, 3, and 4 each receive the p-requests from node 1. And they are then all in the p-unlocked state, so each of them approves the p-request, puts itself in the p-locked state, and responses to node 1 with appr.

Phase 4. Broadcast is the phase when the inturn node generates a new block and broadcasts it to the other nodes, as shown in Fig. 1(d). When node 1 receives *apprs* from more than half of the nodes in the blockchain system, it will start to generate a new block. After the block is generated, node 1 will put itself in the p-unlocked state, and then broadcast the block to the other 3 nodes. After each of the 3 not-inturn nodes receives the new block and inserts it into its own local chain, the node will put itself in the p-unlocked state. At this time, all 4 nodes are all in the p-unlocked state returning to the initial phase i.e., Fig. 1(a). Finally, the 4-node system is again ready for the next consensus cycle.

Block Proposed by the Not-inturn Node

Figure 2 shows how a consensus cycle works when a new block is proposed by the not-inturn node identified by 1. The inturn node is identified by 2.

Phase 1. Initial is the initial state of the consensus process, the same as the initial phase of the inturn node case, as shown in Fig. 2(a). At the beginning of the consensus cycle, the four nodes are all in the p-unlocked state. Also, they are ready to start the consensus process.

Phase 2. Preempt is the phase when the not-inturn node makes a preempt p-request to get the p-right. As shown in Fig. 2(b). Node 1 wants to get the p-right, and it puts itself in the p-locked state first. Then, it knows the inturn node is node 2 and makes a preempting p-request (preempt), and sends it to node 2.

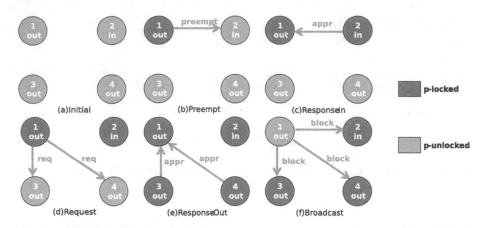

Fig. 2. The consensus process of a new block proposed by a not-inturn node in a 4-node system.

Phase 3. Response-In is the phase when the not-inturn node receives the response from the inturn node, as shown in Fig. 2(c). Node 2 receives the preempt. And node 2 is then in the p-unlocked state, hence node 2 approves the preempt, puts itself in the p-locked state, and responds to node 1 with appr.

Phase 4. Request is the phase when the not-inturn node receives the appr from the inturn node and continues to make p-requests to the other not-inturn nodes, as shown in Fig. 2(d). When node 1 receives the appr from node 2, in order to get *apprs* from more than half of the nodes in the blockchain system, it will continue to make a p-request (req) and send it to each of the rest 2 not-inturn nodes, namely nodes 3 and 4.

Phase 5. Response-Out is the phase when the not-inturn node receives responses from the other not-inturn nodes, as shown in Fig. 2(e). Nodes 3 and 4 each receive the p-requests from node 1. And they are then both in the p-unlocked state, so each of them approves the p-request, puts itself in the p-locked state, and responds to node 1 with appr.

Phase 6. Broadcast is the phase when the not-inturn node generates a new block and broadcasts it to the other nodes, as shown in Fig. 2(f). Very similar to 1(d), when node 1 receives *apprs* from more than half of the nodes in the blockchain system, it will start to generate a new block. After the block is generated, node 1 will put itself in the p-unlocked state, and then broadcast the block to the other 3 nodes. After each of the other 3 nodes receives the new block and inserts it into its own local chain, the node will put itself in the p-unlocked state. At this time, all 4 nodes are all in the p-unlocked state again, the same as the initial phase i.e., Fig. 2(a). After that, the 4-node system is ready for the next consensus cycle.

3   Implementation and Evaluation

For purpose of evaluating the performance of LPoA and comparing it with other analogous protocols, we implement LPoA based on Clique, the PoA consensus engine of Go-Ethereum.

3.1   Evaluation Metrics

There are some common metrics to evaluate the performance of a blockchain system, including throughput and latency [19,26–28]. We adopt the commonly used metrics of the blockchain system and add some necessary metrics to make proper evaluations: throughput, latency, and forking rate. The main evaluation metrics we used in this paper are listed below.

Throughput (TPS). Generally, in a blockchain system, throughput is characterized as the number of transactions successfully processed per second, aka transaction per second (TPS). As Eq. (1) shows, for a transaction set with tx_{count} transactions, t_{st} is the timestamp when the first transaction is sent and t_{ed} is the timestamp when the last transaction is completed. We have $t_{ed} - t_{st}$ denoted as "valid duration", meaning valid time spent during transaction sending process. In calculation, the timestamp of a completed transaction is replaced with the timestamp of the block in which the transaction lies.

$$TPS = \frac{tx_{count}}{t_{ed} - t_{st}} \quad (1)$$

Transaction Latency. For each transaction, there is a time period between the time when the transaction is firstly received by a node and the time when the transaction is confirmed. Denoting the receiving timestamp as t_{recv} and the confirming timestamp as t_{conf}, transaction latency is referred as the time period from t_{recv} to t_{conf}, as Eq. (2) shows.

$$latency_{tx} = t_{conf} - t_{recv} \quad (2)$$

Block Forking Rate. In our experiments, the Block Forking Rate (BFR) of a node is calculated as Eq. (3), where $block_{orphan}$ is the number of orphan blocks and $block_{valid}$ is the number of valid blocks. The "valid blocks", corresponding to the valid duration, are counted from the first block nonempty to the last block nonempty during the transaction sending process.

$$BFR = \frac{block_{orphan}}{block_{valid}} \quad (3)$$

3.2   Transactions and Sending Program

A sending program is created to send a large number of transactions. When the blockchain network is established and ready for consensus, the sending program starts to send transactions with a specific stress model (details in Sect. 3.3). We will first introduce the transaction model for Go-Ethereum [29], Go-Quorum [23], and then introduce the details of these blockchain systems.

For Go-Ethereum and Go-Quorum, they use an account-based model. A regular transaction in Go-Ethereum and Go-Quorum has three basic items, sender, recipient, and transfer amount. In our experiment, all one million transactions share a common sender, and it is generated casually. And the recipients are randomly generated, whose number is the same as the number of nodes, with one node corresponding to one recipient. Transactions are arranged in batches. A batch contains 50 transactions and their recipients are the same. The transactions are sent in batches to every node alternately. The transfer amount is set to 1 for all transactions.

3.3 Stress Model

A stress model is a pattern to reflect transaction stress. There are two models in our experiments and each one has a stress parameter. The bigger the stress parameter is, the greater the stress is.

Stress of Fixed Transaction Sending Rate Model. Stress of fixed transaction sending rate model (i-stress) ensures a steady stress level every time period during the sending process, and thus the duration of the sending process is certain. In our experiments, the time period is set to 0.5 s. Firstly the sending program will send transactions with a quantity of "interval-num" (i-num). Afterward, the sending program will constantly send a set of i-num transactions every 0.5 s until all one million transactions are done.

Stress of Fixed Number of Transactions. Stress of fixed number of transactions model (f-stress) ensures a steady stress level of transactions to be processed in the sending process. Firstly the sending program will send transactions with a quantity of "fixed-num" (f-num). And whenever transactions with a quantity of "p-num" are packaged in a new block, the sending program will send a set of p-num transactions until all one million transactions are done. This sending behavior is triggered by new blocks.

3.4 Experiment Configuration

We conduct our experiments on Tencent Cloud. Each node is deployed on one virtual machine of type S5.LARGE8. Each machine instance has a virtual CPU of 4-core of Intel Xeon Cascade Lake 8255C processer @2.5 GHz, 8 GB RAM, and 50 GB hybrid storage, running Ubuntu 20.04 LTS.

In each experiment, a total of one million transactions are sent as the baseline to make comparisons among the analogous protocols. TPS, Transaction latency, and BFR (if any) are used as metrics. For the blockchain systems with consensus protocols that can generate empty blocks, the block time is set to 1 s. For every set of parameters, experiments are repeated 4 times and the average values are taken.

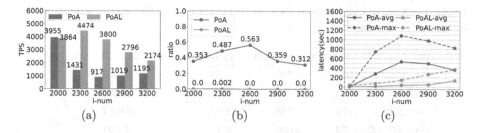

Fig. 3. TPS, BFR, and transaction latency results between PoA and LPoA with the i-stress of i-num of 2000, 2300, 2600, 2900, and 3200 in a 4-node system.

4   Results and Comparisons

In our experiments, greater stress, i.e., bigger stress parameters may cause a node not to respond and even crash. For i-stress, it is a bigger i-num while a bigger f-num for f-stress. This always happens in PoA earlier than LPoA. So we try the stress parameters from smaller to bigger until any node doesn't work. This allows us to push the i-num and the f-num to the biggest extent.

4.1   PoA and LPoA with Different Parameters

In this subsection, we establish PoA and LPoA systems with various parameters. All the nodes in the systems are placed in the same data center. On the premise of ensuring that all nodes work normally without crashing, we try to increase the stress by increasing the i-num. The average results of a 4-node system are shown in Fig. 3. It shows that PoA is able to handle the biggest i-stress with i-num up to 3200. In Fig. 3(a), it shows that with the i-num of 2000, the difference of TPS between PoA and LPoA is tiny. But as the i-num grows bigger, the TPS of PoA decreases dramatically and fluctuates, while the TPS of LPoA increases first and decreases later. This may be caused by reaching the bottleneck of transaction processing rate (BTPR). As long as the i-num reaches the BTPR of the system, the nodes in the system will be too busy to process incoming transactions which will grow more and more and lead to a decrease in TPS. In contrast, when the i-num is smaller than the BTPR, as it grows bigger, the nodes in the system are still capable to process more transactions and the TPS increases as a result. The BFR results are shown in Fig. 3(b). LPoA significantly lowers the BFR to around 0, while PoA holds all the BFRs over 0.3. With respect to transaction latency, LPoA also reduces the mean of both average transaction latency and maximal transaction latency. As Fig. 3(c) shows, the average latency ratio of LPoA to PoA is at least 1/2 and up to 1/20.

4.2   PoA and LPoA Across Data Centers

Taking blockchain systems of nodes in different data centers into consideration, we establish a 4-node system each for PoA and LPoA. The 4 nodes are placed in

Table 1. Comparisons between PoA and LPoA with specific stress parameters in a 4-node system across data centers.

Test item	Avg.TPS	Avg.BFR	Avg.Latency (ms)	Max latency (ms)
PoA-i1700	1637	0.307	184175	651303
LPoA-i1700	3163	0.000	6912	36452
PoA-f20000	1079	0.385	214269	888887
LPoA-f20000	3172	0.000	6302	27921

4 different data centers, which lie in Guangzhou, Shanghai, Beijing, and Hong Kong respectively. Two sets of experiments are conducted to compare the performance of the protocols. The first one adopts the i-stress with the i-num of 1700. The Other one adopts the f-stress with the f-num of 20000. The results are shown in Table 1, where the "Test item" column follows an abbreviation scheme: {protocol}-{stress model}-{stress parameter}. "PoA-i1700" means i-stress with i-num of 1700 tested on PoA for example.

The stress parameters are likewise pushed to the biggest extent for PoA. Compared with the results in the 4-node system in the same data center, the maximum of i-num decreases to 1700. This is mainly due to a reduction in bandwidth. The intranet in the same data center provides higher bandwidth than the public network among 4 different data centers. LPoA has lower bandwidth requirements than PoA. It can be seen that, with the i-num 1700, LPoA still delivers around 2 times TPS and 1/3 average latency compared to PoA. Moreover, in the experiments, LPoA incurs no forking. Similar results are observed in the case of f-stress with the f-num 20000. The results show a better ratio with around 3 times in TPS and 1/4 in average latency.

4.3   Across Systems and Protocols

Go-Quorum. We try to increase the stress as greater as possible. Results with the max i-num and the max f-num are shown in Fig 4. The BFR results are omitted because QBFT and Raft are absent of forking and the BFR results of IBFT are all zero in the tests. For IBFT and QBFT, they get almost the same results in both TPS and transaction latency, with the i-num up to 1500 and the f-num up to 6000 while Raft can only hold the i-num of 1300 and the f-num of 3300. Raft surpasses IBFT and QBFT in transaction latency in both of the two kinds of stress models. Raft has a maximum transaction latency of around 2.1 s. It is lower than the average values of IBFT and QBFT which is around 2.5 s. When it comes to TPS, compared with IBFT and QBFT, Raft gets better results in TPS with f-stress, while with i-stress in contrast. Compared with LPoA, the three kinds of protocols are inferior to it in the maximum of the stress parameters and the best TPS but perform better in BFR and transaction latency in some cases such as with each one's biggest stress parameter.

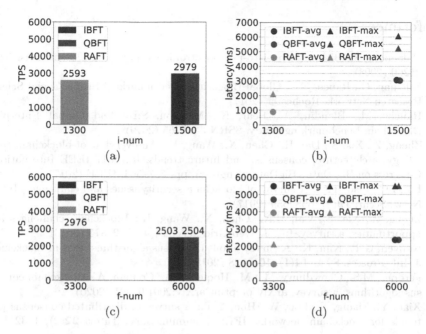

Fig. 4. TPS and transaction latency results of Go-Quorum with both the i-stress of i-num and the f-stress of f-num to the biggest extent in a 4-node system.

5 Conclusion

We propose a novel improved PoA consensus protocol, LPoA, which can handle high transaction throughput, low transaction latency, and low forking rate. The main idea of LPoA is to add a pre-consensus process on which node has the right to propose a new block. The process is realized through a lock mechanism that is simple and of low overhead. The implementation of LPoA is realized based on the PoA consensus engine of Go-Ethereum, Clique. Experiment results demonstrate that LPoA delivers up to 3x throughput, lower transaction latency, and negligible forking rate over PoA. LPoA also shows its capacity of handling greater transaction stress and higher transaction throughput in comparison with other analogous protocols like IBFT, QBFT, and Raft(Go-Quorum).

Acknowledgment. The work described in this paper is supported by the Key-Area Research and Development Program of Guangdong Province (2020B0101090004), the Key-Area Research and Development Program of Shandong Province (2021CXGC010 108) and the Science and Technology Program of Guangzhou, China (202103050004).

References

1. Nakamoto, S.: Bitcoin: a peer-to-peer electronic cash system. Decent. Bus. Rev., 21260 (2008)
2. Hileman, G., Rauchs, M.: Global Blockchain Benchmarking Study. Social Science Research Network, Rochester (2017)
3. Rauchs, M., Blandin, A., Bear, K., McKeon, S.B.: 2nd Global Enterprise Blockchain Benchmarking Study. SSRN 3461765 (2019)
4. Zheng, Z., Xie, S., Dai, H., Chen, X., Wang, H.: An overview of blockchain technology: architecture, consensus, and future trends. In: 2017 IEEE International Congress on Big Data (BigData Congress), pp. 557–564. IEEE (2017)
5. Lin, I.C., Liao, T.C.: A survey of blockchain security issues and challenges. Int. J. Netw. Secur. **19**(5), 653–659 (2017)
6. Zheng, Z., Xie, S., Dai, H.N., Chen, X., Wang, H.: Blockchain challenges and opportunities: a survey. Int. J. Web Grid Serv. **14**(4), 352–375 (2018)
7. Nguyen, G.T., Kim, K.: A survey about consensus algorithms used in blockchain. J. Inf. Process. Syst. **14**(1), 101–128 (2018)
8. Ferdous, M.S., Chowdhury, M.J.M., Hoque, M.A., Colman, A.: Blockchain consensus algorithms: a survey. arXiv preprint arXiv:2001.07091 (2020)
9. Xiao, Y., Zhang, N., Lou, W., Hou, Y.T.: A survey of distributed consensus protocols for blockchain networks. IEEE Commun. Surv. Tutor. **22**(2), 1432–1465 (2020)
10. Sankar, L.S., Sindhu, M., Sethumadhavan, M.: Survey of consensus protocols on blockchain applications. In: 2017 4th International Conference on Advanced Computing and Communication Systems (ICACCS), pp. 1–5. IEEE (2017)
11. Omote, K., Yano, M., et al.: Bitcoin and blockchain technology. Blockchain Crypt Curr., 129 (2020)
12. Dwork, C., Naor, M.: Pricing via processing or combatting junk mail. In: Brickell, E.F. (ed.) CRYPTO 1992. LNCS, vol. 740, pp. 139–147. Springer, Heidelberg (1993). https://doi.org/10.1007/3-540-48071-4_10
13. Vasin, P.: Blackcoin's proof-of-stake protocol v2, 71 (2014). https://blackcoin.co/blackcoin-pos-protocol-v2-whitepaper.pdf
14. Szilágyi, P.: Eip-225: clique proof-of-authority consensus protocol, Mar 2017. https://eips.ethereum.org/EIPS/eip-225
15. Castro, M., Liskov, B.: Practical Byzantine fault tolerance and proactive recovery. ACM Trans. Comput. Syst. (TOCS) **20**(4), 398–461 (2002)
16. Ongaro, D., Ousterhout, J.: In search of an understandable consensus algorithm. In: 2014 {USENIX} Annual Technical Conference ({USENIX}{ATC} 14), pp. 305–319 (2014)
17. Huang, H., Kong, W., Zhou, S., Zheng, Z., Guo, S.: A survey of state-of-the-art on blockchains: theories, modelings, and tools. ACM Comput. Surv. (CSUR) **54**(2), 1–42 (2021)
18. Bano, S., et al.: SoK: consensus in the age of blockchains. In: Proceedings of the 1st ACM Conference on Advances in Financial Technologies, pp. 183–198 (2019)
19. Dinh, T.T.A., Wang, J., Chen, G., Liu, R., Ooi, B.C., Tan, K.L.: BLOCKBENCH: a framework for analyzing private blockchains. In: Proceedings of the 2017 ACM International Conference on Management of Data, pp. 1085–1100 (2017)
20. Gupta, S., Hellings, J., Rahnama, S., Sadoghi, M.: Building high throughput permissioned blockchain fabrics: challenges and opportunities. Proc. VLDB Endow. **13**(12), 3441–3444 (2020)

21. Wood, G., et al.: Ethereum: a secure decentralised generalised transaction ledger. Ethereum Proj. Yellow Pap. **151**(2014), 1–32 (2014)
22. Parity Technologies: Parity - ethereum client (2021). https://www.parity.io/technologies/ethereum/
23. Chase, J.P.M.: A permissioned implementation of ethereum (2021). https://github.com/ConsenSys/quorum
24. Szilágyi, P.: Binance smart chain, a parallel binance chain to enable smart contracts, June 2021. https://www.binance.org/en/smartChain
25. Shahsavari, Y., Zhang, K., Talhi, C.: A theoretical model for fork analysis in the bitcoin network. In: 2019 IEEE International Conference on Blockchain (Blockchain), pp. 237–244. IEEE (2019)
26. Hao, Y., Li, Y., Dong, X., Fang, L., Chen, P.: Performance analysis of consensus algorithm in private blockchain. In: 2018 IEEE Intelligent Vehicles Symposium (IV), pp. 280–285 (2018). https://doi.org/10.1109/IVS.2018.8500557
27. Kuzlu, M., Pipattanasomporn, M., Gurses, L., Rahman, S.: Performance analysis of a hyperledger fabric blockchain framework: throughput, latency and scalability. In: 2019 IEEE International Conference on Blockchain (Blockchain), pp. 536–540 (2019). https://doi.org/10.1109/Blockchain.2019.00003
28. Pongnumkul, S., Siripanpornchana, C., Thajchayapong, S.: Performance analysis of private blockchain platforms in varying workloads. In: 2017 26th International Conference on Computer Communication and Networks (ICCCN), pp. 1–6. IEEE (2017)
29. Ethereum community: Official golang implementation of the ethereum protocol (2021). https://github.com/ethereum/go-ethereum

Phishing Fraud Detection on Ethereum Using Graph Neural Network

Panpan Li[1,2], Yunyi Xie[1,2], Xinyao Xu[1,2], Jiajun Zhou[1,2(✉)], and Qi Xuan[1,2,3,4]

[1] Institute of Cyberspace Security, Zhejiang University of Technology,
Hangzhou 310023, China
jjzhou@zjut.edu.cn
[2] College of Information Engineering, Zhejiang University of Technology,
Hangzhou 310023, China
[3] PCL Research Center of Networks and Communications, Peng Cheng Laboratory,
Shenzhen 518000, China
[4] Utron Technology Co., Ltd., Hangzhou 310056, China

Abstract. Blockchain has widespread applications in the financial field but has also attracted increasing cybercrimes. Recently, phishing fraud has emerged as a major threat to blockchain security, calling for the development of effective regulatory strategies. Nowadays network science has been widely used in modeling Ethereum transaction data, further introducing the network representation learning technology to analyze the transaction patterns. In this paper, we consider phishing detection as a graph classification task and propose an end-to-end **P**hishing **D**etection **G**raph **N**eural **N**etwork framework (PDGNN). Specifically, we first construct a lightweight Ethereum transaction network and extract transaction subgraphs of collected phishing accounts. Then we propose an end-to-end detection model based on Chebyshev-GCN to precisely distinguish between normal and phishing accounts. Extensive experiments on five Ethereum datasets demonstrate that our PDGNN significantly outperforms general phishing detection methods and scales well in large transaction networks.

Keywords: Blockchain · Ethereum · Phishing fraud detection · Graph neural network · Subgraph sampling

1 Introduction

Thanks to the development of blockchain technology, the past few years have witnessed the emergence of more than 1,100 cryptocurrencies in the financial field, further reforming the financial system. In general, blockchain technology can be described as a distributed ledger maintained by a peer-to-peer network through a consensus mechanism. Its non-intermediary trust system changes the traditional mechanism of establishing and maintaining trust-based Internet central institutions, allowing accounts to freely exchange cryptocurrencies or other fiat currencies without relying on traditional third parties.

D. Svetinovic et al. (Eds.): BlockSys 2022, CCIS 1679, pp. 362–375, 2022.
https://doi.org/10.1007/978-981-19-8043-5_26

However, the financial nature of cryptocurrencies makes them the target of various financial crimes [1]. According to CoinGecko data, the current market value of cryptocurrencies has risen to 1.84 trillion, and the 24-h trading volume is 78.687 billion. Moreover, the anonymization and weak regulation of blockchain platforms also exacerbate the problem. According to incomplete statistics, in the first half of 2017 alone, 30,287 users suffered financial fraud on the Ethereum platform, including phishing scams, Ponzi schemes, and ransomware, with a total economic loss of 225 million. Among these frauds, over 50% were classified as phishing scams targeting cryptocurrency [2]. The proliferation of phishing scams can lead to doubts about the security of blockchain technology, thereby hindering the healthy development of the technology [3]. Therefore, researchers have paid more attention to financial security in blockchain, and have come up with various methods to detect phishing fraud.

The openness and transparency of the blockchain makes transaction records available, further providing conditions for phishing detection. Inspired by network science, researchers construct transaction networks from raw transaction records and apply various network analysis methods to detect phishing scams. Existing phishing detection methods [4–6] mainly utilize graph representation learning techniques to generate the account feature vectors, and further achieve phishing detection via downstream machine learning classifiers. However, these methods do not achieve an end-to-end architecture, failing in learning the task-related features. Meanwhile, these methods generally suffer from poor scalability in large-scale Ethereum transaction network.

In this paper, we consider phishing detection as a graph classification task. Specifically, we first introduce a network lightweight strategy to rescale the Ethereum datasets and construct the Ethereum transaction networks. Then we formulate a sampling rule for subgraph extraction, which can efficiently extract subgraphs of similar scales to allow for mini-batch training of subsequent models. Finally, we design an end-to-end Chebyshev graph convolutional network to automatically extract account transaction behavior features and achieve phishing detection. We conduct extensive experiments on five Ethereum datasets, and the results demonstrate that our method significantly outperforms existing phishing detection methods and scale well in large transaction networks.

The remainder of this work is organized as follows. In Sect. 2, we briefly summarize the phishing detection methods and the network representation learning methods. In Sect. 3, we introduce the details of our proposed phishing detection method, including lightweight network construction, transaction subgraph sampling, and the architecture of phishing detection graph neural network (PDGNN). In Sect. 4, we present the experimental setup and analyze the experimental results. Finally, we summarize the main work and contribution of this paper in Sect. 5.

2   Related Work

2.1   Phishing Detection Method

The most existing illegal phishing fraud detection methods concentrate on graph analytics, which rely on the transaction networks constructed from raw blockchain transaction data. Yuan et al. [4] proposed a graph random walk method named trans2vec to extract the account features for phishing detection on Ethereum, which takes the transaction amount and timestamp into account and uses SVM classifier to distinguish the accounts into normal and phishing ones. Chen et al. [5] proposed a phishing detection method based on graph convolutional network (GCN) and autoencoder, which aggregates account features and network topology, and uses the lightGBM classifier to identify phishing accounts in Ethereum. Wang et al. [6] introduced the subgraph network (SGN) mechanism into Ethereum transaction network for extending the feature space of accounts. They constructed the transaction subgraph networks (TSGN) by extracting the first-order subgraphs of accounts, and used graph neural networks such as GCN and Diffpool to identify phishing accounts. Shen et al. [7] proposed a generic end-to-end graph neural network model named I^2BGNN, which can accept transaction subgraphs as input and learn to map the subgraph patterns to the label associated with account identity. Zhou et al. [8] proposed a joint learning graph neural network framework named Ethident, which utilizes a hierarchical graph attention encoder to characterize the account behavior pattern and applies self-supervision mechanism for improving model generalization.

2.2   Network Representation Learning

Network representation Learning aims to learn latent, low-dimensional representations of network nodes, while preserving network topology structure, node content, and other side information [9]. The generated low-dimensional node features can be easily used for downstream graph analysis tasks, such as node classification [10], graph classification [11], link prediction [12], etc. Perozzi et al. [13] proposed to generate a node representation through the co-occurrence probability of the node sequence generated by random walk. Grover et al. [14] proposed biased random walks to balance Breadth First and Depth First sampling, achieving a balance between homogeneity and structural equivalence. The factorization-based graph embedding algorithm uses the connection information between nodes to construct various matrices (such as Laplace matrix and adjacency matrix) and then decomposes the above matrix to obtain node embedding vectors. The models related to matrix decomposition include Graph Factorization (GF) [15], GraRep [16], HOPE [17], etc. Different from the above methods, LINE [18] optimizes the first-order and second-order proximity of nodes by designing a specific objective function to obtain node representation. The graph convolutional network (GCN) proposed by Kipf et al. [19] iteratively aggregates and updates the node features based on network topology, achieving higher expression performance. The Graph2vec proposed by Narayanan et al. [20] can

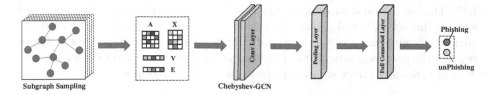

Fig. 1. The overview of PDGNN framework for Ethereum phishing detection.

learn the graph-level representations of networks and serves for graph classification tasks (Fig. 1).

3 Methodology

3.1 Problem Description

Ethereum transaction data can be modeled as a transaction network $G = (V, E, \mathbf{X})$, where $V = \{v_1, v_2, \cdots, v_n\}$ represents the account set, $E = \{(v_i, v_j) \mid i \neq j\}$ represents the set of transactions with timestamp and amount value, $\mathbf{X} \subseteq \mathbb{R}^{n \times d}$ is the node feature matrix constructed from the information of transaction frequence. We consider phishing detection as a graph classification task. Given a set of account subgraphs $\Omega = \{G_i, y_i\}$, graph classification aims to learn a function mapping the subgraph patterns G_i to label y_i associated with account identity, i.e., whether the target account is a phishing account or not.

3.2 Lightweight Transaction Network

Thanks to the openness of blockchain, researchers can crawl transactions from Etherscan platform[1]. However, there are extremely large transaction records and most accounts are not always active, which makes it difficult to mine account characteristics through a large number of transactions. It is imperative to construct a lightweight network to reduce the complexity of phishing detection tasks. In this subsection, we focus on the labeled target accounts and extract transactions associated with them by a second-order Breadth First Search (BFS). Firstly, we collect 1165 phishing accounts from Etherscan and perform a first-order BFS centered on these target accounts to extract transactions. After this, the total transaction information reduce to 1,686,003 accounts, 4,380,616 transaction records and 167 weakly connected components. However, the transaction network constructed from the above information is still large-scale, which is not conducive to those methods with full-graph learning manner. This paper uses only the largest weakly connected component, with a total of 1,684,164 accounts and 4,378,716 transaction records, and further propose a random walk-based sampling algorithm to lightweight the transaction network, i.e., a second-order

---

[1] https://etherscan.io/.

BFS. During the random walk, we firstly select an account as an initial node and specify the network scale. Then we choose one of the neighbor accounts of the current account and move forward until the number of accounts in the network reaches the specified scale. If the neighbor of the current account does not exist, we will randomly select an account from the visited accounts.

3.3   Subgraph Sampling

When extracting the transaction subgraph of the target account, it is reasonable to consider the number of hops and sampled neighbors per hop, because they control the scale of subgraphs. In this subsection, we propose a formula for calculating the number of sampling neighbors, which ranks each node's neighbors and samples its top-k neighbors according to the edge information. The calculation formula is as follows:

$$k = \lceil \overline{D} \times (1 + Density) \rceil = \lceil \frac{|2E|}{|V|} \times (1 + \frac{2|E|}{|V|(|V| - 1)}) \rceil \qquad (1)$$

where $\overline{D}$ is the average network degree, $Density$ is the network density, $\lceil \cdot \rceil$ represents ceil operation, $|V|$ and $|E|$ represent the number of nodes and edges respectively. The calculation formula adaptively extracts subgraphs of suitable scale according to the network topology, which improves the subsequent calculation efficiency compared with the traditional sampling strategy with fixed number of neighbors. In addition, the transaction edges contain two attributes: transaction amount value **a** and times **t**, so that the neighbors of the target account can be sorted separately according to these two attributes. When the number of neighbors is less than k, all neighbors will be extracted to construct subgraph.

3.4   Phishing Detection Based on Graph Neural Network

In this section, we present the details of phishing scam detection graph neural network (PDGNN), which is divided into the following steps: (1) automatically aggregate nodes' information by using graph convolutional network, (2) extract the characteristics of the target node by pooling layer, (3) classify phishing accounts through the full connection layer.

Graph Convolution Layer. We use Chebyshev GCN to automatically aggregate and update account features, and the single-layer Chebyshev GCN is defined as:

$$\mathbf{H} = \sigma \left\{ \sum_{k=0}^{K-1} \beta_k T_k(\widetilde{\mathbf{L}}) \mathbf{X} \right\}, \qquad (2)$$

where $\sigma(\cdot)$ is RELU activation function, K is the number of layers, β_k is the coefficient of Chebyshev polynomial, $\mathbf{X}$ is the node feature matrix. $T_k(\widetilde{\mathbf{L}})$ is k order Chebyshev polynomial and $\widetilde{\mathbf{L}} = 2\mathbf{L}/\lambda_{max} - \mathbf{I}$ where λ_{max} can be solved by

Table 1. Basic statistics of the Ethereum datasets. $|V|$ and $|E|$ are the numbers of nodes and edges respectively, Y is the number of labeled phishing nodes.

Dataset	$|V|$	$|E|$	$|Y|$
EthereumG1	20000	131189	242
EthereumG2	30000	172011	363
EthereumG3	40000	202595	462
EthereumG4	50000	227854	556
EthereumG5	60000	250402	604

power iteration, $\mathbf{L}$ is the Laplace matrix. The transaction subgraph extracted in this paper is a weighted directed network, thus the Laplace matrix needs to be transformed as:

$$\mathbf{L} = \mathbf{I} - \widetilde{\mathbf{D}}^{-\frac{1}{2}} \mathbf{A} \widetilde{\mathbf{D}}^{-\frac{1}{2}}, \ \widetilde{\mathbf{A}} = \mathbf{A} + \mathbf{A}^{\top}, \tag{3}$$

where $\widetilde{\mathbf{D}}$ is the normalized degree matrix of $\widetilde{\mathbf{A}}$. $T_k(\widetilde{\mathbf{L}})$ recursion can be carried out by using the properties of Chebyshev polynomial:

$$T_k(\widetilde{\mathbf{L}}) = 2\widetilde{\mathbf{L}}T_{k-1}(\widetilde{\mathbf{L}}) - T_{k-2}(\widetilde{\mathbf{L}}), T_0(\widetilde{\mathbf{L}}) = \mathbf{I}, T_1(\widetilde{\mathbf{L}}) = \widetilde{\mathbf{L}}. \tag{4}$$

Pooling Layer. Here we use the pooling layer to obtain the target account's representation from the whole graph:

$$\mathbf{Z} = \mathrm{pooling}(\mathbf{H}), \tag{5}$$

where $\mathrm{pooling}(\cdot)$ is a pooling function. Here, we adopt the average pooling function.

Full Connected Layer. We use full connected layer for graph classification:

$$\hat{y} = \mathrm{softmax}(\mathbf{W}\mathbf{Z} + \mathbf{b}), \tag{6}$$

where $\mathbf{W}$ and $\mathbf{b}$ are parameters of full connected layer. The model uses cross-entropy loss function:

$$\mathcal{L} = -\frac{1}{n} \sum_{i=1}^{N} y_i \log \hat{y}_i - (1 - y_i) \log(1 - \hat{y}_i). \tag{7}$$

4 Experimental Results

4.1 Dataset

We evaluate the proposed method on five lightweight Ethereum networks. The basic statistics are summarized in Table 1.

4.2   Comparison Methods and Experimental Setup

We compare PDGNN with seven graph-based detection algorithms, including manual feature (MF), LINE [18], DeepWalk (DW) [13], Node2Vec (N2V) [14], T-EDGE [21], Graph2Vec (G2V) [20] and I²BGNN [7]. For all random walk-based methods including DW, N2V and T-EDGE, we use the same parameter settings: the number of walks per node is 10, the length of walks is 30 and the size of the context window is 5. For all graph embedding methods, the embedding dimension is set to 128. For manual feature method and all graph embedding methods, we use logistic regression classifier for classification. For the end-to-end GNN-based models I²BGNN and PDGNN, the dimension of the two hidden layers is set to 128. We split each dataset into training and testing sets with a proportion of 4:1, we repeat 5-fold cross validation for 5 times and report the average performance measures involving Precision, Recall, F1-score and Accuracy.

4.3   Evaluation Metrics

For a binary node classification problem, the prediction results can be divided into the following four cases according to the real label and predicted label of the node:

- **True positive (TP):** The real label is positive, and the predicted label is positive.
- **False positive (FP):** The real label is positive, but the predicted label is positive.
- **False negative (FN):** The real label is positive but the predicted label is negative.
- **True negative (TN)** The real label is negative, and the predicted label is negative.

Precision, recall, F1-score and Accuracy are most important indicators in node classification, and their definitions will be briefly introduced below:

- **Precision:** It shows how many of the samples with positive category are real positive samples and is defined as:

$$\text{Precision} = \frac{\text{TP}}{\text{TP} + \text{FP}}$$

- **Recall:** Recall indicates how many positive examples in the sample are predicted correctly and is defined as:

$$\text{Recall} = \frac{\text{TP}}{\text{TP} + \text{FN}}$$

- **F1-score:** F1-score is the harmonic average of Precision and Recall without being influenced by unbalanced samples. The calculation formula is:

$$\text{F1} - \text{score} = 2\frac{\text{Recall} \times \text{Precision}}{\text{Recall} + \text{Precision}}$$

Table 2. Results of phshing detection. The best results are highlighted in blod.

EthereumG1

Algorithm	MF	LINE	DW	N2V	T-EDGE	G2V-t	G2V-a	I^{2}BGNN	PDGNN
Precision	0.6968	0.6512	0.8119	0.7331	0.7479	0.7662	0.7816	0.7726	**0.8319**
Recall	0.6161	0.4173	0.7769	0.6651	0.7186	0.7640	0.7398	0.8963	**0.9377**
Accuracy	0.5093	0.5938	0.7979	0.7072	0.7381	0.7649	0.7670	0.8165	**0.8742**
F1-score	0.4477	0.5057	0.7935	0.6916	0.7319	0.7631	0.7595	0.8294	**0.8813**

EthereumG2

Algorithm	MF	LINE	DW	N2V	T-EDGE	G2V-t	G2V-a	I^{2}BGNN	PDGNN
Precision	0.8272	0.6980	0.8061	0.8282	0.8308	0.8272	0.8045	0.8437	**0.8875**
Recall	0.3890	0.4795	0.7041	0.7014	0.7890	0.8164	0.8082	0.8904	**0.9205**
Accuracy	0.6534	0.6356	0.7658	0.7712	0.8137	0.8219	0.8055	0.8616	**0.9014**
F1-score	0.5252	0.5674	0.7497	0.7517	0.8089	0.8211	0.8053	0.8656	**0.9033**

EthereumG3

Algorithm	MF	LINE	DW	N2V	T-EDGE	G2V-t	G2V-a	I^{2}BGNN	PDGNN
Precision	0.6622	0.6328	0.8205	0.8227	0.8041	0.8069	0.8103	0.8269	**0.8551**
Recall	0.6409	0.4501	0.7921	0.7402	0.7533	0.7985	0.7490	0.8699	**0.9068**
Accuracy	0.5232	0.5957	0.8097	0.7795	0.7838	0.8032	0.7870	0.8432	**0.8768**
F1-score	0.4753	0.5252	0.8059	0.7658	0.7763	0.8015	0.7783	0.8470	**0.8800**

EthereumG4

Algorithm	MF	LINE	DW	N2V	T-EDGE	G2V-t	G2V-a	I^{2}BGNN	PDGNN
Precision	0.6687	0.6993	0.8454	0.8210	0.8234	0.8252	0.8192	0.8156	**0.8648**
Recall	0.6017	0.5439	0.8044	0.7720	0.7972	0.8455	0.8563	0.8707	**0.9137**
Accuracy	0.5022	0.6547	0.8287	0.7982	0.8126	0.8314	0.8332	0.8359	**0.8852**
F1-score	0.4249	0.6103	0.8238	0.7919	0.8093	0.8339	0.8367	0.8404	**0.8883**

EthereumG5

Algorithm	MF	LINE	DW	N2V	T-EDGE	G2V-t	G2V-a	I^{2}BGNN	PDGNN
Precision	0.6509	0.6765	0.8015	0.8184	0.8240	0.8160	0.8079	0.8331	**0.8930**
Recall	0.8033	0.5603	0.7934	0.7521	0.7537	0.8413	0.8248	0.8694	**0.8992**
Accuracy	0.6496	0.6463	0.7975	0.7860	0.7959	0.8256	0.8140	0.8463	**0.8950**
F1-score	0.6966	0.6126	0.7964	0.7755	0.7867	0.8284	0.8160	0.8502	**0.8958**

- **Accuracy:** Accuracy means that the correctly classified samples are divided by the total number of samples and is defined as:

$$Accuracy = \frac{TP + TN}{TP + FP + TN + FN}$$

4.4 Evaluation on Phishing Detection

We compare our PDGNN with seven baseline methods to evaluate its effectiveness in detecting phishing accounts, and the experimental results are reported in Table 2, from which we observe that our PDGNN achieve state-of-the-art results with respect to comparison methods.

Across all datasets, the manual feature method (MF) has the worst detection performance, because simple heuristic features are not capable of capturing structural pattern features of accounts. Compared with manual features, random walk-based methods (DW, N2V, T-EDGE) achieve better performance in detecting phishing accounts, because they can learn the structural pattern information of accounts. Graph2Vec and I^2BGNN consider phishing detection as a graph classification task, and outperform other baselines with node classification manner, indicating that the key behavior pattern information of accounts can be preserved in the account subgraphs.

For our PDGNN, it significantly outperforms manual feature method (MF) across all datasets, and yields 28.60%–109.21% relative improvement in terms of F1-score, indicating that the learned account features are better at characterizing the behavior patterns of phishing accounts than the heuristic features. When compared to graph embedding methods, our PDGNN surpasses strong baselines: we observe 6.17%–11.06% relative improvement over best baselines. Our PDGNN uses structural information to update the attribute features of accounts and optimizes them in an end-to-end manner, which significantly outperforms graph embedding methods that only extract structural information of account interactions and detect phishing accounts in a two-stage manner. We also compare with end-to-end GNN-based method I^2BGNN, and observe 3.90%–6.26% relative improvement, which may benefit from the better expression ability of Chebyshev GCN.

4.5   Parameter Analysis

We further investigate the impact of different parameters in our PDGNN.

Impact of Sampling Strategies. We sample transaction subgraphs according to different edge information, and preserve one of the edge information, yielding four types of subgraph datasets: $a - a$, $a - t$, $t - a$ and $t - t$. For example, $a - t$ represent that we sample transaction subgraphs according to the transaction amount value a and preserve the transaction times t as edge weight. Table 2 shows the phishing detection results under different sampling strategies, from which we observe that $a - t$ and $t - t$ achieve better performance in most cases. We have reasonable explanations for such phenomenon. Phishers engage in illegal fraud activities, they usually spread a large number of websites, emails or links containing viruses, unwanted software, etc., and trick the recipient into doing remittances directly. As a result, the center phishing account would receive large number of transactions from those victims, which is significantly different from the behavior patterns of normal accounts. Thus we speculate that the transaction times t (i.e., the number of transactions) would play an important role in distinguishing phishing accounts.

Impact of Directivity. Here, we investigate the impact of the network directivity on the proposed PDGNN, as shown in Fig. 3. As we can see, training with

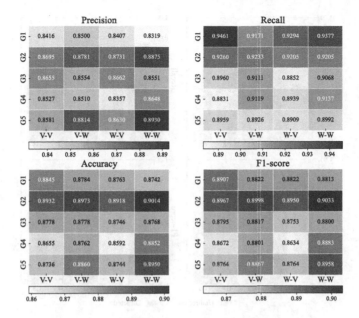

Fig. 2. Phishing detection results under different sampling strategies.

undirected networks seems to benefit the model generalization more, indicating that undirected networks greatly simplify the complex and redundant structure in the Ethereum transaction network and have better detection performance than directed ones.

Impact of Graph Pooling. Here we use max-pooling and average-pooling to test the performance of subgraph representation. Max-pooling can extract the most important features of each node in the subgraph, while average-pooling can keep the information of the whole subgraph and make features smoother. Figure 4 shows the phishing detection results under different graph pooling functions, from which we observe that average-pooling outperforms max-pooling in most cases, indicating that the characteristics of all nodes play an important role in representing the behavior patterns reflected in subgraph.

Impact of Hidden Dimension. GNN is usually applied to shallow networks, and simply stacking more layers will lead to feature over-smoothing. In this paper, we apply two GNN layers in PDGNN. The impact of hidden dimensions is shown in Fig. 5, from which we can observe that the phishing detection performance is proportional to the dimension of the hidden layer to a certain extent, i.e., high dimensional embedding can encode more information. However, when the hidden dimension increases continuously, the performance tends to decrease. The reason is that the model with high dimension GNN layer will be overfitting, resulting in poor model generalization.

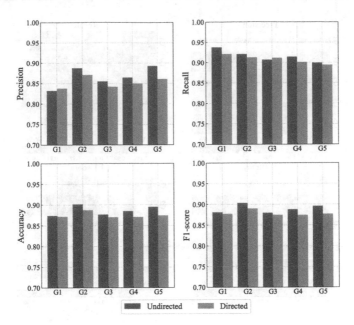

Fig. 3. Phishing detection results under directed and undirected networks.

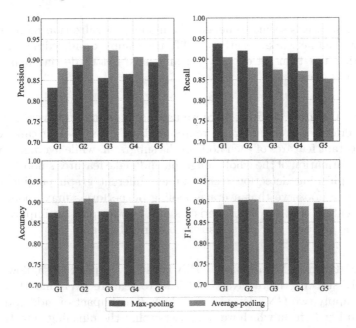

Fig. 4. Phishing detection results under different graph pooling functions.

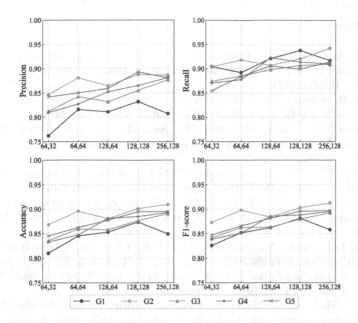

Fig. 5. Phishing account detection results under different dimensions of the convolutional layer.

5   Conclusions and Future Work

In this paper, we propose a deep model phishing detection framework based on graph classification, which provides a novel network perspective of to detects phishing scam. Specifically, we present a lightweight network method to rescale dataset and make subgraph sampling to reduce in resource consumption. Further, we designi an end-to-end PDGNN model to learn user behaviors and detect phishing accounts. Experimental results demonstrate the effectiveness of our proposed phishing detection framework, and indicate that PDGNN is capable of extracting more information from Ethereum transactions.

For future work, we plan to design more comprehensive subgraph sampling rules to make full use of the Ethereum transaction information. At the same time, we hope analyze account behavior from morc application scenarios to create a secure transaction environment.

Acknowledgments. This work was partially supported by the National Key R&D Program of China under Grant 2020YFB1006104, by the Key R&D Programs of Zhejiang under Grant 2022C01018, by the National Natural Science Foundation of China under Grant 61973273, and by the Zhejiang Provincial Natural Science Foundation of China under Grant LR19F030001.

References

1. Holub, A., O'Connor, J.: Coinhoarder: tracking a Ukrainian bitcoin phishing ring DNS style. In: 2018 APWG Symposium on Electronic Crime Research (eCrime), pp. 1–5. IEEE (2018)
2. Conti, M., Kumar, E.S., Lal, C., Ruj, S.: A survey on security and privacy issues of bitcoin. IEEE Commun. Surv. Tutor. **20**(4), 3416–3452 (2018)
3. Bartoletti, M., Carta, S., Cimoli, T., Saia, R.: Dissecting Ponzi schemes on ethereum: identification, analysis, and impact. Future Gener. Comput. Syst. **102**, 259–277 (2020)
4. Wu, J., et al.: Who are the phishers? Phishing scam detection on ethereum via network embedding. IEEE Trans. Syst. Man Cybern. Syst. (2020)
5. Chen, L., Peng, J., Liu, Y., Li, J., Xie, F., Zheng, Z.: Phishing scams detection in ethereum transaction network. ACM Trans. Internet Technol. (TOIT) **21**(1), 1–16 (2020)
6. Wang, J., Chen, P., Yu, S., Xuan, Q.: TSGN: transaction subgraph networks for identifying ethereum phishing accounts. In: Dai, H.-N., Liu, X., Luo, D.X., Xiao, J., Chen, X. (eds.) BlockSys 2021. CCIS, vol. 1490, pp. 187–200. Springer, Singapore (2021). https://doi.org/10.1007/978-981-16-7993-3_15
7. Shen, J., Zhou, J., Xie, Y., Yu, S., Xuan, Q.: Identity inference on blockchain using graph neural network. In: Dai, H.-N., Liu, X., Luo, D.X., Xiao, J., Chen, X. (eds.) BlockSys 2021. CCIS, vol. 1490, pp. 3–17. Springer, Singapore (2021). https://doi.org/10.1007/978-981-16-7993-3_1
8. Zhou, J., Hu, C., Chi, J., Wu, J., Shen, M., Xuan, Q.: Behavior-aware account de-anonymization on ethereum interaction graph. arXiv preprint arXiv:2203.09360 (2022)
9. Zhang, D., Yin, J., Zhu, X., Zhang, C.: Network representation learning: a survey. IEEE Trans. Big Data **6**(1), 3–28 (2018)
10. Abu-El-Haija, S., Kapoor, A., Perozzi, B., Lee, J.: N-GCN: multi-scale graph convolution for semi-supervised node classification. In: Uncertainty in Artificial Intelligence, pp. 841–851. PMLR (2020)
11. Xuan, Q., et al.: Subgraph networks with application to structural feature space expansion. IEEE Trans. Knowl. Data Eng. **33**(6), 2776–2789 (2019)
12. Chen, J., Zhang, J., Chen, Z., Du, M., Xuan, Q.: Time-aware gradient attack on dynamic network link prediction. IEEE Trans. Knowl. Data Eng. (2021)
13. Perozzi, B., Al-Rfou, R., Skiena, S.: DeepWalk: online learning of social representations. In: Proceedings of the 20th ACM SIGKDD International Conference on Knowledge Discovery and Data Mining, pp. 701–710 (2014)
14. Grover, A., Leskovec, J.: node2vec: scalable feature learning for networks. In: Proceedings of the 22nd ACM SIGKDD International Conference on Knowledge Discovery and Data Mining, pp. 855–864 (2016)
15. Ahmed, A., Shervashidze, N., Narayanamurthy, S., Josifovski, V., Smola, A.J.: Distributed large-scale natural graph factorization. In: Proceedings of the 22nd International Conference on World Wide Web, pp. 37–48 (2013)
16. Cao, S., Lu, W., Xu, Q.: GraRep: learning graph representations with global structural information. In: Proceedings of the 24th ACM International on Conference on Information And Knowledge Management, pp. 891–900 (2015)
17. Ou, M., Cui, P., Pei, J., Zhang, Z., Zhu, W.: Asymmetric transitivity preserving graph embedding. In: Proceedings of the 22nd ACM SIGKDD International Conference on Knowledge Discovery and Data Mining, pp. 1105–1114 (2016)

18. Tang, J., Qu, M., Wang, M., Zhang, M., Yan, J., Mei, Q.: Line: large-scale information network embedding. In: Proceedings of the 24th International Conference on World Wide Web, pp. 1067–1077 (2015)
19. Kipf, T.N., Welling, M.: Semi-supervised classification with graph convolutional networks. arXiv preprint arXiv:1609.02907 (2016)
20. Narayanan, A., Chandramohan, M., Venkatesan, R., Chen, L., Liu, Y., Jaiswal, S.: graph2vec: learning distributed representations of graphs. arXiv preprint arXiv:1707.05005 (2017)
21. Lin, D., Wu, J., Yuan, Q., Zheng, Z.: T-EDGE: temporal weighted multidigraph embedding for ethereum transaction network analysis. Front. Phys. **8**, 204 (2020)

Author Index

Printed in the United States
by Baker & Taylor Publisher Services